CSI REPRINT

VIETNAM: HISTORY OF THE BULWARK B2 THEATRE,

VOL 5: CONCLUDING THE 30-YEARS WAR

by Tran Van Tra

COMBAT STUDIES INSTITUTE

Published by Books Express Publishing
Copyright © Books Express, 2012
ISBN 978-1-78039-677-4

Books Express publications are available from all good retail and online booksellers. For publishing proposals and direct ordering please contact us at: info@books-express.com

NOTE

JPRS publications contain information primarily from foreign newspapers, periodicals and books, but also from news agency transmissions and broadcasts. Materials from foreign-language sources are translated; those from English-language sources are transcribed or reprinted, with the original phrasing and characteristics retained.

Headlines, editorial reports, and material enclosed in brackets are supplied by JPRS. Processing indicators such as (Text) or (Excerpt) in the first line of a brief, indicate how the original information was processed. Where no processing indicator is given, the information was summarized or extracted.

Unfamiliar names rendered phonetically or transliterated are enclosed in parentheses. Words or names preceded by a question mark and enclosed in parentheses were not clear in the original but have been supplied as appropriate in context. Other unattributed parenthetical notes within the body of an item originate with the source. Times within items are as given by source.

The contents of this publication in no way represent the policies, views or attitudes of the U.S. Government.

PROCUREMENT OF PUBLICATIONS

JPRS publications may be ordered from the National Technical Information Service, Springfield, Virginia 22161. In ordering, it is recommended that the JPRS number, title, date and author, if applicable, of publication be cited.

Current JPRS publications are announced in Government Reports Announcements issued semi-monthly by the National Technical Information Service, and are listed in the Monthly Catalog of U.S. Government Publications issued by the Superintendent of Documents, U.S. Government Printing Office, Washington, D.C. 20402.

Indexes to this report (by keyword, author, personal names, title and series) are available through Bell & Howell, Old Mansfield Road, Wooster, Ohio, 44691

Correspondence pertaining to matters other than procurement may be addressed to Joint Publications Research Service, 1000 North Glebe Road, Arlington, Virginia 22201.

JOINT PUBLICATIONS RESEARCH SERVICE

2 February 1983

Southeast Asia Report

No 1247

Foreign Broadcast Information Service

JPRS REPORTS

Japan Report
Korean Affairs Report
Southeast Asia Report
Mongolia Report

Near East/South Asia Report
Sub-Saharan Africa Report
West Europe Report
West Europe Report: Science and Technology
Latin America Report

USSR

Political and Sociological Affairs
Problems of the Far East
Science and Technology Policy
Sociological Studies
Translations from KOMMUNIST
USA: Economics, Politics, Ideology
World Economy and International Relations
Agriculture
Construction and Related Industries
Consumer Goods and Domestic Trade
Economic Affairs
Energy
Human Resources
International Economic Relations
Transportation

Physics and Mathmetics
Space
Space Biology and Aerospace Medicine
Military Affairs
Chemistry
Cybernetics, Computers and Automation Technology
Earth Sciences
Electronics and Electrical Engineering
Engineering and Equipment
Machine Tools and Metal-Working Equipment
Life Sciences: Biomedical and Behavioral Sciences
Life Sciences: Effects of Nonionizing Electromagnetic
Radiation
Materials Science and Technology

EASTERN EUROPE

Political, Sociological and Military Affairs
Scientific Affairs

Economic and Industrial Affairs

CHINA

Political, Sociological and Military Affairs
Economic Affairs
Science and Technology

RED FLAG
Agriculture
Plant and Installation Data

WORLDWIDE

Telecommunications Policy, Research and
 Development
Nuclear Development and Proliferation

Environmental Quality
Law of the Sea
Epidemiology

FBIS DAILY REPORT

China
Soviet Union
South Asia
Asia and Pacific

Eastern Europe
Western Europe
Latin America
Middle East and Africa

To order, see inside front cover

JPRS 82783

2 February 1983

SOUTHEAST ASIA REPORT

No. 1247

VIETNAM: HISTORY OF THE BULWARK B2 THEATRE,

VOL 5: CONCLUDING THE 30-YEARS WAR

Ho Chi Minh City KET THUC CUOC CHIEN TRANH 30 NAM in Vietnamese 1982 pp 5-335

[Book by Colonel General Tran Van Tra published by the Van Nghe Publishing House, Ho Chi Minh City. Printed at the Joint Printing Plant, Ho Chi Minh City; 10,000 copies printed. Printing completed on 27 March 1982 and submitted for registration on 27 March 1982]

CONTENTS

Introduction		1
Chapter One	The New Front	6
Chapter Two	The Only Path Is That of Revolutionary Violence	30
Chapter Three	Punishing the Agreement Violators	48
Chapter Four	The Greatest Rainy Season Ever	76
Chapter Five	Beginning of a New Phase	105
Chapter Six	A Once-in-a-Thousand Years Event: The Spring General Offensive and Uprising	136
Chapter Seven	The War-Deciding Strategic Battle: The Historic Ho Chi Minh Campaign	166
Chapter Eight	Final Hours of a Regime: The Ho Chi Minh Campaign Wins Total Victory	194
Last Chapter	The Municipal Military Management Committee	214

INTRODUCTION

[Text] In 1978 the Political General Department of the Vietnam People's Army adopted the policy of having cadres who worked and fought on the battlefields write memoirs about our nation's glorious war against the United States and recommended that I write about the B2 theater during the victorious spring of 1975: "How did the B2 theater carry out the mission assigned it by the Military Commission of the Party Central Committee?" How did it contribute to that glorious spring?"

Along with the other battlefields throughout the nation the B2 theater, in order to fulfill its glorious mission, contributed considerably to our people's great victory. The B2 theater and its people are proud of being part of the heroic Vietnamese fatherland, of the heroic Vietnamese people. Recalling and recording the events that occurred there is an honor and a responsibility of all cadres, enlisted men, and people of B2. I accepted the recommendation.

But I believe that the contributions of B2, one of the key war theaters, were not only its battles, its rice, its routes, and its people who sacrificed their lives, but also things that were much greater and which were valuable strategically and with regard to organizational art, and which by actually furthering the process of victory in the war contributed to the policies and lines of the Central Committee. They included not only heroic victories but also temporary, bitter defeats in certain places and at certain times, for they were all true and were valuable experiences. They are musical notes which are indispensable to composing the heroic symphony of the area. Therefore, to only record some events of the final victory, although it was a very great victory, would be a major deficiency. In order to create a bright spring it is necessary to pass through a gloomy winter, and a victorious dry season can be based only on the rainy season of the preceding year. It is difficult to speak of the foliage without speaking of the roots, and to do so would be inaccurate.

Therefore, I decided to record what I knew and remembered of the B2 theater throughout the long anti-U.S. resistance war. That was not a simple matter, so it was necessary to spend a good deal of time thinking, seeking documents, meeting with cadres I once knew, and returning to the battlefields of the past, in order to find the truth, which changes very faithfully. It was necessary to request many comrades to lend their assistance and cooperation, and to add together the memories of many comrades holding many positions in many areas of the theater. But I was determined to succeed in that project, for I regarded it as my final responsibility toward the liberation war--one which I could not delegate to others--and toward B2, an area which I love and in which I lived and served for most of my life, from the days of secret political activity prior to the August Revolution to the complete victory which unified the fatherland, and which I may select as my final resting place.

I have divided my book into five parts:

Part 1: From the Geneva Agreements in 1954 to the simultaneous uprising movement in 1960.

Part 2: From 1961 to 1965, the period of effective resistance to the special war.

Part 3: From 1965 to 1968--the defeat of the U.S. limited war.

Part 4: From 1969 to 1973, opposing the Vietnamization of the war and chasing the U.S. troops from Vietnam.

Part 5: From the Paris Agreement of 1973 to the complete victory (1973-1975).

I begin by writing about the final strategic phase (Part 5), a phase that is still current because it is appropriate to the requirements of many people, especially the men of B2.

But what was B2? Perhaps even now there are many people who are not very clear about that. To help the reader better understand the events about which I have written, I believe that it is necessary to mention some of the features of the B2 theater.

"B2" was the code name of the land and people in the southernmost part of the homeland during the anti-U.S. war period. Vietnam south of the 17th Parallel was divided into four theaters. B1, usually called Zone 5, included the central coastal provinces from Quang Nam-Da Nang to the present Phu Khanh Province. B3, the Central Highlands region, consisted of the provinces of Gia Lai, Kontum, and Dac Lac. B4 was made up of Quang Tri Province and the former Thua Thien Province. B2 consisted of the rest of South Vietnam, from the former Gia Nghia Province (part of the present Dac Lac Province), Lam Dong, Thuan Hai, and on down to the Ca Mau Peninsula, Con Son, Ha Tien, and Phu Quoc. It included a vast jungle-and-mountains area, the tail of the great Truong Son mountain range. From mountain peaks north of Dalat and Lam Dong 1,500 to 2,000 meters high, the elevation gradually declines in the direction of eastern Nam Bo. Bordering that area is the vast, fertile, highly populated lowland area of the Mekong Delta, the location of such famous resistance war bases of the past and the U Minh forest, Dong Thap Muoi, etc. It is a flat, open, humid area with rice paddies alternating with gardens and hamlets and is intersected by such large rivers as the Dong Nai, Soai Rap, Vam Co, and Cuu Long, and a large number of small rivers, canals, and arroyos. Some areas are inundated practically the year round, or are wet 6 months and dry 6 months. In some places there is a shortage of fresh water the year round. A coast thousands of kilometers long, a vast continental shelf rich in natural resources, and such major seaports and river ports as Vung Tau, Saigon, My Tho, Can Tho, Rach Gia, etc., are advantages for aggressors coming from the sea. The road network in Nam Bo, the most highly developed in South Vietnam, was improved by the Americans to support their mechanized operations. Saigon, the capital of the lackey puppet administration, the largest city--at one time it had a population of 4 million--and the political, military, and economic center of South Vietnam, was situated in the center of the B2 theater and, along with many other large cities such as Da Lat, Phan Thiet, Bien Hoa, Tay Ninh, My Tho, Vinh Long, Can Tho, Ca Mau, and Rach Gia, formed a system of bases from which the U.S.-puppet operations were launched in all directions. It was also the center for the application of the neocolonial policy, a place where the debauched American lifestyle flourished, and a place which consumed American goods and served the large expeditionary armies and the lackey forces. The United States and its puppets organized South Vietnam into four tactical zones. The area south of the Ben Hai River was Military Region I and the Mekong Delta corresponded to Military Region IV. Saigon, situated in the middle of Military Region III, was organized into the Capital Special Zone and was the command headquarters and the center of the U.S.-puppet war apparatus.

Our B2 theater accounted for about half of the land and about two-thirds of the population of South Vietnam, and encompassed part of the enemy's Military Region II and all of their military regions II and IV.

To facilitate guidance and command in the extremely fierce warfare, we divided the B2 theater into Military Region 6 (the southernmost part of Trung Bo [Central Vietnam], Military Region 7 (eastern Nam Bo), Military Region 8 (central Nam Bo), and Military Region 9 (western Nam Bo and Saigon-Gia Dinh).*

It must be added that about three-fourths of the border between our country and Kampuchea lay within the B2 theater. That area included land routes and river routes connecting the two countries, such as national routes 1, 22, and 13, the Mekong and So Thuong rivers, the Vinh Te Canal, and other roads and small rivers. The people of the two countries had always had good relations with each other in work and business. Friends, relatives, etc., usually experienced no problems in crossing the border by road, river, or canal. The destinies of the people on the two sides of the border have always been closely bound together and have fought shoulder-to-shoulder for the common well-being and shared good times and bad. That angered the enemy, who expanded their aggression and tried to sink their talons into both countries.

The people of B2 are honest and loyal and are independent in nature and their deeply patriotic ancestors came from north and central Vietnam. They always think of our beloved Uncle Ho and Hanoi, the capital and the ancient Thang Long, with an immortal sentiment:

---

*The military regions encompassed the following provinces:

Military Region 6: Quang Duc (Gia Nghia), Tuyen Duc (Da Lat), Ninh Thuan, Binh Thuan, Lam Dong, and Binh Tuy.

Military Region 7: Phuoc Long, Long Khanh, Phuoc Tuy (Ba Ria), Binh Long, Binh Duong (Thu Dau Mot), Bien Hoa, Tay Ninh, Hau Nghia.

Military Region 8: Long An (Tan An), Kien Tuong (Moc Hoa), Kien Phong (Sa Dec), Dinh Tuong (My Tho), Go Cong, and Kien Hoa (Ben Tre).

Military Region 9: Chau Doc, An Giang (Long Xuyen), Vinh Long, Vinh Binh (Tra Vinh), Phong Dinh (Can Tho), Ba Xuyen (Soc Trang), Kien Giang (Ha Tien-Rach Gia), Chuong Thien (Bad Lieu), and An Xuyen (Ca Mau).

Saigon-Gia Dinh Special Zone

"From the time we used swords to expand the nation we have for a thousand years remembered Thang Long" (Poem by Huynh Van Nghe, a military commander in Nam Bo during the anti-French resistance war).

The people of B2 are proud of their indomitable national-salvation, revolutionary traditions of the past, such as the anti-French movements of Nguyen Trung Truc, Thien Ho Duong, Doc Binh Kieu, Thu Khoa Huan, and Truong Dinh, of the staunch patriotic spirit of Nguyen Dinh Chieu, etc., with the "clusters of leaves that hide the sky," Can Giuoc, and Go Cong, the "Eighteen Hamlets of Vuon Trau," Hoc Mon, Ba Diem, etc. B2 still cherishes the celebrated feats of arms of the cloth-shirted Nguyen Hue on the Rach Gam River, and still has fond memories of our wise leader Ho Chi Minh who led the way to national salvation, and lived in Phan Thiet City, Ben Nha Rong, etc. Then there was the blood shed by our predecessors in the Nam Ky uprising in 1940, the August Revolution in 1945, etc. All of those things continually reminded and encouraged the people of B2 to be prepared to arise, once they had awakened, and sacrifice everything for independence and freedom.

In writing these thoughts and memories, I hope only to fulfill the obligations of a soldier who was fortunate enough to have lived and operated in a glorious era of the fatherland and of the people, and above all his obligation toward B2 or, more accurately, toward the people of B2, whom I love, all the people in the cities and in the rural areas, living scattered about the jungles, the mountains, and the maquis or concentrated in the subwards and villages. Especially, toward my friends, relatives, comrades, and fellow unit members, people I knew as well as those I didn't know, who were from all over the country, from Lang Son to the Ca Mau Peninsula, who fell in the B2 theater and whose blood stained every inch of the B2 theater so that we could win independence and freedom, and who sacrificed everything so that the North and South could be united and work together in building socialism. They were people who had great merit toward the great recent victory of our people and the homeland. Only they, people who never thought of themselves and contributed their entire lives, are worthy of living in the memories of thousands of future generations. That very sacred mission, which is also an order of history and the people, is to faithfully record and correctly evaluate the developments and events, and the hardships and noble sacrifices of the land and people of B2 which I witnessed, know about, and still remember.

Of course, because my knowledge and writing ability are limited, and because an article or book can only concentrate on a certain number of matters, I unfortunately could not deal with all of the miraculous accomplishments of the Vietnamese in the B2 theater, who resolutely, heroically, and creatively responded to the skilled leadership and guidance of the party Central Committee throughout the long and glorious resistance war and contributed their effort and skill to the historic resistance war. I only hope to record some of those events within the limits of my understanding, in order to make a small contribution to the people who are still alive today and to those of future generations. To do so is also to make a small payment on the debt I owe to the people who gave there lives in the B2 theater for their nation and class.

Because of that heavy responsibility, I decided to write only the complete truth, the truth that everyone knows as well as the truth some people do not yet know, which some people like and other people do not like. History is always truthful and will mercilessly eliminate what is not true, if not today then tomorrow. I hope that the readers everywhere, especially those who operated in the B2 theater, will contribute opinions and supplement the deficiencies and the omissions. I will be very pleased and grateful.

I also would like to express my gratitude for my comrades and friends who encouraged and assisted me, and who have contributed very valuable opinions and cooperated in all regards.

I would like to thank the comrades in the war recapitulation sections of the Ministry of National Defense, Military Region 7, Military Region 9, and Ho Chi Minh City, and the comrades who were members of the provincial unit commands in B2. My special thanks go to comrades Senior Colonel Nguyen Viet Ta and Captain Vo Tran Nha, who devoted much effort to assembling documents and contacting the localities, and who contributed worthily to the contents of this book.

                                              Spring, 1980

CHAPTER ONE

The New Front

A series of violent, incessant B52 bomb explosions shook the headquarters bunker of the Regional Command. Immediately afterwards loudspeakers hanging from tree limbs announced the report of the area duty officer: "Nine B52's divided into three groups dropped three strings of bombs across Zone A and between B1* and B2**. Everyone is safe."

We continued the conference. A staff cadre arrived to report that "The Central Staff has sent a message informing us that the Paris Agreement had been signed!"

I instinctively smiled and thought about those strange final minutes between war and peace, if indeed there was to be peace. It seemed that, significantly, the Americans had made full use of the final minutes of a war that had lasted decades by sending B52 steel crows to send "messages of reconciliation!"

Even so, news that the Paris Agreement had been signed caused everyone to breathe a sigh of relief. Joyful expressions appeared on the faces of the commanders. Those faces were all weatherworn: everyone looked thin but healthy. Was that not a valuable prize for nearly 10 months of continuous fighting all over the theater to force the enemy to sign an agreement to end hostilities and conclude a strategic phase?

Never before had a military activity campaign been as prolonged and as increasingly intensive as during the recent period. The military regions and units reported to the Regional Command the victories they had won, and the positions our troops had taken from the enemy hour by hour, but at the same time there were continual reports about the difficulties, the shortages of troops, food, and ammunition, and especially the fatigue of the cadres and men. The Military Region 9 Command (western Nam Bo) sent a message recommending straightforwardly that the Regional Command order an immediate cessation of hostilities so that we could reorganize our forces. The troops were no longer capable of fighting! But the enemy was extremely obstinate. They had been painfully defeated on the battlefield, had been outnegotiated at the conference table, and had been forced to sign in October, but had then reneged on their promise. So what should we do? Conclude our activities and rest, at a time when our objectives had not been attained? No! We had to continue to fight. We would fight until they understood the will of revolutionaries.

The difficulty was deciding what to do at that time. If we stopped, things would go in one direction. If we made a little more effort and won a few more victories we would bring about a qualitative change and things would go in another direction. That is what we did. We made a little more effort and won a few more victories in South Vietnam at a time when it was thought that we were exhausted and could no longer fight because we were out of rice and

---

* The Regional Command
** The Regional Staff

ammunition. We were steadfast, fought back intelligently and proudly, and shot down large numbers of B52's and other airplanes during 12 long days and nights in Hanoi and Hai Phong, as if something miraculous had happened, as in the ancient myth of Lac and the dragon. And clearly, we were able to create a new quality. The enemy--the leading, most dangerous and cruelest imperialist country of the era--had to bow its head and submit. They had to sign an agreement to end the war and restore peace in Vietnam and agree to completely withdraw the U.S. and puppet troops from South Vietnam and recognize the independence, sovereignty, and territorial integrity of Vietnam.

"Fight until the Americans get out and the puppets collapse.
"Advance! The soldiers and people of the
"North and South will meet in a happier spring."

Dear Uncle Ho! We had carried out to a decisive degree your instruction of a previous year, which manifested the skilled policy of the state. Once the Americans got out the puppets would have to get out and the north and south would be reunited. We pledged to go all-out to achieve his dream as soon as possible.

The decisive turning point of the war had been created. A difficult route had been traversed with great effort and we gathered together all our strength to travel the remaining distance, which might prove to be no less complicated and difficult. But we could see rosy rays of light on the horizon.

On a Monday in January 1973, at the Regional Command Headquarters, in a bunker in the middle of a jungle base area, the atmosphere was bustling and seething. We were monitoring the situation on the battlefield and the units, but our focus was on urgently discussing a plan and measures for implementing the Paris Agreement strictly and effectively. Many tasks had to be carried out: quickly reorganizing our forces, being vigilant toward the enemy, whom we had known well for a long time, etc. Suddenly a staff cadre entered and handed comrade Nam Nga (i.e. Maj Gen Nguyen Minh Chau), regional chief of staff at that time, an urgent message. Comrade Nam Nga quickly read the message then, with a serious expression that could have meant either happiness or worry, handed it to me. The message said that the Central Committee had appointed me head of the military delegation of the Provisional Revolutionary Government of the Republic of South Vietnam to the Four-Party Joint Military Commission in Saigon. Oh! How sudden! The Central Office [COSVN] and the Regional Military Party Committee had decided on the make-up of the delegation in advance, and it had already been approved by the Central Committee, but now there was a sudden, last-minute change. In only 3 more days I would have to be in Saigon!.

During my several decades as a soldier I had experienced many surprises, on the battlefield, in my work, and from people--both friends and enemies--but that surprise both pleased and worried me. It worried me because I was unfamiliar with such work and the time was too pressing: I had to pack and set out before I had time to get a handle on the job, let alone making full preparations for the new struggle front, which was completely different from the battlefield. However, that was not the first time I had been surprised by an assignment from the upper echelon. I was used to it. I had confidence in the leadership of the upper echelon and in my colleagues, and confidence in myself. I calmly accepted my responsibility. In fact, in this instance there was greater enjoyment in it for me. My beloved Saigon! For a long time, during the era of the French colonialists, I had lived, engaged in seething revolutionary activities, won victories, and tasted defeat there. I had been away from the city fighting for decades, and was now returning in full view of the people and my comrades, and within the thick encirclement of the enemy. The streets, markets, factories, poor workers' neighborhoods which I knew in the past had now certainly changed greatly, but even so I still had memories of other people from Saigon, like myself, who decided to leave so that they could later return in triumph. Once before I had tried to return but couldn't. This time, although it was not to be a permanent return, was as delightful as a beautiful dream. Every minute many imagined images of Saigon, both in the past and in the present, passed across my mind like a roll of film. When he saw me sitting in silence, comrade Muoi Khang (i.e. Senior General Hoang Van Thai, then a lieutenant general), asked me, "What else can you do but accept the mission? Congratulations!"

He then came up to shake my hand and hug and kiss me, and suddenly the room was echoing with congratulations and requests, and was tumultuous with the sound of laughter. There was no longer the atmosphere of a meeting. I exchanged a few pleasantries with Muoi Khang, then requested permission to prepare for my trip to Saigon. Muoi Khang would care for everything for me at home.

When I went back to my house and looked around at what had been familiar surroundings for years, I was suddenly saddened by the prospect of leaving. A light breeze blew in, bringing along the sweet scents of a myriad of flowers in the green jungle. In front of the house, in a narrow field extending along the valley, flocks of small birds hastily gleaned the grains of rice which were dropped during the recent harvest. The stream running along the fields was winding its way under rows of trees that were leafless because of the bombing and shelling. There had just appeared a few fresh young saplings. Every object that day seemed to have an overflowing, fresh, affectionate soul. I don't know how long I would have sat there meditating if Chin Vinh (Maj Gen Tran Do) and Hai Le (Maj Gen Le Van Tuong), the deputy political officer and political director of the Regional Command, had not come in and pulled me back to reality.

"Do you need anything else? Are you satisfied with the organization and composition of your Joint Commission delegation?" asked Chin Vinh.

I agreed to maintain unchanged everything that had been arranged, and only requested the addition of comrade Tu Bon (Senior Colonel Nguyen Huu Tri), an intelligence cadre and Army Hero who had lived in Saigon more than 3 years and who had come to the base only a few months previously, after learning that he had been compromised. He was an expert on Saigon and knew all of its streets and many people in various circles in the city. In addition to helping me carry out a number of tasks, he would be my driver if the enemy agreed to let us provide our own drivers.

Hai Le informed me that "The Central Committee had requested you to tell it what name you intend to use so that it can be passed on to Paris. Our delegation must inform the U.S.-puppet side."

Like everyone else, I had never used my real name, but had habitually used a code name, which I had changed now and then to make it difficult for the enemy to monitor me and maintain secrecy for our operations. The usual practice in wartime was for us to use a different name for each task during each phase. Now, faced with a new mission, I would meet the enemy face to face and would of course have to choose a name. Almost without thinking, I took the name "Nguyen Viet Chau," the name of a younger brother with whom I had been very close and who was killed in 1969 when he was presiding over a meeting of the party committee of Can Tho City. My brother and I had lived in Saigon, had participated together in secret revolutionary activity there during the period of French domination, had been released from a French prison at the same time, had participated together in the August 1945 uprising, and had left our beloved Saigon to take part in the resistance war. Now I was returning to that city and naturally thought about my esteemed younger brother, my comrade in death as well as in life. I was happy to take that unforgettable name. But then ond day, during an ordinary meal at the Regional Command at which Bay Cuong (comrade Pham Hung, a member of the Political Bureau and secretary of COSVN) was present, I suddenly remembered that I was not returning to Saigon as a stranger but was going under an assumed name, which would be inconvenient.

Many of the people of Saigon could not forget their children who had gone to fight in the resistance war years ago and in whom they had placed their confidence and hope. And a considerable number of the enemy, such as Tran Thien Khiem, the puppet premier, Lam Van Phat, a puppet major general, and a number of others, knew me. After graduating from the French military academy in Dalat they went to Dong Thap Muoi to join the resistance. As the commander of Military Region 8 at that time, I accepted and sent them to study and practice at the military region military administration school. But then, because they could not bear the hardships and did not love their country or their people, they deserted, surrendered to the French, and continued to serve their French, and the American, masters. Even the Americans might have dozens of photographs of me. Thus it would be best to use a name with which everyone, friend and foe alike, was familiar. The members of COSVN and the Regional Military Party Commission agreed. Thus I recommended that the Central Committee agree to the change and send a message to Paris so that the other side could be informed that the head of the delegation of the PRG of the RSVN would be Lt Gen Tran Van Tra.

Within a short period of time I drafted a plan to prepare in all ways for my new assignment, reviewed the organization of the delegation, and discussed in detail with Ba Tran (Maj Gen Tran Van Danh) the mission, personnel, documents, and facilities, especially the communications-liaison facilities, foresaw contingencies, decided on the measures, and assigned Ba Tran, the deputy delegation head, to represent me in directing all implementation tasks.

Ba Tran, who was born in Hoc Mon, grew up in Saigon and joined the anti-French resistance war in 1945, was the regional deputy chief of staff and was responsible for organizing and guiding the delegation and for strategic guidance.

He was an expert on Saigon and knew a good deal about the enemy. I had confidence in his ability and thought that the enemy would also respect him because he was robust, fair-skinned, stout, muscular and proper.

I attended a Regional Command meeting, in which the staff, political, rear services, and other organs participated, to discuss in detail all measures for coordinating struggle between the conference table and the battlefield. I emphasized that if the enemy respected us at the four-party conference table in Saigon and we were victorious in implementing the Paris Agreements, that it would principally be due to the strength of our troops and to our comrades on the outside. We promised that we would be worthy of being representatives of the heroic people's armed liberation forces of the South in the middle of the enemy's capital and in the bosom of our beloved compatriots.

We were due in Saigon on 28 January 1973. We had agreed to a time for the Americans to pick us up by helicopter at Thien Ngon, a location in northern Tay Ninh on National Route 22. In the past, Thien Ngon had been a small settlement of people who earned their living in the forest. During the war the Americans chased away all the people and built a strongpoint there for a U.S. brigade. It had an airfield, a supply depot, and a drill ground. From it were launched sweeping operations in the surrounding areas. At the beginning of 1972--by that time the puppet army had replaced the Americans--Thien Ngon was the main focus of the "Nguyen Hue" campaign.* In the course of our campaign we completely eliminated that strongpoint. Thus Thien Ngon was then only an old, desolate battlefield on which the vegetation had been burned and the surface of which was scarred by bomb and shell craters and littered with the hulks of U.S. tanks, armored vehicles, artillery and trucks, which were strewn all over. There remained only a runway usuable only by helicopters. After informing the enemy of the pick-up time we sent a reconnaissance team to Thien Ngon to rebuild some old bunkers, in which we would await the enemy before, during and after the appointed time. The members of that team reported to us every 15 minutes on all developments in the situation there. Meanwhile, a fully equipped delegation of cadres prepared our actual departure point at the Loc Ninh airfield. Our delegation organized a leisurely Tet celebration in advance. We knew that when we arrived in Saigon we would have to urgently begin work, even though the lunar New Year was only 4 or 5 days away, so we wanted to enjoy a Tet "at home," in our free, liberated area, that was embued with friendship between those leaving and those remaining behind. Celebrate Tet in advance! We were only repeating something that had happened several times in the history of our people's combat. Quang Trung-Nguyen Hue had his troops celebrate Tet in advance in 1789 at the Tam Diep bivouac area before they advanced on Thang Long, destroyed the Manchu-Ch'ing army, won a brilliant victory at Dong Da, and permanently ended the Chinese protectorate in our country. In the spring of 1968 the South celebrated Tet in advance--Tet Mau Than-- so that it could carry out the general offensive and uprising, smash the aggressive will of the U.S. imperialists, create a crisis in the White House, scare the Pentagon to death, and force the United States to deescalate the war, negotiate with us at Paris, then conclude the endlessly long conference during the spring of 1973. This spring--the spring of 1973--we were again celebrating

---

*Our offensive campaign in eastern Nam Bo in 1972.

Tet in advance so that we could go into the very lair of the enemy, force them to correctly implement the agreements, and see what tricks they would play and what they truly wanted.

The Tet feat in the bunker of the Regional Command was very flavorful. It was not very elegant but there were Tet cakes, including glutinous rice cakes, pork, both from pigs we had raised and from wild pigs, and with watermelon, liqueur, local products, and products from Hanoi. The comrades at COSVN, the Front for the Liberation of South Vietnam, the government, and the Regional Command, representatives of the mass association organs, and even a reporter from the liberation press, etc., joined in the festivities with the members of our delegation. The atmosphere was truly intimate and cosy. Happiness spread over everyone's face. The happiness increased with every glass of liqueur. We toasted the victory, pledged to meet again under even more auspicious circumstances, and toasted the success both at the conference table and on the battlefield. In the midst of the Tet meal, when the conversation was deafening, we received a message from Thien Ngon: "At the appointed hour the U.S. helicopters did not arrive to pick up the delegation. Instead, two enemy airplanes circled twice and dropped bombs around the air strip. Bomb fragments and fragments of the hulks of tanks and armored vehicles flew over our bunker. Then there was silence." Everyone poured some more liqueur and lifted their glasses to toast the health of the delegation members, to toast our cleverness and vigilance, and to warmly toast our delegation's first victory over the cowardly treachery of the Americans and their puppets. The conversation during the meal became even more resounding because of discussions about the Thien Ngon incident, the U.S.-puppet capability to violate the Paris Agreements, and the complications of our mission and of our work on the battlefield. Despite all that, everyone was burning with strong confidence, confidence in the inevitability of our victory under any circumstances. Everyone's eyes were alive with the brilliant vitality of spring. Outside, rays of sunlight shining through the foliage illuminated the jungle. The weather was dry, cool and pleasant. Everywhere, along the roads, there were streaks of white flowers, interspersed with the shiny golden color of wild apricot blossoms. This year spring came early in the base area, and the vegetation seemed to compete in responding to the happiness of victory.

Loc Ninh, a highly populated, prosperous town in the liberated area of eastern Nam Bo, was situated 100 kilometers from Saigon on National Route 13, which extends into Kampuchea and then Laos. Extending northward was National Route 14, which went to Ban Me Thuot and the Central Highlands. Extending southward was Route 17, which connected with our northern Tay Ninh base area. After it was liberated in April 1972, Loc Ninh became an important military position which threatened the enemy's defense of Saigon, and was a political center of the liberated B2 area. Loc Ninh, in the fertile red-soil area, which was appropriate for the growing of tropical crops, had vast rubber plantations left over from the French colonial period and luxuriant orchards of all kinds of fruit-- durians, rambutans, mangos, milk fruit, etc.--and hundreds of hectares of valuable pepper and coffee. In the past Loc Ninh had been a district seat in Binh Long Province, a strong point which lay within the puppet III Corps' outer perimeter for the defense of Saigon. During our "Nguyen Hue" campaign, Loc

Ninh was the principal objective and the most important position that had to be taken on the enemy's outer defensive perimeter. We not only wiped out a fortified brigade-level base but also wiped out many tank and armored regiments and many powerful task forces of the puppets' III Corps, and captured many POW's and officers, including Colonel Vinh, whom we later, out of humanitarianism and to demonstrate our good will, returned to the United States and its puppets. For those reasons, Loc Ninh had come to symbolize our victory and the disgraceful defeat of the enemy. We wanted the enemy to send helicopters to pick up our delegation at Loc Ninh so that they would remember that terrible blow. From that glorious spot, our delegation would proudly enter the puppet capital.

Immediately after they committed treachery by bombing the designated Thien Ngon location, we vigorously protested and demanded that they pick us up at Loc Ninh. Each time they disgracefully failed in an attack on us they had to be brought to their senses by the strength of their adversary. We hoped that they would not dare play any more dirty tricks, although we were fully prepared, for we knew that the enemy's nature would never change. After bombing Thien Ngon in order to wipe out our delegation to the Central Joint Military Commission, which we protested, they sent troops to carry out sweeping operations and bombed the locations designated as pick-up points for our delegations to the joint military commissions in the Pleiky and My Tho regions and to the local joint military teams in Phu Bai, Da Lat, Kontum, and Tan An. They continually took advantage of every small opportunity, regardless of reason or of the provisions of the agreement, to carry out schemes and plots in hopes of annihilating us--every person and every hamlet--if they could. Every time they did so we vigorously protested their acts at the four-party meetings in Saigon and they apologized and blamed the local security forces, whom they promised to punish. We were well aware that they were making empty promises just to get us to think that the Americans and their puppets had a plan to sabotage the Paris Agreement on both a small scale and a large scale.

Was not history repeating itself? The French had been heavily defeated and had to sign the Geneva Agreements in 1954, after which the Americans endeavored to prevent the agreements from being implemented. Today, the Americans and their puppets had suffered a heavy defeat and were trying to sabotage the Paris Agreement. However, we were people who were experienced. We had fought and negotiated in order to achieve agreements favorable to the revolution. We would struggle to implement all articles of those agreements. For the independence and freedom of the people, we were prepared to sacrifice and fight to the end. At the same time, we held out a hand of national reconciliation and concord in order to save those who had gone astray. But in view of our bloody experience in the past we were not so foolish as to believe that our enemies would sincerely carry out the agreements. Therefore, we were not surprised by such perfidy. We had drafted two plans to cope with two possible developments: first, because our struggle bore results and because of pressure from our people and the people of the world the enemy was forced to correctly implement the Paris Agreement; second, they would sabotage and abandon the agreements. It was all up to the enemy. We were attempting to bring about the first contingency, but we were prepared to cope with the second one.

On 1 February 1973, at the appointed hour, a flight of U.S. helicopters commanded by an American lieutenant colonel who was accompanied by a puppet officer, and flying along the course and at the altitude we had designated, made a circle around Loc Ninh and, one after the other, from the northern end of the air strip. While they were circling around they had clearly seen the air strip, the town and, more importantly, the large number of anti-aircraft positions and tanks, deployed in many perimeters around the town, which were prepared to respond if they tried any funny business. On that day the town of Loc Ninh was like a large festival. Revolutionary flags few everywhere. Especially, at the airfield there was a solemn, orderly atmosphere. A large number of people of all categories, cadres, and neatly dressed troops assembled and formed ranks. There was a forest of gold-starred red flags, mixed in with half-blue, half-red flags and countless banners and slogans applauding the victory of the Paris Agreements on Vietnam, demanding the strict and absolute implementation of the agreements, acclaiming the military delegation of the PRG of the RSVN, etc. A quick, seething, and spirited rally was held beside the waiting American helicopters. Many delegates representing the various circles and mass associations arose to make brief speeches in which they demanded peace and national concord, congratulated our delegation, and expressed confidence in the inevitable victory of the delegation's struggle. On behalf of the delegation, I expressed its gratitude to the cadres, enlisted men, and people who had come to applaud and solemnly see off the delegation, acknowledged the advice given the delegation, and promised to be worthy of that confidence. The U.S. officers and flight crews tried to appear civilized and stood looking on in silence, but the puppet officers were perplexed and angry and remained seated in the helicopters, not daring to come out.

After the rally was over, as ordered by the commander of the Loc Ninh airfield the U.S. helicopters started their engines. I turned and glanced at the comrades and people and gave a loving look at the scenery of Loc Ninh, then shook hands with everyone. I hugged and kissed comrade Van Pha, deputy head of the Regional Political Office, with whom I had participated in the "Nguyen Hue" campaign at Loc Ninh several years previously, and comrade Le The Thuong, in charge of propaganda-training in the region, with whom I had once traveled the entire length of the Truong Son trail. Comrade Thuong promised, "I'll send you a photograph I took of the people seeing you and our delegation off to Saigon." Our delegation members waved to the people, then the comrades, two abreast, solemnly boarded the helicopters, amidst the affection of the people and the forest of flags and flowers. The U.S. major commanding my helicopter was very polite, carefully inspecting my seat, then stepped down, stood at attention and saluted, invited me to board the helicopter, fastened my safety belt, then sat down in his seat. The helicopters took off in an orderly formation, circled once above the airfield, then headed straight for Saigon along Route 13. The large number of people at the airfield were not the only ones seeing us off: nearly everyone, people traveling along the road, standing in their yards and on the streets, or working in the rice paddies and potato fields around Loc Ninh stopped work to wave at us. That was an extremely moving, very peaceful scene in an area scarred with the devastation of war. What did the Americans in the helicopters, and the puppets think about that scene, which was completely in contrast to the scene a few days ago. The same helicopters had caused much death and separation for countless families; when they flew overhead there was nothing below them, not a single person on the ground below! Suddenly the American major turned toward me and half jokingly, half seriously said, "You have won the war!"

The flock of helicopters followed Route 13 past Binh Long, Tau O, Chon Thanh, Bau Bang, Lai Khe, Ben Cat, etc. All of those places had been the location of many fierce battles between us and the American and puppet troops over the course of many years and still bore the marks of the glorious feats of arms of the diligent and heroic eastern Nam Bo troops. I looked down at the jungle, which previously consisted of thick growths of large and small trees but was now denuded and desolate. There were many bomb craters on the surface. Many long scars of devastation caused by B52 carpet bombing succeeded one another and criss-crossed one another in the devastated jungle. When they looked down from above, the Americans thought that nothing could survive where their B52's had passed over, so they boasted that the B52 were terrible gods of war. Then we flew over the Saigon River, the Binh Loi Bridge lying between two thick nets of steel, then An Phu Dong, then Tan Son Nhat. The helicopters landed in the military part of the airfield. Our delegation thanked the crew members and shook their hands. Looking neat in the tidy insignia-less liberation army uniforms, we formed into an orderly line on the runway. The officers carried briefcases and wore revolvers. The enlisted men wore floppy jungle hats and carried backpacks and AK rifles. Everyone wore the famous rubber sandals. I don't know whether the Americans and their puppets understood the significance of that or not, but the many Vietnamese and foreign reporters who were present at the airfield that day were very observant. They photographed us with movie cameras and still cameras. I smiled with delight when I noticed them photographing our rubber sandals. They said, "Wearing simple, proud rubber sandals, they sat foot on Tan Son Nhat. They entered Saigon, capital of the Republic of Vietnam, in the same rubber sandals they wore during Tet of 1968." (UPI, 1 February 1973). The reporters told the truth. Those rubber sandals had left their proud imprints on the streets of Saigon, at many important objectives, and even at Tan Son Nhat airfield, as well as all the other towns, cities, and municipalities in South Vietnam during Tet Mau Than, so that there could be the scene on that day--rubber sandals entering Saigon with good will-- and so that some day it would be certain that the rubber sandals could return to Saigon yet another time--to a liberated Saigon. I looked at the line formed by the cadres and men of the delegation from one end to the other and felt very happy and proud. They had bright eyes and bright smiles and stood erect, looking correct and imposing, all of which expressed the confidence of victors. They were cadres and men from all battlefields and holding many different positions, and they were from many different components and of many different age groups. Some had served since the anti-French resistance war and some had answered the call of the simultaneous uprising. Some of them took up arms in Saigon during the Tet Offensive, and others had been in the army only a year but had contributed to the immortal Loc Ninh-Route 13 victory. They stood there like simple, ordinary, natural people before the lenses of the reporters and before the inquisitive, curious, and surprised eyes of the U.S.-puppet MP's who were standing around. From the crowd there came toward us people wearing the uniforms and insignia of the Hungarian and Polish armies. It turned out that they were our Hungarian and Polish comrades in the International Commission for Control and Supervision who had come to the airfield to greet us and offer our delegation all necessary assistance. I intimately greeted those comrades and expressed my deep gratitude. After completing several simple forms, we got into black American Fords and Chevrolets to go to the delegation's headquarters--which the Americans and their puppets called "Camp David"--in Tan Son Nhat airfield.

Camp David, formerly a U.S. military camp, had been renovated. It consisted of many temporary wooden, sheet-metal roofed barracks arranged in straight rows, between which there were broad paths and occasionally a shade tree. It was very hot, especially at midday. In addition to the heat there was the roar of all kinds of airplanes and helicopters. The noise, which came from all directions, made everyone angry and irritable. It was difficult to think, work and relax. Fortunately, after the sun went down at dusk the area naturally became cooler, but there was no way to turn off the incessant noise. It was indeed a military camp. It was entirely adequate for soldiers in wartime, but fell far short of the minimum standards of a diplomatic delegation. They were clearly playing a dirty trick on us there. Perhaps they had spent a lot of effort to find an "appropriate" headquarters for both of our delegations: the military delegation of the government of the DRV and our delegation.

As soon as we entered the gate of the camp, Le Quang Hoa, Luu Van Loi, Ho Quang Hoa, Bui Thanh Tin and many other people I knew, practically the entire DRV delegation, rushed up and surrounded our convoy. Just after we got out of the car brother Hoa presented me with a bouquet of fresh lilies from Hanoi, then everyone hugged one another. There were sounds of laughter and backslapping. It was truly moving--especially the spirit of brotherhood among the children of the same mother--the motherland--who had writhed in misery and pain during years of warfare. It was truly heartwarming and happy when comrades-in-arms who had lived and died together on the battlefield and faced a cruel enemy, now met in the bosom of the enemy, surrounded by enemy troops, with one noble objective: struggling for peace and national concord.

I turned to hug and kiss Doang Huyen, deputy head of the military delegation of the PRG of the RSVN, who had gone to Saigon in advance to participate in meetings of deputy delegation heads and discuss the work procedures. Duong Dinh Thao, a member of our delegation who had also arrived at Saigon via Paris, anxiously relayed to me a letter and warm salutations and congratulations from Nguyen Thi Binh and our delegation in Paris.

The camp was divided into two parts: one side was reserved for brother Hoa's delegation and the other was reserved for my delegation. But the Americans and their puppets had the good intention of preparing for the two delegation heads a relatively decent house built in the duplex style: each of us had half of the house, including a living room, an office, a dining room, a bedroom and a bathroom. There was a door to each of the rooms, and there were airconditioning, bright lights, a telephone and other conveniences. We clearly understood their "good intentions." Therefore, we moved into other rooms and lived and worked with the others. We turned that house over to specialists so that they could inspect it. After searching around for days they showed us some very small microphones they had found under tables in the offices and livingrooms. We joked with one another that we didn't know whether they had been put there by the Americans or by the puppets, or put there as a practical joke by carpenters who were also electronic technicians. There were many other such stories: jamming the radio channels we used to communicate with the base areas, obtaining copies of our telegrams, etc. But enough! It does no good to talk. Doubtlessly, that was a common story to the Americans in the age of electronics. What were those stories compared to the Watergate affair in Washington? The important thing was that we were aware of, and were on guard against, even the smallest detail. That was nothing less than the continuation of a war that had not yet ended. The enemy used every trick they could use, from modern weapons that could kill many people at a time to the most sophisticated electronic machinery, the radar and lasers used in the viewing and listening devices, from MacNamara's fence to Camp David. In its 15 March 1973 issue THE STARS AND STRIPES, the newspaper of the U.S. Army in the Pacific, admitted that "The United States had fought three long wars in this century. The Vietnam war was the largest war with regard to the number of bombs dropped and was also the largest with regard to the use of science and technology in warfare!"

That was a matter of abusing modern U.S. technology for aggressive purposes, to kill people and deceive others. As for the puppets, they had neither technology nor intelligence, so their U.S. masters assigned them the task of playing vile, petty tricks every day to give our delegation a hard time, such as limiting the food and goods a contractor could bring into Camp David, preventing the press, and especially the people, from meeting with and talking with our delegation, and seeking to restrict our travel, especially through Saigon, by causing delays, damaging our vehicles, having the escorting MP's arrive late, etc., then intimidating us with helicopters and tanks, and plotting to use money and women to bribe us. With regard to our regional delegations and local teams, the enemy's behavior was even worse. They provided bad, unsanitary, crowded, hot housing quarters which lacked all conveniences. For example, in the My Tho region they provided a recently remodeled chicken-coop in the Dong Tam base. The stench was still very strong. They provided poor-quality food. In one instance, at Hue, the canned goods were so old that they were wormy. At the four-party conference table in Saigon we continually and vigorously protested their treatment and demanded the formation of an investigating team. The Americans blamed the puppets. Major General Woodward, head of the U.S. delegation, pretended that "It is unfortunate that the U.S. delegation knows nothing about such deficiencies. The Republic of Vietnam is resonsible for such things. They have informed us that everything is in good shape." On such occasions, the puppets either clammed up or blamed the lower echelon, the local officials, or people who had not done their jobs properly, and then agreed to send an inspection team and promised to fix up the housing and provide additional equipment, but that was the end of it.

Furthermore, they organized gangs of hooligans and thugs to cooperate with their MP's and police to commit acts of violence against PLA officers who were members of the joint military commissions and teams by throwing rocks and trash, and even using steel rods, knives, and hammers to wound our men, such as Major Le Thanh Nhon and two captains on the Buon Me Thuot team, and six of our comrades at Hue. Comrade Tran Hon Ngo was hit on the head and knocked unconscious at Duc Pho in Quang Ngai Province while he was working with an investigation team of the joint commission. All of our officers and men in the joint commissions and teams were people who had achieved many accomplishments in war on many battlefields and had fought very heroically, like tigers, in the battles. Now, on the new struggle front in the area controlled by the enemy, they always had confidence in the just cause and in the inevitable victory of the revolution, were very calm and steadfast, and did not waver in the face of ugly acts, intimidation, or attempted bribery. We are very proud of them and are grateful to the troops of Uncle Ho who were very ordinary but were indomitable, had military bearing and didn't blink an eye.

Why did the Americans and their puppets play such cheap tricks? Certainly not to create a wholesome atmosphere in order to cooperate in correctly implementing the agreements, and certainly not to create an atmosphere of national reconciliation and concord after years of enmity because of the destructive warfare. How could reasoning people subjected to such acts by the United States and its puppets still believe that they truly wanted to end the war and bring about peace? Clearly, they brazenly and without hiding their perfidious faces intended to sabotage the agreement.

The most important aspect of the agreement, and the first matter that had to be implemented, was the ceasefire. Articles 2 and 3 of the agreement and the protocol on the ceasefire made clear and specific stipulations about the complete cessation of hostilities, the forces remaining in their original positions, etc. But after 28 January 1973, the day on which the ceasefire took effect (and until 30 April 1975), it was ironic that there was not a day on which the guns fell silent on any of the battlefields in South Vietnam.

On the very hour the ceasefire was to take effect, Thieu's puppet administration sent a task force led by tanks on an operation to take Cua Viet from us. There we put up a very stiff resistance, annihilated the encroaching enemy troops, and maintained the liberated area. Thus at the four-party conference table our side held the upper hand in denouncing their violation of the agreement. Lt Gen Ngo Du, head of the puppet delegation argued that we had occupied Cua Viet at 0758 on the morning of 28 January (the ceasefire was to take effect at 0800 on the morning of 28 January). I responded, "But we liberated Cua Viet in May 1972. We have all kinds of clear evidence about the illegal encroachment by your army after the ceasefire. But I would like to inform you of a report we have just received that thanks to their high degree of vigilance our liberation troops have annihilated the encroaching troops and defeated that adventuristic act, after having tried to use loudspeakers to appeal for them to retreat and not violate the agreement, but to no avail. That is a lesson for those who do not want to respect the agreement and not respect their signature." Their faces paled and they were bitter.

In order to prevent enemy airplanes from flying over areas under our control, we demanded an immediate discussion of Article 3 of the protocol regarding the ceasefire: "The joint military commissions will reach agreements regarding the corridors, routes, and other stipulations regarding the movement of military transport aircraft and military transport ships and boats of one side which must pass through an area controlled by the other side." Both the U.S. and puppet delegations regarded that matter as being unnecessary. But during the meeting on 16 February the American side urgently announced that a C47 had been shot down south of An Loc and two U.S. crewmen had been seriously wounded. During all of the following meetings the Americans protested and demanded the appointment of an investigating team. I agreed to the investigation but stressed that since the Four-Party Joint Military Commission had not yet reached agreement regarding the flight paths, altitude, etc., of airplanes flying over areas controlled by the liberation troops, no one can accept responsibility for their safety. Ultimately, the Americans had to shut up and forget the incident. Clearly, by basing ourselves on the legality of the agreements while resolutely protesting the violations we forced the Americans and puppets to respect us. In places where we were weak and careless on the battlefield, even if the enemy was 100 percent guilty of a violation it would still argue obstinately, regardless of our protests. An example was the puppets' taking of Sa Huynh in Quang Ngai which we had liberated in 1972, along with a relatively long stretch of National Route 1. After the ceasefire took effect the puppets launched a division-sized operation to retake that area in order to restore their communications on Route 1. We vigorously exposed that violation and demanded that an investigation team be sent there, but the Americans and puppets ignored our demand and considered the incident closed. After 28 January the enemy also launched continuous operations to take villages and hamlets along Route 4 in My Tho which we had controlled prior to 28 January, and set up outposts deep in our territory. In that area, because our forces were not on guard and were afraid that if they retaliated they would violate the agreements, the enemy was able to occupy those places and fraudulently claim at the conference table that the area belonged to them. The ceasefire was the heart of the agreement but the Thieu puppet regime completely ignored it and brazenly sabotaged the heart of the agreement. Their 1973 "Ly Thuong Kiet" plan set forth five major strategic goals:

--Encroachment and pacification were the central measures.

--The pillar was building a strong army and a strong governmental administration. Within 5 years the ARVN would be made younger and more effective, and would be modernized.

--Sabotaging the parts of the Paris Agreement on Vietnam which were not beneficial for the Republic of Vietnam.

--Restoring the economic level of 1973-1974 in the 1973-1978 long-range plan, especially with regard to industry, accompanied by the economic blockading of the enemy.

--Maintaining the deterrent force of the U.S. air and naval forces in Southeast Asia.

They also endeavored to carry out "land grabbing" operations and "flag planting" operations in which infantry and helicopters were used to plant flags. They prepared 1.6 million three-barred puppet flags for that task.

The 6 April 1973 report of the Committee To Denounce War Crimes in Vietnam concluded that "In the 2-month period between 28 January and 28 March 1973, the Saigon administration violated the Paris Agreement more than 70,000 times, including 19,770 land-grabbing operations, 23 artillery shellings, 3,375 bombings and straffings of liberated areas, and 21,075 police operations in areas under their control."

According to enemy data, as of October 1973 they had set up 1,180 outposts in South Vietnam and controlled 7,258 hamlets more than they did prior to 28 January 1973.*

Clearly, although the United States and its puppets had signed the agreement they continued to act imperturbably in accordance with their existing plans, and endeavored to pacify, encroach, and build a strong army in order to change the balance of forces in their favor and gain complete control of South Vietnam. At a meeting of the two South Vietnamese delegations in March 1973, Lt Gen Du Quoc Dong, who had replaced Ngo Du as head of the puppet delegation, when he had been put in a bad position showed his true face by saying, "I don't approve of the Paris Agreement because it only benefits your side." I sternly criticized him, "So it is clear: Lt Gen Du Quoc Dong is representing the Republic of Vietnam in the implementation of an agreement of which he does not approve, and indeed opposes. It is evident and clear that your side is violating and sabotaging the agreement." He hastily corrected himself, "I personally do not approve of it...but...because the agreement has been reached, we must carry it out!"

As everyone knows, before the Paris Agreement was signed the United States urgently sent weapons and war facilities to South Vietnam to bolster the puppet army, make up for the puppets' heavy losses in 1972, and build up a sufficient stockpile so that the puppet army could continue to be strong after the Americans withdrew. Kissinger had often declared during press conferences in the United States that "After the Americans withdraw, the Republic of Vietnam must continue to be strong." That work continued at a rapid pace after the agreement took effect. Many documents have clearly recorded the figures, the world press had written much about them, and there are ample statistics, so I believe that it is unnecessary to repeat them here.

Furthermore the U.S. and vassal troops were required to withdraw completely from South Vietnam in accordance with the agreement, but they turned over to Thieu's army their modern equipment supply depots, and bases.

Articles 5 and 6 of the agreement stipulated that all troops, military advisers and military personnel, including military technical personnel, military personnel attached to the pacification program, and the weapons, ammunition, and war materiel of the United States and the other foreign countries, would have to be completely withdrawn from South Vietnam within 60 days after the signing of the agreement, and that all military bases of the United States and the other foreign countries were to be dismantled. The protocol on the ceasefire also stated in Article 8 that "The United States and the other foreign countries mentioned in Article 5 of the agreement will take with them all of their weapons, ammunition and military equipment."

---

*Documents captured from the enemy after the liberation and now held at the B2 War Recapitulation Section of the Ministry of National Defense.

In order to insure the correct implementation of those articles, Article 3 stated clearly that beginning with the ceasefire the forces of the United States would remain in their original positions while awaiting a troop withdrawal plan. The Four-Party Joint Military Commission would stipulate the procedures.

The Four-Party Joint Military Commission was responsible for coordinating monitoring and investigating the implementation of Articles 3, 5 and 6. Especially, the International Commission was required to control and supervise the implementation of those articles.

During the meetings of the delegation heads of the four parties at Tan Son Nhat we continually requested the U.S. delegation to inform us of its plan to withdraw troops and dismantle its military bases so that joint inspection teams could monitor and inspect its implementation. It was the same every day: Major General Woodward, head of the U.S. delegation, hemmed and hawed and turned to other matters. But one day he solemnly announced "The results of the strict implementation of the agreements on the part of the United States, which has disarmed torpedoes and mines...." He spoke distinctly about numbers, time, space, etc. When he reached the part about withdrawing troops he said, "Eight thousand troops, including those of the Allies, have been withdrawn from South Vietnam." I immediately protested, "We cannot accept such a perfunctory report by the U.S. delegation. No one can believe the 8,000 figure or any other figure Major General Woodward gives out, without thinking that it could be false. I believe that any withdrawal of U.S. troops or the troops of any other foreign country must be announced in advance so that there can be on-the-spot monitoring and inspection by the Four-Party Joint Military Commission as well as the control and supervision of the International Commission, as has been stipulated. Otherwise, no figures can have any value. As far as I am concerned, to date not a single U.S. soldier, or a soldier from any other country, has left South Vietnam."

Many days later, on 16 February 1973, the Americans sent us a diplomatic not officially agreeing that joint four-party military teams could go to the various locations to observe the withdrawal of U.S. and South Korean troops and could take photographs. Thus they had to make a concession. From those observations it was clear that although when they arrived in Vietnam the U.S. and South Korean troops had been armed to the teeth, when they left they carried no weapons at all, but only sleeping bags, personal effects, and such tacky souvenirs as earthenware and porcelain elephants, stonewar from Marble Mountain, etc. When our men asked about that they were told, "Our weapons and equipment have been sent by ship." Such was their deception!

Only after their total defeat in 1975 did the Americans, dumbfounded over the fact that although they used every trick to provide the puppet army with much equipment it was still defeated, angrily admit the truth: "With the enormous quantity of equipment and materiel left behind when our forces withdrew, added to the aid provided subsequently, the ARVN forces should have been fully capable of coping with the enemy." (From the concluding Chapter 10 of the book "The Last Helicopter," by Weldon A. Brown.)

How about the dismantling of military bases?

The American Major General Woodward solemnly reported that "We are authorized to reply to you that at present we have no bases in South Vietnam. All of them were turned over to the Republic of Vietnam prior to the signing of the agreement. The American troops are now stationed in camps temporarily borrowed from the Republic of Vietnam."

That was a deception that was brazen beyond words.

Once the imperialists had drafted a plan and had objectives, they acted in the style of aggressors, lying brazenly no matter to whom they were talking.

The International Commission should have been fully capable of exposing those dishonest acts, and of reaching accurate conclusions and condemning violations of the agreement by the Americans and puppets in order to prevent them from sabotaging the agreement and continuing the war. Four countries--Hungary, Poland, Indonesia and Canada--participated in the International Commission. After Canada withdrew it was replaced by Iran, which worked in accordance with the principle of consultation and unanimity.

It must be frankly said that Canada practically belonged to the Americans and took the Americans' part in the International Commission, arguing, glossing over and, when necessary, vetoing. The head of the Canadian delegation, Ambassador Gauvin, was outwardly courteous but was said to be a person who was dogmatic, overbearing, domineering and looked down on others. One day Gauvin indicated that he wanted to make a courtesy call on the delegation of the PRG of the RSVN. We were quite willing and regarded that as a good opportunity to speak frankly with that representative of the International Commission. I received him in a living room that had been prepared as decently as conditions in Camp David allowed. I went out to his car to greet the ambassador, escorted him inside, and invited him to sit with me on a divan, the most ceremonious seat in the living room. Accompanying him were a political aide of the Canadian delegation, and a number of others. The person who did most of the interpreting during that meeting was our interpreter, comrade Dung, who interpreted for me during all of the meetings of the heads of the four-party delegations. Dung was a remarkable youth who spoke English fluently in a strong voice and knew how to stress the essential passages.

After the exchange of pleasantries Gauvin spoke of the role and accomplishments of the International Commission, especially during the period in which Gauvin served as its chairman, regarding the ceasefire, the exchange of prisoners, the withdrawal of U.S. and vassal troops from South Vietnam, etc. By doing so he wanted to speak of the effectiveness of the International Commission and its objectivity and fairness and, especially, unjustly criticize us in an accusatory, threatening voice by saying that there had as yet been no ceasefire because of our many violations on the battlefield. I sat listening to him very calmly and politely, both patiently listening and understanding the significance of each word. Even the ambassador realized that he had spoken too long and looked at me inquisitively. I calmly invited my guest to eat some fruit and smoke a cigarette. Then I began to speak:

"My dear Ambassador Gauvin, you have spoken very accurately of the very important role and the very necessary objectivity of the International Commission for Control and Supervision in implementing the agreement. I am sincerely sorry that the sound of gunfire can be heard all over, that although agreement has been reached to end the war and restore peace in Vietnam the devastating war of the past several decades is continuing. I believe that no people in the world desire peace more ardently than the people of Vietnam, who have fought and borne hardships in the cause of justice. But, Mr Ambassador, there is a reason for everything. I would like to turn for you a few pages of recent history. Our nation won independence in 1945. The French colonialists again invaded our country. Only by fighting 9 years, the outstanding victory during which was the battle of Dien Bien Phu, were we able to achieve the signing of the Geneva Agreement. During that period there was also an International Control Commission of which Canada was a member. I'm sure you are well aware of that." Gauvin nodded his head in agreement. I continued, "But Nixon, who was then the U.S. vice president, declared to the press that 'Although France has signed a treaty to end hostilities in Indochina, the United States will act alone if necessary and will send troops to that part of the world.' That was reported by THE NEW YORK TIMES. That is indeed what the United States did."

Gauvin made a motion with his hand to interrupt the interpreter and began to speak at length. I said to Dung, "Continue to interpret what I say. Only after I have finished should you listen to and interpret what he has to say." Dung, unperturbed, continued to interpret for me.

"I would like to bring some figures to your attention, Mr Ambassador. Between 1955 and 1960 more than 800 U.S. ships carrying weapons and war facilities of various kinds arrived at the ports of Vietnam, especially Da Nang. During the same period $600 million worth of aid was given to the Ngo Dinh Diem regime. The whole world knows about that. That was a brazen violation of the Geneva Agreement. But the International Commission at that time did not stop those illegal acts because it ignored them, covered them up, or was under pressure. So the guns continued to fire and the war continued on our Vietnamese soil. Canada was an important part of the International Commission at that time and cannot, of course, deny its great responsibility."

Gauvin again interrupted and would have gone on talking if I had not instructed Dung to continue to interpret what I was saying and to speak in a voice louder than Gauvin's.

Dung, who was indeed a remarkable youth, drowned out what Gauvin was saying, forcing Gauvin to stop talking and listen to me. He appeared to be surprised, perhaps because he had never before failed to dominate others and been restricted in such a way. I continued, "Events are now repeating themselves. Before and after the Paris Agreement the Americans shipped weapons and equipment to the ARVN so that it could sabotage the agreement and carry out land-grabbing and pacification campaigns. Furthermore, although the U.S. and other foreign troops returned to their countries they left their weapons, facilities, supply depots, and bases to the army of the Thieu regime, which was a brazen violation of the Paris Agreement."

At that point Gauvin, as if he could stand no more, jumped up, waved his hand vigorously, and mumbled a few words. I had to calm him down: "Mr Ambassador, please take it easy. I only want to say a few more words, then you may have your turn." Then I continued.

"This time, if we, the International Commission, and the Four-Party Joint Military Commission do not cooperatively closely with one another, try to operate together objectively and effectively, and stop all such violations, I believe that the sound of gunfire will continue to be heard. That will not be surprising, and the reason will be clear. Our responsibility to history is great but we have not met the desires for peace of the people of Vietnam, the people of Canada, and the peace-loving people of the world. What will the Canadian government, which has twice participated in the international commissions under two treaties, think about its role?

Now Gauvin no longer appeared so eager to speak. His attitude softened. "Dear Lt Gen Tran Van Tra," he said, "I admit that I know nothing about the Geneva Agreement. I know nothing about what happened then." Then the ambassador changed the subject and talked about the weather in Saigon and the various kinds of fruit in Vietnam.

I pleasantly invited my guest to drink beer and soft drinks. Everyone tried to maintain a friendly atmosphere.

Gauvin again spoke and recalled a big reception he had organized in Saigon for Sharp, the Canadian Secretary of State for External Affairs who came here on an official visit. In addition to all the "bigshots" of the Saigon puppet regime and the U.S. Ambassador Bunker, he invited members of the International Commission and of the Four-Party Joint Military Mission, including ourselves.

"General Tran Van Tra was truly the star of that reception, a star in the sky of Saigon that day," he said. "Dear Mr Ambassador," I replied, "that was the star of the just cause of the PRG of the RSVN, which I have the honor of representing here!" "No, no," he said, "I was speaking of your outstanding individual role."

He was attempting to avoid praising the PRG of the RSVN, although it had long had indisputable prestige, not only in Saigon but at Paris and in the world. In order to oppose it, the United States and the puppet Thieu regime adopted the principle that in South Vietnam there existed only one government, that of Thieu's Republic of Vietnam. The United States and China had agreed to that principle during the "Nixon-Mao Zedong-Zhou Enlai political conference which resulted in the Shanghai Communique.

He continued, "You are a great soldier," Now I was truly at a loss. I clearly understood his posturing but did not suspect that he would praise me so highly. Luckily, I suddenly remembered an appraisal of our soldiers by UPI in 1964: "The Viet Cong guerrillas are mythical figures. They are an enemy worthy of fearing, a foe everyone must respect." In 1965 the magazine U.S. NEWS & WORLD REPORT wrote that "The Viet Cong guerrillas are the most skilled and the greatest in the history of mankind."

I smiled broadly and said, "I thank you for your compliments. The truth is that out of patriotism and love for the people, and because 'there is nothing more precious than independence and freedom,' our liberation fighters have sacrificed their lives in combat and have won victory. The American press and news agencies, as well as those of the world, have called them mythical figures, the most skilled, greatest fighters. I am truly proud to represent them in Saigon in order to struggle for the correct implementation of the agreement they won only by shedding much blood."

Then Ambassador Gauvin excused himself and left. He suggested that we have a souvenir photograph taken. Gauvin handed the camera he had brought along to our photographer so that he could take a few snapshots.

The 60 days we spent in Saigon with the Four-Party Joint Military Commission were pressing, tense days. Our two military delegations did all they could to struggle for the implementation of the agreement, but the results were limited. The comrades of the Hungarian and Polish delegations to the International Commission, with an international spirit and ardent brotherhood, cooperated closely with us in struggling, protecting one another, and helping one another.

Our comrade Major General Xuyt"[phonetic], deputy head of the Hungarian delegation to the International Commission, a big man who looked husky in his Hungarian army uniform, during the first working session said in a sincere voice, "The party, state, army and people of Hungary have sent us to Vietnam for the sake of the peace and well-being of the Vietnamese people, and for world peace. We regard the success of the Vietnamese revolution as our success and are thus ready to lay down our lives for it. That is the principle which guides all of our actions. We are not afraid of death and of course are not afraid of hardship."

I was very grateful for the heartfelt words of the emissary of the working class who had come from a faraway land to help us during a difficult period, in a spirit of noble international proletarianism!

It would be impossible to relate everything we accomplished or failed to accomplish during those 60 days. Because the Americans and puppets had objectives and plans that had been prepared in advance, the key problem--the ceasefire-- could not be resolved. The war continued. Let us listen to what Thieu had to say to the puppet officers at Thu Duc:

"The Republic of Vietnam will implement the ceasefire provisions only when:

"1. The Army of the Republic of Vietnam no longer supports me.

"2. When American military aid is only sufficient for defensive purposes.

"3. When the military forces of the Republic of Vietnam are no longer capable of defending the important areas of South Vietnam."

Clearly, the loyal lackey of the Americans thought that he would be victorious, so he obstinately sabotaged the ceasefire and continued the war as if there had been no agreement!

The American and vassal troops had withdrawn. The vassal troops of the Americans who had sold themselves to the Americans to participate in killing our people, such as the Australians, New Zealanders, Thai, and South Koreans, had completely withdrawn from our country. In the morning of 15 March 1973 USARV, the U.S. Army Command in Vietnam, conducted a flag-folding ceremony and bugged out. In the afternoon, MACV, the U.S. Military Assistance Command in Vietnam, actually the U.S. GHQ which commanded all U.S. troops, the vassal troops, and Thieu's army and the imposing U.S. aggressive war apparatus in Vietnam, the Tan Son Nhat headquarters of which had been dubbed the "Pentagon of the East" by the press, also pulled down and folded its flag.

Whether by accident or by clever design, the next day the military delegations of the DRV and the PRG of the RSVN drove into the courtyard of that "Pentagon of the East." The two delegations got out of their cars and advanced directly into the reception room, past two rows of American MP's who stood at attention and saluted, in order to attend a party organized by the major general who headed the U.S. delegation. We laughed, drank American whiskey, and talked about the weather and peace in Vietnam, in the "Pentagon of the East."

Thus the U.S. troops also got out. But, as stated above, they left behind all kinds of weapons, military bases, and even officers in civilian clothing, to prop up the Thieu regime.

With regard to the exchange of prisoners in accordance with the agreement, we succeeded in securing the release of our people who had been captured during the war. Maj Nguyen Thi Dung, a member of our military delegation, was responsible for the POW exchange. She was very active and aggressive, visiting all of the puppet prisons, from Bien Hoa to Con Dao and Phu Quoc. She was the only female member of the four military delegations, spoke French and English fluently, was attractive and polite, and struggled resolutely, which won the respect of the Americans and puppets. We were proud of her. She worked at disseminating the articles of the agreement regarding the exchange of POW's to our men who were still imprisoned, struggled for the improvement of prison conditions, and demanded the return of those who were still detained. The enemy did not return everyone and were not sincere, but we were able to liberate a considerable number of our cadres and men, people who had fought heroically but had fallen into the hands of the enemy and had been subjected to their barbarous treatment.

We returned all American and puppet POW's we were detaining.

But another important matter was that in the course of the 60 days of face-to-face meetings with the enemy we gained better understanding of them. The Americans were only interested in obtaining the release of their POW's as a gift to the American people, and in bringing the U.S. troops home, as demanded by the American people. Otherwise, they continued to implement their policy of Vietnamizing the war so that they could remain in Vietnam. The puppets adhered to Thieu's "four nos" slogan: no concession of land to the "communists," no neutrality, no coalition with the "communists," and no talking with the "communists." Although the puppets were forced to negotiate with us at the two-party talks at Tan Son Nhat, in fact they continued to adhere to their "four nos" principles and did not negotiate with us in good faith, but argued about everything, made careless statements, and agreed to something one day only to change their minds the next day. They even reneged and refused to implement the first and smallest matter--the color of the flag and the insignia--of the Four-Party Joint Military Commission--which was agreed upon at the meeting of deputy delegation heads on 31 January 1973. That decision was that the flag, arm bands, and insignia on the vehicles, boats, and aircraft of the Joint Military Commission were to be orange in color. During a meeting of delegation heads they recommended that the matter be reconsidered and that another color be selected. We rejected that recommendation. What had been agreed to should be carried out, and not reneged on. In the middle of a meeting, during a break, Brig Gen Phan Hoa Hiep, deputy head of the puppet delegation, sat down beside me and whispered, "You don't know me but I know you well." I asked him, "When did we meet?" Hiep replied, "I was a soldier in the 3d Division (at the time of the August Revolution 1945). It's too bad the bigwigs at that time were at odds with one another. Otherwise I might still be a resistance fighter under your command." He chuckled when he said that. What he said was correct. The "big wigs" to whom he referred included me. At the beginning of the resistance war I commanded a unit called the Hoc Mon-Ba Diem-Duc Hoa Interdistrict Liberation Unit, which operated around Saigon. Nguyen Hoa Hiep was commander of the 3d Division and Ly Hue Vinh was commander of the 4th Division. The 4th Division fell apart as soon as the French returned in 1945. The 3d Division disintegrated and surrendered to the French within a brief period of time. I disarmed some of the units of those two divisions which had been robbing and attacking the people in Nhuan Duc, An Nhon Tay, Hoc Mon-Gia Dinh, My Tho, and Duc Hoa (Long An). It was said that Phan Hoa Hiep's family name was in fact not "Phan" but a transliteration of "Francois" into "Phan Hoa," for his real name was Francois Hiep, son of a French father and a Vietnamese mother. When I related that rumor to him he tried to ingratiate with me, called himself my youngest brother and pleaded for his "older brother" to agree to change the color of the flag.

"Orange is close to red," he said, "It makes us mad to see it." He had degraded himself to youngest brother, so I took the part of the eldest brother and said, "Why do you get mad? Red is the splendid, brilliant color of the future, and is nothing to be afraid of. You should know that orange is in common use internationally. It is very visible, even from far away. That color is the most appropriate and is attractive. Furthermore, what has been agreed to should be carried out, not haggled back and forth, which wastes time. There are still many things remaining to be done." He continued to plead with me but I resolutely turned him down. Even so, the puppets refused to carry out the agreement. There were many stories similar to the orange color story.

According to the agreement, the Four-Party Joint Military Commission would cease operations after 60 days. But near the end of that period, according to American sources and the Saigon press, the Four-Party Joint Military Commission would be extended. We didn't know what they were up to. Was it in order to prolong the legal presence of the U.S. delegation? Was it that the puppets wanted to remain under the protection of their American masters? Was it to keep the DRV delegation there in hopes of resolving a number of other problems that benefited the Americans, such as searching for missing U.S. military personnel? Was it to weaken the role of the PRG of the RSVN? But we resolutely prepared for the U.S. military delegation to return to America and for brother Hoa's delegation to return to Hanoi. As for our delegation, when the change was made to the Two-Party Joint Military Commission, the Central Committee decided that Maj Gen Hoang Anh Tuan would head the military delegation of the PRG of the RSVN. Of course, I would leave, but my departure became a problem. Would I go to Hanoi? There was reason to do so. Would I go to Loc Ninh? The Americans and puppets would give us a hard time, and would either not provide facilities or carry out some nefarious plot. We knew that at least the Americans and puppets wanted to keep me at Tan Son Nhat. To allow a top-ranking officer--in their estimation--to return to the battlefield would be to "turn a tiger loose in the jungle." It would be useful to keep such a person in their grasp as a hostage.

We had long known that everything was decided by the American masters. The puppets were merely the dutiful servants. The preceding 60 days had made us even more convinced of that. In that matter as well as in many others, if the Americans agreed everything would go smoothly. We had to get the Americans to agree to take me to Hanoi.

On the night of 29 March I invited Woodward, head of the U.S. delegation, to our delegation's headquarters at Camp David. At the designated hour Woodward, Brigadier General Wickham--deputy head of the U.S. delegation--and the interpreter Major Sauvagio, who wore a green beret and had been an advisor for the puppet regime's pacification cadre training school at Vung Tau, arrived.

I informed Woodward that because our communications were difficult I had only just received a delayed message that there was one additional American POW our forces were holding in Tra Vinh Province. In order to express our good will and correctly implement the Paris Agreement, we wanted to turn him over to the Americans. On the following day the two sides would assign cadres to carry out the turning over of that last American POW. I said that personally I regarded that as a friendship gift to the lieutenant general to commemorate the 60 days we worked together on the Four-Party Joint Military Commission (my intention was to suggest that because of that Woodward would be commended and promoted).

Woodward was openly very pleased, thanked me profusely and, in order to express his gratitude, inquired about my health and asked if I had any plans for the future.

It was a question that was asked at the right place and at the right time. That was all I could hope for. I replied that I planned to take a trip to Hanoi and, along the way, visit Laos. Woodward and Wickham thought that I intended to help resolve the question of American and puppet POW's in Laos, but could not say so. Woodward appeared to be very anxious and asked, "When do you plan to go?" "I'll go tomorrow if you'll provide the means." He replied, "You will have the means. I'll arrange for a C130 flight to Hanoi tomorrow morning."

I expressed my gratitude and reminded him that on the following morning one of our officers would meet with the American officer to arrange the turning over of the POW at Tra Vinh. He thanked me and asked me whether the C130 should wait to bring me back. If not, how would I return? (the U.S. delegation would cease operations and return to the United States on 31 March. After that date it would be necessary to use a puppet facility).

I smiled and said that I might return to Saigon by way of Paris, so that I could visit another famous European capital (Woodward thought that I needed to meet with our delegation in Paris).

Woodward was very pleased, said that that was a good idea, and said goodbye. He did not forget to affirm that an airplane would be available on the following morning.

On the morning of 30 April 1973 the puppet officer who brought a convoy of sedans to pick me up at my residence and take me to the ramp of the airplane was very deferential. Accompanying me to the airfield to see me off to Hanoi were Maj Gen Le Quang Hoa, Major General Woodward, head of the U.S. delegation and his wife. I warmly shook hands with and said goodbye to everyone. The warm, affectionate, and extremely moving handshakes secretly signified a victory and the sympathetic handshakes secretly expressed mutual gratitude. Woodward wished me a safe journey and good luck, and said that he would send an airplane to Hanoi to bring me back, even though I had not requested him to do so. I wished Mr and Mrs Woodward good fortune, stepped aboard the airplane, and waved to everyone. Thus aboard the American C130 (the Americans were courteous enough to provide a seat for me in the cockpit) I, Lt Col Nguyen Quang Minh (a research cadre with the Joint Commission), Dr Le Hoai Liem, the intepreter Dung, the bodyguard Hoa, and a number of other cadres, would fly from Saigon to Hanoi, thus ending 60 days of very seething and tense activity in the bosom of the enemy.

Sitting aboard the airplane and for the first time flying the length of the country, from Saigon to Hanoi, I felt disturbed and moved. There it was, a country that had existed 4,000 years and had been built by the blood and sweat of countless generations, in the past and in the present. The fresh green villages, the endless mountains and jungles, the long coastline with white sand beaches, and the immense blue continental shelf were truly a phantasmagoria. The gentle rays of the bright March sky embellished the scene with marvelous, sparkling colors. It was very beautiful, that homeland of ours. Also very beautiful were the heroism, intelligence, creativity, and persistent labor, generation after generation, of the millions of Vietnamese who built the beautiful country of today. I was very grateful for my ancestors and suddenly I remembered Uncle Ho and what he once told our troops in the Hung Temple on the side of Mt. Nghia: "The Hung kings achieved merit by founding the nation; you and I must work together to preserve it."

The words of Uncle Ho have been deeply engraved in the hearts of the Vietnamese people. No enemy, even the chief imperialists from across the Pacific or the shameless expansionists from the north, will be smashed to smithereens and be chased out of our country. Le Chieu Thong in the past, and Nguyen Van Thieu in the present, will live in infamy. Our homeland was certain to be independent, free and unified by any means.

The airplane was flying over the Red River Delta! Hanoi--our beloved capital and the heart of the homeland. I had lived in Hanoi for a long time and had worked there. Several times I had left it and returned. But this time was somehow different: I was strangely excited and moved, as if I were a child who had been far away for a long time wrestling with the difficulties and dangers of life and now was suddenly able to return to my warm home and be with my sweet, beloved mother. I was home: the child had returned to his sweet mother, so that he could again prepare to set out on another distant journey completely different from the one he had just taken.

Three days later a C130 from Saigon landed at Gia Lam airfield to pick me up-- just as Woodward had promised. I sent Lt Col Nguyen Quang Minh to inform the American officer commanding the airplane that I was not yet able to leave. Comrade Minh wrote a notice stating that Lt Gen Tran Van Tra was busy and could not leave, and authorizing the airplane to return to Tan Son Nhat without having to return to Hanoi at a later date to pick him up. He did not forget to express my thanks.

In my extreme happiness over being able to return to our beloved capital, and with a feeling of freedom and relaxation from being with my friends, comrades and compatriots, I thought fondly of my comrades who were still at Tan Son Nhat. Because of a mission that was indispensable in the present phase of the struggle, those comrades had to live and work in a tense atmosphere while surrounded by the enemy, for how long no one knew. In the future, what would happen to those comrades at the hands of the obstinate and insidious enemy? I calmed myself by thinking that those of us in the liberated area must go all-out and cooperate closely with those comrades in order to win victory for the revolution. It was certain that those comrades would not be isolated, for they had us and the people, even in Saigon. One day we would meet again to celebrate the victory.

CHAPTER TWO

The Only Path Is That of Revolutionary Violence

Immediately after I arrived in Hanoi I met with leaders of the party, the government, the Ministry of National Defense, and the Ministry of Foreign Affairs to report on the work of the Four-Party Joint Military Commission, on what had been accomplished and what had not yet been accomplished, on my conclusions after 60 days of face-to-face meetings with the Americans and puppets, on my observations regarding the situation, etc. I listened to their good observations and evaluations regarding the work of the Four-Party Joint Military Commission, the enemy plots, and what we would do next. Then I was granted several days' leave, after which I prepared for and participated in a plenary session of the Political Bureau of the party Central Committee regarding the situation and mission of the revolution in South Vietnam.

The members of COSVN and the Regional Command--Pham Hung, Muoi Cuc (Nguyen Van Linh, deputy secretary of COSVN), Hai Hau (Tran Nam Trung), Muoi Khang, and Sau Dan (Vo Van Kiet) came to Hanoi via the Truong Son route. We held a separate meeting regarding the B2 theater in order to reach agreement on our evaluation of the situation and our observations regarding the recent developments and our estimates of future developments. We exchanged experiences with Nam Cong (Vo Chi Cong) and Chu Huy Man of the Military Region 5 theater and Hoang Minh Thao of the B2 theater, who had come to Hanoi to participate in the conference.

During the last third of April 1973 the Political Bureau of the party Central Committee, along with delegates from the South Vietnam theaters, was in session. It was an extremely important conference. After the various parties signed the Paris Agreement, i.e. after we had won a decisive victory in the anti-U.S. war, forced the United States to end its war of destruction in the north, and forced the U.S. and vassal troops to withdraw from Vietnam, and especially after 60 days of implementing the agreement, during which there were a number of actual developments on the battlefield, that conference was held to reevaluate the situation, evaluate the balance of revolutionary and counterrevolutionary forces, and delineate the path of advance of the revolution in South Vietnam during the new revolutionary phase. That was a desire of everyone, of the cadres as well as the enlisted men and people.

Until that time, not everyone in the ranks of the cadres at the various echelons, on the battlefields, or even in the Central Committee, agreed about the value of the Paris Agreement, the balance of forces between ourselves and the enemy on the battlefield, and especially how the agreements should be implemented and how to cope with the enemy, who were increasingly violating the articles of the agreement. Even the developments on the battlefields differed because on each of them our conditions and those of the enemy were completely different, the strategic value of each battlefield in comparison to the war as a whole differed, and the leaders on those battlefields had different outlooks and acted differently. That was a reality that could be no other way.

Therefore, if common evaluations and policies were based on the actual developments, dangerous mistakes would be made if the theater was not representative of all the rest or was not strategically important with regard to the war as a whole. If, while the war situation was changing, we did not correctly evaluate the role of each theater, mistakes would be made in organizing and deploying forces, and in adopting strategic, campaign and tactical policies, which would of course affect victory or defeat in the war. It was not that no mistakes were made in our war against the U.S. aggressors to liberate the nation. But thanks to the wise, democratic and centralized leadership of our party we were able to promptly correct our mistakes and win victory. Revolution is an undertaking of the masses. Each success or defeat of the revolution in each phase is a success or defeat of the thought and acts of millions of people, especially the collective leadership. It was never a case of "failures are due to you and successes are due to me." In each phase of the revolution, at each historical turning point, correct policies and actions are always the results of collective thought and knowledge, of the combination of many minds, from the mind of the highest leader to the minds of the enlisted men and ordinary people when, out of patriotism and love for the people, they plunge into the actual, specific, lively tasks on the battlefield: No one is always right and no one is always wrong, for everyone is human. What is noblest and wisest is to recognize one's mistakes and resolutely and promptly correct them. Even collective leadership is not always right. But it is certain that the collective leadership makes fewer mistakes than individual leaders. President Ho, the talented leader of our party and our nation, recapitulated and heightened the tradition of our party and nation by means of a very concise but very profound sentence: "Solidarity, solidarity, complete solidarity. Success, success, complete success."

Solidarity in this case is not merely solidarity in action but also in all other spheres: thought, cognizance, ideology and will. It was because he was embued with that tradition that he was a person who was extremely simple and modest. In him was concentrated the intelligence of everyone, and his thoughts became everyone's thoughts. The virtue of Ho Chi Minh spread light throughout the nation and illuminated the soul of Vietnam. He not only fully understood himself but fully understood everyone else; he was just, upright, and full of love.

Our people forged their tradition in the process of founding and defending their nation by means of the saying, "One tree alone amounts to nothing, but three trees clustered together form a high mountain." The Vietnam people are like that and Ho Chi Minh was like that!

I still remember many questions asked by many cadres from the various theaters, such as, "The Agreement has been signed, so why haven't the puppet army and the puppet administration collapsed?" Or else they made such observations as "The Americans have left but the puppets not only haven't collapsed but have become stronger," or, "The Americans have been defeated but at the same time the puppet administration has not only continued to exist but has become stronger politically, militarily and economically."

There was some superficial evidence which, added to the nefarious, obstinate plots and highly subjective plans of the Americans, prevented those comrades from understanding the true nature of the situation.

Immediately after the Paris Agreement took effect the puppets sent troops to take a number of important areas we were occupying, such as Cua Viet (Tri Thien), Sa Huynh (Quang Ngai), Route 4 (My Tho), Route 2 (Ba Ria), the Bay Nui area (Long Xuyen), etc. They not only took many areas we had expanded into prior to 28 January but also took some areas we had controlled for some time. At the same time, they impetuously launched many sweeping and police operations in areas that previously had been contested by us and the enemy. In the areas under their control, they carried out pacification operations and eliminating our enclave guerrilla bases, in order to eliminate our interspersed positions and expand and fill out their areas. On nearly all battlefields they set up additional outposts in the areas they had just taken and further expanded the areas they controlled along the strategic routes and around the large cities. In the provinces of My Tho, Go Cong, Kien Tuong, and Ben Tre, between January and April 1973 they established 287 additional outposts in 129 hamlets of 24 villages. Also during that time, the Americans brought in weapons and war facilities from the Philippines, the United States and Japan, to bolster and develop the puppet army. They provided additional modern weapons for the puppet army, such as M48 tanks, 175mm "king of the battlefield" cannon, F5E aircraft, etc. The puppets employed all measures to conscript soldiers on a large scale. On the average, every month they conscripted 15,000 youths. Therefore, they were able to rapidly supplement their regular army. The rest of the youths--a rather large reserve force--were trained in the recruit training center, all of which were full. The regional forces and civilian defense forces were greatly increased. By forming mobile Regional Force groups to fight locally in place of the regular army units, during the first 6 months of 1973 the number of RF battalions increased from 189 to 337. In the cities, they strongly developed the police forces. Many police field force battalions were formed, especially in Saigon. The U.S.-puppet plan was to continue to develop the puppet army into a 1.1 million-man army that was modernized, younger, and more effective, especially by strengthening the technical combat arms. The air force would be increased to 1,500-1,800 aircraft of various kinds. There would be 31 to 35 armored regiments, etc.

In addition to consolidating and developing the puppet army, they went all-out to consolidate the puppet regime from the central level down to the basic level. They sent pacification cadres to the villages and hamlets and sent army officers to set up village subsectors--the main tools of fascist suppression--in order to gain tighter control over the people by such activities as consolidating the interfamily system, developing the "regiment the masses" program, etc. They developed agents and spies in all hamlets and sent them into the contested areas and our liberated areas. In order to back up the puppet Thieu regime, and be prepared to support its lackey armies in Indochina--mainly in South Vietnam--the United States stationed in Southeast Asia a mobile military force made up of four aircraft carriers, 735 tactical aircraft and 173 B52 strategic bombers.

All of the above were pursued vigorously by the Americans and puppets as soon as the agreement was signed. It may be said that after the agreement was signed they stepped up their attacks and exercised even tighter control over the people, thus creating considerable difficulties for us.

Meanwhile, for our part, because they had been in continuous action since April 1972 our cadres and men were fatigued, we had not had time to make up for our losses, all units were in disarray, there was a lack of manpower, and there were shortages of food and ammunition, so it was very difficult to cope with the enemy's attacks. In some places we had to retreat and allow the enemy to gain control of the land people. In addition, a number of cadres and some localities, in a spirit of implementing the upper echelon's directive to fully implement the Paris Agreement, were afraid to retaliate against the enemy out of fear of violating the agreement, carried out the work of proselyting among the enemy troops to neutralize the puppet troops in a rightist, dangerous manner, concretized in the form of "five forbids": It was forbidden to attack the enemy; it was forbidden to attack enemy troops carrying out sweeping and land-grabbing operations; it was forbidden to surround outposts; it was forbidden to shell puppet outposts; and it was forbidden to build combat villages. They thought that that would stabilize the situation and avoid creating tension, in order to achieve national conciliation and concord. In a number of places forward units were sent to the rear to be reorganized and consolidated. They thought that if such units were not withdrawn to the rear they would be annihilated. In fact, when one of our armed units was pulled back the enemy methodically destroyed the mass infrastructure, wiped out our party infrastructure, and eliminated the "leopard spot" there.

Against such a background, when they witnessed such initial confused events a number of cadres from the central level down to the local level thought that since the agreement we had grown much weaker and the enemy had grown much stronger. The enemy was winning many new victories while we had suffered additional losses. Thus they concluded that the enemy was stronger than we were, that the balance of forces on the battlefield had changed in favor of the enemy, and that the revolution was in danger. Because of such observations, there were a number of incorrect policies and actions. I will return to that subject later.

That conference of the Political Bureau of the party Central Committee fully resolved all worries of the cadres and war theaters. It scientifically and correctly analyzed the balance of forces between ourselves and the enemy, profoundly analyzed the situation, and set forth a wise policy for guiding the revolution in South Vietnam to victory. The party Central Committee reached unanimous agreement on the results of that conference and issued the 21st Resolution of the party Central Committee. But in order to arrive at that unanimity, the Political Bureau conference passed through a rather animated, and at times very tense, discussion. There was a clashing of many different opinions and interpretations regarding the developments on the battlefields. As a participant in the conference, I was deeply impressed by the strong sense of responsibility of all of the comrades participating in the conference, their spirit of straightforwardly reflecting the actual situation on the battlefield, their spirit of struggling strongly for truth, and their spirit of patriotism, solidarity, and objectivity. That was the democratic, centralized working method of our party, the secret of all correct policies and successes.

The matter that was discussed most seethingly from the very beginning was the question of who was stronger, we or the enemy. It is not easy to evaluate strengths and weaknesses. If one speaks in generalities without getting into specifics, one cannot determine what is strong and what is weak. If one gets into specifics that are not the most universal ones, conclusions about weakness and strength may not be entirely correct, and indeed the opposite may be true. There is also the question of whether a strength or weakness in a certain place or at a certain time is temporary or basic, and the capability of such weaknesses or strengths to change. And it must also be understood what strength is. For example, after the agreement was signed the puppet regular army battalions were rapidly increased to between 400 and 550 men, with ample food and ammunition, while our main-force battalions had not yet been augmented and totaled at most 200 men, with insufficient ammunition and food. After the American and vassal troops withdrew, the puppets' total troop strength was between 700,000 and 1.1 million, while our forces on the battlefield amounted to at most one-third those of the enemy. It would be incorrect to conclude from that that the puppets were strong and we were weak. In addition to those material numbers, it is necessary to add together many other factors, such as the morale of the soldiers, the deployment of units and their missions in campaign and strategic plans, in attacks and defense today and tomorrow, etc. That is not to mention much broader factors, such as the political factor, the combat objectives, the factor of the people. Our just liberation war, as pointed out by many party resolutions, is waged by both military and political forces. We attack the enemy with both political forces and mass political forces. In speaking of strengths and weaknesses one cannot consider only the military aspect, but must consider all aspects, including the political situations of the two sides.

During several decades of war we had to evaluate the balance of forces between ourselves and the enemy many times. In 1959, the most difficult period of the revolution in South Vietnam, the Ngo Dinh Diem puppet regime dragged the guillotine everywhere and carried out a bloody fascist suppression. There was only one army--that of Diem--holding sway on the battlefield, like a martial arts performer demonstrating his skills in a ring without an opponent. Even so, Resolution 15 of the party Central Committee created a simultaneous uprising movement with stormlike strength which liberated many large areas and caused the Americans to panic and launch a special war to prevent the Diem clique from collapsing. If, at that time, we had not had a revolutionary, dialectical point of view we could not have realized that we still had latent strength among the people, but would have seen only the specific strength of the enemy. In 1965, the number of people supporting the revolution in the various areas was quite large, especially in the Mekong Delta, but that number could not have been larger than the number of people under enemy control (but don't think that the people under enemy control belonged to the enemy). In our armed forces, the guerrillas were relatively strong but only a small number of main-force regiments had been formed. In the B2 theater at that time there were only two combat-ready regiments. As for the enemy, in addition to regional forces and militia they had a dozen divisions with strong technical equipment and tens of thousands of U.S. advisers, and they were supported by U.S. helicopter units, combat aircraft, and naval ships which participated directly in the fighting. Despite that, we launched the Binh Gia campaign, wiped out many strong battalions of the enemy and armored squadrons, shot down many airplanes, and began a new era in the war. After the attack on the Bien Hoa airbase, the Binh Gia campaign, and then the victorious battles at Ba Gia and Pleiku, the Americans and puppets clearly realized that the puppet army would be annihilated and the puppet regime would collapse. Thus the Americans had to impetuously send in U.S. troops to save the puppets, put out the fire, and transform the special war into a limited war, in correct accordance with America's "flexible response" global stragegy, so that it could play its role of international gendarme.

Prior to the arrival of the U.S. troops, if the balance of forces between ourselves and the enemy had been viewed simply in terms of specific, materiel forces, who would have thought that we were strong and were capable of annihilating the puppet army and overthrowing the puppet regime? Later, when the United States sent in at the same time about 200,000 troops who had modern equipment and relied on the strength of overwhelming firepower and rapid mobility, to carry out a strategic counter offensive during the 1965-1966 dry season, we concluded that the Americans and puppets were not strong but were passive, and continued to press the strategic offensive, launched the Bau Bang-Dau Tieng offensive campaign, gained the initiative on the battlefield, and won many victories. In 1968, when the U.S. troops numbered nearly 500,000, with all kinds of modern weapons except the atomic bomb and with the purchasing of the services of lackey vassal troops in addition to Thieu's army, we could clearly see the enemy's weakness and our strength, and exploited that strength to a high degree in carrying out the general offensive and uprising of Tet Mau Than, a unique event in the history of war. During Tet we not only attacked the enemy simultaneously in all urban centers, including the U.S. war headquarters in Saigon, the puppet capital, but also wiped out an important part of the U.S.-puppet manpower. That strategic blow defeated the U.S. limited war strategy and forced the United States to deescalate the war, begin peace talks in Paris, and adopt the strategy of "de-Americanizing the war" and then "Vietnamizing the war." We thus smashed the U.S. imperialists' strategic global "flexible response" strategy. The international gendarme became terrified of the role it had taken for itself; and the illusion of the "absolute military superiority of the United States" was shattered.

However, during Tet of 1968 we did not correctly evaluate the specific balance of forces between ourselves and the enemy, did not fully realize that the enemy still had considerable capabilities and that our capabilities were limited, and set requirements that were beyond our actual strength. In other words, we did not base ourselves on scientific calculation or a careful weighing of all factors, but in part on an illusion based on our subjective desires. For that reason, although that decision was wise, ingenious, and timely, and although its implementation was well organized and bold, there was excellent coordination on all battlefields, everyone acted very bravely, sacrificed their lives, and there was created a significant strategic turning point in Vietnam and Indochina, we suffered large sacrifices and losses with regard to manpower and materiel, especially cadres at the various echelons, which clearly weakened us. Afterwards, we were not only unable to retain the gains we had made but had to overcome a myriad of difficulties in 1969 and 1970 so that the revolution could stand firm in the storm. Although it is true that the revolutionary path is never a primrose path that always goes upward, and there can never be a victory without sacrifice, in the case of Tet 1968, if we had weighed and considered things meticulously, taken into consideration the balance of forces of the two sides, and set forth correct requirements, our victory would have been even greater, less blood would have been spilled by the cadres, enlisted men, and people, and the future development of the revolution would certainly have been far different. In 1972, after a period of endeavoring to overcome many difficulties make up for the recent losses, and develop our position and strength with an absolute revolutionary spirit on the part of the soldiers and people, our troops participated in winning victories in Kampuchea and Laos. However, not all of our main-force units could return to South Vietnam. In that situation, we correctly evaluated the positions and forces of the two sides, destroyed many fortified defense lines of the enemy in Quang Tri, the Central Highlands, and eastern Nam Bo, and created many integrated liberated areas at Dong Ha, Dac To, Tan Canh, Loc Ninh Bu Dop, and northern Tay Ninh then, in coordination with the great "Dien Bien Phu in the air" victory in the North, attained our goal of smashing the American's scheme of negotiating from a position of strength, and forced the Americans to sign in Paris, agreements which benefited us.

Clearly, in each phase of the revolution and of revolutionary war, the correct evaluation of our strength and that of the enemy, correctly realizing the weaknesses of the enemy and ourselves, and correctly evaluating the balance of forces between the two sides are the most basic conditions for the adoption of correct policies to guide the revolution from one victory to another. Our party's leadership of the Vietnamese revolution to complete victory was also based on an evaluation of the balance of forces between revolution and counterrevolution, not only in our country but in the world, was generally correct, although at times and in places, and in some specific details, mistakes were made. But correctness was dominant and determined victory. In actuality, nothing is completely correct. One should not fear speaking about mistakes, but only fear not realizing or correcting mistakes. But every time the balance of forces between ourselves and the enemy it is possible to be rightist and fear the enemy or to be leftist, subjective and faltering in policies and actions. For that reason, evaluations of the situation and of the balance of forces must be based on lines and policies, collective intelligence and on actual developments.

The signing of the Paris Agreement was the clearest manifestation of the balance of forces on the battlefield at that time. The Americans and puppets also carefully evaluated the balance of forces between the two sides after having contended with us in South Vietnam to avoid losing additional land, and carried out the barbarous, evil scheme of using B52's to bomb Hanoi and Hai Phong, and blockading the North. Only after evaluating their capability and will and those of their adversary were they willing to pick up a pen and sign the agreement, and agree to a number of conditions which did not benefit them. We also carefully weighed the strength of the enemy, their schemes, and the possibility of concluding agreements with many points that benefited us. Thus the Paris Agreement was signed on the basis of the enemy and ourselves weighing the strengths and weaknesses of each other and the balance of forces in the world. By signing the Paris Agreement the Americans were willing to accept a partial defeat, but that was all. We had won a victory, but not yet a complete victory. But that defeat for the United States and victory for us proved that the revolution was stronger than counterrevolution. So how could we be weak and the enemy strong?

The most important provisions of the agreements, one which affected the war as a whole, were that all U.S. and vassal troops had to withdraw from South Vietnam and that the United States had to end its war of destruction in the north of our country. The interesting thing about those provisions was that they seemed to fit in with the Vietnamization strategy and with the Nixon Doctrine of "regional alliances and self-defense," so that the United States would not have to flee even though it had been defeated. It was interesting in that it helped the United States withdraw its troops to America, satisfy the demands of the American people, and extricate itself from a dilemma: it was no longer being able to maintain a U.S. army abroad but was being increasingly defeated to the point of complete defeat. That withdrawal from South Vietnam as stipulated by the agreement, i.e., with the agreement of the two sides, helped the United States to avoid losing face. As for us, those provisions were extremely important for the development of the revolution in our country and in Indochina. Prior to the agreement we had to fight both the puppet troops and hundreds of thousands of U.S. and vassal troops strongly supported by U.S. naval and air forces, including B52 strategic bombers. Once the agreements took effect and the U.S. and vassal troops withdrew from the battlefield, the puppet troops could no longer rely on the U.S. troops and no longer were strongly supported by U.S. air and naval forces. The puppets' firepower was much weaker than that of the Americans. Although the puppet troops were increased in number and were provided additional facilities and weapons--some of which were more modern than those they had in the past--by their U.S. masters, in order to develop the effectiveness of the new combat arms and new forces, a period of training and tempering was required. However, meeting the technical requirements of the puppet army and of modernization was not an easy matter and could not be achieved in just a few years. That is not to mention the morale status of the puppet troops, who were perplexed by the reaction of the popular masses after the Paris Agreement was signed. In actuality, on the battlefield--according to the reports from all units and localities--after the agreements took effect the firepower of the puppet artillery and air force decreased appreciably and was increasingly tending to decline even more. The puppet artillery and air support given the infantry was very poor, for their firing was inaccurate and the number of shells was limited. The puppet troops, who were accustomed to relying on the U.S. troops, now had to fight alone without the effective aid and support of the United States, so their morale clearly declined. Thus after the agreements the balance of forces on the battlefield changed in an important way in our favor. The fighting strength of the puppet troops declined clearly and our position and strength developed strongly. Even so, there was no basis for thinking that after the Americans withdrew the puppets got stronger, and were stronger than we were, which was no different from imagining a ghost in order to scare oneself.

The agreement stipulated the ending of all U.S. military activities against the territory of the DRV by all forces, on the land, in the air, and at sea, no matter what their point of origin. Thus the socialist North would have very good conditions to develop the great effectiveness of the base area of the entire conditions, and would have good conditions for fulfilling as well as possible its role of being the great rear area of the revolution in South Vietnam. If we had good position and strength in the South and throughout the nation it was certain that we would victoriously fulfill our glorious revolutionary enterprise, although we would have to overcome many difficulties. But we also had to realize our remaining weaknesses and not be subjective, so that we could endeavor to overcome them. Our armed forces were in disarray and had to be urgently supplemented and consolidated. Our local troops and guerrillas were still too few and there were still many deficiencies in our proselyting work among the enemy. But we would overcome those weaknesses from a position of victory and strength and with a spirit of enthusiasm and self-confidence.

Due to a lack of such understanding, there was worry that our forces exposed to the enemy would be annihilated and that our free areas would be lost, so a number of mistaken viewpoints were rectified by the conference of the Political Bureau and its 21st Resolution. Otherwise, countless calamities would have resulted. One of those viewpoints was that we should urgently stabilize the situation by abandoning the contested areas and take the initiative in forming two areas: our area and the enemy's area. One was that we should readjust and reorganize our forces and withdraw our forces from enemy areas to our areas so that they could be consolidated and reorganized. One was that we should carry out those tasks as soon as possible. Another was that we must have clearly defined areas in order to have appropriate struggle slogans, and could not waver.

Clearly, the puppet regime of Nguyen Van Thieu desired that very much. They were very afraid of the interspersed, "leopard spot" configuration on the battlefield. Our forces were everywhere, even in their urban areas and in their capital. They were able to evaluate the operational and combat effectiveness of each of our party members, commandos, and guerrillas. They were also able to evaluate one of our small armed units in an area under their control and in enclave guerrilla areas. Each such person and each such unit was a gun-barrel pointed at the enemy's temple, a source of support for the people's morale, and a pillar of the local secret mass organizations. Each of their actions was a source of propaganda which bolstered patriotism and the revolution and opposed suppression, oppression, and injustice. Their actions spoke louder than their words. Their image was that of a light in darkness, a light which although small at first was spreading over an increasingly larger area and could never be extinguished. Each party member and soldier, and each small unit, in turn, had a source of support in our larger units--platoons, companies, battalions, or larger units--scattered all over the various areas, in temporarily occupied areas, the contested areas, and the areas contiguous to our free areas. That was a system from which we could not lose a single link. It was an all-encompassing strategy of revolutionary war which caused the enemy troops to suffocate, to worry apprehensively day and night, and think that all places had to be defended and they could be safe only with large forces. Had not the Americans calculated that to cope with one of our men they had to have 5, and then 10 to 20 men?

Despite that, should we voluntarily withdraw our forces from the areas controlled by the enemy and the contested areas to the rear in order to consolidate them, and ourselves erase the very effective "comb's teeth" position of the revolution, which terrified the enemy? By doing so would we not give the enemy a hand so that they could do other, more important things, which they had been unable to do after many years of fierce attacks and pacification? If it was argued that that was a temporary measure for a certain time, while we consolidated our forces, so that after we had regained our strength we could return and operate more effectively, that was due to the imagination of impractical people. In fact when, in the B2 theater, we withdrew or abandoned a certain base, even on our own accord, within a few days the enemy would occupy that area, gain control of the people, launch sweeping operations, and set up outposts. When we wanted to send forces back to open up an area or an enclave, and organize our masses, we practically had to start from the beginning. It was even more difficult than work in areas in which we had never had a base, and much blood had to be shed by our comrades and compatriots. The comrades who operated behind enemy lines and in contested areas have much experience in that regard. Each comrade and each unit remaining in a base and creating the core of a political or guerrilla base was extremely valuable in a life-and-death struggle such as that between ourselves and the enemy. Every loss of an infrastructure or a base nucleus was a source of worry and pain which we had to find all ways to overcome.

Here I would like to mention the example of unparalleled heroism on the part of the cadres and men of the 320th Regiment who, in 1969-1970, were assigned the mission of operating in Long An Province, in the Duc Hue, Ben Luc, Can Duoc, Can Giuoc, Tan Tru, Chau Thanh, and Tan An areas. During that period, none of us could forget that after Tet Mau Than [1968] the Americans sent additional troops to Vietnam, stepped up shipments of all kinds of weapons and ammunition, attained their highest troop level during the war, and insanely counterattacked us. The Americans and puppets continuously attacked, and carried out very fierce sweeping and pacification operations. In many places our people were massacred and herded into strategic hamlets. Many infrastructures were lost and many comrades were lost, especially in the areas adjacent to cities and the highly populated areas which were important strategically. Long An was such an area. It surrounded Saigon from the northwest to the southwest and was a highly populated, fertile area, was the gateway to the Mekong Delta, connected the delta with Saigon, and connected our Dong Thap Muoi area with the northern Tay Ninh revolutionary base. Long An was also a province with a long revolutionary tradition of fighting the French and the Americans. The National Liberation Front of South Vietnam bestowed on its people, who were very patriotic and resolute, the golden words "Loyal and resolute, all the people fight the enemy." For those reasons the Americans and puppets concentrated their attacks there and at times made Long An a pacification test point. But they still suffered a bitter defeat.

In addition to all kinds of puppet forces, the Americans used part of the 25th "Tropical Lightning" Division and the 3d Brigade of the 9th Division. I remember that the Long An cadres said to me, "It's true that the enemy is climbing down the ladder of [deescalating] the war, but they have placed the feet of the ladder in Long An Province!" Long An was the last rung, so the more they deescalated the more troops they sent there and the more fiercely they attacked and bombed! It was truly a strange metaphor--everyone laughed when they first heard it--but it described well the developments at that time. We definitely would not allow the enemy to succeed there, for that would considerably influence the common movement. The Regional Command held many discussions, weighed all factors, and decided to strengthen our forces in Long An. It sent the 320th Regiment, along with the local forces, to fight the enemy, maintain the movement, and maintain our infrastructure and guerrilla bases. The 320th Regiment was a unit with many accomplishments which had undergone much testing in combat and in bearing terrible hardships. It had been an independent main-force regiment which had long operated as a whole unit in a mountains-and-jungle environment, but now it was sent to a highly populated lowland area with open terrain that was intersected by many rivers and canals, and had to fight flexibly, by individual companies and battalions, and often had to disperse into platoons and squads. It not only had to fight to annihilate the enemy but also had to proselytize and organize the masses, proselytize enemy troops, eliminate spies, kill tyrants, and guide and coordinate with the guerrillas and district troops. Sending a concentrated main-force unit to operate in such a dispersed manner, so that it could be said to be no longer a main-force unit, was a reluctant necessity under those circumstances and at that time.

In a war in which our varied operational forms are many and varied and the situation on the battlefield changes every day, such decisions are not unusual. At a time when the guerrillas and local troops in that area had been worn down and had not yet been consolidated, but we had to maintain the movement, that was a correct decision. But there are also instances in which it would be incorrect to use main-force troops in lowland areas, or think that by sending in main-force units it would be possible to open up the lowlands. That is not the case (I will have more to say on that subject later).

On 18 December 1968, on behalf of the Regional Military Party Committee and the Regional Command, I went to a location in Tay Ninh Province to work and assign missions to the regiment in its assembly area, in order to prepare in all ways for the new task. I walked for about 10 days; with a pack on my back, using a rattan walking stick, with my pants rolled up above my knees, and wearing well-worn rubber sandals. I and a heavily armed bodyguard squad made our way along twisting jungle paths and open areas flooded with stagnant water. In the wild tropical jungles there were all kinds of big trees intertwined with vines that had become tattered and denuded, and trees that had lost their tops and leaves because of bombs, shells and chemical poisons. It was a pitiful sight. Comrade Hung, my loyal bodyguard, who was small but wiry and was from Be Cat, which also has many jungles, lay in a hammock near mine in a clump of trees that had not yet been defoliated. After a hard day's journey, he was quietly swaying his hammock. I asked, "Hung, why don't you get some sleep so you'll be fresh when we set out early tomorrow morning? We still have a long way to go." Hung replied, "Oh! I saw you laying there quietly so I thought you were asleep! I'm so sad that our jungles have been so devastated. It takes decades for a tree to grow so big." Hung pointed to a large tree near us that had been uprooted by a bomb and continued, "My home area has also been devastated." To console both Hung and myself I said,

"After we kill all of the enemy troops our country will be much better. Our people are able and creative, so why worry? Our jungles will again be green."

In the regiment's bivouac area the jungle was a little better. There were temporary huts made of small branches and roofed with "trung quan" leaves (leaves as large as a man's hand which do not burn even when dry and grew all over the jungles of South Vietnam). Each hut was big enough for a squad. My squad and I were also assigned a hut. Representatives of the Long An Party Committee and provincial unit had arrived on the previous day to participate in a work session and discuss a coordination plan with the regimental staff. I met comrade Nguyen Duc Khoi, the regimental commander; Le Van Minh, the political officer; and Hong Hai and Trinh Ngoc Cham, the deputy regimental commanders. Those beloved, brave cadres would gloriously sacrifice their lives in battle in 1969 and 1970. I also met many other outstanding cadres in the regimental command, the regiment's staff, political, and rear services organs, and the battalion commands. Some of them became martyrs and others matured, gained experience, and added to the glorious tradition of the regiment, or were assigned elsewhere.

The meeting took place an hour after I arrived, just as soon as the cadres could be convened. We needed no assembly hall and there were no desks and chairs--the men sat on mounds of earth and logs in a cleared area in the jungle under a canopy of green leaves. We worked only during the day. At night, under the light of the stars and the moon, I visited the huts and talked with the cadres and men about their home areas, their families, the war situation in South Vietnam, Hanoi and even the situation in the United States and the world. We talked about all sorts of things, serious subjects, frivolous subjects, and even private thoughts and problems. Every night I visited the huts and returned to my hut late at night to go to sleep. Even so, I didn't have enough time to visit all of the huts.

Standing before a map of eastern Nam Bo--including Long An and Go Cong Provinces and part of Dong Thap Muoi--hanging from a tree trunk, and holding a bamboo stick I had just taken from a nearby cluster of bamboo, I solemnly and directly assigned missions to the regiment. Then I discussed the terrain and our situation and that of the enemy in the places in which the enemy would operate. None of the regimental cadres knew anything about the area. Because I had served since the anti-French resistance war and had waded and walked over the entire area, I was the only one who knew about the people and terrain there and gave the men an initial briefing. I gave them specific instructions about the operational missions, guidelines, and modes, the tactical forms the enemy had used and would use in each area of the province, and the tactics and techniques we needed to apply to win victory. I spoke about the mass proselyting methods, the task of organizing guerrillas and assisting the local troops, and the task of combining the regiment's unit with the local village and district units and the regiment with the provincial unit. Finally, I instructed them about the party work and the political work, and about the spiritual and material lives of the cadres and men in all forms of activity: in large units, in small units, and in individual, scattered teams.

After that briefing the men had 2 days in which to discuss all aspects. I cleared up their remaining questions.

I could never forget those days of urgent and serious work and the sincere, overflowing sentiment in the 320th Regiment. Its men, both the cadres and enlisted men, accepted their mission enthusiastically, discussed it excitedly, and tried to envision the coming battles and the hardships awaiting them.

Not enough can be said about the extremely difficult period during which the cadres and men of the regiment shared hardships with the local cadres and with the guerrillas and people, holding their ground despite bombing and shelling that were so fierce that their only fortifications were the roots of coconut trees. Who wouldn't remember their strange lives: every day living in the mud and stagnant water, firing at helicopters and airplanes, resisting the sweeping operations and "hit and run"* operations of the 3d Brigade of the U.S. 9th Division, and every night discussing with the people plans to attack the enemy or buying food and ammunition from strategic hamlets. How could one forget the tense, worrisome night crossings of the Vam Co River? It took a company 5 to 7 days to cross from one district to another, then it had to cross Route 4, along which the enemy had placed outposts, barbed wire, minefields, etc. In addition, for month after month we had to carry our wounded to the rear and bring up weapons, ammunition and recruits via a route nearly 100 kilometers long in the interspersed area, with the slogans "Persistence, stalwartness, and taking the offensive," and "living and fighting here, and also dying here, for the success of the revolution." (Today, before Tet the people in the Can Duoc, Tan Tru, Duc Hue and Chau Thanh areas tidy up the graves of the unknown soldiers of the 320th Regiment in remembrance of them!) The regiment and the localities were able to maintain the revolutionary infrastructures and bases of the districts, villages, and guerrilla enclaves during the most difficult period. During the spring of 1975 the regiment, then part of the 8th Division of Military Region 8, along with the other forces participated in the annihilation of each battalion and regiment of the puppet 7th Division, in coordination with the uprising of the people, in order to liberate the Tien Giang area. With its example of glorious combat, the regiment, along with the other units and localities all over the battlefield, provided the B2 theater with valuable experience. Because of such models on the battlefield, the comrades in COSVN and the Regional Party military Commission would not agree to withdraw their forces to the rear, but gave the order to consolidate and reorganize on the spot and maintain the interspersed position in the three areas, and positively reported that opinion to the Central Committee.

There was also the question of two areas or three areas. Throughout the life-or-death struggle between ourselves and the enemy, a fierce, tense struggle

---

*"Hit and run" was a local term describing a widespread tactic of the U.S. troops in Long An at that time. That tactic was carrying out a surprise attack by landing small units from a few helicopters which flew low and slow. The troops would fire indiscriminately and fiercely into a few suspected positions of our troops, bases of local cadres or places where people were concentrated. Then they would quickly jump aboard the helicopters and make a quick getaway.

took place in all parts of the theater, and on that basis there took form three areas. One was the area in which we were strong, our large units stood fast, and the people participated in all activities and in attacking the enemy by all means, political, military proselyting, and military. Another was the area in which the enemy was strong, exercised military and political control, and heavily suppressed and exploited. In that area, we secretly organized the masses and had guerrillas, commandos and sappers. We had political cells in which the people secretly had the cadres and helped the revolution by deceiving the enemy in many ways and operating openly and legally. There were guerrilla bases in which weapons and food were cached; there were guerrillas, and sometimes local troops and spearhead main-force units which operated in place. Of course, there were party chapters to provide on-the-spot leadership, the central factor of the movement. Between our area and that of the enemy there was a so-called contested area, which was large or small depending on the location. That was an area in which the two sides were equally strong and were fiercely competing with each other; it was constantly undergoing upheaval and change, at times every day and every hour. In that area most of the popular masses supported the revolution and there were all kinds of revolutionary forces and organizations. District and provincial local troops often operated there, and at times a main-force unit of the military zone or of the upper echelon came into the area to fight the enemy and support the local forces. The enemy often launched sweeping operations, shelled and bombed, and herded the people into areas under their control. It may be said that the struggle there, waged by all means at the disposal of both sides, took place every hour, night and day. Some places were controlled by the enemy during the day and by us at night. Each side tried to push out the other so that it could gain full control. Therefore, the contested area changed continually, like a strip of sand buffeted by winds from two directions. If the wind blew more strongly from one direction the sand would pile up on the other side and spill over on that side, and vice versa. As long as there were two sides--revolution and counterrevolution--and they continued to struggle to control the land and people there would be a contested area. It would disappear only when there was no longer a struggle between the two sides, i.e. when one side yielded and the other side won complete victory. The Paris Agreement did not end the struggle between revolution and counter-revolution and could not immediately end the armed struggle, for the enemy committed violations and grabbed land as described above, hoping to achieve the result of there being only one regime--the puppet regime--and one army--the puppet army. Thus the viewpoint that we should form only two clear areas--the enemy area and our area--in order to have struggle guidelines appropriate to each other in order to immediately stabilize the situation, and so that we could consolidate and rebuild our weakened armed forces and build up economy and governmental administration was completely inappropriate. I still remember that in the meeting held by the comrades in COSVN to prepare for the Political Bureau conference they agreed unanimously that on the basis of the actual situation in the B2 theater it was necessary, under all circumstances and at all times, to keep up the struggle in all three areas. Only if we gave up the struggle would we lose the contested area. In fact, if we did so, the area under our control would gradually become a contested area and then would become an area controlled by the enemy, so that eventually there would not be both our area and a contested area but only an area under enemy control.

According to an analysis by those comrades, there could never be a stable situation on the battlefield because neither we nor the enemy would give up the struggle; even if there was no longer armed struggle there would be political and economic struggle.

During the plenary meeting of the Political Bureau comrade Tran Huu Duc, who had been sent to the Tri Thien [Quang Tri-Thua Thien] theater to study the actual situation, returned to report to the conference that Tri Thien had completed a territorial realignment: the enemy's area extended from the railroad to the sea and our area extended from the railroad to the Laotian border. Our units had been withdrawn to our area so that they could be strengthened. The situation had stabilized and our men were enthusiastic, etc.

We expressed our viewpoint that to do so was dangerous. Such stability would be only temporary. After the enemy had time to reorganize they would attack west of the railroad and if we resisted the contested area would reappear. But this time the contested area would be entirely west of the railroad. Without meaning to we would voluntarily turn over additional land to the enemy and help them destroy our interspersed position, eliminate the "leopard spot" configuration, and fill out their area, an area with fertile land, good roads and a large population which included nearly all of the towns and cities. Anyone could see what the prospects for the future were. As far as the enemy was concerned, such a territorial realignment was ideal. The puppet Thieu regime and the U.S. strategic research companies had researched three territorial realignment modes to serve as a basis for the struggle at the conference table in Paris.

1. A territorial realignment by dividing South Vietnam along a parallel. The area north of that parallel would belong to the Viet Cong (the PRG of the RSVN) and the area south of that parallel would belong to the puppet Thieu regime.

2. A division along the length of South Vietnam. The mountainous area along the Laotian and Kampuchean borders, which had few people, was poor economically, and had poor roads, would be the "Viet Cong" area and the area along the sea, which had a large population and was advantageous in all regards, would be the area of the puppet Thieu regime.

3. An in-place ceasefire, with forces remaining where they were and interspersed zones of control would be formed.

Of those three modes, the puppets were most afraid of the third, with its interspersed "leopard spot" areas of control, for they felt there could be no ceasefire with such an arrangement and that it was quite possible that the people would arise to oppose and annihilate them. If their area were not an integrated whole it would be very difficult for them to develop their economy, effectively control the people, etc. They preferred the vertical division according to the second mode, for such a dvision would be entirely beneficial to them. They thought that before long, with U.S. aid they would become rich and strong, control large numbers of people, and eventually annihilate the PRG of the RSVN and gain sole control of South Vietnam.

We struggled at the conference table, but only by shedding much blood on the battlefield were we able to force the enemy to reluctantly accept an in-place ceasefire. So would we now voluntarily bring about a vertical division?

Resolution 21 stated clearly that "At present the positon and strength of the revolution in South Vietnam are stronger than at any time since 1954" and that "The new victory of the people of Vietnam, Laos, and Kampuchea has led to a change in the comparison of forces in the Indochinese Peninsula that is more favorable than ever for the South Vietnamese revolution."

The actual development of the situation proved increasingly that those observations were very correct. The revolutionary forces had become much stronger than the counterrevolutionary forces in South Vietnam.

Later, at the plenary conference of the Political Bureau of the party Central Committee held in December 1974 to discuss the 1975-1976 strategic plan, i.e. nearly 2 years after the true situation became clear, Le Duc Tho stated that since the Paris Agreement we had, in general, evaluated the enemy too highly and ourselves too lowly. The actual situation on the battlefield had clearly shown that Zone 5 was afraid that if it attacked, the enemy would attack from the rear, but when the upper echelon ordered it to attack it was victorious. Tri Thien also feared the enemy. In the Mekong Delta, in December alone we eliminated more than 500 illegally placed enemy outposts. In only 1 month we attained 70 percent of the 6-months dry season norm. Now, the actual situation was clearly that we were stronger than the enemy.

Resolution 21 also confirmed that "The path of the revolution in the South is the path of revolutionary violence. Under all circumstances we must take advantage of the opportunity, maintain the line of strategic offensive, and provide flexible guidance in order to advance the revolution in the South." The resolution set forth the strategic guidelines and modes for each area: "The liberated area...must build and consolidate," "the contested area...must maintain our position and strength and gradually improve them..." and "the area controlled by the enemy...must lead the masses in struggle."

The determination of that strategy and the assignment of those missions weakened (although not entirely ending) the belief that the Americans and puppets could observe the agreement, and that there could be peace and stability. It also lessened fears that the enemy was strong. During that Political Bureau meeting it was also decided that we must resolutely retaliate against the enemy for having violated the agreement. Resolution 21 stated that "At present the active, positive direction most beneficial to the revolutionary cause of the entire nation is always holding high the flag of peace and justice, and struggling politically, militarily, and diplomatically to force the enemy to carry out the Paris Agreement, in order to defeat the enemy." Clearly, our party affirmed at the very beginning that the Paris Agreement was a victory for us, and that we had to struggle to force the enemy to strictly implement them and that our cause was just and we were certain to be victorious. We signed the agreement and honored our signature. We would also force them to honor their signature. We would not allow the Americans and puppets to sabotage the agreement. In order to maintain the accomplishments of the revolution, we had to punish the enemy for violating the agreement by its land-grabbing and pacification activities. We would not retaliate passively in places where the enemy thought it advantageous to violate the agreement and attack us. We had to take the initiative by retaliating against them very painfully and attack the places from which their attacks originated and in places disadvantageous to them. In that spirit, in September 1973 we made an open declaration over our radio station to warn the enemy and so that the world could clearly understand our legitimate actions.

We hoped that after that warning the Americans and puppets would awaken so that we would not have to act and actually open fire. There were still conditions for carrying out the agreement; the door was still open at Paris and Tan Son Nhat. But Thieu may have thought that he was truly strong and that his U.S. master was still a solid source of support. Therefore, Thieu increasingly stpped up the fighting, despite the agreement and despite our warning, and hoped to rule forever in South Vietnam. The United States, for its part, thought that once it withdrew its troops it could still, by means of its Vietnamization strategy, remain permanently in South Vietnam.

Let us listen to a story told by an American, Weldon A. Brown, in his book "The Last Helicopter":

"Thieu continued to think that with U.S. aid and with the secret commitments made by Nixon, he had nothing to worry about. The commitments were still valid and he had been strengthened because the United States had provided him additional jet combat aircraft and very modern weapons, so much so that in 1975, when the U.S. Congress forbade the continuation of combat aid, Thieu still felt secure because of the commitments made by Nixon. The aid program and our promises caused Thieu to have a false sense of security, as a result of which Thieu turned down all efforts toward reconciliation or negotiations with the opposition and ignored the Paris Agreement. During the first year after the signing of the agreement, Thieu carried out small attacks and pushed the communists from a number of areas in the Mekong Delta and along the coast, set up outposts there, and resettled refugees in the newly occupied areas, and even had his troops raid Kampuchea."

"Thieu did not want the political process to succeed and weaken his regime, no matter in what form." Anthony Lewis wrote the following:

"Thieu prevented people from traveling from one area to another, and changed political prisoners into common criminals so that he could continue to detain them, and forbade all political parties except his own to operate. Thieu not only refused to observe the provisions of the Paris Agreement but regarded propaganda in favor of those agreements in South Vietnam to be a crime. When the ceasefire was about to take effect Thieu launched harassing operations. Thieu needed our tacit support for those acts, which violated the agreement, and it appears that he got his wish. Just before the ceasefire took effect Washington quickly shipped Thieu weapons valued at $1 billion. According to one source, at the beginning of February 1975 Thieu told an American reporter that since the Paris Agreement was signed the United States had never pressured him to make political concessions to the communists, that is to observe the peace-keeping provisions. Shipler wrote that Ambassador Martin and the United States did nothing to prevent those foolhardy acts and did nothing to persuade Thieu to carry out the Paris Agreement."

Thus it is clear which party violated the agreement and deliberately stepped up the war. It was essential that the violator be punished.

CHAPTER THREE

Punishing the Agreement Violators

After the Political Bureau meeting we met with the Military Commission of the party Central Committee to discuss the specific implementation of the Political Bureau's Resolution. On 1 June 1973 the B2 delegation met to discuss the contents of a preliminary guidance message to be sent back to our theater and make preparations for our return. I still had a lot of specific things to do with the General Staff, the Political General Department, the Rear Services General Department, and the combat arms commands, so that they could clearly understand the actual situation in our theater, listen to our opinions, and give their specialized guidance, and to obtain their valuable assistance with regard to planning, materiel, and technical matters. I then hastily prepared to set out.

I was about to return to the green jungle, the battlefield aflame with combat, and my combat units after a period of absence. I felt very anxious and happy. That spontaneous happiness enabled me to discover a feeling that had long been inside me: I regarded the base as my home, the battlefield as my home area, and the cadres and men of the organs and combat units as my relatives. When I was assigned the mission of leaving the battlefield to go to Saigon and participate in the Four-Party Joint Military Commission I thought that I wouldn't return and I felt anxious and nostalgic, as if sadly bidding adieu to my home area. Now that I was about to return to the base and the battlefield, I was as happy as if I were about to return to my old village and my loved ones. Perhaps the decades I had lived on the battlefield, in the wide open spaces, with constantly changing scenery, the jungle birds, and the fish, had conditioned my soul to respond only to the green jungle. Or perhaps I had yearned all my life for independence and freedom and had pledged to take up arms and fight until the final objective was attained, so my life had been tied in with the battlefield. That was not entirely the case. Even as I take pen in hand to write these lines I understand even more clearly the nostalgic reason for the life and society of soldiers during many long years of war. How beautiful and how noble is the sacred comradeship for the goal of liberating the homeland and the people. During the difficult days of hunger and thirst we shared each piece of jungle root, and each bit of firewood and custard apple, and shared with one another each drink of spring water we had brought from the other side of the mountain. On the Truong Son route, every year, after months of carrying heavy burdens, climbing mountains and fording streams to the point of exhaustion, we shared each spoonful of sugar or bit of salt, or offered one another our last quinine tablet to help one another reach the objective. Each human life was precious and the homeland needed every soldier, but we regarded our joys and sorrows. If one heard that the other won a battle and did a better job than he did, he would enthusiastically study the other's example. If one heard that the other had been defeated he would be worried and seek ways to help out. Everything was for the common cause. Everything was for the revolution. One for all, all for one. Such was life in the "green jungle." Such was life among comrades in arms in two wars of resistance, in the Duong Minh Chau, War Zone D, Dong Thap Muoi, and U Minh Forest bases. Love for one's comrades and fellow unit members, the jungle, and the streams were immense and unlimited. That was love we learned from Uncle Ho, from his immense love for the nation and for the workers and fighters. That love transcended space and time and was the same everywhere and at all times.

Anyone who had lived such a life would be indulgent and nostalgic. It was not that the battlefield had captivated me, but that my heart and morality made me attached to it.

All along the Truong Son route during that trip south there was much less enemy bombing and shelling. All activities became much more pleasant and animated. From one troop way-station to another and from one segment to another there was specialization and efficiency was many times higher than in the past. The men were happy when they met our delegation traveling south from Hanoi. Everyone wanted to know whether there was anything new with regard to lines and policies. Had the Political Bureau issued a resolution on the new situation and missions? The cadres in charge of the units and stations whispered in my ear, "What does B2 intend to do?" and "What are the prospects?" They promised to do all they could to aid the battlefield. I was very moved. Those comrades would give us their all-out assistance and support the battlefields, but that area itself was a battlefield. They were not only aiding the battlefields but were also fighting heroically under fierce bombing and shelling, no less so than at the front. They had a truly noble spirit of thinking only of their comrades and the total victory of the revolution. The same was true all over the country during wartime. Millions of people acted as one, believed in the party, and worked, fought, and sacrificed everything for victory, for the success of the revolution in the South, and for the unification of the homeland.

Of course, it was unavoidable that certain backward elements would violate discipline in a cowardly* manner: some were afraid of dying and sought ways to avoid going to the front, but they were a small, insignificant minority.

During that arduous, dangerous trip I dreamed of the battlefield. After the victory we would have a country extending from Lang Son to the Ca Mau Peninsula, from the border to the islands, with an immense sky and immense seas. We would have 40 to 50 million Vietnamese who lived new-style lives. We would build a new society, a socialist society, and would create the new socialist man, just like the society and people the heart and morality of which had formed me. It was necessary to eliminate the bad customs which the way of life of selfish individual competition in the artificially prosperous society and consumer society left behind by U.S. neocolonialism. We had to put an end to thankless habits and vile individual desires which resulted in husbands mistreating wives, children abandoning their father, and friends being changed depending on one's needs of the moment. The new society had to be a society in which there is no oppression, exploitation, or injustice, in which everyone is able to develop their talents and participate in building the nation and

---

* That is, fearing death and remaining in the rear, or transferring to other, less dangerous units.

in a free, well-off, happy life for everyone. The new man must be exemplary, virtuous and talented.

Virtue is manifested in behavior between people, between the general and the specific, in the family and in society. Everyone must love and respect each other, and be faithful, sincere and loyal. Such people have nothing in common with people who smile cordially in one's presence but betray one behind one's back, who "stabs you in the stomach with a dagger while praying to Buddha." It must be Vietnamese morality and communist morality, which combine to form the virtue of Ho Chi Minh.

Talent is manifested in the specific results of completed tasks and missions, not in superficial boasting and exaggeration. If words are not accompanied by action they have no value, theory not demonstrated by reality is only empty theory. Every individual must be exemplary in study, work, combat, production, and one's way of life, and life in an exemplary, close-knit family and an orderly, harmonious society. If we are not exemplary no one will listen to us, and if families are not harmonious and exemplary there is no way to create an orderly, just society. I think that our society of the future must be a pure society made up of pure people. That society differs from the Maoist society described by comrade P.P. Vladimirov in his book "Yanan Diary":

"The principled nature of the party is replaced by reverent minds, a personality cult, and a self-effacement of the individual. The self-effacement had, in general, become a characteristic of life in Yanan. While trying to avoid making waves at any price, and keep one's position, or even rise higher, people appear to have gone crazy. Honor, virtue, friendship, etc., are forgotten."

Such people clearly are not communists. Such a society is not a socialist society.

I had a dream about a road. I had an enthusiastic exchange with the comrades in the Command of Group 559 at the Group's headquarters. We decided that once the revolution succeeded and our country was unified we would develop that Route 559, the eastern Truong Son route, the famous "Ho Chi Minh Trail," into a truly modern Ho Chi Minh road. It would be a highway running north-south along the Truong Son, following the old 559 route, which would be improved, broadened, and meet standards. Along the way there would be erected monuments to commemorate the feats of arms of each segment of the road, of the heroic martyrs, so that future generations could always know about the backbone road of the homeland which passed down the length of the nation, a road that unified the nation even then. That backbone extended from Hanoi, the nerve center, and from the socialist North to the South, which was engaged in a life-and death struggle. In the future, if we were capable of doing so, we would also build a parallel railroad. The Ho Chi Minh highway and the Ho Chi Minh railroad would in fact be backbone routes for a country that was developing strongly. All of our dreams would become reality. We were sacrificing ourselves in combat to achieve success so that future generations could continue to build a rich and strong state so that our people can have a civilized, happy life.

At the end of June the water level of the Sekong River had risen and the current was flowing swiftly. Two well-built boats of Group 471 (under the 559 Command) took us downstream through many rough rapids. Each time we passed through a rapids my entire body shook. A soldier sat in the stern, his hand on the tiller and looking ahead intensely. Another stood imposingly on the bow, his two hands clutching a long pole, prepared to push the boat away from dangerous bolders sticking up out of the water or submerged below the surface. Meanwhile, the boat continued to rush along with the swift-flowing current. Many times I thought it was about to be smashed to pieces against a rock. We got out of a vehicle and boarded a boat, then left the boat and resumed the journey by land. On each occasion we were greeted warmly and given all-out assistance, and the partings were reluctant. It is impossible to remember all of the people along that wartime route. They included cadres and enlisted men and there were females and males. They were all alike: they had calm expressions in the face of danger and had bright smiles and loved their country, and had a will of iron. We became friends immediately after we met, and parting was difficult.

As soon as I came ashore I met comrade Cuu (Colonel Huynh Van Cuu), deputy head of the Regional Protection Bureau, accompanied by several others, who had brought several "command cars" to take us back to the base. Cuu was a cadre who specialized in organizing our official trips and visits to the battlefield. He was very experienced in insuring safety and rapidity. I hugged him and firmly shook hands with everyone. He looked me over and said, "You look thinner but are still firm. When we heard that you were returning we were all happy. I thought that I wouldn't have the opportunity to escort you again!" "Did you think that I would remain in Saigon?" I asked, "In fact I wanted to stay there, as a member of the Four-Party Joint Military Commission and Concord, if it were set up. But the enemy wanted no part of it. They don't want peace, but only war, so I had to return to the green jungle with you."

Our convoy arrived at the base at dusk. Over a period of half a year many things had happened, but the scenery, the land, and the sky at the base were practically the same.

Comrade Tam Hoa, i.e. Nguyen Xuan On, the chef de cabinet of the Regional Command, along with comrade Le Van Xup, a bodyguard who had been an aide since I first returned south, and Misses Xuan Thu and Huong of the military medical team, and Lien and Tam of the mess team, ran out to the gate to give me a rousing reception.

When I entered the house I looked around. In the rich green garden there were fresh greens, fruit trees, bananas, grapefruits and luxuriant pink plums. Comrade Chin Dung, who was old and had served with the old 309th Battalion during the anti-French resistance, and now diligently tended the garden, boasted to me about his accomplishments and observed, "For a long time now the enemy have reduced their bombing and strafing here, so the vegetation is healthy. When peace is achieved this entire denuded jungle area will become fruit orchards and fields of green vegetables. I will be able to return to my home village of Cam Son in My Tho and live out my old age." Chin Dung turned around and continued his introductions. "This is the young man Tai and this is Miss Thao. The secretarial team will prepare for their wedding so that we can drink some wine in celebration.

While Thao and Tai were blushing and trying to hide their smiles, Kien Chien, the deputy chef de cabinet, and the youths Diep, Cach and Luu of the Civil Affairs Team laughed aloud and shouted encouragement. Everyone crowded around asking all sorts of questions. I didn't have time to respond adequately to any of the questions. It was truly moving, as if we were a family. I suddenly asked comrade "Five Poison" (i.e. Nguyen Van Hoanh), my secretary, to take from the car the gifts I had brought from Hanoi and distribute them to everyone. He was called by that name because his name was Nam [Five] and he was a chemical corps cadre, and to distinguish him from comrade "Five Red Medicine," a military medical doctor who also worked at the organ. The gifts didn't amount to much, a package of "Capital" cigarettes for the men and needle, thread and hair clasps for the women. They had only sentimental value.

As if suddenly remembering something pleasant, brother Tam Hoa pulled me to one side and asked, "Do you know that the puppets have openly complained, demanding that you return to Saigon? It's so funny. They said that Hanoi had placed you under 'house arrest,' and that Hanoi must return you to them!" "It's nothing but a psychological warfare trick," I said. Tam Hoa continued, "When brother Hai Khiet,* a member of the Joint Military Commission, reported that you had gone to Hanoi for good they became enraged. They threatened our delegation that if Lt Gen Tran Van Tra did not return they would send vehicles to take away our entire delegation. They may really do that, for the puppets have stopped at no vile act in the past. Thus our comrades there must have plans to fight to defend themselves. The tense situation has lasted several months. I'm really concerned about them."

I replied, "We will struggle to force them to observe the Paris Agreement. They won't dare do anything to our people, for we are strong legally, politically, and militarily."

After I rested a few days COSVN held a meeting to disseminate Resolution 21 and organize its implementation. Toward that end, a conference of military administration cadres from all over the B2 theater was held in September 1973 in an attractive bamboo grove in the base area. In attendance were large numbers of leadership cadres of the provinces, military regions, mass organizations, and regiments and divisions. The discussions were very seething and enthusiastic. Those comrades reported on the actual situations in the localities and units, our good points and deficiencies during the recent period, related them to theory and to the resolution, and evaluated what was correct and what was incorrect. The main features of the situation--the question of whether we or the enemy were stronger, whether there should be two areas, whether our forces should be consolidated on the spot or withdrawn to, how we should retaliate, etc.--were analyzed. The discussions were very specific

---

*Bui Thanh Kiet, a senior colonel and deputy head of the military delegation of the PRG of the RSVN to the Two-Party Joint Military Commission.

and dealt with each detail and aspect, so that implementation could be correct and in order to avoid leftist or rightist deviation. Especially, those comrades spent a good deal of time discussing the military proselyting policy after the agreements. According to one view, we had to stress political struggle and military proselyting should be our strategy; it was necessary to use many military proselyting stratagems by the masses to paralyze the enemy's military operations, and that was a form of attack. We had strong military forces but we would avoid using them, for using military forces would be very entangling and would cause a lack of mutual confidence and tension. We had to dare achieve national conciliation and eliminate enmity.

Such one-sided views were based on our subjective thoughts and desires and did not take into account the actual plots and acts of the enemy, and would cause the lower echelons to have pacifist, rightist thoughts and cease to fight. One cadre said of the lower echelons, "The men have been fighting for decades. Isn't that enough? Now we must "be green on the outside and red on the inside," promote military proselyting, and transform supporters of the enemy into our supporters." According to another, "We still have troops, weapons, and ammunition. We can take what we need from the United States and Thieu and we will not have to worry about insufficient supplies, etc." Although they dared not say so openly, in their hearts the lower echelons wanted to say to such cadres, "We don't want to keep on fighting merely to satisfy our personal desires. We want the country to be at peace and for the killing of the people to cease. But if the enemy launches sweeping and land-grabbing operations and shoot at us, and plot to eliminate the revolutionary gains we have made recently, what are we to do? Put up our hands and shout the slogan 'Peace forever'?" No. We sincerely did not want a recurrence of the grievous naivete of the 1954-1959 period. In my heart I still mourn the many comrades who fell in battle--with weapons in hand but not daring to fire--during that period, and mourn the many local movements that were drowned in blood. Because they were afraid of being criticized and of acting contrary to the (military proselyting) policy, the guerrillas in My Tho had to attack on the sly (without the knowledge of the upper echelon) the enemy outposts that had been set up illegally in their base area. In Mo Cay and Ben Tre, where our troops had to retreat continually in the face of enemy land-grabbing operations and not retaliate against them, they lamented, "How could we sink any lower?" and ultimately were able to recover the district's base area by retaliating on their own accord.

After the conference of military administration cadres, I met with the military cadres to discuss the details of the military plan for the 1973-1974 dry season, the first full dry season since the signing of the agreements. In essence, the plan reconfirmed our explicit attitude of observing and defending the agreement, and thus punishing the violator. We endeavored to do what we had declared we would do: resolutely and actively punish the enemy, even in the places from which they launched the agreement-violating attacks. If we were to carry out that plan we had to be strong politically, legally and militarily, and strong not only with regard to forces but also with regard to our deployment of the various kinds of forces in the various areas, in accordance with a strong strategic posture which provided for all contingencies. We had to consolidate and rectify our armed forces on the spot and had to develop the position and strength of the revolution in all three areas: our area, the enemy's area and the contested area. All localities had to use all political forms to proselytize and win over the enemy troops, and force the withdrawal of or wipe out the outposts and positions illegally set up in all areas after 28 January 1973. It was necessary to insure the democratic rights of the people--their right to travel and earn a living--and their right to dismantle the strategic hamlets and return to their old village if they so desired. We had to annihilate all forces launching attacks, carrying out sweeping operations, robbing the people, or interfering with the people's livelihood. All such activities were illegal. We informed our delegation to the Two-Party Joint Military Commission of our plan so that it could coordinate its struggle at the conference table.

A review of the situation since the agreement was signed showed that there had been many changes in the B2 theater. Between January and April 1973, in all military regions and provinces the enemy had used all types of troops to attack and encroach upon our areas, and endeavored to achieve pacification, herd the people, conscript recruits and clear terrain. Especially around Saigon they used bulldozers to flatten the people's houses and gardens, and used soldiers and prisoners to cut down vegetation, clear out mangrove trees, set up additional outposts, and sent out "Phoenix" spies to uncover, arrest and kill patriots they called "Viet Cong infrastructure." After May 1973, thanks to the close guidance of COSVN and the Regional Command, and of the local leadership echelons, we retaliated fiercely so the enemy forces were stopped and were gradually repulsed. Outposts which had illegally been set up were wiped out, surrendered, or were withdrawn, increasingly larger numbers of enemy troops deserted, and the enemy's regular and local units were hit hard and revealed weaknesses and suffered increasingly larger losses in the various areas.

The situations of our side and the enemy developed in two increasingly contrasting directions. For our part, the cadres, enlisted men, and people realized that the United States had been defeated, the puppets had weakened, we were victorious, and our status was improving, and were enthusiastic and confident and participated positively in all tasks of opposing the enemy. For the enemy's part, the officers and enlisted men of the various kinds of forces realized the truth--that the United States had been defeated--and were tired of the war, were afraid the war would continue, and wanted peace. When carrying our military operations they did so perfunctorily, and sometimes did not carry out the operations at all but falsified their reports (this happened at the regimental and battalion levels). The number of draft-dodgers and deserters increased steadily. The forces controlling the people were also negative and relaxed their control. Therefore, the people struggled and engaged in livelihood increasingly far from home, and one by one returned to their old villages and our liberated area. At the same time, the upper-echelon Americans and puppets, who were very obstinate and subjective, drated one plan after another and ordered the lower echelons to implement them. Thieu instructed the sector (provincial) echelon as follows:

1. Expand your territory, gain control of the population, maintain the area under your control, maintain security, and do not lose a single village or

hamlet. (The overall norms were to control 11,000 of the 13,000 hamlets in South Vietnam, and that by February 1974, 65 percent of hamlets must be Class A--tightly controlled--hamlets.)

2. Take and defend all strategic lines of communication.

3. Annihilate the enemy armed forces and supply and transportation forces in all areas, especially those crossing the border.

4. Isolate and blockade the enemy economically, and sabotage and destabilize the enemy's base areas and liberated area.

5. Step up monitoring, espionage, and the use of airborne reconnaissance commandos to grasp the situation, study objectives, and draft contingency plans while awaiting the opportunity to retake the areas we held prior to 29 March 1972.

He also issued specific instructions to each area:

1. In the areas under our control and the cities, wipe out the seeds of uprising and prevent uprisings by patrolling, ambushing, eliminating the Viet Cong infrastructures, tightly controlling the people, stepping up psychological warfare, organizing the people, consolidating the governmental administration, normalizing the people's lives and creating conditions for economic restoration and development.

2. In the consolidation area (i.e. the contested area), made up of the Class and Class D hamlets, push back, stop and annihilate the Viet Cong political and military forces; restore and consolidate the governmental administration, raise the level of security, expand the area under our control, and use political and economic means to bribe the people, but rely principally on military means. The territorial military forces will gradually be concentrated to carry out attacks in that area.

3. In the Viet Cong mopping-up area (i.e. our liberated and base areas), concentrate on attacking the transportation corridors to achieve an economic blockade, and on reconnaissance and intelligence activities. Depending on the situation, use air power and artillery to attack supply depots and transportation facilities, win over the people, maintain a government in exile, and create instability. Maintain military activities and draft plans to retake the area.

With regard to their pacification plan, they stated that it was necessary to launch many pacification campaigns in each sector and military region, as well as nationwide, and increase the density of small unit operations; set up many additional outposts; and bulldoze the terrain in the contested area and our liberated area. In 1973 alone their norm was to destroy 12,000 hectares. In areas under their control, they were to relocate the people, set up hamlets, clear wasteland, and encroach upon our liberated area. Their 1973 plan called for the relocation of 100,000 people and the establishment of 20 hamlets in the provinces of Long Khanh, Phuoc Tuy, Binh Tuy, Lam Dong, Kien

Phong, Ninh Thuan, and Dac Lac. Expenses would total 50 billion puppet South Vietnamese piasters.

The enemy made the following national objectives: taking and holding as much territory as possible; endeavoring to control the people, especially the peasants; and increasing actual military and political strength. Military Region III and Military Region IV constituted the enemy's heartland. On 6 March 1973 Thieu met with the Military Region commanders and province chiefs and said, "I place the life-or-death struggle on the shoulders of the high-ranking commanders of those two military regions (Military Region II and Military Region IV).

Thus the puppet Thieu regime not only ignored the Paris Agreement but took advantage of it and of the honesty of its adversary, which believed in peace, stability and national concord, and endeavored to consolidate and develop their forces, step up their land-grabbing attacks, and eventually completely eliminate the liberation troops and the PRG of the RSVN. If we were not vigilant, if we were rightist and gave ground, the puppet forces would become increasingly strong and their position would improve, and the situation would have developed differently. Clearly, after the end of April we reacted and retaliated, while the enemy revealed weaknesses and deficiencies, were stopped and retreated. Following the Political Bureau conference COSVN, in a spirit of debate, guided opposition against the enemy more resolutely and the situation on the battlefield developed increasingly to our advantage.

Even in the period from January to April, when we were losing much of our land and population on the other battlefields, in Military Region 9 (western Nam Bo), where the enemy concentrated the largest number of troops and which they regarded as the center of their land-grabbing attacks--especially in the Chuong Thien area and the area between Can Tho, Soc Trang, Ca Mau, and Rach Gia Provinces--we held our ground. We were able to do so because comrade Sau Dan (Vo Van Kiet) at that time secretary of the Military Region 9 Party Committee, agreed with the military region command, headed by comrade Le Duc Anh, that the enemy would never willingly observe the agreement, that war was still war, and that nothing had changed. Therefore, the main-force regiments of the Military Region remained in place and, along with the local forces and guerrillas, operated as usual, attacked resolutely, retaliated fiercely, and annihilated entire enemy battalions (the 3d Battalion of the 16th Regiment of the puppet 9th Division and the 86th Ranger Battalion). That clearly did not indicate that our forces had weakened and the enemy forces had become stronger since the agreements, as some comrades imagined.

By means of those activities, Military Region 9 liberated an area 20 kilometers long along the Nuoc Duc Canal in southern Chuong Thien, and a number of other areas. The population of those newly liberated areas amounted to 600,000, in 11 villages and 152 hamlets, not counting the people in the contested area who returned to our area to produce. At the same time, Military Region 9 wiped out all of the land-grabbing outposts illegally set up by the enemy, after which the garrisons of some enemy outposts that had been established prior to the agreements also fled in panic. The heroic actions and brilliant specific results of the soldiers and people of Military Region 9 were outstanding and unique in comparison to the other military regions, and were praised by the Political Bureau and set an example for the other battlefields. But surprisingly those specific acts were completely contrary to a whole series of policies at that time, just after the signing of the agreement: that we should urgently stabilize the situation, create two zones, one controlled by us and the other controlled by the enemy, withdraw our forces to the rear so that they could be consolidated, and not use troops rashly but struggle politically, principally by military proselyting. Using military proselyting, using the masses to paralyze the enemy's military operations and neutralize the enemy's outposts, were types of attacks, as mentioned above. Especially, the actions of the military forces of Military Region 9 were based on the viewpoint that there had been no agreements, that nothing had changed, and that it was necessary to keep on fighting. That was an incorrect understanding of the Paris Agreement and the new strategic phase. But it was correct in that it correctly evaluated the obstinacy and perfidy of the enemy, just like during the Geneva Agreements period, and resolutely retained the revolutionary gains that had been made. It was in accord with the actual situation and was not illusory and utopian. "Luckily," that was a distant battlefield, so upper-echelon policies were often slow in reaching it and the rectification of mistakes was often not prompt. Let us here mention one point: reality is extremely valuable, whether it is the reality of something mistaken or something correct; it is the basis of theory and of policies and lines. Any theory, policy or line not based on reality is mistaken.

In one of their long-range plans the enemy intended to:

"Between February and August 1973, endeavor to occupy and control the major part of the territory of South Vietnam.

"Between September 1973 and February 1974, endeavor to consolidate the gains that had been made and defend them solidly.

"Then, in 1974 or at latest 1975, there would be a political solution and a general elections to make things legal. There will be only one governmental administration (i.e. that of Thieu) and one strong army (i.e. the Army of the Republic of Vietnam). The war will wither away. The Viet Cong will only be an opposition party which engages exclusively in political struggle, nothing more and nothing less.

"Otherwise, we will use large-scale warfare to completely eliminate the Viet Cong in 1976 and 1977."

With regard to the economy, to accompany that political-military plan they drafted a long-range 1973-1980, 8-year plan which was promulgated on 20 May 1973. The plan was divided into three periods:

"1973-1974: restoration and rebuilding.
"1975-1976: development and consolidation.
"1977-1980: self-sufficiency and a reduction of aid."

The aspirations, plans and acts of the enemy were one-in-the-same from the very beginning.

On the basis of the actual developments on the battlefield between them and the middle of the rainy season, we could see what the schemes and actions of the enemy were. We studied the implementation of Resolution 21 of the party Central Committee and concretized it in the form of COSVN Resolution 12, on the basis of which we drafted the B2 theater's operational plan for the 1973-1974 dry season. After presenting the plan and obtaining the approval of COSVN, I reviewed the plan for the last time and approved it in September 1973 so that the staff and the battlefields could have time to meticulously organize its implementation and report to the Military Commission of the party Central Committee.

The main battlefield that was selected was the Mekong Delta, which the enemy had selected as the focal point for their pacification, land-grabbing, population-grabbing, and plundering activities. We had to stay the bloody hand of the enemy and resolutely punish them. We had to regain and retain the liberated area we had prior to 28 January 1973. In order to attain that goal we had to closely coordinate our activities with the other battlefields and not allow the enemy to make peace in places they were weak and at a disadvantage in order to concentrate troops to attack in places where they had the advantage and in places strategically important to them. We decided to strengthen the forces--both the manpower and weapons of Military Regions 8 and 9, the delta battlefield, so that those two battlefields could fulfill their mission of being the principal battlefields in that phase. At that time, a problem that was posed within the ranks of military cadres, as well as among the civilian cadres, was how the forces of the delta should be strengthened.

Since we had selected the delta as the main battlefield we had to deploy strong forces of all three types there in order to defeat the enemy. Thus many main-force troops were concentrated there.

In the short range as well as in the long range, the question was whether the two sides should continue to fight in the eastern part of the theater like two water buffaloes clashing with each other or whether we should surprise the enemy by selecting another area, i.e. the Mekong Delta, in which to concentrate our forces and attack.

Those who shared that opinion wanted to redeploy our forces and send the region's main-force troops to augment the rural areas in the delta. They thought that to liberate the highly populated, rich delta would be to win the war. In fact, that was not a new viewpoint but had persisted for a long time. According to that viewpoint, we had to liberate the rural areas before liberating the cities. It was contrary to our party's line regarding the anti-U.S. war. That was a strategy of attacking in all three strategic areas: the lowland rural area, the jungle-and-mountains area, and the cities. It was a strategy of attacking with both military forces and mass political forces, and of always combining offensives and uprisings. Therefore, the position of cities was very important. In that strategic offensive the main-force attack would be the decisive blow, but our increasingly well-equipped main-force units could be concentrated to fight on a large scale in an open delta area with many rivers and canals and with marshy terrain. In that area the enemy held the lines of communications, which were defended by a system of strongly fortified outposts. The enemy also had fleets on the river and had complete control of the air. Our experience had shown us that when fighting the U.S.-puppet troops it was best if we concentrated troops in regimental units equipped with light military equipment. If divisions were organized, they had to be light divisions, and the method of command and tactics could not be the same as on the jungle-and-mountains battlefield. At the same time, we had to develop extensive guerrilla forces, large numbers of elite sappers, and strong local troops in order to wage marvelous, continuous, seething guerrilla warfare and revolutionary people's war, flexibly combine the three types of troops on all kinds of terrain, and in all kinds of weather, by means of the three combat columns, combined campaigns, and both military forces and the political forces of the masses. We were entirely capable of fighting in that manner, had large numbers of revolutionary people, had superiority and had experience. Each battlefield was different with regard to conditions, missions, objectives and capabilities. We had to have appropriate methods for organizing and deploying forces and could not be imitative, and certainly could not base our actions on our subjective desires.

The Regional Command had always affirmed that the eastern Nam Bo battlefield, including Saigon, the principal battlefield of B2, was the war-deciding strategic battlefield which would determine the outcome of the war. There we were capable of bringing into play the great role of main-force units. The terrain was favorable for the concentration and use of large main-force units and the use of all weapons and technical facilities. It was an area in which we were capable or organizing, deploying and stockpiling rear services facilities and materiel-technical support facilities for a large army and for major campaigns. That battlefield had an important strategic position. We could threaten the enemy, force the enemy into a passive defensive position, and annihilate much enemy manpower, combining lightning attacks with storm-like uprisings to smash the U.S.-puppet war center and ultimately knock out the enemy there.

The delta battlefield played a very important role throughout the course of the war, for both we and the enemy relied on the treasury of people and materiel there to build up military, political and economic forces and change the balance of forces between the two sides. At times we made it the main battlefield in that sense, but only at certain times in the course of the war, such as during that dry season and the rainy season of 1974 or, in the past, in 1962 and 1963. However, it was not the battlefield that would decide the war. Therefore, B2 had long made its strategic deployments and force deployments on the basis of the role and position of the battlefield, in a strategic offensive plan of a truly revolutionary war. It was vital that the eastern Nam Bo main-force units not be weakened; on the contrary, they had to be further strengthened. I remember that in 1965-1966, when the Americans were sending large numbers of troops into South Vietnam, a number of comrades in charge of the city of Saigon directly asked me, "The Americans are bringing in large numbers of troops and strong weapons, and are changing over to a limited war, so should we change our strategic line? Should we disperse our main forces so that we can wage a protracted guerrilla war in order to defeat the enemy? I emphatically said no. I explained the passive, fire-extinguishing role of the Americans; that they had large numbers of troops but were not strong and we were still attacking them; and that we would not disperse them to fight as guerrillas but would organize many additional divisions--at that time only one division had been organized in B2--and advance to the formation of crops. There was absolutely no question of changing the strategic line, or of defeating the enemy by waging a protracted guerrilla war. However, that attitude did not die away entirely; the struggle against it was prolonged. A long time had passed since then. The Americans had to get out and the puppets were aggressive but that aggression was in its death throes, so the eastern Nam Bo main-force troops had become even more important. We had endeavored to strengthen the main-force units of eastern Nam Bo and decided to reinforce the forces in the delta by many different means. We would positively and quickly send many additional troops, weapons and ammunition, and facilities in order to promote the development of the three types of on-the-spot troops; assign to the regional main-force divisions the mission of urgently organizing and training a number of technical combat arms companies and battalions so that they could be sent down to the military alliance; send to Military Region 9 the 1st Regiment of the main-force 1st Division of the Region, which was operating in the Bay Nui-Ha Tien area; step up close guidance of plans and modes; and guide a plan for closely coordinating the battlefields, including those of the main-force units, so that the enemy could not concentrate on attacking in the lowlands as they saw fit.

During that dry season B2 carried out the task of protecting, consolidating, and expanding the communications-transportation corridors connecting the Regional base in eastern Nam Bo with the Dong Thap Muoi base, and on down to the U Minh Forest base, along three routes:

--The route along the Kampuchean border to Bay Nui, Ha Tien, Rach Gia and the U Minh Forest.

--The My Tho route through Ben Tre, Vinh Tra and Ca Mau.

--The river route via the Tien and Hau rivers.

At the same time we strengthened the route connecting eastern Nam Bo with the great rear area via the Truong Son 559 route. With the agreement and positive assistance of the Rear Services General Department, the Regional Rear Services Department worked with the military regions in urgently building up the materiel reserves of the region and the military regions, starting with the beginning of the dry season, so that they could continue to take the initiative and develop strongly.

The weapons and equipment supplied by the General Staff to B2 in 1973 were being received and transported efficiently. But there was as yet no upper-echelon distribution plan to transport and stockpile the supplies for 1974 early and positively. If we waited for a decision, we would lose transportation time and slow things down, and if unexpected obstacles were encountered, the stockpiling plan could be upset. I had been thinking about that problem since I attended the plenary meeting of the Political Bureau in Hanoi in May, but could find no solution to it. I went to meet with comrade Dinh Duc Thien, then head of the Rear Services General Department. Comrade Thien was straightforward and enthusiastic; enthusiastic toward his friends and comrades and toward the common endeavor. A large man, he was a person who dared to think and to do, was open, kind, easy to get to know, and especially was good-natured. The military cadres of the north and south, the old revolutionary cadres who had been active in the past, both men and women, and the enlisted men, knew about and sympathized with his good nature and folksy "obscenity." After I explained the problem and expressed my concern that I had not been able to resolve it, he laughed it off and said, "There's no problem. Why can't a battlefield commander think out the solution to such an easy problem?"

I was surprised and looked at him inquisitively. After hesitating a moment he said very slowly, with a very sympathetic expression, "Let me be the chief of the general staff for an hour. I will immediately sign an order giving B2 several thousand additional tons of weapons, then I will sign similar orders for the other military regions."

I burst out in laughter when I realized that he was joking. I joked with him in turn, "If I had unlimited powers, I'd let you be the 'Son of Heaven' for 24 hours so that you could be granted all your wishes and marry a beautiful princess just like Hassan did. But I won't assume responsibility if you, like Hassan, are sent to an insane asylum and receive 50 lashes a day!"*

We laughed together merrily. But then he presented a plan: "If you agree, I'll lend you in advance 2,000 tons of weapons of various kinds from the total to be distributed to B2 in 1974."

I was extremely happy. We had reached agreement about a loan. He did not forget to emphasize, "Later I will deduct what supplies I'm sending you in advance. Tell your men to take good care of them. If you use them up and demand more, I'll have you all thrown in jail."

There remained the problem of transportation. I was certain in advance that the people responsible for transportation would be prepared to take on that additional difficult task. That turned out to be the case.

It was a dry season in which the two sides were trying to gain control of the land and the people. The enemy's objective was to gain control of the areas they controlled prior to 29 March 1972. They acted as if the Paris Agreement did not exist. Our objective was to retake the areas under our control prior to 28 January 1973. That objective was legally in accord with the Paris Agreement. The central focus of Military Region 9's plan was to punish the enemy troops for encroaching on our U Minh base area and retaking the highly populated areas in Go Quao and Giong Rieng in Rach Gia, and in Vinh Long and Tra Vinh, which made up a strategic area between the Tien and Hau Rivers. The central focus of Military Region 8's plan was to punish the

---
* From a story about a dreaming youth in the book "A Thousand and One Nights."

enemy for occupying the heart of our Dong Thap Muoi base and retake the highly populated Cai Be and Cai Lay areas in My Tho Province, which lay astride strategic Route 4, the backbone of the delta, along with areas in Ben Tre Province which bordered Vinh Long and Tra Vinh in Military Region 9. Another objective of those dry season activities of the two sides was to control rice. On 24 August 1973 Thieu convened in Can Tho a so-called Rice Conference. The quota they set for that dry season was stealing 1 million tons of rice. On 29 August 1973 the puppet general Vinh Nghi, commander of Military Region IV, directed the 16 province chiefs in the delta to steal and turn over more than 400,000 tons of husked rice (equal to 1 million tons of paddy) by the end of 1973. We had to combine punishing the enemy with breaking up that rice-stealing plan, protect the people's property and build up our stocks. Military Regions 8 and 9 were not the only ones fulfilling that mission. Military Region 7 (eastern Nam Bo) and Military Region 6 (southwest Trung Bo) also had to combine retaliation with gaining control of the rice harvest so that they could have rice stocks and readily available rice.

During that dry season the regional main-force units also had a rather difficult mission. In addition to gaining time so that we could build, consolidate and organize, especially the combat arms, step up tactical and technical training and improve our ability to carry out coordinated combat arms operations, and support the localities, the 9th and 7th divisions were deployed along the enemy's intermediate defense line of Saigon in the provinces of Tay Ninh and Binh Duong to coordinate with those provinces and help them fulfill their dry season missions. The principal missions of those two divisions were to threaten the intermediate line and inner line (the outskirts of Saigon) of the enemy's Saigon defenses and to pin down the 5th, 25th and 18th divisions, and the ranger groups of the puppets' III Corps, so that they could not withdraw to reinforce the delta or launch attacks in other places, and so that they could not complete and strengthen the defenses of their capital.

More must be said about the enemy's plots and acts in the Saigon area, as part of their general strategic scheme, after the agreement. Prior to 1972, Saigon was protected by three solid defense lines. With our "Nguyen Hue" campaign and our 1972 dry-season military operations throughout the region we smashed the outermost defense line and penetrated the middle defense line, so that only the inner line remained intact. Thus the defenses of Saigon were rather thin and unreliable. After the Paris Agreement was signed the Saigon puppet regime launched sweeping operations to occupy the contested areas and our liberated area, and consolidated and filled out the areas under their control. Especially, they paid all-out attention to bolstering the defenses of Saigon, their nerve center. They continually launched large and small operations to wipe out our political and guerrilla infrastructure in the outskirts of the capital. After launching those sweeping operations they used bulldozers to flatten the gardens and houses of the people in such areas as Cu Chi, Hoc Mon, Thu Dau Mot, etc. They used deserters from their army who had been captured to cut down the vegetation in the Lai Thieu and Thu Duc areas and the nipa palm groves at Binh Chanh, Nha Be, Can Duoc and Can Giuoc. They set up additional outposts, placed obstacles, laid mines and dug antitank trenches in the Bien Hoa area in order to further strengthen the capital's inner defense line.

In places they did not control, such as our long-established guerrilla bases around Saigon, including the six maquis villages at Thu Duc, the Rung Sat Zone, Duyen Hai, An Son, Lai Thieu, Tan My, Binh Ly, Hoc Mon, and the three villages of southern Ben Cat--which they called the "Iron Triangle"--Vuon Thom, Ba Vu, Tam Tan, Binh Chanh, the Can Duoc area, Can Giuoc, Nha Be, etc., they bombed and shelled day and night, pursued a scorched earth policy, created a "free fire" area, and tried to eliminate those guerrilla bases. The puppets' 1973-74 dry season plan was to take 60 of our liberation base enclaves in eastern Nam Bo, especially around Saigon. They plotted to restore the middle defense line by retaking Route 2 at Ba Ria, the Dat Cuoc area north of Tan Uyen, the Dau Tieng, Long Nguyen, and Thu Dau Mot areas, the Boi Loi area in Tan Ninh, Ho Bo, An Nhon Tay and Cu Chi. They launched a large, division-sized operation in the Long Nguyen and Dau Tieng areas, which were in our liberated area and were gaps in their middle defense line to the north. But we defeated them, wiped out entire puppet battalions, and prevented them from attaining their objective. But strengthening the defenses of Saigon was still a matter of life and death, so they still did not abandon their plan to occupy our areas so that they could restore their defense lines.

Our plan was to not only hold on to the liberated areas, stop their encroachment, and annihilate the troops carrying out the sweeping operation, but also to prevent them from completing their defenses of Saigon according to their plan to form a strategic enclave, thus forcing the puppet III Corps forces to always be passive and on the defensive in an unstable battlefield position, and to always worry that the Saigon defense line would be penetrated. Furthermore, their very skimpy strategic reserves could not withdraw to the other battlefields. That created an additional fierce contradiction for the puppet troops with regard to Thieu's stupid strategic line of spreading his troops out to defend every place, in order not to lose a single village or hamlet, thus forcing them to always be passive strategically and tactically, and to have no way of escape from that entirely disadvantageous situation.

The Regional main-force 5th Division directly supported the delta by counterattacking the enemy troops encroaching in the Kien Tuong area along the Kampuchean border, and expanded the corridor connecting eastern Nam Bo with the delta via the western part of Tay Ninh Province. Meanwhile a small mainforce detachment, along with sappers, punished the enemy in the Bu Bong and Tuy Duc areas in Quang Duc Province to protect the corridor connecting with the Truong Son 559 route, while also supporting the soldiers and people of Military Region 6, in which enemy troops were encroaching in the Binh Thuan and Binh Tuy areas.

Bu Bong was an enemy strong point near the Kampuchean border. The enemy troops stationed there continually launched sweeping operations and attacks in the surrounding villages, raided our transportation corridor, and used artillery to interdict that corridor day and night, which created considerable difficulties for the transportation of supplies to us. In order to punish the enemy at the point of origin of their violations, and to begin the 1973-74 dry season campaign, we used the 429th Regiment, a strong sapper regiment reinforced by an infantry detachment, to take that 4 November 1973. Then we expanded the liberated area around Bu Bong and took the Tuy Duc intersection, thus insuring that our transportation corridor was unimpeded and safe. Just as we had hoped, the puppets sent the 22d Division of their II Corps, along with three Regional Force regiments, and an armored regiment which was land-grabbing in the Ninh Thuan-Binh Thuan coastal area to attack us, in hopes of cutting our transportation corridor. We retaliated fiercely, wiped out part of their manpower, held on the entire liberated area, and created conditions for our forces in Military Region 6 to effectively oppose the enemy in western Phan Thiet.

Also in order to carry out our warning that we would punish the enemy where their attacks originate, on 5 and 6 November we used artillery of the 13th sapper regiment to shell Bien Hoa AFB and destroyed a number of aircraft and installations at the air base. For a long time enemy airplanes had taken off from that base to bomb such places in our liberated area as Loc Ninh, Bu Dop, Lo Go and Ka Tum, and the enemy used the Rang Rang airfield, which was situated in the midst of one of our base areas (War Zone A), for target practice. At those places we shot down 30 enemy airplanes between October and December 1973. Beginning in November 1973, every time the enemy bombed and strafed our liberated area we shelled, or carried out sapper attacks on, enemy airbases. Furthermore, we inflicted even more painful blows by destroying enemy fuel depots no matter where they were located. On 2 December 1973 the Nha Be gasoline depot, the largest fuel depot in South Vietnam, was infiltrated by sappers of the 10th Regiment who blew up a large number of tanks. Millions of liters of gasoline and oil were destroyed and smoke and flames rose hundreds of meters into the air, lighting up the Saigon sky. That resounding feat of arms of the 10th Sapper Regiment let the enemy know that we would do what we said, and warned them to watch out. That tank farm on the outskirts of Saigon was surrounded by a thick network of marshy rivers and canals. It had been attacked many times in the past, so the enemy had taken very careful precautions. They increased their forces, changed their defensive employment, placed obstacles and laid mines, used dozens of German Shepherd dogs and used radar, etc. Before the attack I personally reviewed the plan and all details had been prepared. Bay Uoc (Colonel Le Ba Uoc), political officer of the 10th Regiment, reported that "The unit selected to carry out the attack, made up of more than 10 cadres and enlisted men, entered the depot area for a first-hand inspection and inspected each fuel tank. We guarantee that the attack will be victorious."

The sappers' tradition was to penetrate through to their target and win a certain victory. The men of the 10th Regiment made good on that pledge.

Thus at the beginning of the rainy season we and the enemy were both very active all over the B2 theater. We achieved rather close cooperation among the military regions and between the local and main-force units, stretching out and pinning down the enemy everywhere, and winning many victories. In the Mekong Delta the enemy had to change the focal point of their activities. Between the signing of the agreement and the end of the 1973 rainy season the enemy took the Hau Giang area in our Military Region 9 and concentrated the entire 21st and 9th Divisions, a number of ranger and Regional Force units, and river patrol boats in order to carry out land-grabbing operations. Because they met with fierce retaliation, the enemy could not achieve their objectives and suffered heavy losses. Although they set up a number of additional outposts in such places as Bay Nui, Ha Tien, and Song Trem in the U Minh Forest, in many other places we expanded our liberated area and the enemy's plan to take the area which included parts of four provinces was completely defeated. At the beginning of the dry season they had to send some river patrol boats from Can Tho to Cat Lai in eastern Nam Bo and send the 9th Division to Kien Tuong and some ranger battalions to III Corps, leaving behind in the Hau Giang area only the weakened 21st Division and a number of ranger battalions and Regional Force troops. They concentrated their troops in the Tien Giang area of our Military Region 8 principally to encroach upon Dong Thap Muoi and the Kampuchean border area, interdict our transportation corridor to the Mekong Delta, and cope with our 5th Division. By concentrating troops there they intended to hold the area southwest of Saigon, a very important area between Saigon and the Mekong Delta, so that Saigon would not be isolated and so that the puppet regime could have a base that was strong socially, politically, militarily and economically. That clearly demonstrated the U.S.-Thieu scheme to closely combine Military Region III and Military Region IV (the old Cochin China) into the vital strategic area of all of South Vietnam. They strengthened those two military regions in all regards so that they could advance to defeating the enemy or, if necessary, withdraw into a strategic enclave there in order to continue to exist. But that scheme was carried out only half-heartedly, with a lack of spirit, by a greedy and blind strategy: "Under all circumstances it is necessary to hold on to everything and not lose a single village or hamlet to the Viet Cong." That is usually the case: people who lack actual experience and are short on courage and boldness think one way and act another. As they act they are scared to death, even in their thoughts.

The overall strategic design of the B2 Command at the beginning of the 1973-74 dry season may be summarized as follows: keeping the pressure on Saigon, keeping the enemy pinned down, and forcing them to passively defend their capital--their nerve center--so that we could take the initiative in effectively punishing them for violating the agreements, expand our rear area and the highly populated areas, and create an unimpeded supply corridor so that we could stockpile material-technical means. We would improve our position and strength and change the balance of forces in a manner favorable to us in all regards. We deployed the 9th and 7th Divisions and the sapper and commando forces (I will say more about them later) around and close to Saigon, and even inside the capital, along with the local forces, guerrillas and popular mass forces, to struggle against and punish the enemy in order to lay siege to Saigon and prevent the enemy from acting freely. We deployed the 5th Division and sappers in Kien Tuong to draw the enemy in that direction and prevent them from concentrating their attacks in our highly populated Hau Giang area. We opened the Bu Bong-Tuy Duc corridor to connect the 559 route with the corridor in western Tay Ninh, the eastern Nam Bo route, the Mekong Delta route, and the other routes, in order to transport supplies to and build up reserves on the various battlefields for that important strategic period.

We expanded our rear area so that our bases and liberated areas could be integrated, support one another and form a solid bloc, while in forward areas we actively developed the guerrilla forces, local troops and organized masses.

Having gained experience with regard to our method of attacking Saigon, and the enemy's defensive methods, during Tet 1968, we studied and drafted a contingency plan for a general offensive and uprising, if it should occur. For as stated above, the Americans and puppets had obstinately sabotaged the Paris Agreement, refused to observe the ceasefire, and launched increasingly larger military operations against us, so of course the war continued and developed and could end only with the victory of one of the sides. In diplomatic negotiations, on the basis of each other's strength the two sides should make concessions to and understand each other. But in war, to hesitate and be unprepared is to die. The enemy, furthermore, planned to completely annihilate us in 1976 and 1977. We had to prepare in advance for a general offensive and uprising so that we could win total victory. In 1968, on the basis of the situation, the terrain, and the key objectives within the enemy's capital, we delineated five offensive directions and deployed our forces in those directions. We used the method of coordinating military attacks with mass uprisings and outside attacks with inside attacks, with the inside forces being the revolutionary masses, the commandos, and the sappers, followed by the shock troops and local forces, and the outside forces being the main-force units. During Tet of 1968--a real, large-scale exercise--we won a great victory. It was not a complete victory only because the situation and balance of forces did not permit it. Now, the enemy's objectives had not changed very much. The basic changes were in the situation and in the balance of forces between the two sides. The forecasting of the situation and the planning strategic contingencies must be done early, for only then can we carry out some specific tasks of the strategic contingency plan. Such preparations require time and we cannot wait until things become too clear, which causes haste and prevents preparations from being made in advance, perhaps to the point that the opportunity is lost. In 1972, because we lacked foresight and did not prepare in advance, when we defeated them in Quang Tri the enemy left Hue practically wide open but we did not take full advantage of that favorable opportunity. Of course, in addition to lacking foresight and advance preparation we also lacked flexibility and failed to boldly exploit that opportunity. Strategic commanders must be able to think broadly and deeply, look far ahead, foresee how the situation will develop, and make preparations in advance. By his efforts he must create conditions for the lower echelons to win certain victory. By his dynamism he must propel and guide the situation in the direction of winning victory for us. By his daring, he must act promptly when an opportunity arises.

Beginning in September 1973 the Regional Staff, along with the B2 strategic intelligence operatives who had been planted in the headquarters organs of the puppets and Americans, reviewed the enemy objectives we had to take, monitored the situation on a daily basis, and kept abreast of the enemy's plans and orders. It must be emphasized that during the war the B2 theater--which encompassed the jungle-and-mountains, lowland and urban areas, including Saigon, the enemy's capital--was an all-encompassing battlefield and one with the largest enemy forces and many important strategic and campaign objectives. All developments there affected the overall situation, so the upper echelon authorized the Regional (B2) Command to organize and guide its most important secret strategic intelligence element, which also aided the upper echelon.

That intelligence unit helped us learn the details of many U.S.-puppet plans and obtained from the enemy a number of valuable documents, so we were able to promptly assess the situation and take effective countermeasures. Our intelligence agents, except for a small number who became corrupted--it was inevitable that some would be--had a loyal revolutionary nature. Many of them heroically sacrificed their lives, many achieved merit, and many of them become Heroes of the Armed Forces. In accordance with the force organization and deployment that had been approved by the Regional Command, I assigned comrade Ba Tran the mission of withdrawing the 367th Regiment--one of our sapper-commando groups that had been responsible for the Phnom Penh (Kampuchea) battlefield to help our friends but for which there was now little need--in order to reinforce Saigon. We had completed the organization and deployment of our commando and sapper regiments inside the capital and in the outskirts. At the B2 level we organized a Sapper Command--called Group 27--headed by comrade Dang Ngoc, who called himself "Phong." Si was a robust, sincere cadre who was ready to struggle in defense of justice and was not afraid of personal danger, which was a precious virtue, especially at a time when there were unwholesome phenomena in society. Si himself was a sapper cadre who had matured in combat. He was calm, resolute, said little but did much and finished what he began. On 30 November 1973, when I inspected the 27th Group, it had more than 6,000 cadres and men who were trained and experienced in combat. In addition to the headquarters organ the group consisted of forces which engaged directly in combat and were deployed in the various areas in the outskirts. North of Saigon there were the 115th and 119th sapper regiments; east of Saigon there were the 116th Regiment at Long Thanh and the 10th Regiment at Rung Sat; west of Saigon there was the 117th Regiment and the 113th Regiment, which was responsible for Bien Hoa. We were forming an additional regiment south of Saigon. Group 27 also directly controlled a sapper regiment that had achieved many feats of arms: the 429th Regiment. With regard to commandos, within the city there was organized Group 316, commanded by comrade Nguyen Thanh Tung (i.e. Muoi Co). It was organized into many "Z," each of which was responsible for an important objective. The sappers and commandos were deployed by area or objective. They had the missions of continually consolidating their organization, training in combat skills, studying and grasping the objectives they had been assigned to take, perfecting their operational plans, and training the cadres and men on the terrain and around the objectives for which they were responsible. They also had to immerse themselves in the masses, understand the people in the area they were operating, and create a political base to serve as a source of support from them. On 15 December 1973 comrade Dao, the political officer of the Sapper Command of the High Command, who had come south to inspect the sapper situation in the B2 theater, said, "The B2 sappers have developed and matured, have participated in combat and campaigns with good results, and at present have been assigned missions and organized and deployed in accordance with a new strategic status. That is due in part to the guidance of the Regional Command, which drafted a strategic plan early and has specific guidelines and modes. Furthermore, the sappers have a tradition and have much combat experience." He also contributed many valuable opinions regarding the organization and training of B2 sappers.

During the 1973-1974 dry season there was another problem that was no less vexing for us: the defense of the Loc Ninh liberated area, the regional base.

For a long time the enemy had continually threatened and attacked that area by air, and was determined to prevent us from stabilizing our base area, despite having to pay the price of losing many airplanes to our anti-aircraft forces. The puppet III Corps had a plan to use strong forces to take Loc Ninh and were only awaiting the opportunity and order of its supreme command and U.S. master. Aware of that, we had to prepare a plan to stop and defeat them in order to hold on to our base area. The questions were what forces we should use, how many troops we should use, what our fighting method should be--defensive, counteroffensive or offensive--and whether we should fight on a small scale or a large scale? When could the enemy attack? Should we deploy forces in advance to await the opportunity to strike a lightning blow against them? If so, how long should we wait? Would we tie down our limited forces in a passive status? We had to think carefully about a whole series of such problems in order to make correct decisions at a time when the battlefield was in a state of flux.

The Military Commission of the party Central Committee sent us a message which emphasized that Loc Ninh was not only important militarily but had a great political significance in the present situation. Therefore, the enemy was continually plotting to take it. We had to hold it at all costs, immediately send a main-force division there, and draft a plan to counterattack and annihilate the land-grabbing enemy troops.

Carrying out the order of the Military Commission, we immediately convened a conference of staff, political and rear services cadres to study a plan to defend Loc Ninh. The discussion was quite animated. Everyone realized the importance of defending that base, as the Military Commission had just pointed out. It was also a matter of the honor and prestige of our Liberation Army.

We assessed the general situation in the B2 theater and in the region, reviewed the enemy's forces, and estimated their method of attack. Which forces could the enemy use? What would be the scale of the attack, what would be the points of origin? What were their other capabilities? We knew that in order to attack Loc Ninh the enemy would mainly draw their forces from III Corps, with the puppet 5th Division serving as the backbone, along with part of the 25th and 18th Divisions, a number of ranger units, and the 81st Airborne Brigade, part of their general reserves. It was certain that they would use Lai Khe, the base of the puppet 5th Division, as the starting point, and that the main line of attack would be along Route 13 through Binh Long, a city that had been heavily damaged. But the 5th, 25th, and 18th Divisions also had to concern themselves with defending Saigon and with mending its defense lines, which were then in tatters. Especially, the puppet 5th Division was responsible for defending Saigon to the north, a very important direction, and faced large enemy forces and our liberated area, which restricted its freedom of movement. They were also well aware that taking Loc Ninh would be no easy matter, and that one or two divisions alone would be insufficient. The experience of the clashes over a period of many years on the eastern Nam Bo battlefield, even when the U.S. troops were still there--the "Big Red One" 1st Infantry Division, the "Tropical Lightning" Division, the 1st Cavalry Division, their most modern division, etc.--which the puppet troops had often accompanied, could not escape smelling defeat. Could the enemy send additional forces from the 1st, 2d, and 4th Military Regions? That would be very difficult, and not many forces were available, for if they were to carry out the "don't lose a single hamlet or village" strategy and grab land in order to become the masters of all of South Vietnam, as they aspired to do, where would they get the troops to concentrate in one spot?

Thus in order to attack Loc Ninh they would have to have a meticulous plan, make very careful calculations, use many forces and have skilled command--something even they were suspicious about. What then should we do? We reached the decision that we would, by means of a plan to gain the initiative, force the enemy to concern themselves with defending Saigon, tie their hands and feet, and prevent them from sending forces from Saigon to attack Loc Ninh. Thus we would not bring in a division to defend Loc Ninh but would, on the contrary, move up close to Saigon and prepare to strike at their heart if they adventurously set out to attack us. At Loc Ninh we organized a front made up of local guerrillas and headquarters guerrillas, combined with the regional anti-aircraft and mechanized forces there and a recently consolidated main-force regiment, the 201st Regiment, serving as the backbone. Those forces would appear everywhere, wear down and stop the enemy wherever they attacked, even on the fringes of the base. Meanwhile, our main-force units would, if necessary, leisurely concentrate at a predetermined assembly point and strike lightning blows to annihilate enemy units which we selected. That was the valuable experience of our counteroffensive campaign against the U.S. Junction City operation in northern Tay Ninh in 1967. Westmoreland was struck a painful blow in that operation, and after the dazzling blow of Tet 1968 he had to endure the disintegration of his military career, even though at one time he had been called "the most skilled U.S. general." Thus we carried out the order of the Military Commission creatively and in a manner completely in accord with the situation in the B2 theater at that time. We pressured the enemy, forced them to defend Saigon, struck them a mortal blow, and ended for all their plots to consolidate and complete the Saigon defense lines and to concentrate forces to attack and take Loc Ninh.

That was in May 1974, when the puppet III Corps was eager to take An Nhon Tay in order to link up with Ben Cat along Route 7 and across from Thai My-Go Noi (Trang Bang)-Provincial Route-15 An Nhon Tay to Rach Bap-Ben Cat. Their plan was to make the Rach Bap post a fortified bridgehead on the eastern bank of the Saigon River. A post that would be placed on Provincial Route 15 at An Nhon Tay would serve as a bridgehead on the western bank of the Saigon River and connect with Route 7, Go Noi, and Trang Bang. Thus they would create an intermediate defense line which, although it contracted a bit in comparison to the old one, would form a continuous, solid defense line north of Saigon. Once that plan was fulfilled, the forces of III Corps would be relatively free to concentrate in order to attack Loc Ninh or some other place. In order to carry out that plan, in March and April they assigned a number of additional ranger battalions and armored squadrons to the 25th Division, which attacked from Dong Du to Trung Lap along Route 2 past Cu Chi and Trang Bang, and Go Noi on Route 7, setting up outposts in order to encroach on our liberated area and clearing away vegetation. They used forces stationed at Jinet and Rach Bap to attack north in the direction of Bung Cong in a coordinated, mutually supporting operation. Having grasped the enemy's plan, we resolutely retaliated against the land-grabbing and smashed the enemy's plot to complete their defense line along Route 7, east and west of the Saigon River.

West of the river, the independent 16th Regiment, under the direct control of the Regional Command, along with the "Determined To Win" Battalion of the Saigon Military Zone, and the local forces and guerrillas of Cu Chi, fiercely retaliated against the puppet 25th Division and successfully defended the An Nhon Tay liberated area east of the river. In mid-May our 9th Division, which was stationed at Long Nguyen in Ben Cat District, deservingly punished the enemy at Jinet, wiped out that post, and isolated the Rach Bap post, the garrison of which was forced to flee in panic. We liberated a segment of Route 7 east of the river from Rach Bap to Kien Dien and directly threatened Ben Cat. Meanwhile the 7th Division, coordinating with the 9th Division, attacked and heavily damaged the Phuoc Hoa base on Route 16 near Tan Uyen, wiped out some enemy manpower and armored vehicles, and forced the abandonment of a number of illegal land-grabbing outposts. Thus the enemy was unable to carry out its plan and was unable to take An Nhon Tay to extend its area of control west of the Saigon River. On the eastern side of the river we took a 10-kilometers-long area, pushed the enemy farther from the river, and connected our Long Nguyen base north of Route 7 with our An Thanh base, i.e. the three villages south of Route 7 in Ben Cat District, the famous "Iron Triangle." The northern doorway to Saigon was not closed, but was opened wider, and the enemy's defense line was not completed but was further breached. The enemy responded vehemently to that development. They concentrated there most of the III Corps forces, the entire 3d Armored Brigade, and strong air and artillery support, and launched one counterattack after another over the course of several months but each time was defeated. The enemy was able to concentrate such forces in part because of the insufficiency of the activities of our 7th Division in the area of Phuoc Hoa in Tan Uyen District. It was unable to draw in and disperse the enemy in order to reduce the burden on the 9th Division. But our liberated area there was kept intact. Thus in May and June just one of our divisions--the 9th--effectively coped with practically all of the forces of the enemy's III Corps in an extremely fierce, heroic and resourceful manner, stood its ground, maintained the liberated area, inflicted heavy losses on the enemy and created a great strategic advantage for us.

By the spring of 1975, only 9 months later that area had been further expanded to the rear and became the starting point of one of our important offensive columns in the Ho Chi Minh Campaign. Our 9th Division had been worn down because it had to fight continuously for nearly 2 months with an enemy force that was more than three times larger, but the campaign and strategic value of those battles, as well as the political significance of their effect on the morale of the puppet troops and the psychology of the people in Saigon, were very great. Frank Snepp, a CIA specialist stationed in Vietnam, where he was responsible for strategic research and analysis and for drafting "field evaluations" for the CIA to serve the drafting of policies by the U.S. Embassy in Saigon and in Washington, wrote of those battles during the summer-fall fighting as follows: "Although the North Vietnamese troops only launched probing attacks to the north and northeast of Saigon and had themselves recently been battered, the South Vietnamese 5th and 18th divisions suffered heavy losses, especially in the "Iron Triangle," and were now exhausted and no longer capable of fighting."*

At that time there was some criticism of those battles, that it was unnecessary to suffer such losses and that it was a mistake to select that area for the battles. That was because such people did not fully understand the significance of destroying the enemy's ability to defend the Saigon enclave during the final strategic phase, and the significance of forcing the enemy to assume a passive defensive position and tying their hands so that we would be free to act on the critical battlefield during that decisive period. The accomplishment of those objectives required a process of resolute struggle, resourcefulness, and bravery, especially at a time when there was not much difference in the balance of forces between the two sides (although if we had not been strong we would not have been able to accomplish that). That our strength was able to overwhelm the enemy was as clear as day, so what's the use of arguing." That was also an important test for better understanding of the enemy on that strategic battlefield, of their strength and capability, and how they reacted.

Evaluations of different battles only express the evaluation of a strategic period and the role of each part of the battle. But the battlefield commander must have specific and actual understanding of our position and strength and those of the enemy. He must seek every way to place the enemy in an unfavorable position and place ourselves in an advantageous position. He must promptly and correctly evaluate each strategic period and know what must be done to promptly prepare for the successful war-deciding battle on his battlefield, especially when that battlefield will play the role of ending the war. With regard to strategy, unlike tactics, he waits until the final hours before breaking through.

In June 1974, the Regional Command reviewed all aspects of the situation in B2 after a dry season of challenges, challenges to the actual strength of both sides on the battlefield and to the will of both sides and the implementation of plans they drafted in the 1973 rainy season, with both sides trying to win victory. The beginning-of-season rain poured down in torrents, foreshadowing a season of heavy rainfall, like every other year in B2. The enervating midday heat of summer had given way to a comfortable coolness. Here and there the green jungle was sprinkled with the gold of ripe "gui" fruits. The soldiers of eastern Nam Bo were familiar with the bittersweet taste of the "gui" fruit. Since there were deficiencies in all regards, and meat and fish were scarce, "gui" fruits were valuable foods to our main-force troops. How delicious were the pots of soup consisting of wild green and ripe "gui" fruit. It was a sweet-sour soup which cooled one's insides. During operations in the mid-day heat of summer, when they were carrying heavy loads, if the troops drank a small glass of "gui" juice during their 10-minute break they would have enough energy to reach their destination. During the meeting held to review the situation, everyone was able to drink pleasing "gui" juice, but what was the most pleasing were the brilliant results of our dry-season activities in all parts of the theater, at a time when the enemy had entered the threshold of a period of essential defeat. We had completely bankrupted their insane

---
*From the book "Decent Interval," by Frank Snepp. Published by Random House, New York and Toronto, November 1977.

plan to retake all areas they held prior to 29 March 1972, an excessively greedy plan which regarded the enemy lightly and was the clearest evidence that they were trampling the Paris Agreement. They were defeated in their plan to pacify the highly populated areas and the areas under their control were not only unstabilized but were reduced. They were unable to steal the planned amount of rice from the people and to blockade the enemy economically. Except for the Dong Thap Muoi base of Military Region 8, which they took and in which they set up nine large and small outposts, they failed to take or destabilize 60 "Viet Cong" guerrilla enclaves in eastern Nam Bo and around Saigon. They remained intact although the enemy caused trouble at times. Not only was the enemy unable to mend their lines defending the capital, but those lines were further penetrated, both to the north (Route 7 at Rach Bap in Ben Cat District) and to the east (Route 2 at Ba Ria), which caused the enemy's defensive position to become even more vulnerable and unbalanced. They could never gain the initiative on that battlefield, even though Thieu had told his military region commanders that that battlefield--Military Regions III and IV--was "of life or death importance to all of South Vietnam." Furthermore, they had become bogged down in a defensive position and their forces were spread out all over. They wanted to take and pacify the highly populated coastal areas in Binh Thuan and Ninh Thuan, but had been drawn to and suffered losses in the mountains and jungles of Quang Duc. They wanted to expand their control and plundering of rice in the rich Hau Giang area but they were drawn to Kien Tuong, along the Kampuchean border, by the enemy and tied down there. Afraid of exposing its western flank, III Corps had to send six task forces to attack the Queo Ba and Duc Hue areas, so it had to accept the loss of Route 2 at Ba Ria, thus shattering the middle defense line of Saigon at that point, while we connected our two base areas north and south of Route 2. They were not only unable to concentrate forces to take the enemy's famous Loc Ninh base but had their hands full trying to defend their nerve center! From that point the enemy corps was capable of concentrating forces in a certain area only if the other areas were not being attacked. Their strategic reserves were too small, at that time consisting solely of the 81st Airborne Ranger Brigade. The airborne and marine divisions were tied down in Tri Thien [Quang Tri-Thua Thien]. There seemed to be nothing the General Staff or, more accurately Nguyen Van Thieu, could do to affect the situation in a certain military zone than watch as one disastrous defeat followed another. That was the result of a stupid strategy which did not correctly evaluate the strengths and weaknesses of the two sides but greedily wanted to hold each village, hamlet, and outpost and not give an inch to the "Viet Cong." Their forces were spread thinly all over the place, to the extent that they no longer had any mobile reserve forces.

That situation of the enemy, which lasted until the end of the war, caused the enemy forces, which were three or four times larger than ours, to be annihilated piece by piece, until they were totally annihilated.

After May, the enemy also realized that it lacked strategic reserves, so it decided to withdraw the Airborne Division from I Corps to serve as general reserves, but in carrying out that decision, it could only bring the division to Saigon brigade by brigade, slowly and over a long period of time. Even during that dry season there were events that allowed the enemy to evaluate its capability and realize how mistaken its strategic line. Throughout the dry season, especially during the latter months, most of the IV Corps forces in the Mekong Delta were drawn to My Tho and the Kampuchean border in Kien Tuong. In Hau Giang, the 21st Division had to disperse into battalions but still could not bolster the morale of the regional and self-defense forces. Many outposts were abandoned and many villages and hamlets were lost. The IV Corps commander had to take the initiative of abandoning a number of small, squad and platoon-sized outposts in order to reinforce more important outposts of company size or larger to obtain additional troops and make up for attrition. Only when they had no other choice and faced the peril of annihilation were they willing to abandon some outposts, villages and hamlets. They began that task during the dry season of 1974 and eventually had to abandon the Central Highlands during the 1975 dry season.

The tendency of defeat for the U.S.-puppets and victory for us in the war, which began with the 1973-1974 dry season and ended with the total defeat of the enemy, had its origins in an erroneous strategy that was pursued from the beginning by the Americans and puppets: the strategy of defending all parts of the country, of spreading troops thinly to prevent the "Viet Cong" from taking a single inch of the land, in accordance with Thieu's "four no's" policy.

How about the army that propped up the traitor regime? Although the Americans endeavored to strengthen and equip it so that it could replace the U.S.-troops, the fighting quality and numbers of the puppet army continued to decline. After the Paris Agreement they feverishly conscripted troops and rapidly increased the number of regular and regional troops. Beginning in June and July, their troop strength steadily declined. They admitted that between January and May 1974 the number of troops lost in combat and through desertion was more than 100,000, an average of more than 20,000 a month. During that time, the number of youths they conscripted to supplement their armed forces amounted to only a little more than 10,000 a month. Their IV Corps suffered the highest losses; each battalion had only about 200 troops--some units had only 150 to 180 men--and there was no way to build up those units. The ratio of equipment losses rose to a high level. Of more than 1,800 aircraft of the various kinds, they could use only about 1,000. Of their more than 100 F5 jet aircraft they could use less than half. They were forced to take such stern measures as making a census of their troops and opposing the evils of "ghost soldiers" and "rear echelon warriors." Even the table of organization of the General Staff declined by 20 percent. Unnecessary units and miscellaneous support units were eliminated. Troops were taken from self-defense units and put into regional force units, and were taken from regional force units and put into regular units. Conscripts were brazenly rounded up and monks were taken from pagodas and forced to do military service. Even so, their situation did not improve in the least, but continued to decline.

For our part, by the end of the dry season we had retaken all the areas we had held prior to 28 January 1973, including the area north and south of Route 4 in My Tho, in which the enemy feverishly grabbed land after the agreements.

We not only expanded the liberated area to more than 20 villages with a population of more than 300,000 people, principally in the Mekong Delta. That was a result of our punishing blows; when we wiped out one illegal land-grabbing outpost, the enemy troops abandoned four or five others in panic. (When we annihilated an enemy battalion on a land-grabbing operation in violation of the Paris Agreement, the enemy abandoned three or four nearby hamlets.) Clearly, the puppet troops were aggressive when we drew back, but when we resolutely attacked they became dispirited and ran for their lives. In all three areas our organized mass forces, guerrilla forces, and local troops were developed. The contested area was extended into the area under enemy control in all military regions in the B2 theater. The main-force troops of the military regions and of the Regional Command were augmented, trained and rationally deployed to create a potent offensive status, especially in eastern Nam Bo and around Saigon. While we held on to the base areas and the guerrilla enclaves in eastern Nam Bo and around Saigon, our rear-area base areas were expanded and consolidated to the greatest extent ever. It was an integrated liberated area extending from Quang Duc Province to Phuoc Long, Binh Long, and Tay Ninh along the Kampuchean border. Our Loc Ninh base was connected with the large liberated area of Long Nguyen in Ben Cat District because we wiped out the Nha Bich outpost on the Be River and the puppet's Tong Le Chan outpost--which was secretly abandoned during the night--on the Saigon River. Those two puppet ranger bases were isolated in our liberated area. The enemy tried to hold them to serve as staging areas from which to send spies deep into our area to gather intelligence, and to send rangers to attack our transportation corridor, supply depots, and organs, if we were careless. They would also be tactical bridgeheads for large-scale operations to take our bases in the future.

After the agreement, one of the enemy's difficulties was supplying those two positions and rotating its garrisons, for it was surrounded entirely by our liberated area at the conference table of the Four-Party Joint Military Commission, and later of the Four-Party Joint Military Commission. On the basis of Article 3(b) of the Protocol on the ceasefire in South Vietnam we continually demanded that the Americans and puppets discuss the determination of military transport corridors, so that one side could pass through an area controlled by the other side when necessary. But the Americans and puppets obstinately ignored us. Once, out of humanitarianism, although no such agreement had been reached, we allowed puppet helicopters to evacuate wounded from the Tong Le Chan base. But we resolutely refused to allow enemy military vehicles, military boats, or military transport planes with the mission of supplying food and ammunition or bringing replacements to pass through our area before an agreement had been reached as called for by the Paris Agreement. In April 1975 the enemy troops at Nha Bich, foolhardily launching an operation to open the road to Chon Thanh to obtain supplies, passed through our area. Our 7th Division punished and wiped out the troops carrying out the operation, as well as those in the outpost. The enemy knew that they had made a mistake and were completely silent and bit their lips. Having learned from that experience, the enemy troops at Tong Le Chan, taking advantage of an overcast night, secretly abandoned the post and fled through the jungle to safety in their area. Then the enemy played a slanderous propaganda trick by claiming that we had wiped out the Tong Le Chan camp, thus violating the Paris Agreement.

Their protest led nowhere because there was no evidence. But our rear area was expanded and filled out. The Loc Ninh base was connected with the "Iron Triangle," only about 30 kilometers from Saigon. Also during that dry season our transportation corridors from the rear to the front--from the Truong Son route to the eastern Nam Bo base, and from there to the military regions--were unimpeded. Even the most distant and difficult places, such as the central coastal areas of Military Region 6 and the U Minh Forest in Military Region 9, received shipments of fresh troops and materiel, some for supplementation, some for reserves.

Thus after the 1973-1974 dry season the situation in the B2 theater had become clear. Our position and strength had grown. The enemy was caught in a passive position which it could not reverse because it was becoming increasingly weak but its methods were outmoded and confused and its extremely obstinate and illusory political and strategic line was continuing to sabotage the Paris Agreement and seeking ways to completely annihilate its adversary. Such was the situation at the beginning of the 1974 rainy season.

We were not the only ones who analyzed the transformation of the situation after the end of the 1974 dry season in that way. On the American side there were also people who realized, more or less, that that was the case. Weldon A. Brown wrote in the concluding part of his book "The Last Helicopter," as follows:

"David Shipler, a NEW YORK TIMES correspondent and an experienced observer in South Vietnam during the last months before the collapse of South Vietnam, declared that the illusion of American strength had blinded Thieu. Shipler observed that in the summer of 1974 Hanoi had begun to step up its pressure all over South Vietnam. Shipler wrote that during that critical time an American diplomat predicted that if Washington continued to supply weapons to Saigon, but didn't pressure Saigon into a political accommodation, Washington and Saigon were certain to lose the war."

It is praiseworthy that an American diplomat was able to realize the reason for the inevitable defeat of the Americans and puppets, and when it began.

CHAPTER FOUR

The Greatest Rainy Season Ever

In general, with regard to weather the B2 theater was divided into two seasons, a rainy season and a dry season, both of which lasted 6 months. In the mountainous region, the rain arrives early and is heavy. In the lowlands the rain arrives late and is lighter. Especially during the rainy season the water flows down from the high-elevation watersheds in large volume and at a rapid rate, overflowing the basins of low-lying rivers and canals, especially the Mekong River basin, before slowly draining into the South China Sea. During the dry season it is possible to walk all over the Dong Thap Muoi area, a low-lying depression in the lowlands, but during the rainy season it becomes a vast sea, with the water reaching depths of 4 to 5 meters in some places. The principal means of travel is by boat. In eastern Nam Bo, although the jungle-and-mountains area is high-lying the rainwater also inundates the fields and roads and the red soil becomes muddy. Such weather and soil conditions exerted a considerable influence on the activities of the concentrated units and the technical combat arms. Therefore, in the rainy season our large units and those of the enemy were forced to scale down their activities and take advantage of that time to prepare for the coming dry season, when they would send powerful forces to attack each other. Over the course of many years of the war, that had become the rule. But the 1974 rainy season was an unusual rainy season in the B2 theater. We were determined to break that rule and act urgently to create a new opportunity and change the gloomy rainy season into the brilliant dawn of a new period. During the June conference, during which the Standing Committee of COSVN reviewed the 1974 dry season and discussed the coming direction, its secretary, Pham Hung, concluded that:

"In this year's dry season a new factor has appeared: We are winning victory and ascending while the enemy is weakening and descending. We must not stand still but must win even greater victories and force the enemy into even greater decline. During this year's rainy season we have many advantages and many capabilities for winning greater victories than during any previous rainy season, even greater than those of the past dry season. Regardless of the weather and the difficulties, we must step up our activities in all regards, create a new status and new strength, materially and with regard to morale, for the military regions, provinces, localities, and main-force units so that they can begin the 1974-1975 dry season with a strong, vigorous spirit. In 1975, especially during the 1975 dry season, we will be capable of winning victory, transforming the situation, and creating a new turning point, one of decisive importance."

There was nothing mysterious about COSVN's prescience. It was based on the actual situations of ourselves and the enemy on the battlefield and reflected the results of the activities of millions of comrades and compatriots in all hamlets, and of tens of thousands of guerrillas, local troops, and main-force troops, who contended with the enemy for each person and each inch of ground, every day and every hour, all over the theater. It was a result of profound understanding of ourselves and the enemy. It was a result of full understanding of the objectives of our revolution, firmly grasping revolutionary methods, and clearly understanding what we had to do and where we had to go, and at the same time profoundly understanding the plots, acts, desires and capabilities of the enemy.

At that time questions were asked that caused us to think a good deal: "Why, when facing that hopeless situation, did the puppet Thieu regime continue obstinately to adhere to its reactionary political line and deny the true situation in South Vietnam--that there were two zones, two regimes, two armies and three political forces--but refuse to admit there was a third force, was unwilling to form a coalition with the 'Viet Cong,' and was determined to sabotage the Paris Agreement and continue the war?" "Why did they continue to hang on to the stupid military stragegy of defending everything, land-grabbing all over the place, and trying to wipe out the liberation armed forces and liquidate the PRG of the RSVN?"

We had long known that the puppet Thieu regime was only a lackey, a tool of the U.S. imperialists. All of its thoughts were under the guidance, and all of their actions were under the command baton, of their masters. Thus the answer to those questions lay in the plots and policies of the United States.

In his book "A Soldier's Report" Westmoreland admitted that "He (P. Harkness) and the other U.S. officials went to Vietnam to implement a national policy that had been drafted in Washington." As for the statements of the South Vietnamese military and civilian leaders quoted in a report prepared for the U.S. Office of the Secretary of Defense titled "The Collapse of South Vietnam," "According to Tran Van Don, General Vien admitted the dependent role of South Vietnam. Another general agreed that the South Vietnamese leaders had been pressured into the implementation of American plans." Nothing could be clearer than words that slipped out of the Americans and puppets after their complete defeat.

Our people's war against the U.S. imperialists was very complicated with regard to both content and form from the very beginning and--through its developmental processes--to that time. It was not merely a national liberation war against aggression and was not merely a class war between revolution and counterrevolution in our country, but was more complicated, a war which manifested the struggle between the forces of progress and reaction all over the war, which converged on the key battlefield: Vietnam! Immediately after France was forced to sign the Geneva Agreements, the United States opposed them and was determined to intervene in Indochina and throw out the French, so that it could assume the role of international gendarme. The U.S. plot to occupy South Vietnam and make it the first line of defense against the socialist camp and prevent the influence of socialism from spreading, so that it could become the masters of the rest of the world (except for the socialist countries). The Americans thought that Vietnam, although a small country, occupied an important strategic position in the world. The United States, rich in dollars and modern weapons, was capable of and had to defeat the socialist bloc there without having to clash with the Soviet Union or China

(China was at that time still a country in the socialist bloc). The U.S. leaders thought the prospects of that strategy were high; they were self-confident, did not deeply study the Vietnamese nation and people, disregarded the experience of their French friends, and ignored the just voice of Americans who protested the war and of the progressive people of the world. As a result, the more bogged down they became the more they had to escalate the war, and the more they escalated the war, the greater were their losses in men and materiel. Like a greedy, addicted gambler they continued to lurch from one defeat to another. After they had escalated to the top-most rung they of course had to deescalate, but both escalation and deescalation were measures for carrying out the global strategy of the U.S. imperialists and carrying out their plot to achieve global hegemony and oppose the socialist bloc. When the strategy of "massive retaliation," based on a monopoly on nuclear weapons, was bankrupted and the three revolutionary currents were attacking victoriously all over the world, the United States had to shift over to a strategy of "flexible response" with its three types of war--special, limited and general--in order to take the initiative and win under any circumstances, and especially in order to oppose the national liberation wars. After that strategy was applied on the Vietnam battlefield in 1961, the special war was defeated at the end of 1964 and the beginning of 1965 and the special war was bankrupted in 1968, but the balance of forces in the world and the conditions at that time did not permit the United States to start a general war and use nuclear weapons, so the strategy of flexible response was rendered impotent. Perplexed and confused, Johnson hastily came up with the "de-Americanization" policy in hopes of pulling his feet out of the Vietnam quagmire. But the U.S. imperialist leaders and strategists were unwilling to accept the disgrace of defeat and still believed that the United States was destined to rule the world. They were very afraid that if they lost Vietnam they would lose a whole series of other countries according to the "domino theory." Therefore, after Nixon became president he adopted a strategy of "regional defensive alliances" which was in fact a policy to mobilize and win over the forces of the world to oppose the socialist bloc, so that the United States would not stand alone. In Vietnam they transformed that strategy into the Vietnamization--not the de-Americanization--of the war. People were partially correct in saying that Johnson wanted to get out of Vietnam by "de-Americanizing," while Nixon wanted to remain in Vietnam by "Vietnamizing the war." In fact, Nixon, unlike Johnson, had not been demoralized, so he tried hard to pursue the unchanging objectives of the U.S. imperialists. Before and after the Paris Agreement the United States implemented its strategy of Vietnamizing the war by seeking all ways to make the puppet army and regime strong militarily, economically and politically so that they could defeat the liberation armed forces and annihilate the PRG of the RSVN, keep South Vietnam as a nation dependent on them and permanently divide our country. Those objectives had never changed. The only change was using Vietnamese blood to replace American blood. The Americans were forced to sign the Paris Agreement although its contents were not advantageous for them and their puppets. But they signed it anyway, thinking that they could reverse the situation by dishonest and crooked schemes, by the economic strength of the United States and by its intricate, insidious diplomatic activities all over the world. They regarded the Paris Agreement as only a means, as a tactic, during a certain strategic phase. They signed the agreement so that they could implement the provisions beneficial to them while misrepresenting and rejecting those that were not beneficial. Their objective was still to serve their victory. The strength of weapons and dollars are the true "laws" of the U.S. imperialists in the world today. Their own words have very clearly revealed their insidious plot. Lt Gen Tran Van Don of the Saigon puppet regime, said in his book "The Unending War in Vietnam" (published by the Presidio Press, California and London, 1978), "He (i.e. Charles Whitehouse, the deputy U.S. ambassador who accompanied the Kissinger delegation to Saigon in mid-October 1972 to explain the Paris Agreement and persuade Thieu to sign them) said to me, "The agreement has some good points and should be signed. It is only a piece of paper and will change nothing, you will see."

At the beginning of January 1973 Tran Van Don and Bui Diem, heading a special delegation sent by Thieu to Washington to learn of the U.S. intentions, reported to Thieu that Alexis Johnson, a U.S. undersecretary of state, said privately to me (i.e. Diem): "We have been friends many years, and I am speaking to you as a friend. The fact is that the United States has not changed its objectives in Vietnam." And in a Top Secret message sent to Thieu at that time, Nixon stated that "The freedom and independence of the Republic of Vietnam are still supreme objectives of America's foreign policy."

Thus it is clear. The deep-lying plot of Nixon and Kissinger was to, by signing the Paris Agreement, send the U.S. troops home, secure the release of the U.S. POW's, calm down U.S. and world opinion, and shore up the U.S. military forces, which were no longer prepared to carry out the U.S. global strategy, while having a period of several years of breathing space in Vietnam in order to carry out the following insidious plots:

1. Providing additional equipment, weapons, and modern technical equipment in order to transform the puppet army into a strong force capable of annihilating the liberation armed forces. Increasing economic development aid and investment for the puppet Thieu regime in order to develop that regime, which the United States recognized as the only legal regime in South Vietnam, into a Southeast Asian regime that was strong militarily, politically and economically.

2. Providing reconstruction aid for North Vietnam, using material-technical bait to tempt North Vietnam, infiltrate and monopolize it, and by that means restricting the north's aid for the NLFSVN, using the north to restrict activities in the south, and plotting to achieve the peaceful transformation of the regime in the north.

3. Using the policy of U.S.-style detente on a worldwide basis to create pressure and limit the aid of the socialist bloc for both the north and the south, in hopes of strangling our ability to fight. In fact, after reaching agreement at Shanghai to retain Thieu and keep South Vietnam in the U.S. orbit, China limited its aid to Vietnam, especially with regard to large weapons and transportation facilities. In the "Nixon's Trip to China" chapter of his memoir "The White House Years," Kissinger recounted the working sessions of Zhou Enlai and Nixon: "Zhou's position on Vietnam was a masterpiece of tortuous circumlocution; he objected to Nixon's opinions more out of sorrow than anger. He expressed 'sympathy' for the people of North Vietnam but said

nothing about common interests. He referred to China's obligation to help Hanoi not in terms of the solidarity ideal, or in terms of legitimate national rights, but in terms of the historical debt owed Vietnam because of the Chinese Empire in the past.

"His principal argument regarding the necessity of an early end to the war was that it caused the United States to become bogged down and to waste much energy which should be expended on more important parts of the world. Zhou criticized our negotiating position in a very perfunctory manner. He demanded that we withdraw our troops from South Vietnam. He never supported Hanoi's political program--and of people who criticize us--regarding a coalition government and the overthrow of Thieu."

Then Kissinger concluded, "Our diplomatic activity was about to succeed in isolating Hanoi." The United States truly believed that its scheme to divide the countries of the socialist bloc, and its worldwide detente policy, were about to bear results.

4. Along with the above plots, it was necessary to flout their strength by retaining a strong U.S. military force in Southeast Asia to serve as a deterrent force, intimidate weak-willed people, and support the Thieu clique.

By means of schemes, the Thieu regime would gradually become stronger, the PRG of the RSVN would become increasingly stronger, Thieu would be capable of eliminating the opposition and gaining full control of South Vietnam, and South Vietnam would be transformed into dependency of the U.S. imperialists in that strategic location on the western shores of the Pacific.

In accordance with that scheme, the United States was continuing to implement its strategy of Vietnamizing the war in South Vietnam despite the Paris Agreement. The President and the other key officials in the U.S. administration at that time stressed that in order to persuade Thieu that the United States would always be by his side, it was necessary to provide him with all kinds of aid and be prepared to reintervene in South Vietnam if necessary. Even Kissinger had promised Thieu, in the course of his trip to Saigon in October 1972, that the United States would use military forces to attack and occupy North Vietnam by attacking north from the 17th Parallel. Thieu gleefully suggested that it would be necessary to land troops nearer the objective than attacking north from the 17th Parallel. Although Thieu and his clique were concerned about their fate as servants, were ordered around and treated with contempt by their U.S. masters, and had weak position and strength, they were still confident of the support of their masters and thought that if they got into trouble their masters would certainly not go back on their word but would protect and assist them. The puppet Brig Gen Le Trung Truc, who had been an aide as the chairman of the Interministerial Committee to Coordinate the Ceasefire, admitted that "The United States always bragged about its peerless strength. Thieu had absolute confidence in the military strength of the United States, and thought that since the United States was involved in Vietnam it would remain involved to the end."

Because it was so confident of that, the Thieu clique was blind to the real situation and continued the war in order to fulfill its subjective desires and the intentions of its masters. Such were the plots of the United States and the acts of Thieu. He was under no illusions that the disciple and master would strictly adhere to the agreement. The United States not only wanted to occupy South Vietnam but had the even more insane desire of invading and occupying the North, in order to divide and control the socialist bloc. That illusion had the very encouraging support of his new ally--China--and had been tested during the recent period and events. If the Chinese rulers during the 1960's had not given one signal after another, by many different means, so that the United States could understand that it was free to act in Vietnam provided that they did not clash with China--"If you don't bother us we won't bother you"--in 1965 the United States would not have dared to brazenly send troops to South Vietnam, and then wage a war of destruction against and blockade the North. If in 1972, at Shanghai, they had not promised to save Thieu and South Vietnam for the United States--as Luigi Sommarugia wrote in the Italian newspaper IL MESSIGORIO on 3 April 1979, "China accepted the U.S. recommendation that Thieu be retained in South Vietnam, with the result that Vietnam would, like Korea, be permanently divided. In return, Nixon promised that China could join the United Nations and take a seat on the Security Council, and that the United States would abandon its policy of supporting Taiwan"--the United States would not have boldly withdrawn its troops from Vietnam and changed its strategy, but still believed that it could remain permanently in South Vietnam.

In brief, that meant that whether the United States remained in Vietnam or left Vietnam it had the assurance, ironically, of its gigantic friend to the north, a country bordering ours.

It had been a year and a half since the Paris Agreement was signed. The actual developments in South Vietnam did not follow the meticulous arrangement the United States had made, or the plan that had been drafted by Nixon and Kissinger. The reason for that was something Nixon and Kissinger did not take into consideration and could not comprehend. That was the effect of their adversary's intelligence and courage in thought and action. If after 1973 we had believed that by one means or another the Paris Agreement would be implemented, just as we had believed that 2 years after the Geneva Agreements there would be a general election, or if we had incorrectly evaluated our strength and that of the enemy, and had been guilty of leftist or rightist mistakes in thought and action, the situation would have been different. Of course, faltering steps could not be avoided during the initial period. But a faltering period of the first 3 or 4 months of a new strategic phase of a long war was a short period. It was not sufficiently long for the enemy to take advantage and win victory. On the contrary, we were vigilant, our party's guidance was acute and timely, and our people and armed forces were closely united in combat and revolutionary struggle, so we were on the ascent and the enemy was on the decline and could recover. The enemy's wily, cruel schemes were not timely and could not be carried out. The puppet military forces could not become stronger, but were becoming dispirited and were falling apart. They wanted to augment their large civilian self-defense forces and build strong, mobile regional forces capable of occupying and defending all areas, but now those two forces were now declining numerically, many surrendered or deserted, and outposts and bases were abandoned. They wanted to concentrate their regular forces into completely mobile forces with modern, highly sophisticated equipment and weapons in order to reduce the number of troops and save money for economic development while still maintaining a strong military, but now they were forced to urgently increase their troop strength and the number of units, but still did not have sufficient forces to hold the localities and there were no mobile forces. They wanted to expand and stabilize their area in order to appeal for foreign economic construction investment, but that area shrank and was unstable, and no one dared invest in it. They had a serious budget deficit and U.S. aid had to be used for military expenditures. They wanted to create a strong ruling party, the "Democratic Party," but they forced everyone to join "Mr Thieu's Party," which was made up entirely of opportunists and political speculators who joined in hopes of attaining promotions and getting ahead, who stole and bribed to their heart's content, and bullied the people. How could there be a strong ruling party? Thus the puppet Thieu regime did not become stronger in all respects, as the United States hoped, but was becoming weaker in all regards--militarily, politically, economically, etc.--and was in ruins and going downhill.

After the U.S. imperialists were defeated, they had to retreat militarily and shift over to employing all sorts of devilish plots to set up a "prestigious puppet" to replace them and firmly control South Vietnam. But that puppet did not stand erect but had begun to collapse, so at that time what was needed was a shove sufficiently strong to push it into the abyss so that neither the pupil nor the master could save it. That was an opportunity.

The correct evaluation of that situation and a correct realization of the opportunity were extremely important with regard to strategic guidance on a key battlefield that was representative of all of South Vietnam.

Lenin said that "Revolution is a science, but at the same time it is an art. It demands sensitivity toward the situation and timely positive response to changes in the situation. Revolution is always creative." COSVN and the Regional Military Party Commission evaluated and were aware of that changed situation in order to guide all rainy season plans and activities, while also drafting a 1975 plan, especially for the 1974-1975 dry season, and reporting it to the Military Commission of the party Central Committee.

During the July 1974 conference of COSVN the secretary stressed that "The winning of a decisive victory in 1975-1976, especially our efforts during the 1974-1975 dry season, is within the purview of Resolution 21 of the party Central Committee and COSVN Resolution 12, which call for the winning of a decisive victory during the next few years. We must fulfill our rainy season mission and positively prepare to fulfill our 1975 mission. Great efforts are required on the part of the entire party. The basis of our decisions was the situation during the recent period, especially during the past 4 months of 1974. A directive will be issued to the military regions and provinces to review the implementation of Resolution 12, make all-out efforts during the rainy season, and make truly good preparations for the 1975 dry season, with a truly resolute spirit. We will make a full report to the Central Committee and recommend that it guide the combining of diplomatic struggle and coordination on all battlefields in South Vietnam."

The contests of the 1974 rainy season activities, according to the guidance of COSVN and the Regional Military Party Commission included:

--Continuing to defeat the enemy's pacification plan by launching counter-offensives and offensives, expanding the area under our control, and developing the political struggle movement for the masses to arise to become the masters in the various areas, especially in the Mekong Delta and the area around the capital. Holding a conference in September 1974 to recapitulate the task of opposing pacification throughout the B2 theater.

--Strengthening our forces militarily and politically in order to create the position and strength to enable them to fulfill their 1975 mission. We had to be strong in each village, each district, and each province so that we were capable of developing those areas on our own. In comparison, in 1960 there were nearly 5 million people in the liberated and contested areas but were brilliantly successful in the simultaneous uprising. In 1968, when we controlled nearly 4 million people, we won a victory in the Tet Mau Than general offensive and uprising. Thus the norm regarding the number of people we had to control by the end of that rainy season, and prior to the 1975 dry season, was equal to the 1968 level.

--Concentrating on rapidly accelerating the urban work. At that time, the contradiction between the ruling comprador bourgeois-bureaucratic-militaristic clique and the various strata of people was becoming fierce, especially in the cities. We were capable of creating a strong urban fist.

--Firmly grasping the armed forces and being concerned with development, training and combat. The time had come when all three types of troops had to be developed rapidly and strongly so that they could fulfill their key mission of being the decisive forces.

--Building up the liberated area and base areas and insuring the transportation corridors. Despite the handicaps of the rainy season and the efforts of the enemy to stop us, we had to, by all means, augment the supplies and rear services of the forces, areas, and military regions so that they could be prepared to win big victories during the dry season.

--With regard to the party's leadership, it was necessary to motivate the cadres, enlisted men, and masses ideologically. We had to enable the entire party, the entire army, and the entire population to clearly understand the insidious plots of the Americans and puppets, clearly understand our new victories and the new factors of the situation and enthusiastically endeavor to advance. In view of the insidious plots of the enemy, they had to realize that there was no other course than to use revolutionary violence to oppose counterrevolutionary violence, and that it was necessary to attack strongly in order to defend our right to live. Everyone had fully to bring into play their capability and responsibility in order to win a big victory. It was necessary to oppose rightist tendencies and vagueness regarding the enemy.

--The echelons and sectors had to rectify their table of organization and working methods so that they could be appropriate to the new situation, streamlined, appropriate to the actual situation and the grassroots situation, and have the highest effectiveness.

One of the most urgent tasks during the rainy season was preparing military forces for the dry season. Since all of the forces had to participate in fighting the enemy in all three areas and attain the norms assigned by the upper echelon for the rainy season, all three types of troops and the military organs had to be concerned with organizing and developing units, and with training in order to increase their combat effectiveness and complete our deployment on all parts of the battlefield. That Regional Command force development plan was approved by the Military Commission on 6 June and immediately afterward disseminated to the military regions and the various echelons, down to the base level. The intention of the plan was to mobilize the localities, to the greatest extent possible, to achieve the unlimited expansion of the village and hamlet guerrillas and local district troops, so that the districts could have battalions, and the villages companies, with which to defend themselves and expand the liberated areas without requiring the aid of the provincial forces. That was based on the actual experience of My Xuyen District in Soc Trang Province and of a number of places in Kien Phong Province. During the recent dry season we effectively retaliated against enemy land-grabbing and by that means expanded the liberated area, so that it was made up of many hamlets and villages which formed a contiguous area. In such places, the popular masses arose and participated enthusiastically, along with the guerrillas and local troops, in attacking the enemy and wiping out, or forcing the abandonment or surrender of, many outposts set up by the popular PF and RF troops in the villages.

The provinces had to expand efforts to encourage youths to enlist and, along with recruits assigned by the upper echelon, supplement existing units or be organized into strong provincial battalions. Depending on its circumstances, each battalion should have between one and four battalions. The provinces capable of doing so, and required to do so by their missions, could organize a light regiment and a few independent battalions. During that period, except for Military Region 6 and Saigon the other military regions--7, 8 and 9--were to have a number of independent regiments directly under their command. In order to enable the military region commands to remain fully abreast of all military and political forces, and command the offensives and uprisings throughout the military region, and in order to streamline organization and have a strong main-force fist, in August 1974 the Regional Command decided to organize a light division for each of the military regions by consolidating the independent regiments, strengthening the combat arms, and organizing division command organs commanded by a deputy military region commander. Military Region 9 organized the 4th Division, made up of the 10th, 20th, and 30th regiments and commanded by comrade Nguyen Dinh Chuch. In Military Region 8 there was the 8th Division, commanded by comrade Sau Phu (Senior Colonel Huynh VAn Nhieu) and consisting of the 18th, 24th and 320th regiments. In Military Region 7 its two independent regiments--the 33d and 4th--were organized into the 6th Division commanded by comrade Dang Ngoc Si (code name Hai Phong). In Military Region 6, where our conditions were difficult in all regards, which was distant from the aid and command of the upper echelon, and which lacked manpower, materiel, and transportation facilities, in order to be appropriate to the mission and operational guidelines and mode there, we had only organized independent infantry battalion, sapper units, guerrillas, and armed work teams. In view of the new situation and the missions that would be assigned to the military regions, in May and June 1974 the Regional Command ordered the merging of the 186th, 840th and 15th infantry battalions, and the artillery, communications and other companies, to form the 812th Regiment, which was to undergo urgent training and make Binh Tuy and Binh Thuan provinces its main area of operations. Because it did not clearly understand the intention of the Regional Command, the military region was not yet clear about forming that regiment. The Regional Command explained to it the necessity of organizing the regiment and ordered that it be organized immediately to promptly fulfill its mission and avoid missing the opportunity. In 1975 that regiment, along with the local forces and other units, liberated most of Binh Tuy and Lam Dong provinces, all of Tuyen Duc Province, and part of Ninh Thuan Province, thus brilliantly fulfilling the mission of the military region.

In the Saigon Special Zone, in addition to the forces deployed by the Regional Command inside and outside the city, because of its special conditions we only organized separate battalions, such as "Determined To Win" battalions 1, 2, 3 and 4, along with the district local troops, guerrillas, armed security forces and armed youths. (The Gia Dinh Regiment was formed later.)

By that time the Regional Command directly controlled the 5th, 7th and 9th Divisions, the 201st, 205th, 16th and 271st independent regiments, the 27th Sapper Group, the 316th Municipal Commando Group and a very limited number of combat arms units. In the B2 theater there were five battalions of vehicle-pulled artillery of the various kinds, including two battalions of 105mm and 155mm artillery pieces captured from the enemy which were very short of ammunition, and three battalions of tanks and armored vehicles which were under-strength and included M41 tanks and M113 troop carriers captured from the enemy. The combat engineering and communications units were even weaker. There was only one river-crossing combat engineer battalion with insufficient equipment, a construction battalion, two battalions of combat engineers, three bridge-and-road battalions, two wireless radio battalions, and a wired communications battalion. For a long time we had complained to the comrades with the General Staff and in the Combat Arms Command of the High Command that our forces were too small at a time when we were responsible for a large, key theater such as B2, and of course had often demanded additional personnel, facilities, equipment, weapons and ammunition. What commander would not want to control ample combat forces and have reserves so that he can fulfill his mission as well as possible. Perhaps that was why some of the comrades at the General Staff complained that B2 had a localistic, partialistic attitude and demanded more than the B1, B3 and B4 theaters. We heard many such complaints, not directly, but from others who related those biased observations to the extent that when we discussed military forces we often said, "Let us heed what the Greek philosopher Pythagoras said: "If you suffer an injustice, console yourself; the person truly worthy of pity is the one who caused the injustice." We added that a skilled general did not always have to have plentiful forces in order to win.

Even so, when we felt that it was necessary to do so we still made recommendations to the upper echelon, and continued to demand additional forces. We decided to organize a corps for the B2 theater by combining the 9th and 7th divisions and a number of existing combat arms units, and recommended that the High Command give us an additional division and tank and artillery units, and that those units arrive at the battlefield at the beginning of the dry season so that a strong corps on that important battlefield. After receiving the approval of the High Command, at the military conference held in July 1974 the Regional Command officially decreed the formation of the corps, called the 4th Corps, of which comrade Hoang Cam would serve as commander and comrade Hoang The Thien as political officer. In addition, the 271st and 205th independent regiments were formed into the (understrength) 3d Division, commanded by comrade Do Quang Hung, to facilitate command. The 3d Division, as well as the 5th Division, the 16th and 201st Regiments, the 27th Sapper Group and the 316th Commando Group were directly under the Regional Command so that they could be used wherever necessary.

The formation of a corps at the B2 theater level and of divisions for the military regions was a positive preparatory step with regard to the theater's main-force units, in order to meet the demands of the situation and the operational policy adopted by COSVN and the Regional Military Party Committee for the coming period. It was warmly applauded by the people, the sectors and the echelons who helped carry it out. It inspired the soldiers and people of the B2 theater to enthusiastically advance to the winning of new victories. It also demonstrated the greatest period of large-scale force development ever in the B2 theater, with regard not only to main-force units but also provincial and district local troops and village and hamlet guerrillas. The armed forces were not the only ones to be developed rapidly during that period; the party forces at the base level and the mass political forces also grew much larger and stronger, even in areas in which we had been very weak. For example, Cho Moi District in Long Xuyen Province was a district in the weak area, and was a narrow strip of land between two large rivers, the Tien Giang and Hau Giang. Prior to 28 January 1973 there were only two party chapters in the district and very few of the masses were organized, although the people there were very good and had a long revolutionary tradition. By the end of the 1974 dry season, however, we had eight party chapters which encompassed 11 of the total of 13 villages. We were able to create hundreds of secret and special guerrillas and had 79 agents in 15 civilian self-defense groups and intergroups of the enemy. Our cadres could move about and mobilize the masses to struggle everywhere in the province. Another example was Cho Gao District in My Tho Province, which lay immediately east of National Route 4 and was bordered by the Tien Giang River, the Cho Gao Canal, and a branch of the Van Co River. The terrain presented many difficulties for our cadres operating there. There were 20 villages in the district. In 18 of them there were party chapters and mass infrastructures. In all, at that time our military and political forces numbered 4,336, while the enemy had 3,318 RF, PF and civilian self-defense troops. We gained superiority in a district which had been one of our weak districts. Furthermore, a number of village officials and families of puppet soldiers contributed tens of thousands of dong to the district's resistance war fund. According to combined data, by the end of 1974 there were 3.4 million people living in the liberated and contested areas in the B2 theater, in low-level and high-level revolutionary organizations, which was not far below the 1968 level. During the rainy season we could endeavor to increase that number even more. The reason for that was that COSVN continually monitored and guided the military regions and provinces, by direct contact with the localities and by means of directives 01 to 08, the principal contents of which were urgently creating position and force and changing the comparison of forces between ourselves and the enemy. The norms regarding the development of actual military and political strength in the localities, and activities to oppose the enemy and expand the liberated area, which were assigned by COSVN and the Regional Military Party Commission to the military regions and provinces for the recent dry season had been attained and surpassed. COSVN also was confident that the norms that had been set forth for the rainy season in the B2 theater would be surpassed to an even greater extent. All of the cadres who participated in the military conference in July expressed determination to overcome all norms assigned by the upper echelon. Those comrades brought up a very new situation: the popular masses all over were aware of the decline of the enemy and our victorious position, just as stated in the party resolution, which proved that the masses had caught up with the guidance of the party or, in other words, that the masses were marching in step. Whenever that is true, whether in wartime or in peacetime, the revolution will have the strength to do everything, to resolve many difficulties which were seemingly unresolvable.

During that July military conference we disseminated and explained the April 1974 resolution of the Military Commission of the party Central Committee which had been approved by the Political Bureau in order to, on the bases of the most recent developments in the situation, supplement Resolution 21 of the party Central Committee. The resolution evaluated the new U.S. plot as follows: "The basic plot of the U.S. imperialists is still to carry out the 'Nixon Doctrine,' impose neocolonialism in South Vietnam, and transform South Vietnam into a separate, pro-American country, but shift over from using U.S. military forces directly in the fighting to using the puppet army and regime, with the effective aid of the United States with regard to military advisers, economics, and finance."

"In order to implement that scheme, the United States has from the beginning consistently carried out a policy of both signing the agreement to restore peace and helping the Saigon puppet regime continue the war."

The resolution observed that "In places in which we have resolutely counterattacked and attacked the enemy have been confused and passive and have encountered difficulties. They have been pushed back in Military Region 9 and have been stopped in Military Region 8, and although they had succeeded in grabbing a little land in Military Region 5 they were stopped. We have wiped out a rather large part of the enemy's manpower, defended our liberated enclaves in the Mekong Delta and around Saigon, defended our vast liberated areas and base areas, and maintained our strategic threat to the enemy."

The resolution gave specific guidance to the battlefields: "Go all-out to take advantage of time to strengthen forces, strengthen material resources, and concentrate guidance on insuring that the lowland areas, especially the Mekong Delta, undergo a clear transformation in our favor.

"Military Region 5 must correctly evaluate the situation, clarify the thinking of cadres and the operational mode, cooperate closely with the main-force units, the local troops, and the militia and guerrilla forces, achieve close coordination between the Central Highlands and the lowlands, essentially restore the movement to the 1972 level and further expand it, and defend and gradually fill out the liberated areas and base areas in the Central Highlands and the western parts of the lowland provinces.

"In eastern Nam Bo we must defend the liberated enclaves around Saigon and consolidate them into strong staging areas which form an increasingly tighter noose threatening Saigon, and further consolidate and expand the corridors connecting the outskirts of Saigon with the vast liberated and base areas.

"Tri Thien must consolidate its position in the contiguous area, penetrate deeply down into the lowlands, create political and guerrilla bases, weaken the enemy's control, advance to coordinating the three spearheads (political, military and proselyting among enemy troops), advance the movement, reconstitute the three areas, destroy the enemy's multiple defense line position, and continually threaten the enemy in order to pin down the airborne and marine divisions and create advantages for the other battlefields in South Vietnam, while at the same time maintaining and strengthening the liberated area."

At the conference there were also presented a detailed evaluation and assessment by COSVN of the rainy season plan and a preview by COSVN and the Regional Military Party Commission of activities necessary to win a great victory during the 1974-1975 dry season. The cadres attending the conference, who had battlefield experience and had been in constant contact with the base levels and with danger during the different periods, agreed unanimously with COSVN's assessment of the situation. That unanimity became collective strength with which to implement the party's resolution and strength which was passed on to the party members and masses.

Immediately after the military conference, comrade Pham Hung, as secretary of COSVN, secretary of the Regional Military Party Commission, and political officer of the Regional Command, joined us in explaining the resolution in detail to groups of cadres from each military region. Especially, we discussed with the cadres from the Saigon Municipal Unit the development and deployment of the various kinds of military and political forces, both secret and open, as well as the operational forms, especially the form of armed activity in the outskirts and in the city. Comrade Pham Hung personally resolved questions in the consciousness of the city's cadres regarding the deployment of sapper regiments in the outskirts and military activities in those areas. Many cadres had the mistaken viewpoint that the party organization and mass organization in the outskirts were still weak and that sappers and local troops should not be deployed there because they might be exposed, because they feared that the enemy and launch sweeping operations had destabilized the situation, thus preventing them from building infrastructures. They were especially afraid that if the sappers or local troops fought the enemy there, all of their bases would be broken up. If armed forces were stationed there, would they not fight if the enemy arrived? Thus the question of "How should we fight to avoid breaking up the bases?" greatly confused them. A number of places withdrew their armed forces or forbade them to fight. He emphasized that "Our party's line is to attack the enemy in all three strategic areas-- the jungles-and-mountains, the lowlands, and the cities--and to attack them with both armed forces and political forces. If that is to be accomplished it is necessary to organize and deploy military forces combined with mass forces. The only differences among the areas is how to organize forces and what types of forces to deploy. We must attack the enemy by means of all three offensive spearheads, so it is necessary to study how the attacks by the three spearheads should be carried out and where in order to win small and large victories. We absolutely must not fight a protracted guerrilla war and not refrain from combat. In war, we cannot hope for stability in order to organize forces, and forces organized under such conditions of artificial stability cannot be of high quality. In the present strategic phase we must further tighten the noose on Saigon, and must be prepared to achieve coordination among the various areas in order to win a victory during the coming dry season. We must not be tardy. When cadres have correct viewpoints and struggle bravely, and when there is close coordination between the local party committee echelons and the military command echelons, there will be correct modes. We must be bold, and dare to think and do."

A very important, unforgettable example of daring to think and do was the transporting and stockpiling of food and ammunition for the B2 theater during the rainy season by warriors who truly were "the first to go and the last to return," in the tradition of the Nam Bo resistance war, warriors who endured difficulties and hardships but were taciturn and were so happy over the victories of their comrades that they all but forgot their own victory. They were the rear services warriors? Throughout the rainy season, with its heavy rain and mud, tens of thousands of rear services troops, along with hundreds of thousands of people worked day and night on all routes from the rear to the front, through muddy, flooded fields, and the rivers and water of Dong Thap Muoi, the U Minh Forest, and all over the Mekong Delta, to the mountains and jungles of Military Regions 7 and 6, to the outskirts of Saigon, and into the capital. Perhaps the rear services branch of B2 reflected most clearly the skilled combination of all elements in our anti-U.S. war: combining the army's rear services with the national rear area, combining on-the-spot purchasing and production, combining specialized rear services with the people's rear services, combining military forces and mass forces enlisted men and civilian laborers, regular troops and guerrillas, large-scale and small-scale, open and secret, secretly carrying supplies across enemy areas at night, secretly using trucks and boats to transport supplies on roads and rivers, transporting supplies into the cities, combining the modern with the primitive (ox carts, cargo bicycles, motorboats, rowboats, backpacks, etc.), and combining the supply work with combat to annihilate the enemy and defend our supply forces. Even in the command structure of the Regional Rear Services Department combination was necessary to insure a high degree of effectiveness of its work. Comrade Tu Khanh (Maj Gen Dao Son Tay), the department's political officer, who had been a worker in the Ba Son factory in Saigon, was born in Gia Dinh Province, participated in the revolutionary movement at an early age and joined the Indochinese Communist Party. In the anti-French war he was a deputy commander of the Military Command of Gia Dinh Province. During the anti-U.S. war, before changing over to the rear services sector he was the regional artillery commander. Thus he knew a good deal about the military, the city and the people of Saigon, and the eastern Nam Bo region. He was loyal and sincere and loved and was deeply concerned for the cadres and men and knew how to insure that the troops would fight victoriously. The department commander, Bui Phung, from the outskirts of Hanoi, had served as a staff officer of the Rear Services General Department and was expert at his profession. Comrade Tu Vo (Vo Phat), the department's deputy commander, who had been secretary of the Long Chau Tien provincial party committee during the anti-French period and had engaged in revolutionary activities in the Mekong Delta and in Kampuchea, was a person with many accomplishments in creating local sources of materiel for the sector. The lower-echelon cadres made a similar deployment so that they could combine their talents, virtue and knowledge of their work, familiarity with the battlefield, ability to locate sources of materiel, and knowledge of human nature. The assignment of great tasks must be accompanied by organizing and selecting people who are capable of carrying out those tasks, in order to insure their success. It would be impossible to relate all of the combinations that were made to create the combined strength which enabled the B2 rear services sector to support all battles and campaigns, no matter where or when they took place, from the beginning to the end of the war. Even during the period in which the B2 theater was experiencing the greatest difficulties and shortages with regard to food and ammunition, especially in War Zone A in northern Bien Hoa in 1966, the region deployed and kept there the 81st Rear Services Group commanded by comrade Muoi Thien.* Therefore, when the 9th Division had to fight in that area it had rice and ammunition without having to take them along and be slowed down. While en route to an assignment in 1966, I visited the 81st Group. Comrade Muoi Thien and his men assured me that they were determined to "hold their ground" no matter what the situation. In addition to being attacked by bombs, shells and poison chemicals, the men serving there had another dangerous enemy: malaria. For that reason, during "the 9 years"** the men had a saying, "The Ma Da and Song Be--heroes meet their end" (the place where the Ma Da River flows into the Song Be River was famous for being insalubrious and caused the death of many of our soldiers from malaria during the anti-French period.

There, "miraculous speed" must be understood as preparing the battlefield in advance, and having supplies where and when they are needed. If that was to be accomplished, it was necessary to foresee developments early, accurately and promptly, and be an organization that was skilled in making preparations in advance, efficient, and made up of brave and resourceful people. There can be no miraculous speed if we "wait until the water reaches our feet before jumping." If one waits until something happens before acting, how can one act in time? The Americans and puppets had large and small transport planes and many helicopters and could not get the job done in time, let alone having to meet requirements under urgent conditions. The B2 rear services had the technique of "feathering the nest in advance." It cached hundreds and thousands of tons of food, weapons and ammunition in the guerrilla enclaves and

---

*Senior Colonel Vo Van Lan, now commander of the Rear Services Department of Military Region 7.
**"The 9 years" referred to the anti-French period.

the areas in which the main-force and local troops would operate when necessary, and cached explosives, weapons and ammunition in the outskirts of cities and next to the enemy's airfields, ports and supply depots; and inside the cities, near important objectives, such as for the sappers and commandos in Saigon, whom we used in accordance with plans drafted by the upper echelon. Without cleverly organized forces commanded by suitable, capable cadres and without revolutionary masses, such tasks could not have been carried out. In order to prepare for the 1974-1975 dry season, during the rainy season the rear services sector transported to the military regions, including Saigon, more than 3,000 tons of weapons and ammunition, and supplied to the units sufficient quantities of base ammunition loads and food for combat and for reserve stocks. It stockpiled in areas in which the dry season battles would take place, especially in eastern Nam Bo, nearly 30,000 tons of materiel, including nearly 8,000 tons of ammunition and 1,500 tons of POL. Something else noteworthy about the B2 rear services sector was that it tried to create local sources of materiel whenever possible, and only requested from the upper echelon what it could not obtain locally. In 1973 and the rainy season of 1974, the materiel obtained locally by the B2 rear services sector amounted to 73 percent of the theater's needs, so only 27 percent were requested from the central echelon. Correctly carrying out the order of the Regional Command, the rear services sector insured that there were always on hand stocks of food, medicine and military medical equipment; enough POL for from 3 to 6 months; and sufficient weapons and ammunition for 1 year. Achieving those feats on a distant, key, extremely fierce battlefield was a very significant accomplishment. When I met with them, those rear services troops who gave their all in all campaigns, they were spontaneously happy despite the hardship and danger, and said nothing about their work.

At the beginning of 1975, I went to the Ta Lai ferry crossing on the Dong Nai River in War Zone A in northern Bien Hoa. I talked with the driver of a truck full of ammunition who was robust and lively. He was bending over feeling the tread of a worn tire but suddenly stood straight and said, "I'm from Ha Bac and came south in 1973. My name is Pham Van Mieng." The comrade who was driving the motorboat that was pushing the ferry across the river was older, and was thin but wiry. He said, "I'm from Ca Mau, and enlisted during the simultaneous uprising. My name is Ut Den. I'm studying new things up here. Back home I only knew how to drive a boat with an outboard motor to take my wife to the market." "So you have a wife," I said, "Do you have any children yet?" He replied, "I had a 3-year-old boy who was shot to death by the PF on a sweeping operation. Then I enlisted for good because I was determined to get revenge." I felt sorry for him. I asked, "How about comrade Mieng?" He replied, "I don't have a family yet. After we win I'll volunteer to stay on here." "So," I said, "are you interested in some girl?" "No, sir," he replied, "I have to take care of my truck night and day." I remember that in 1968, when crossing the Saigon River at night, I met at a ferry crossing in a bamboo grove that had been tattered by bombs and shells but was still capable of camouflaging small groups, several very young girls who were carrying heavy boxes of ammunition to bunkers on the bank. I recognized two of them, Miss Tham and Miss Lien, Warriors of Emulation who had participated in victory celebrations at the regional base and at the Rear Services Department. Most of the girls were from the outskirts of Saigon and had enlisted to do rear services work in the Saigon-Gia Dinh Zone. When they recognized the commander they were very pleased and gathered around, excitedly asking, "When will Saigon, Tan Thoi Nhat village, and Be Diem be liberated?" Another interrupted, "How About Tan Hiep village in Hoc Mon? You only think of your own village." "Will we be able to go home after Tet?" I wonder where Tham, Lien Mieng, and Ut are now! So many people, including rear services cadres, fell on the battlefield. The first rear services director of B2, comrade Nguyen Van Dung, a worker from Saigon, his hair grey after two resistance wars, also sacrificed his life in the line of duty. In that war there was no division into rear area and front line. The rear services personnel always had to advance to the force and enthusiastically go in advance to prepare the battlefield.

In August and September 1974 the Regional Staff, along the lines delineated by COSVN and under the guidance of the Regional Command, drafted an operational plan for the 1974-1975 dry season that foresaw the winning of a decisive victory within the next few years. At the beginning of October, COSVN discussed and approved the plan. During the meeting, each comrade in COSVN clearly and specifically analyzed the situation on the battlefield and the overall situation, and unanimously decided to win a decisive victory and complete the national democratic revolution in 1975-1976; 1975 would be the pivotal year and in 1976 we would victoriously conclude the war. It was not easy to reach such unanimity. There was much hesitation and reflection, and much analyzing and going over problems again and again. Everyone spoke of the decline of the puppet army and regime in the various areas. In the cities there had appeared a mass political struggle movement to oppose the corruption and impotency of the puppet Thieu regime, and that situation had considerably affected the morale of the enemy troops. Everyone concluded that our position and strength had become stronger and had developed uniformly on all battlefields. Our village and hamlet guerrillas had wiped out and eliminated enemy outposts. But there was still concern about a number of remaining weaknesses: although the guerrilla and local forces had recently developed strongly, numerically they did not yet meet requirements; our main-forces had not yet fought a major annihilating battle; and although the mass movement had become stronger it was not yet strong enough to carry out an uprising and overthrow the puppet regime. Our three strategic blows--main-force, rural and urban-- were not yet uniform. Our urban attacks were still weak. Although the United States had been defeated and had to withdraw its troops from Vietnam, and the situation in the United States was in upheaval politically and the United States was in poor shape economically and financially, it was essential that we be clever in order to limit U.S. intervention and insure that we won a rapid, efficient victory. All of those concerns were very correct. They were the truth and everyone realized that it was necessary to make great, continual efforts in order to insure victory within that period of time.

The participants reached unanimity in determining the stage of the revolution and the stage of the war we were in, and agreed with the opinions of Muoi Cuc (comrade Nguyen Van Linh, deputy secretary of COSVN): "The Thieu regime is in a state of serious decline, in part because its contradictions are developing and in part because our attacks are becoming increasingly strong. We must attack even more strongly and more often, and not allow them to regain their strength. We are now capable of pushing the enemy back step-by-step, winning partial victories, and eventually winning total victory. The puppet regime cannot hold out beyond the 1975-1976 dry season." Bay Cuong concluded that "The enemy is undergoing an all-round crisis that is also affecting the central regime, not merely just one aspect or a certain area. The puppets will decline at an increasingly greater rate, like a truck going downhill, and there is a possibility that that rate will suddenly increase. We still have deficiencies and weaknesses, but we are capable of overcoming them and are in the process of doing so. We are winning a big victory even during the current rainy season. We are capable of making good preparations for the coming dry season. We estimate that we can complete the national democratic revolution in 1976. The year 1976 will present an extremely important opportunity. But 1975 must be the pivotal year; only if we endeavor to win victories that year can we create conditions for winning a decisive victory in 1976. We say 1975, but in fact the decisive period will be the 1974-1975 dry season. It is necessary to fully grasp the spirit of the dry season plan discussed by COSVN and the Regional Military Party Commission, fully explain the significance and contents of the dry season from top to bottom, and understand that this year's dry season plan is a closely coordinated campaign plan encompassing all the military regions--the Military Region 6 to Military Region 9--both the main-force and local troops, and the rural, jungle-and-mountains, and urban areas. It must be coordinated very harmoniously. This time, more than at previous times, we have a plan for coordinating, discussing and carefully preparing, from top to bottom, and in both the military and the party echelons. We are determined to win a big victory. Thus the leadership and guidance of COSVN and the Regional Military Party Commission must be tight during this year's dry season. There must be close coordination between the party committee echelons and the equivalent military echelons in guidance and command. We must do a truly good job of carrying out the dry season plan, while also preparing to develop strongly if the situation develops in our favor. We must try to win the greatest, most timely victory in 1975."

During that COSVN meeting we also discussed the eventuality of the situation developing rapidly and the puppet army and regime collapsing earlier than we had foreseen, especially if there occurred a military-political development in Saigon itself. In such an event the B2 theater would, by itself, have to launch the final attack on the enemy's headquarters lair and conclude the war, and must not fail to take advantage of such an opportunity. I reported to COSVN that we would go all-out to step up the development of local armed forces and guerrillas, and have the localities intensify the development of revolutionary mass forces in order to prepare for such an opportunity. But with regard to main-force units the B2 theater was still very weak, and lacked both the infantry and the technical combat arms to fulfill such a difficult mission. I recommended that the Military Commission of the party Central Committee immediately assign the B2 theater three or four divisions so that we could insure success in that final battle. From the point of view of the possible development of the situation, the strategic line, our method of organizing, deploying and using forces, and the position and role of the B2 theater, sending us three or four additional divisions during that phase would have been entirely rational. I reported in outline our plan for attacking Saigon and spoke of the necessity for those additional main-force units.

After discussing the situation the comrades in COSVN agreed unanimously and decided to request those forces from the central echelon immediately. But so that those divisions could reach our theater in time we would request the central echelon to assign those units on a rotational basis, i.e. send divisions from the Central Highlands to the B2 theater, then send replacement units from the Tri Thien theater to the Central Highlands, and so forth, until a sufficient number of units were deployed on the battlefield. By doing so we could reduce the time required to move the units.

COSVN and the Regional Military Party Commission reported our plan to the Central Committee and its Military Commission, and recommended that the Political Bureau convene a meeting of representatives of all theaters to discuss a unified plan for all of South Vietnam during that phase.

The 1974-1975 dry season plan approved by COSVN was in fact a plan to prepare for a general offensive and uprising in the B2 theater, a plan to create conditions for advancing to winning victory to end the war in that key theater. Therefore, it had to be based on the preparation in advance of a plan for a general offensive and uprising throughout the B2 theater. In fact, we had nurtured that contingency plan for a long time beginning with the preparation and execution of the General Offensive and General Uprising of Tet Mau Than [1968]. During decades of combat in that theater, first against France and then against the United States, our military cadres had practically memorized each terrain feature, village, river and canal. We also fully understood our enemy and their capability to defend and respond in each period. More importantly, we fully grasped our party's leadership line in that war. We attacked the enemy by both military forces and political forces. Parallel military and political efforts would inevitably lead to a completely victorious general offensive and general uprising. Unanimously approving of and confident in that leadership line, we were always certain that the time would come when we absolutely had to carry out a general offensive and general uprising. Therefore, after the adoption of party Central Committee Resolution No 9 in 1963, a resolution which delineated that line very clearly, we in the theater that included Saigon-Gia Dinh, the capital of the puppet regime, continually thought about how the general offensive and general uprising should be carried out. In 1964 the B2 theater delineated five lines of attack on Saigon, then organized the Saigon Special Zone into subzones 1, 2, 3, 4 and 5 for the purpose of organizing and deploying forces and direct the general offensive and general uprising of Tet Mau Than. During that time we selected the objectives inside and outside the city, and organized appropriate types of forces to combine attacking from inside out to attacking from outside in. Tet Mau Than was an extremely valuable practical experience. Every day the war was developed by the use of many different forms and scales was also a day which further enriched our thought and provided us with additional experience. Now we were standing in the threshold of a second general offensive and uprising in Saigon and all over the B2 theater. Having mulled it over in our minds for many years, we had little difficulty in drafting a plan for Saigon and all of the B2 theater to serve as a basis for the 1975 dry season plan.

It was not a plan to launch a general counteroffensive against the enemy troops from a certain front, as in a regular war. We would not use exclusively military forces--powerful main-force corps--to wipe out the enemy and chase them from the Central Highlands, or advance from Quang Tri to Thua Thien, Quang Nam, and Da Nang, then down to Saigon, then pursue the enemy to Cau Mau, Con Son, Phu Quoc, etc. Indeed, we would be incapable of doing so even if we wanted to, and it would be dangerous to do that if we were capable of doing so, for there was the danger that the enemy would gradually draw in their troops to form an enclave in a certain area and then, with the support of superior U.S. air and naval power, counterattack. The "Gavin Plan" had called for such a strategic enclave in the Mekong Delta. Gavin was a well-known U.S. general who came to Saigon in 1972, when the Americans and puppets were being knocked about and were being heavily defeated from Quang Tri to eastern Nam Bo. Against that background, is recommended a strategy of gradual retrenchment and withdrawal if the puppet forces were defeated. The last area to be defended would be My Tho-Vinh Long-Can Tho. He reasoned that the Mekong Delta was a manpower pool, the source of sustenance for Saigon, and the heartbeat of the "capital." The Mekong Delta would be a place for consolidating forces and aiding Saigon. There it would be possible to strengthen defensive forces and create the capability to counterattack the enemy under even the worst possible conditions. He remembered the lesson learned when puppet troops were sent from My Tho to save Ngo Dinh Diem in a certain year. He also thought that the Mekong Delta, which fronted the sea and Con Son, Tho Chu, Phu Quoc, and other islands, afforded a strong position and would facilitate the entry of U.S. forces from the Pacific. The ways the colonialists viewed things differed very little. In 1946, a directive sent to the D'Argenlieu, the French High Commissioner in Indochina, Moutet, the French minister for overseas colonies, stressed that: "Cochin China is the true focal point of our overall policy in Indochina. We must succeed, and succeed rapidly, in Cochin China because the future of the presence depends almost entirely on our victory or defeat there." D'Argenlieu also had the viewpoint that "Cochin China is the key to the Indochinese Federation in the French Union. If the authority of France is consolidated there, the Indochinese Federation in the French Union will become a reality." "The importance of Cochin China must never be forgotten. It will be the long-range foundation of the Indochinese Federation and the foundation of our influence."

Nguyen Van Thieu vehemently opposed Gavin's plan and thought that it was stupid and a surrender to the "Viet Cong." But that was a time when Thieu thought that he was still firmly in power and relied on the strong supporting pillar of the United States. But now that his tenure was no longer secure, was not the Gavin plan the best solution? The Western Press commented that "With a population of about 10 million in the Mekong Delta, could not Nguyen Van Thieu be the president of a Southeast Asian country with an area of about 60,000 square kilometers?

But we had thought all that out before Gavin, as well as possibilities Gavin hadn't thought of.

*According to documents of the Historical Office of the Military Science Department.

From the very beginning, our party adopted a strategic plan of a marvelous general offensive and general uprising of a revolutionary people's war developed to a high degree. We attacked the enemy by means of military forces organized in many appropriate forms, combined with mass uprisings, on both a small scale and a large scale, in all areas: the jungle-and-mountains area, the lowland rural area and the urban area. In view of the fact that the enemy had complete superiority in the air, at sea, and on the rivers and canals, had modern weapons and facilities, could move rapidly by helicopter on all kinds of terrain, and had strong firepower, our principal forces were those deployed on the spot. Everywhere there were revolutionary forces, so everywhere the enemy troops went they were attacked by both military forces and mass political forces, by large forces and by small, elite forces, and by visible forces as well as by invisible forces. Even our main-force units fought only mobile warfare, but they remained within certain areas and cooperated closely with the local forces. There were no main-force units that operated all over the theater and apart from the localities. Our superiority was that the localities were very decisive in nature, but all the localities were united very closely from the central level. Did not Tet Mau Than in 1968 demonstrate that? On the same day, at a signal given by the central level, hundreds of cities, and thousands of villages and enemy objectives were attacked fiercely, to the point that the enemy troops, so much so that the enemy troops didn't know where to turn, and had no place to which to withdraw or retreat. The enemy were dizzy in Vietnam and even in the United States. Such was our miraculous speed, miraculous speed which encompasses a vast space in a short period of time, miraculous speed in combat activities, in campaigns, and more important in a strategic phase, in a method of concluding a war. Don't think of miraculously rapid attacks merely in terms of large, mobile units traveling long distances, for if you do you can't understand the actual situation.

Firmly grasping those strategic viewpoints, throughout the 1974 rainy season COSVN and the Regional Military Party Commission went all-out in monitoring the localities and in supervising them in rapidly developing their military and political forces, and in creating position and strength, so that each place could expand its liberated area. In October 1974, COSVN issued a directive which stressed that "villages must liberate villages, districts must liberate district, and provinces must liberate provinces, throughout the B2 theater." The introduction of that immortal action slogan, based on the strategic viewpoint of combining offensive and uprising and on the actual developments on the battlefield, at that time created a terrible strength. The B2 theater's 1974-1975 dry season plan was based on the assumptions that B2 itself would have to carry out a general offensive and uprising in Saigon and that each military region and province would have to take care of their own battlefield needs without waiting on forces from the upper echelon, but cooperate closely in a common plan with regard to objectives and time, under the leadership of the central echelon. The contingency plan for a general offensive and uprising throughout the B2 theater was drafted on the basis of the following important factors:

First of all, it was necessary not to push the enemy back from one line of resistance to another, and not to allow them to withdraw into strategic enclaves in any area, in Saigon, in the Mekong Delta, or even on the islands in the South

China Sea and the Gulf of Tonkin, as Gavin had planned. As for withdrawing into an enclave at Saigon, we had gradually taken steps to prevent the enemy from creating solid lines of defense and had gradually eliminated the possibility that they could form an enclave in Saigon. As for withdrawing into enclaves in the Mekong Delta or on islands, the most effective measures were carrying out timely and strong attacks and uprisings by the on-the-spot military and political forces, by strategicially cutting the Mekong Delta up into many segments, and by annihilating the enemy in each area in order to prevent them from concentrating in a certain place to assume the defensive.

The second element was that we had to interdict, surround and isolate the enemy troops by means of both campaigns and individual battles, in order to annihilate them and prevent them from concentrating, supporting one another, and reinforcing one another. The enemy forces in the B2 theater were relatively large and consisted of the forces of more than two military regions, in addition to the forces of their Capital Special Zone and their general reserves. Wherever the enemy troops were they had to be attacked simultaneously, so that many would become few and strength would become weaknesses. If that was to be accomplished we had to firmly grasp the method of "two feet and three spearheads, and launch unexpected, timely, continuous, and repeated attacks all over the place and at the same time.

The third was eliminating the enemy's strengths and exacerbating their weaknesses. Throughout the course of the war, the Americans and puppets relied principally on a strong air force, control of the skies, strong air support, and mobility by transport aircraft or helicopters. Then there were the naval forces, the river flotillas, the mechanized troops and the artillery. Without strong air support the puppet troops would quickly lose their will to fight, which could easily lead to disintegration and surrender. In the B2 theater there were three large airfields—Bien Hoa, Tan Son Nhat, and Lo Te in Can Tho—which were their ultimate sources of support and strength. Other than those airfields they would have to rely on the aircraft carriers of the U.S. 7th Fleet offshore. We had to have a plan and deploy special forces in advance, in order to interdict those three airfields to the greatest possible extent, along with antiaircraft forces to guard against air attacks.

The fourth element was an attack on the enemy's nerve center to liberate Saigon, the most heavily defended place. Since it was a political, cultural and commercial center there were many roads connecting it with all parts of the country. Most important were Route 1 and the railroad, which connected Saigon with central Vietnam, and Route 4, which connected Saigon with the delta, which was the rice basket and manpower pool, and also Military Region IV, which still had relatively strong military forces. There were also Route 15 and the Long Tau River, which connected Saigon with the Pacific at the port of Vung Tau, which could be used for landing U.S. troops to save the puppets or as a port of debarkation for puppets returning to the motherland. Since Saigon was the war command headquarters, there were all kinds of lines of communication extending to the regions, the units and even the U.S. 7th Fleet. In order to liberate Saigon, it was first necessary to isolate it from the surrounding areas so that forces could not be withdrawn into Saigon to form an enclave, so that the enemy could not flee, so that there could be no reinforcements or way out. The result would be chaos and disintegration.

The fifth factor was that the attack on Saigon had to be strong, rapid and effective, and that the key objectives had to be taken practically at the same time in order to insure a miraculously quick victory and prevent the enemy from defending the city, consolidating their forces and using buildings in the city for defensive purposes, thus turning the city into rubble and creating difficulties for the attackers. There was yet another problem: we could not allow the political sorcerers to have time to build a stage and bring out the marionettes in order to produce a miracle and prevent the victory of the revolution. In order to do so, we had to closely combine storm-like attacks from many directions on the outside with attacks and uprisings all over the city. We had to avoid having to fight for each street and each house, and to take each objective. Strong main-force units would attack into the city from many directions, while the sappers and elite troops attacked objectives inside the city, the masses arose to take over the neighborhoods and government offices, defend the factories, etc. We had to prevent the enemy troops from having even the slightest bit of morale, so that they would disintegrate en masse. We would wage a revolutionary war within our compatriots' hearts: our party had directed us to firmly grasp the strategy of general offensive and uprising, with attacks and uprisings, with attacks from outside in and from inside out, and simultaneous attacks. That was miraculous speed. In order to accomplish that, COSVN and the Saigon-Gia Dinh Municipal Party Committee studied the deployment of each party chapter, each party member, each leadership activist, and each organized mass cell--youths, women, middle school students, and college students--in all important neighborhoods and organs. The armed forces included armed youths, armed security forces, commandos, and sappers, who were assigned objectives in the city and in the outskirts; they had been steeled and had a tradition. How about the main-force units which would attack into the city from the outside? They would be a very decisive factor in our success, so they had to be strong and we had to make very careful calculations. Even in a coordinated combat arms attack there also had to be coordination among the various kinds of armed forces and semi-armed forces, and coordination between the military forces and the political forces of the organized and unorganized political forces.

The plan called for the main-force units to attack from five directions. That part of the plan was based on the most essential objectives inside the city that we had taken quickly, practically at the same time. It was based on the nature and deployment of those objectives in the city and their relationship to the areas outside the city. It was based on the terrain and topographical features around the objectives and around the city. It was based on the enemy's defensive deployment and the capabilities of the staging areas from which we would launch our attacks, etc. Of those five directions, the northwest and north were the most advantageous. The terrain in both of those directions was good, dry, level and open, which facilitated the use of technical equipment, mechanized equipment and large main-force units. In attacking from those directions it would be necessary to cross open, sparsely vegetated areas near the An Ha bridge, the Rach Tra River and Lai Thieu, but those areas were narrow and easily crossed. The staging area for the attacks--although we would have to fight to further consolidate the staging area prior to launching the attacks--bordered our vast rear area and facilitated the movement and deployment of forces, supplying from the rear, and communications with the rear area and the campaign headquarters. In their defensive deployments the enemy troops paid much attention to those two areas, for they were contiguous to our base area and our main-force units operated there continually. The enemy had deployed two relatively strong divisions in those areas, but they had been dispersed with regard to both width and depth and thus could not form a fortified defense line made up of fortified outposts. for their defenses had already been fragmented. The key objectives those two attacking columns had to take were not situated in the city and the attack routes were not complicated.

To the east, the terrain was favorable but the people did not fully support us. Our organized masses were still weak. An attack would be launched from that direction because it was necessary to attack and take such large and strongly defended objectives as the Bien Hoa AFB, the city of Bien Hoa, and especially the headquarters of the puppet III Corps, the corps with the mission of commanding the main forces defending Saigon. It would also be necessary to cross two large rivers, the Dong Nai and the Saigon. Although the roads were good, if the enemy destroyed the bridges it would be very difficult to reach the objectives in time. The staging areas of the attacks in that direction were distant from the rear area base and many difficulties would be encountered in transporting food and ammunition. Only if we fought to expand the direct rear area of that column in advance could we create supply routes and build up rear services stockpiles, for the enemy still occupied those areas.

The western and southern directions were the most difficult and complicated. In both of those directions the terrain, before we reached the staging areas and in the staging areas themselves, was low-lying and marshy, and was crisscrossed by many rivers and canals. Especially to the south troops on foot could not leave the road, not to mention mechanized vehicles and artillery. Drinking water had to be brought along. If vehicles and artillery were to reach the staging areas from which the attacks were to be launched, they would have to fight their way through and place a pontoon bridge across the Van Co River. Our supply lines would be long and difficult, because there were no roads. If the cadres and units had not operated in the area for years and did not have expert knowledge of the terrain, the localities, and the enemy, they could not overcome the many difficulties in order to create valuable lines of attack. But once the obstacles were overcome so that the attacks could be launched, there would be formed very lethal offensive columns the enemy did not expect which would insure the coordinated success of the entire campaign.

To the west and east we had a mission that was extremely important to insuring the victory of the campaign: completely surrounding and isolating Saigon before the attacks were launched on the center of the puppet capital. That mission included cutting Route 4 connecting Saigon with the Mekong Delta, cutting Route 1, and cutting the railroad to central Vietnam and Route 15 and the Long Tau River to the sea.

In order to insure that all five offensive columns could enter Saigon at the same time to take the most important objectives in accordance with a closely coordinated campaign plan, at a time when each direction had such differing conditions and characteristics, there had to be meticulous advance preparations and a number of extremely important tasks had to be carried out many months in advance. One of those tasks was preparing forces for the western and southern directions. As stated above, those two directions required forces which knew the terrain well, were accustomed to operating in the marshy river and canal areas, etc. Especially, to the south we could not use vehicles and vehicle-towed artillery, but had to use portable artillery. The units had to be accustomed to fighting on complicated terrain under difficult conditions and take along their weapons, ammunition and food, and would be supported only by light artillery. There it was only possible to use regiment-sized units that were lightly organized and streamlined. They had to know how to disperse and concentrate flexibly, know how to cross rivers by using on-the-spot facilities and even without facilities, etc. They had to be units which were accustomed to living with the local people, knew how to coordinate closely with the guerrillas and local troops, and know how to persuade the people to fight with and support the combat forces. To the west we could use vehicles and artillery, even heavy vehicles and artillery, but we had to be expert at moving vehicles and artillery on complicated terrain, secretly crossing rivers at night, clever camouflaging, etc. In both directions it was necessary to meticulously prepare the approach routes from distant locations to the bivouac areas, and prepare the assembly areas and assault positions, which was a very difficult task because some of those areas were interspersed with those of the enemy. It would also be very difficult to stockpile supplies in those two areas, with regard not only to transportation but also to the erection of supply depots and medical aid stations, the transportation of wounded, etc.

On the basis of the draft plan for a general offensive and uprising in the B2 theater, the staff drafted a 1974-1975 dry season plan for the B2 theater which would begin in December 1974 and was divided into two phases:

--Phase 1, from the beginning of December 1974 to the beginning of February 1975.

--Phase 2, from the beginning of March to the end of May 1975.

The principal contents of the dry season plan were to continue to disrupt the enemy's pacification plan in the Mekong Delta, expand the liberated area, bring many additional people over to the revolution, expand and fill out the rear base area and the corridors connecting it with the battlefields, especially the principal eastern Nam Bo base and the areas east and west of Saigon, annihilate whole battalions and regiments of the puppet troops, liberate the district seats, continue to improve our position and strength, accelerate the decline of the puppets and be prepared to create and take advantage of opportunities in order to win victory. The locations and objectives of the attacks to annihilate the enemy and expand the liberated area, etc., had to be appropriate to the draft plan for a general offensive and uprising all over the B2 theater, as mentioned above. To accomplish those tasks and meet the norms that were set would be to positively prepare all conditions for the decisive victory.

In the Mekong Delta the key objectives of the attacks against the enemy were in the provinces of Vinh Long, Tra Vinh and Ben Tre. Vinh Long and Tra Vinh were situated between the Tien Giang and Hau Giang Rivers in the center of the Mekong Delta. Route 4 and the Mang Thit River were two strategic routes passing through the provinces. To expand the liberated area and control of the population we would have to create conditions for cutting Route 4, gaining control of the Mang Thit River, and closing the Can Tho and My Thuan ferry landings, i.e. to cut the Mekong Delta into three parts and cut the enemy's Military Region IV into many isolated segments. That would be a strategic blow which would quickly smash the U.S.-puppet illusion that they could withdraw into a strategic enclave there after being heavily defeated elsewhere, so that they could stage a counterattack. Ben Tre, a province with favorable terrain, bordered on Go Cong, Can Duoc and Can Giuoc. Our victory there would both support the Vinh Long and Tra Vinh fronts and create a good staging area for the attack on Saigon from the south. In order to insure the southern attack on Saigon, the Regional Command planned to create two lines of advance: the first from the Long Dinh area in My Tho across Cho Gao, Tan Tru and Tan An, and then to Can Duoc, Can Giuoc and Nha Be; and the second from Ben Tre through Go Cong, then Can Duoc, Can Giuoc and Nha Be, then attacking into Precincts 7 and 8 in Saigon. Both lines of advance passed through areas that were strategically important to the enemy, which had set up many outposts in them. The terrain in those areas was difficult and they were far from the liberated areas. Therefore, if we did not act to create the necessary conditions many months in advance, and did not have expert units, it would be difficult for us to fulfill the plan.

In addition, Military Region 9 had the secondary mission of expanding the U Minh liberated base in the direction of Can Tho in order to prepare for the interdiction of the Lo Te airfield in Can Tho and the attack on the "Western Capital" [Can Tho], the headquarters of the enemy's IV Corps. Military Region 8 had the secondary mission of expanding the Dong Thap Muoi liberated area to Route 4, in order to prepare to cut Route 4 in the My Tho area and wipe out the puppet 7th and 9th Divisions to prevent them from reinforcing Saigon. The Regional Command also assigned Military Region 8 the mission of preparing regiments to participate in the campaign to liberate Saigon from the south, for only with the forces of Military Region 8, and active preparations of that military region, could we have conditions for carrying out that lethal surprise attack. The region also provided for the possibility of sending two Military Region 9 regiments from Tra Vinh to participate in the attack on Saigon from the south.

The main-force units of the region and of Military Regions 7 and 6 had to launch attacks to expand and complete the base areas and make preparations for the forces north, northwest, east and west of Saigon to surround, isolate and exert increasingly greater pressure on Saigon. At the very beginning of the dry season it was necessary to liberate Route 14 from Dong Xoai to the Quang Duc border in order to expand the regional base to the rear until it bordered on the Central Highlands, connect the Regional base with the area east of Saigon, and create conditions for opening up that route and building up material-technical stockpiles for that area in advance. In order to liberate Route 14 and attain those objectives, it was necessary to eliminate, at all costs, the key Dong Xoai objective, after which the provincial capital of Phuoc Long would be completely isolated. We needed only to surround the enemy there, for they were incapable of reacting. But if conditions permitted we would liberate all of Phuoc Long Province, thus filling out our rear area base and causing psychological and political repercussions that would be very beneficial to us. The forces of Military Regions 6 and 7 had the missions of liberating the districts of Hoai Duc and Tanh Linh in order to create an area in which to assemble our troops and stockpile food and ammunition for the attack from the east on III Corps headquarters and then on Saigon. Then they were to coordinate with the upper-echelon forces to cut Routes 1, 20 and 15.

The regional main-force units also had to extend the corridor in western Tay Ninh, and liberate the Ben Cau and Queo Ba areas in Duc Hue District and the northern part of Duc Hoa District, in order to create a staging area from which to blockade Saigon from the west and create an area from which to launch the attack on Saigon from that direction. It was necessary to take the enemy position on Mt. Ba Den, a high point which controlled the areas north and northwest of Saigon, which was an observation point for monitoring movements in our base area and a communications center for relaying communications between the enemy's III Corps and all of its forces in those areas. We had to expand and fill out our base to the front by taking Binh Long, Chon Thanh, and Dau Tieng and controlling Route 26 for our forces and a staging area for the attacks on Saigon from the northwest and the north.

Thus the 1974-1975 dry season plan for the B2 theater was in essence continuing to attack the enemy to accelerate their decline, changing the balance of forces so that it was even more in our favor, and creating the opportunity for winning a decisive victory, which would in a practical way prepare for--or it could be said begin--the theater's general offensive and uprising and create conditions for the assault on the enemy's final lair.

The soldiers and people of the B2 theater began their dry season activities with very clear awareness of that important strategic phase, with confidence in victory, with a high degree of determination and with an enthusiastic spirit. The Regional Command, working directly with each military region and with each unit, reviewed their plans and inspected their preparation in all regards. Never before had a campaign been so meticulously and diligently prepared militarily, politically and with regard to both the attacking forces and the uprising forces, under the direct command of COSVN. Those seething, secret and urgent tasks were carried out very positively throughout the 1974 rainy season, the greatest rainy season ever!

In order to inspire them as they began that long-awaited dry season, in November 1974, the Regional Military Party Commission and Regional Command sent to all main-force, local and guerrilla cadres and men a letter of encouragement which included the following passages:

"The entire party, army and population are very determined to win a truly great, all-round victory in 1975 in order to bring about a turning point with the decisive significance of changing the balance of forces in our favor and creating a solid foundation on which to advance to winning a total victory.

"The 1974-1975 dry season victory will be decisive with regard to all in 1975.

"...Living in the sacred area of the Bulwark of the Homeland, the home area of the Nam Ky uprising, the general offensive uprising of Tet Mau Than, and many brilliant feats of arms, you must clearly manifest a heroic spirit and be determined to record the 1974-1975 dry season in history with truly dazzling feats of arms.

"Overcome all hardships and difficulties and trod upon the heads of the enemy in advancing to win victory."*

At the end of October, COSVN received a message from the Politibal Bureau ordering comrade Pham Hung and me to Hanoi to participate in a meeting of the Political Bureau of the party Central Committee, along with representatives of the theaters all over the South, to discuss the plan for the coming period.

Our delegation set out on 13 November. During the same period, the forces all over the B2 theater were also busily setting out to the assembly areas to begin the dry season fighting according to the plan. I instructed comrade Le Duc Anh, the regional deputy commander, who would replace me during my absence, that in addition to making regular reports to the General Staff he should report to me on all developments in all parts of the battlefield. I would very enthusiastically receive news of victories, but I would be even more concerned with and monitor the difficulties and obstacles in the process of carrying out the plan.

Comrade Duc Anh reminded me, "Try to explain things to the Military Commission and request additional forces for our theater. The 4th Corps is still crippled and weak, the weakest of all the corps, but it is the main force of the key theater. I just can't understand." I promised that I would fulfill that mission. Both those who were going and those who were staying behind were full of confidence in our victory.

We once again set out on the route that follows the nation's mighty Truong Son range, along route 559, the Ho Chi Minh Trail. But this time we traveled much faster and with less hardship, for we traveled the entire distance from Loc Ninh to Hanoi by motorboat or automobile. The route passed through eastern Kampuchea, crossed southern Laos via Route 9 past Cam Lo and Dong Ha, passed through the former Zone 4, and went on to Hanoi. The "Ho Chi Minh Trail" was no longer a trail but was a system of motor roads with many north-south and east-west branches which were supplemented by the Mekong River, the Sekong River, etc., and had been further embellished by communications lines stretched taut by the wind and POL pipelines that crossed streams and climbed mountains. Here and there POL stations, machine shops, truck parks, and headquarters were operating busily. On one hill after another there were cleverly camouflaged gun emplacements and antiaircraft proudly and imposingly pointing skyward. That was a far cry from May 1959--the birthday of the trail--to the early 1960's, a period during which I was in charge, and assigned to comrade Vo Bam and a number of other "old reliables" the task of gropingly tracing out the route. As they went they had to make their way step-by-step, and when returning they left no footprints, yet the comrades in the Political Bureau and the Military Commission of the party Central Committee continually admonished us to "be careful, be secret and be sure of yourselves."

---
*From the archives of the Military Science Office of Military Region 7.

Maj Gen Vo Bam, a member of the Communist Party in the 1930's, was from My Lai in Quang Ngai, the scene of a terrible atrocity by the United States. His spirit of revolutionary enlightenment, added to his love for his home area, caused him to have an iron will as strong as his husky body. During the first days of cutting a path through the jungles there were countless hardships. Heavy things were carried on the backs and shoulders of rubber-sandaled troops. Now, everyone who traveled the "Ho Chi Minh Trail" was full of confidence in the bright future and realized the mighty development of that vital route, which grew miraculously in the style of Phu Dong and the immortal bamboo of Vietnam. The Vietnamese bamboo, which still stood proudly all along the route, was victorious and will always defeat all reactionary powers, and all bombs, shells, poison chemicals, electronic equipment or anything else in the future.

CHAPTER FIVE

Beginning of a New Phase

I arrived at Hanoi before the Political Bureau meeting began. I reported to the General Staff on the situation in the B2 theater and listened to briefings on the overall situation and on the situations of the other theaters. I inquired about the possibility of assigning additional forces, weapons, and facilities to the B2 theater, something I had worried about a good deal, so that the theater could meet the requirements of the current situation. All along the route, and in Hanoi, a thought that never left my mind was that we had a good opportunity and that if B2 received some additional forces it would win a big victory and thus considerably affect the course of the war all over South Vietnam. Comrade Le Ngoc Hien, at that time in charge of operations at the General Staff, informed me that our reserves of weapons and ammunition were still very thin, especially large offensive weapons, artillery and vehicles. Thus the upper echelon had directed that their issue and use be very tightly regulated. We had to use weapons captured from the enemy to fight the enemy. With regard to forces, he could only let me know about the number of troops that would be sent to the theaters. The B2 theater had to set aside 40 percent of the troops supplied it for the Mekong Delta, in order to strengthen the provincial and district forces. In addition, it was necessary to rapidly develop militia and guerrilla forces so that the on-the-spot forces would be sufficiently strong to fight the enemy, so that the main-force troops in the military region could be more concentrated and mobile.

With regard to the 1975 plan, he informed me that the General Staff intended to make the Mekong Delta the principal battlefield, to concentrate all efforts on smashing the enemy's pacification plan, gaining control of additional people and resources for the revolution, and changing the balance of forces significantly in our favor. Eastern Nam Bo would concentrate on opening unobstructed corridors to the battlefields and on tightening the noose around Saigon. The only main-force blow would be in the southern Central Highlands, with the objectives of extending the strategic corridor past Duc Lap in order to complete that route and annihilating enemy manpower. We would save our strength for 1976, when we would carry out a large-scale strategic annihilating campaign, advance to a general offensive-general uprising, and win a complete victory.

The year 1975 would be divided into three phases:

--Phase 1, from December 1974 to February 1975. During that phase only B2 would be active because it had already drafted a plan.

--Phase 2, from March to June, would encompass all of South Vietnam.

--Phase 3, beginning in August, would be a phase of small-scale activity in preparation for 1976.

When I listened to the General Staff briefing on the plan I was anxious and worried, for the spirit and content of the B2 plan were not in accord with those of the General Staff. The Regional Military Party Commission and COSVN assessed that the situation in the theater had changed in a very fundamental way, that our position was improving and we were winning many victories, while the puppets were on the decline. We could not allow them to recover, or give the United States time to shore them up. Thus in 1975, from the beginning of the dry season, all over South Vietnam we had to attack strongly and were certain to win a great victory and create a new opportunity for the decisive phase of the war. The B2 dry season plan had been based on that spirit and had been reported to the party Central Committee, and we had recommended that the Political Bureau and the Military Commission of the party Central Committee draft a plan to guide and coordinate all of South Vietnam. But according to the General Staff plan, only the B2 theater would be active during the first phase, which was certain to limit our victory, and the enemy could cope with our attacks more easily. The 1975 plan of the General Staff called for only small-scale attacks, the disruption of pacification, the opening of supply corridors, and putting pressure on Saigon, in preparation for the large-scale fighting which would begin in 1976. It thought that the opportunity would not stand still and wait for us, but that it would slip by and the situation would develop in a different direction without our strong and timely influence on it.

Later, during a private working session with Le Duc Tho, he said to us, "The situation is very clear and the tendency is also clear and cannot be reversed. We must have a strategic plan for the 2-year 1975-1976 period. The opportunity in 1976 will be very important. We must go all-out to prevent the enemy from withdrawing into large strategic enclaves in 1976.

"Our materiel stockpiles are still very deficient, especially with regard to weapons and ammunition. The situation in our country and the situation abroad are very complicated and it will be difficult to augment our strategic reserves very much. Therefore, we must limit the fighting in 1975 in order to save our strength for 1976, when we will launch large-scale attacks and win a decisive victory. Only if our strategic intention for 1976 is clear can we have a direction for guiding plans and activities in 1975. We should not and cannot prolong the war indefinitely."

Because the meeting was not held to discuss plans I merely presented my opinions in brief. I strongly agreed that the enemy would try to withdraw into strategic enclaves after they had been heavily defeated, and we had to guard against that eventuality by many different means, beginning at an early date. We should not limit the fighting in 1975 in order to save our strength for 1976. On the contrary, only if we attacked strongly in 1975 could we victoriously conclude the war in 1976. The opportunity was at hand and should be grasped in order to create further opportunities. We must not let the opportunity slip by. Our COSVN had discussed and reached agreement about that problem and would submit a detailed report to the Military Commission of the party Central Committee and the Political Bureau.

I studied the messages sent to us from the theater. Only after reading a message from Le Duc Anh did I learn that B2, implementing a message from Van Tien Dung and brother Ba (comrade Le Duan, the general secretary), had adjusted the plan with regard to the B2 forces, i.e., we would not attack Dong Xoai, would not use large main-force units, heavy artillery and tanks, but would only launch small-scale attacks. Thus Military Regions 6, 7, 8 and 9 and Saigon-Gia Dinh in the B2 theater would continue to act in accordance with the plan we had drafted, with a little readjustment: the regional main-force units would not fight on a large scale and would not attack Dong Xoai but would be sent to attack the Bu Dang or Bu Na areas on Route 14 far to the north. In addition, the General Staff had decided to assign to B2's 7th Division and 429th Sapper Regiment the mission of preparing to attack Gia Nghia during the second dry season phase (March 1975) in order to coordinate with the principal focus of the campaign organized and commanded by the General Staff: Duc Lap (in the southern Central Highlands). I was even more disturbed, for the overall B2 dry season plan encompassed the entire theater and not only closely combined the lowland and jungle-and-mountains areas and the local and main-force troops, but also actively prepared for the second dry season phase and for all of 1975. To readjust the plan and shift around forces in that manner would be to hinder the B2 plan and enable the enemy to react strongly, especially in the delta. Why was that so? We drafted the B2 1974-1975 dry season combat plan on the basis of an assessment and evaluation of the common situation of ourselves and the enemy, in order to attain an important part of the objectives of a strategic phase, as mentioned above. In order to win victory in the various parts of the B2 theater, as planned, the plan had to include measures to keep the enemy pinned down so that they could not be free to move forces to cope with our attacks in places of their choosing, and we had to divert and disperse the enemy. Our B2 theater had two strong divisions--the 9th and 7th--which had achieved many feats of arms in fighting the puppets and Americans in eastern Nam Bo. Especially, the 9th Division was the first main-force division in South Vietnam to travel the long route from Binh Gia, Bau Bang, Dau Tieng, Tet Mau Than and Loc Ninh to the present. The enemy continually monitored each movement of those divisions in order to find out about our intentions and operational plans. During the first phase of the dry season we had intended to use only part of the 7th Division and the independent regiments. The rest of the division was to remain in place in the Tan Uyen and Phu Giao areas in Thu Dau Mot Province. The 9th Division, stationed in Long Nguyen area of Ben Cat District, would not yet participate in the fighting but would carry out feints in order to tie down III Corps forces in the intermediate area and in the outskirts of Saigon so that they could not be sent elsewhere, especially to respond to our attacks in the Mekong Delta. The plan was based on the enemy's assumption that during the dry season we would attack to liberate Tay Ninh Province so that we could make Tay Ninh City the capital of the PRG of the RSVN. We would use feints to make the enemy think that they had guessed right and so that they would tie up forces in the defense of that area. Meanwhile, we would use a regiment of the 7th Division, reinforced by a company of tanks and two companies of heavy artillery, to launch a surprise attack to take Dong Xoai, and use regiments 271 and 201, along with local forces, to liberate Route 14 within the enemy's Military Region III. We sent another regiment of the 7th Division to block the only road between Phuoc Vinh and Dong Xoai and had a contingency plan to annihilate enemy reinforcements brought in by air. The Dong Xoai position was the key base in Phuoc Long Province and along that stretch of Route 14, for it was the throat, the doorway, the lifeline connecting the entire province with the other areas of the puppet

III Corps. If Dong Xoai were lost the rest of Phuoc Long Province and Route 14 would be isolated and it would become difficult to supply that food-poor mountain region province. The objective of our liberation of Route 14 was to open up a corridor to the east in order to transport weapons, ammunition, and food for stockpiling in the War Zone A base and east of Route 20 in preparation for the column that would attack Saigon from the east. That corridor had to pass through Dong Xoai, or near it, and extend northward. If we could not liberate Dong Xoai, our transportation corridor would continue to be blocked, i.e., the objective of the plan would not be attained. If we were able to take Dong Xoai, the enemy troops in Phuoc Long would be desperate, which would create conditions for us to liberate the entire province if necessary. Thus although Dong Xoai was only a position, a district capital and a relatively fortified subsector, it was an important link of the overall dry season B2 plan, and an opening battle that would surprise the enemy and inspire our armed forces. If we did not attack Dong Xoai and open up the corridor to the east, but sent the 7th Division from the area, it was clear that the B2 plan would be considerably affected.

For that reason, I was very worried. I promptly reported my thoughts to Pham Hung and Hai Van (Phan Van Dang, a member of the standing committee of COSVN). Hai Van, who was present in Hanoi, joined the B2 delegation, which now had three members. We recommended that we be allowed to meet with the Military Commission of the party Central Committee and the General Staff so that we could express our opinions and request that we be allowed to retain our old plan and that the 7th Division not be sent to the Central Highlands. The meeting took place on 3 December. I explained as best I could B2's dry season plan and the justifications for it--on the strategic, campaign and battle levels--perhaps not eloquently but clearly and sincerely, for the sake of our theater and in the common interest. One comrade asked what would happen if we attacked Dong Xoai and the enemy reacted by sending in a division, and suggested that we would be forced to use all of the 7th and 9th Divisions to wipe out those reinforcements, thus tying up our main-force units at the very beginning of the dry season. I had to explain in detail our situation and that of the enemy in the theater as a whole, and asserted that if the enemy responded they could not send more than a regiment to Dong Xoai. (In fact, when we did attack Dong Xoai the enemy sent no troops to save the puppets there, and even when we attacked the Phuoc Long provincial capital the enemy sent only about 200 rangers of the 81st brigade.) I was able to make that assertion and reflect the actual situation because we in the B2 theater knew the enemy and the terrain well, and knew what roads the enemy would have to use to go to Dong Xoai and Phuoc Long, what their manpower and air transport capabilities were, and our capabilities and methods for stopping and annihilating them. I had confidence in our plan to keep the enemy pinned down in Saigon. When a military commander on a battlefield briefs and reports to the upper echelon he must have a strong sense of responsibility and must be accurate, clear and definitive.

I requested that the 7th Division not be sent to the Central Highlands because in the present strategic phase we believed that it was necessary to send additional forces from the other theaters to eastern Nam Bo and apply pressure in the Saigon area, and not send forces in the opposite direction, away from

Saigon. That was not a matter of localism but was in the interests of the strategic phase and of 1975. If needed for the General Staff plan, I agreed to send the 429th Sapper Regiment to Gia Nghia, which would be sufficient. During that meeting it was agreed not to transfer the 7th Division but only the 429th Regiment. I was very pleased and expressed deep gratitude for the attention given the lower echelon. As for attacking Dong Xiao, that matter had not been fully resolved. Many participants expressed opinions, but no conclusion was reached:

--We should take the initiative in using our main-force units and not let the enemy draw them out, wear them down, and try them out.

--We were fighting mainly to wipe out enemy manpower. It was not necessary to hold land during the coming phase, so it was not necessary to attack Dong Xoai.

--The 1975 situation was not urgent. We should be prudent, so there was no need to attack Dong Xoai.

--The strategic foci of 1975 would be the lowlands, Gia Nghia, the transportation corridors, and Tri Thien-Da Nang.

--Only by large-scale enemy-annihilating blows could we change the balance of forces in our favor and transform the situation.

Pham Hung expressed disagreement with such reasoning. He said, "This is a matter not only of Dong Xoai but also of the B2 plan. If we change it, I'm afraid that the lowlands and the common direction will be affected. We must understand that in this war we attack the enemy by both military forces and political forces; we attack and arise, arise and attack, and advance to a general offensive and general uprising. Therefore, on the basis of many conditions, there must be many ways to transform the situation; annihilating large numbers of the enemy is not necessarily the only way to bring about a transformation. For example, when we control several million people and master the battlefield, numbers are not a decisive factor. The fact that the enemy's military forces are large is not a sign of strength. We must first of all reach agreement with regard to our battlefield, and which phase we are in, and only then talk about what actions we should take."

After that meeting Pham Hung, Hai Van, and I often discussed and evaluated the situation, the present strategic phase, and the overall plan and the B2 plan in particular, on the basis of the discussions in COSVN before we left, in order to prepare for the coming Political Bureau meeting.

I thought that in war, annihilating large numbers of the enemy troops in a few battles or in a few campaigns is a real requirement for transforming the situation. That is entirely correct, if not the only condition in a conflict between the regular armies in an ordinary war. But in the national liberation war against U.S. aggression, our line was not a regular, ordinary war. Confident in the strength of the people, who arose to determine their own destiny, our party advocated a revolutionary war combined with an armed uprising of the people. We had to use military forces combined with popular mass forces.

We fought the enemy with weapons, politically, and by proselyting enemy troops. We had to carryout attacks and uprisings simultaneously, culminating in a general offensive and general uprising. The nature of our war was both opposing foreign aggressors and waging a civil war against the militarists and comprador capitalists in our country. For that reason, the revolutionary consciousness of the people was a notable strength, a valuable strategic weapon. The political program of our National Liberation Movement was a rallying point, a flag, a rallying of the masses to advance to the creation of a new life, one with freedom, independence, well-being and happiness. It was a strength, a factor in victory and not merely in transforming the situation. If that was true strategically, our war was also unlike ordinary wars with regard to campaigns and tactics. During decades of fighting the Americans and puppets, we continually searched and thought about, experimented with, and made appropriate changes in, our fighting methods, in order to achieve the greatest possible effectiveness and expend less blood, rice, ammunition, etc., so that we could fight for long periods of time, if necessary, and bring about decisive victories in relatively short periods of time. We did not fight the enemy with their methods but forced the enemy to fight our way. We did not compete with the enemy with regard to materiel and technology, or merely in terms of military strength, but with regard to will, determination, intelligence, bravery, cleverness, virtue and persistence, and with regard to both force and position. Our country's patriotism and thirst for freedom and happiness would inevitably defeat the slavery and exploitation of the Americans and puppets. Therefore, if we continued to think in the old way, only understood things the way we understood them in the past, and continued on our usual path, that would be completely inappropriate to the new phenomena and to a new war, which was not a carbon copy of the previous war. If COSVN and our Regional (B2) Command concluded that immediately after the 1974 dry season there had been a clear transformation all over South Vietnam, that we were victorious and on the ascent and the enemy had been defeated and was on the decline, and then took the stand that it was necessary to attack continually, carried out all tasks during the greatest season ever, and then drafted an all-round plan for the 1974-1975 dry season and for all of 1975, in order to win a decisive victory, we did not do so thinking that only when we launched attacks to annihilate the enemy on a large scale would the situation be transformed. That change in the situation was clearly due to a large number of factors, military and political, military forces and popular forces, material and spiritual, domestic and foreign, on the part of the enemy and ourselves, and with regard to position and force. When a certain point is reached, forces will undergo a qualitative change. Guidance must be responsive in order to realize that point and understand the new quality that has appeared, and not wait for or try to bring about a large-scale annihilating blow in order to transform the situation.

Due to such a concept, and on the basis of the actual situation on the battlefield, we concluded that that point had arrived, the situation had been transformed, the opportunity was evident, and if in 1975 we attacked strongly the opportunity would give rise to other opportunities, which we would endeavor to grasp in order to win victory. That was a matter of the science and art of the leadership and guidance of war and revolution. Regarding 1976 as an important opportunity was correct, but was only correct if we would work to create that opportunity throughout the course of 1975, and even prior to that. An opportunity does not create itself, so we should not sit and await the opportunity. An opportunity has objective conditions but it must be created primarily by subjective means.

A few days later, after supper, I was walking along the corridor emerged in deep thought when the telephone rang. Pham Hung invited me to go with him to visit brother Ba [Le Duan] at his home. I was pleased, agreed immediately, and set a time to arrive at Pham Hung's house so that we could go together. Up to that time, because I was busy and had many things to worry about, I hadn't had an opportunity to meet with brother Ba. At exactly 1930 hours Pham Hung and I arrived. Brother Ba came to the door, greeted us warmly, and led us into the living room. He appeared to be healthy, agile and very happy. Not waiting for us to inquire about his health, he asked whether the change of climate we had experienced in Hanoi had affected our health. Then he inquired about the comrades in COSVN and the Regional Military Party Committee, then about a number of others he knew in the military regions and provinces. But that was just a way of starting the conversation. He then went directly to the point and talked about matters everyone was thinking about. That was characteristic of him. When he met with cadres he spoke, spoke that the cadres could understand clearly and deeply and remember carefully. When during a conference, a cadre stood up to make a comment about something about which he was concerned, brother Ba would begin to talk and often would talk 5 to 7 minutes at a time, then let the cadre continue. He said, "The situation is very good and we are winning many victories. We are winning because we are strong, strong politically and militarily, in the rural areas, in the cities, among the people, with regard to our fighting methods--main-force fighting, guerrilla fighting, sapper fighting, fighting by female troops, etc. Only by such combination can we win. Combination with regard to strategy, forces and revolutionary methods. In fighting us the United States used a global strategy: they fought us and the socialist bloc. We also must use a global strategy. Independence, democracy and socialistism cannot be separated from one another. We must use the combined forces of Vietnam and the world. We must use combined revolutionary methods to the highest degree, attack and arise, arise and attack, and use political forces and military forces, main-force units, local forces, and guerrillas, fight in all three areas, and use the three offensive spearheads. That is science. In order to have a correct line there must be such correct methods.

"Militarily, in the present phase we must think, think, continually think, think, to clarify the problems. In 1975, how will we win victory? What political and military developments will there be in 1975? Have you wiped out any subsectors yet? Can you hold Rach Bap? What are the deployments in eastern Nam Bo? With regard to the encirclement of Saigon, how does the present phase differ from the past 2 years? With correct deployment, victory is 60 to 70 percent assured. How should we fight during this phase? Annihilate and achieve mastery, achieve mastery and annihilate, or what? Should we fight to annihilate all of the enemy or to rout all of the enemy?

He spoke in such a way as to explain, and asked a series of questions that needn't be answered. Perhaps he brought up matters, provoked ideas, and gave guidance so that the cadres would have to think and try to come up with the right answers by themselves. But I noticed that he was concerned with the defense of Rach Bap and with breaking up the enemy's strongly defended defensive enclave at Saigon. He was concerned about the deployment of our forces in and around Saigon, to form a solid offensive battlefield position. It was true that correct deployment was 60 to 70 percent of a victory. I truly believed in that saying. Intelligence, resourcefulness, courage, and meticulousness should be used when organizing and deploying forces to form a solid strategic battlefield position, for only then can one talk about defeating the enemy. The strategy of Sun Tzu of the Warring States period in ancient China paid much attention to deploying formations and arranging forces. According to that strategy, "Generals reach the peak of military art only when they know how to bring into play the greatest strength of the forces at their disposal, when they know how to change those deployments so that they can be appropriate to the changing circumstances, and when they know how to create an opportunity to cause the enemy troops to become divided and dispersed, so that strength becomes weakness and many becomes few."* A person who is a general in the present era, an era of revolution and science, with the leadership of a Marxist-Leninist Party, must know not only how to arrange the forces at his disposal into the most rational formations, but must also know how to create forces, organize many kinds of forces with many fighting methods, and combine all types of military forces with the political forces of the masses, forces in our country and forces abroad. He must know not only how to deploy formations to attack the enemy at the front but also in the enemy's rear area and within their ranks.

Just after Pham Hung finished speaking of the prospects of our winning victories during that dry season, I asked brother Ba, "You just sent a message instructing us not to attack Dong Xoai. Why did you do so?" He replied, "The General Staff reported to me that you were going to throw main-force units into the fight from the very beginning of the dry season. To attack Dong Xoai, and then fight a whole series of other large battles, would not be appropriate. We must fight in such a way as to conserve our strength. In the present situation you must always have available powerful forces so that when the opportunity arises you will be able to win victory." I explained to him my intentions and method of using forces. I said that at the beginning of the dry season we would still have a strong reserve force: the 9th Division and a number of regiments. Pham Hung added, "We won't have to use large forces to attack Dong Xoai but are certain of winning a victory. We have thought things over carefully." Brother replied, "If that is so, then go ahead and attack. There's no problem." I couldn't believe what I heard and immediately asked for a confirmation, "So you'll allow us to take Dong Xoai so that we can complete our corridor to the east, as called for by our plan?" He replied, "But you must be certain of victory and not use large forces." When I heard those words I felt as if a great burden had been lifted. I was very happy and couldn't wait to send a guidance message to the theater. That night I drafted a message so that Pham Hung and Hai Van could approve it and send it to COSVN and the Regional Command instructing them to carry out the original plan, i.e., to begin the dry season main-force activities by attacking Dong Xoai. But it

---

* AIR UNIVERSITY REVIEW, 1981, July-August issue.

was too late. Implementing the directive of the party Central Committee, the B2 Command had changed the plan and would not attack Dong Xoai but would only use small units to attack some small posts on Route 14 in the Ba Dang or Bu Na areas. It was too late to return to the old plan. On 6 December a message was received from Le Duc Anh, who reported, "On the day we received the message from brother Ba we convened a meeting of the Regional Military Party Commission to adjust the plan, rearrange our combat formations, send the tanks and 130 mm back to the base area, explain the situation to the troops, etc. Therefore, we cannot begin the attack in the Route 14 area before 12 December, while all over the B2 theater the fighting will begin during the night of 6 December and the early morning of 7 December. If we return to the old plan now we will have to rearrange our deployments, move the tanks, explain the situation to the troops, etc. Under the guidance of the COSVN standing committee, we should carry out the adjusted plan and not delay the date of the offensive. We will proceed in accordance with our 5 December message to the High Command, brother Bay (Pham Hung), and brother Tu (Tran Van Tra)."*

Prior to that, when I departed from the theater on 16 November to represent the B2 Command, brother Le Duc Anh e.e. Le Duc Anh, sent the following message to the High Command:

"Received brother Dung's message of 24 October. We are reporting some points the High Command must know immediately.

"...The winning of a good victory during the first phase of the dry season will create additional conditions for winning great victories throughout the dry season and in 1975. If we wait until phase 2 before attacking strongly, the 1975 victory will be limited. Therefore, we recommend that the High Command approve the plan we have drafted....

"Everything will be reported (by Pham Hung or myself)** in detail directly to the High Command."***

On 18 November brother Sau Nam sent the following message:

"...Received message 484 from brother Dung, with opinions of brother Van**** and have just received message 491 from brother Ba. We have discussed them and concluded that we do not yet fully grasp the intentions and overall plan of the Central Committee and its Military Commission as regards the relationship between the B2 theater and the other theaters in the South. We will carry out the directive of the upper echelon and adjust our plan as follows:

---

*From the archives of the B2 War Recapitulation Section of the Ministry of National Defense.
**Note by the author.
***From the archives of the B2 War Recapitulation Section of the Ministry of National Defense.
****Comrade Vo Nguyen Giap.

"1. With regard to regional main-force units:

"--During Phase 1, the main-force operations will be intended to wear down and annihilate part of the enemy's manpower, and draw in and stretch out the enemy so they cannot concentrate in the delta and around Saigon, help the localities retain their rice, and free the people, while also continuing to consolidate, train and conserve our strength so that during Phase 2 they can operate strongly, in accordance with the requirement of coordinating with the other theaters, as directed by the Central Committee.... Meanwhile, we will continue to prepare for the Phase 2 high-point, such as by preparing the battlefield, training troops to attack objectives along the lines of using portable artillery--nothing heavier than 85 mm direct-fire guns--and without using tanks or 130mm artillery.

"These are some adjustments in Phase 1 plan. After brother Hai Nha* returns and brother Tu** goes north to make his report, we will make additional changes as directed by the High Command.

"But to guard against the possibility that brother Tu may arrive in Hanoi later than expected and before Hai Nha returns, recommend that the High Command provide additional guidance so that we can implement it in time."***

The matter of Hai Nha's return, mentioned in the message was, according to Hai Nha, as follows:

"In November 1974, after being released from Hospital 108 in Hanoi I prepared to convalesce at Sam Son beach. Le Ngoc Hien came to see me and inquire about my health. He said that the General Staff needed someone who was capable and reliable to take orders to the B2 theater and report on a number of situations and the 1975 plan, and asked me whether I was healthy enough to return. I was very pleased to be able to return to the theater immediately to participate in the fighting, so I said that I was healthy enough to undertake that important mission. Brother Hien accepted my offer and told me to go to meet with Le Trong Tan, deputy chief of staff, the following night. As scheduled, I went to meet with brother Tan, who said, 'We need you to return to B2 immediately, and take instructions, regarding the 1975 plan and the intentions of the Military Commission of the party Central Committee. Pham Hung and Tran Van Tra are about to come north. But they have been sent a message telling them not to come, because you can return to report on the decisions that have been made up here. The 1975 plan does not call for large-scale fighting but for the conservation of weapons, ammunition, and forces, and for training, in order to await the 1976 opportunity.' Brothers Tan and Hien gave me a detailed briefing so that I could take mental notes and brief others when I returned. They told me to meet the following morning with Van Tien Dung, the chief of staff, to receive my mission and instructions.

"The next morning
*Maj Gen Lyong Van Nho
**Tran Van Tra
***From the archives of the B2 War Recapitulation Section of the Ministry of National Defense.

"The next morning I went to meet with brother Dung at the 'Dragon House,' at that time the offices of the Military Commission of the party Central Committee and the Ministry of National Defense in Hanoi. After inquiring about my health he asked whether I fully understood my mission. I reported that brothers Tan and Hien had briefed me in detail, and that I understood the mission. He asked me to repeat what I had been told to make certain that I understood everything. I repeated everything from beginning to end. The main contents were the following.

"I will return immediately with instructions for B2 from the General Staff. Brothers Hung and Tra would no longer have to come north.

"In 1975 we will not fight on a large scale, but will be concerned only with disrupting pacification in the Mekong Delta. In eastern Nam Bo, the main-force units will not fight on a large scale. B2 intends to attack Dong Xoai and Phuoc Long, but the General Staff disagrees. It should only fight on a small scale and take a few small positions on Route 14. This year it should fight on a small scale in order to conserve forces and await an opportunity. It should not use tanks and heavy artillery without the case-by-case approval of the General Staff.

"Brother Dung said, 'Your understanding is correct! It is necessary to conserve forces and await the opportunity. This year we will only fight in the delta and disrupt pacification. We are still very short on ammunition, especially heavy artillery shells. We should not fight on a large scale, then not have the forces to fight when the opportunity arises. You must understand that staff cadres such as yourself are responsible for making recommendations to the commander, and that the commander does not bear sole responsibility. So you now fully understand the opinions of the upper echelon. But I will compose a message going over the same points, so that brother Ba can sign it and send it to the B2 theater in advance.'

"I also took along that message from brother Ba (i.e. message No 491, referred to above in the message from Sau Nam to the General Staff) and delivered it to brothers Sau Nam and Hai Le."*

As it happened, Pham Hung and I, not having received that message, set out on the designated day and, fortunately, did not meet Hai Nha. If we had met him, perhaps we would have hesitated a little between continuing and returning. However, as early as mid-October we had recommended the holding of a meeting of the Political Bureau and all theaters in the South, so even if we had encountered Hai Nha and he had passed on to us those opinions of the Military Commission and told us not to go to Hanoi, I'm certain that we would have requested permission to continue our journey so that we could report directly our assessment and evaluation of the situation, based on the actual conditions in the theater, of COSVN and the Regional Military Party Committee, and to recommend an operational policy for 1975, in order to fulfill the 1975-1976

---

*"Sau Nam" was Le Duc Anh, deputy commander of the Regional Command. "Hai Le" was Le Van Tuong, deputy political officer of the Regional Command.

2-year plan. It is very important that the lower echelon report on the situation accurately and promptly, and recommend its opinions bravely and with a sense of responsibility. The upper echelon must do everything necessary to solicit the opinions of the lower echelon, listen closely to the opinions of all sides, and seriously and objectively analyze and consider in order to reach correct conclusions. To do so is to insure success. That has always been the truly democratic and centralized working method of the Political Bureau of the party Central Committee. We felt that we had a responsibility to go to Hanoi to accurately report on the situation.

So that our comrades back in the B2 theater could be at ease when guiding the activity phase we sent a message to COSVN and the Standing Committee of the Regional Military Party Committee that was signed by both Pham Hung and myself. It included the following passages:

"After a preliminary exchange of opinions with a number of comrades in the Political Bureau and the Central Military Party Committee, a high degree of unanimity was reached regarding the assessment and evaluation of the overall situation and the direction to be taken in the coming period. But more specifically, there are still many problems that we must continue to discuss, especially our dry season plan.

"We will recommend that our old plan for the Regional main-force units be left unchanged...."*

After learning that B2 was operating in accordance with the adjusted plan I sent back a guidance message (message No 567/ZK):

"...After Bu Dang and Bu Na, go all-out to take Dong Xoai which, although not a large position, will have both a campaign and strategic effect. The 7th Division may be used to attack Dong Xoai...."**

On 20 December 1974 brother Sau Nam sent a message reporting that "On Route 14 we have completely liberated the segment from bridge 11 near Dong Xoai to beyond Bu Dang on the border of the Kien Duc subsector.... At Bu Dang, Vinh Thien and Bu Na we captured four artillery pieces and 7,000 artillery shells, more than 3,000 weapons of the various kinds, and more than 300 POW's, and are continuing to track down others."***

On 27 December 1974 there was another message:

"...In order to avoid missing the opportunity for a campaign to win a big victory when conditions permit, we have readied a tank company to serve as a reserve force. On 26 December we wiped out the Dong Xoai strongpoint complex without using tanks."****

---

*Archives of the Committee to Recapitulate the War in the B2 Theater of the Ministry of National Defense.
**From archives of the B2 War Recapitulation Section of the Ministry of National Defense.
***Ibid.
****Ibid.

Immediately afterward we received the following message from Hoang Cam, commander at the Phuoc Long front:

"Group 301* to R,** copy to General Staff: Attacked Dong Xoai subsector at 0035 hours 26 December. By 0830 had taken all of Dong Xoai subsector."

-Nam Thach-***

Thus Route 14 within the sphere of responsibility of B2 had been completely liberated. Our rear area base and transportation corridor had been expanded. Although our attack plan had been changed and then changed again, and our forces had been deployed and redeployed, and we had to attack gradually and step-by-step, from a small scale to a large scale and more slowly than we had desired, the enemy troops still were incapable of reacting and did not send any infantry reinforcements, but were resigned to the loss of all three subsectors: Bu Dang, Dong Xoai, and, before that, Bu Dop which had been taken by a local battalion of the Phuoc Long Province unit. The enemy also sent in airplanes to strafe and bomb, but to no effect. The enemy troops remaining in Phuoc Long were perplexed and very shaken up. In view of that favorable situation we requested permission from brother Ba and the Military Commission of the party Central Committee to liberate all of Phuoc Long Province, as provided for by our old plan, should the opportunity arise. I expressed the opinion that our troops could fulfill that mission and said that I was certain that the enemy was incapable of sending strong reinforcements to Phuoc Long if it were attacked. I explained the campaign and strategic value of liberating Phuoc Long Province. After carefully weighing the situation, they agreed. I was delighted, but in order to insure victory I requested permission from brother Ba to use a company of tanks and a company of 130mm artillery. I promised that I would personally command the operation to insure success. He agreed. Phuoc Long was a mountain-region province with rough terrain. To the north and east of the provincial capital there were many high mountains, and the deep, swiftly flowing Be River flowed through those areas. To the west and south the land was more level, but at the southern gateway to the province was situated Mt. Ba Ra, the highest mountain in that area. It is 735 meters above sea level and had many rock cliffs, large boulders and green vegetation. The enemy had long ago set up on the peak of that mountain a wireless communications relay station and an observation post equipped with optical and electronic equipment capable of monitoring a large area. If necessary the enemy could use a regiment to use the complicated, dominating terrain of that mountain to strongly defend the Phuoc Long provincial capital. Because of the rough terrain of Mt. Ba Ra and of Phuoc Long Province, during the period of French domination the French colonialists used the Mt. Ba Ra area as a place for concentrating and keeping under surveillance the patriotic political activists. Many of our cadres and party members were detained there for many years, living apart from society, miserable and sick because of rampant malaria. They

---

*Forward HQ of the Regional Command.
**Code designation of the Regional Command.
***Hoang Cam.

included such women as Hai Soc Ba Diem, Nguyen Thi Luu, Nguyen Thi Dinh,* Hai Be An Giang, Hai Ninh Hau Giang, and many others. Five kilometers to the west of Mt. Ba Ra there was situated Phuoc Binh, a relatively bustling district seat. In Phuoc Binh there was an intersection of roads going to Bu Dop, Dong Xoai, the provincial capital, and to Route 14, at the Lieu Duc intersection. In Phuoc Binh there was also a relatively good Class-2 airfield, the province's air base, that was used for Phuoc Long Province and to support air force operations in that entire mountains-and-jungles area.

Because of the natural terrain of that mountain region province and the enemy's defensive deployments, if we were to attack and liberate Phuoc Long Province with our limited forces we had no other choice than to first take Dong Xoai in order to isolate all of the remaining troops in the province. We had to take, at any cost, the communications station and observation post on Mt. Ba Ra and the Phuoc Binh intersection and airfield. Only thereby could we punch through to the provincial capital and annihilate the enemy troops, whose defensive deployments relied on the rough and complicated terrain consisting of mountains, rivers, lakes and ponds.

We sent a message to the B2 Command to guide the development of the Dong Xoai victory by rapidly taking Mt. Ba Ra and the Phuoc Binh airfield and completely liberate Phuoc Long Province. I did not forget to mention that we had been authorized to use a tank company and a 130mm artillery company. I composed the message, signed it, and had the General Staff send it. But that afternoon, when sitting before a map, studying the enemy's deployments in Phuoc Long Province and envisioning how the enemy might react to our attack, comrade Le Ngoc Hien arrived. He handed me the message I had written and said that he had not yet sent it because I had stated that we had been authorized to use tanks and heavy artillery, which the upper echelon had forbidden us to do. I was a little perturbed, because I was afraid that that message, like the one a few days previously (instructing the B2 Command to implement the original dry season plan) would be received too late. To express my displeasure, I told comrade Hien that as a theater commander I should have the right to send a command message to my forces. I was not about to have my message censored and be forced to amend against my wishes. I had received permission to use heavy weapons and bore full responsibility. I requested him to send the message and told him that he would be responsible if it arrived late and we missed the opportunity.

Thus everything necessary to liberate Phuoc Long Province had been amicably agreed to. There was unanimity from top to bottom. Later, during discussions held to recapitulate the war, a number of cadres who did not understand the situation thought that the liberation of Phuoc Long Province along the lines of "peeling off layers of defense" from the outside in, from Bu Dang, Bu Na, Dong Xoai, Phuoc Binh, then the provincial capital, was a matter of fighting at first on a small scale and then on a large scale, that it differed from another method of using strong forces to strike at the center, at the enemy's

---

*Maj Gen Nguyen Thi Dinh, formerly deputy commander of the Regional Command whom the PLA cadres and men usually affectionately referred to as "Sister Ba." During the period of the 1960 simultaneous uprising she was secretary of the Be Tre Party Committee. At present she is chairman of the Vietnamese Women's Federation.

heart, and then attack from inside out, like a blossoming flower. That is an interesting description, but it is not in accordance with the truth. A lesson based on such a conclusion would have no value. Military strategy is a science. It cannot be understood by muddled thinking remote from reality. With regard to attacks on provincial capitals, there are hundreds of ways to attack hundreds of provincial capitals--a different method for each provincial capital--and not just two ways. The selection of a fighting method is not based on the subjective thinking of one person or another, but must be based on a series of specific factors: where is the provincial capital located, and what are its campaign and strategic positions in the enemy's defensive system? What key objectives must be taken to liberate that provincial capital? How are those objectives distributed on the battlefield? What are the fortifications and forces defending it? What are the terrain and vegetation of the provincial capital? Where will the enemy troops make their stand? Where will the enemy reinforcements originate and by what facilities will they be brought in? What are the scale and capabilities of our forces in all regards? What are the staging area, approach route, etc? Even by asking such simple questions it is evident that the selection of a fighting method must be based on the actualities of space and time, and on our situation and that of the enemy; we cannot sit and think about an existing fighting method then automatically apply it to a provincial capital, making adjustments as we go. The skill of a commander is demonstrated in his ability to grasp the actual situation, and accurately analyze the enemy's situation, our situation, the terrain, the important objectives, and the opportunity that is to be created or already exists, in order to make a decision that is appropriate, creative, and leads to victory. That is not to mention the developments, the factors which arise every minute and every second and must be dealt with. Often battles in fact end in a way unlike that envisioned in the original plan. Sometimes a plan is very good but the person in direct command of the attacking unit makes a mistake in dealing with a complicated development, or deals correctly with a disadvantageous situation, with the result that the battle ends in a very different way. In making recapitulations it is necessary to the objective historical truth to make an accurate analysis, in order to learn valuable lessons.

Thus prior to the Political Bureau conference our delegation, representing B2, had endeavored to report on and discuss our position and won the approval of the Political Bureau and party Central Committee for the dry season plan B2 had drafted on the basis of unanimity in evaluating our actual situation and that of the enemy. We had been authorized to attack Dong Xoai and Phuoc Long. On 22 December Pham Hung sent a message to the Standing Committee of COSVN which included the following contents.

"1. The opinions brought back by Hai Nha reached B2 before we had arrived at our destination. During our work sessions it was decided that the 1975 plan envisioned to COSVN and prepared after the June 1974 conference is entirely correct. You must oversee, and closely monitor and guide its implementation, especially during the present dry season phase. We and the others here are very pleased over the results of the first phase of the dry season. Because of the developing situation you considered things carefully and made rational, timely changes, but the 1975 plan remains essentially as we drafted it. If we are able to fulfill the 1975 plan, especially during the present dry season,

In the second phase of the dry season campaign there will be coordination among the theaters, which will be the best way to insure the fulfillment of our dry season plan and does not represent a major change."*

On 29 December, Pham Hung and I signed the following message to the Regional Military Party Committee and the COSVN Standing Committee:

"1. The situation at the beginning of the dry season in our theater is that the localities and units have endeavored to win victory and have achieved rather good results, although some places are still not up to par. We are very pleased and are confident that we have many good prospects for attaining and surpassing the plan if the various echelons firmly grasp the situation, are not subjective and complacent, and are prepared to overcome difficulties in order to win greater victories. We will thereby have a solid basis for the coming phases, in correct accordance with the strategic design. Those of us here are very pleased and are endeavoring to guide all aspects so that the plan can be carried out well..

"2. ....

"Because of the decision to win a bigger victory this year and create conditions for the coming period, our aid plan has been adjusted. We have been authorized the full amount we requested--27,000 tons--not the 11,000 tons reported earlier. We are now discussing and arranging transportation. Thus you should study the truly appropriate and economical use of those supplies, and pay attention to increasing supplies to the military regions and to using them well, accompanied by utmost economizing...."**

During the period prior to the Political Bureau meeting I had the time and the opportunity to meet with a number of cadres I knew who worked with the Ministry of National Defense and the General Staff. Because of the nature of their missions they monitored the situation on the battlefield on a daily basis and also know the latest news about me. To meet and chat with them was a rare opportunity. We discussed with one another everything from what was going on in the capital to what was going on in our theater, so we could not escape talking about our work. Some responsible cadres informed me about the General Staff's plan to attack Duc Lap and extend our transportation corridor. It would use three main-force divisions of the B3 theater and the General Staff, reinforced by a tank battalion and a battalion of 130mm artillery. It was certain that the strategic corridor would be extended and that the B2 theater could be supplied more easily and rapidly. The B3 staff and comrade Vu Lang were enroute to study the battlefield and make preparations in all regards. I asked why it was necessary to use three divisions, tanks and heavy artillery to take Duc Lap, which was merely an isolated subsector, and a few small positions on Route 14.

---

*Archives of the B2 War Recapitulation Section of the Ministry of National Defense.
**Ibid.

They replied that the objective was not only to take Duc Lap and a few small positions but also to draw in the enemy in order to inflict losses--perhaps large losses--on them. We would take the initiative by selecting the battlefield and drawing in the enemy in order to inflict large losses on them, as well as extending our corridor.

I expressed to those comrades my opinion that the terrain around Duc Lap was rough and restricting, that Route 14 passes between relatively high mountains and there was thick vegetation, so the enemy would not be so stupid as to send forces there so we could annihilate them. Would not the enemy react mainly by using their air force to strafe and bomb our formations? Furthermore, at that time the enemy realized that they needed their forces for much more important objectives than distant, remote Duc Lap. Although we needed Duc Lap to extend our strategic corridor, it did not have much bearing on the enemy's strategic defense plan for South Vietnam as a whole. If we were going to send such strong forces there, why not strike directly at Ban Me Thuot instead of attacking Duc Lap? If we liberated Ban Me Thuot, we would take an objective of campaign and strategic importance and shake the entire Central Highlands. Our corridor would automatically be extended and solidified. Such forces would be sufficient to attack Ban Me Thuot, where the enemy was vulnerable and which it regarded as a rear area divisional and regimental base. Although the province was large and the terrain was advantageous, it was weakly defended, the enemy had few forces there and, especially, the enemy would not suspect that we would send such large forces there and attack Ban Me Thuot. Furthermore, such a move would be appropriate to the present strategic phase of the war, in which we had to launch large-scale attacks to annihilate the enemy and liberate land, and to create a major opportunity. We were no longer in a period of extending our strategic corridor.

They argued as follows:

That matter required further discussion, but if the time had come to launch a large-scale Central Highlands campaign more than those forces would be required. The General Staff was drafting such a plan. We would use large, overwhelming forces and begin with a direct attack on Kontum, annihilating the enemy and liberating that province. Then we would immediately attack the headquarters of the puppet II Corps at Pleiku. We would wipe out the 22d and 23d Divisions and the puppet forces there and liberate the entire Central Highlands. By beginning with an attack on Kontum we would have favorable conditions, for it was adjacent to our vast liberated base, road network and 559 supply depots, which were sufficient to support the campaign. We had many favorable conditions for concentrating large forces and using all kinds of technical equipment.

I disagreed. I smiled and said in a pleasant voice, "You are indeed soldiers of the king. You have fought, and always think about fighting, with plentiful forces, weapons and ammunition. That is far different from us, poor soldiers on a distant, difficult battlefield who count every bullet and are very envious of you. So that is why Le Ngoc Hien the other day reported to the General Staff that in 1972 there were consumed in South Vietnam as a whole 220,000 heavy artillery shells, and that Quang Tri alone consumed 150,000 of them!

I think that to attack Kontum and Pleiku is to attack where the enemy is strongest. They have built up their forces over a long period of time. To do so would be to fight the enemy on their terms. The enemy has long predicted that we would attack Kontum so it has concentrated its forces and attention there. Although we were capable of concentrating large forces and preparing all necessary conditions, the enemy was on guard and we would not have an easy time of it. But to attack Ban Me Thuot would be to completely surprise the enemy and to attack the enemy's undefended rear. They would be quickly annihilated and disintegrated and we would not have to use large forces. If their rear area was taken, the enemy in the forward area would be perplexed and shaken. Ban Me Thuot was an important strategic position, for the large "Hoa Binh" airfield was located there, strategic Route 21 connected Ban Me Thuot with Ninh Hoa and Nha Trang, and beyond Ban Me Thuot lay Gia Nghia and Dalat, so if Ban Me Thuot were lost the entire puppet II Corps in the Central Highlands would have at its disposal only Route 19, which passed through rugged mountainous terrain and was easily cut, and only the Pleiku airfield would be left for receiving supplies and reinforcements. The other routes, such as No 5 and No 7, also passed through mountainous terrain and there were many bridges, which were very weak, and it was not certain that they could handle the traffic, especially mechanized equipment. If we cut off those roads, it was certain that hundreds of thousands of people and the enemy's technical equipment would be endangered and could not be rescued. I compared the effect of attacking and taking Ban Me Thuot on the remaining Central Highlands provinces to chopping down a large tree at its base: all of its branches and the trunk would have to fall. Only such an attack would be an effective campaign and strategic blow which would afford us a certain victory and a big victory.

I reported that conversation to Pham Hung and Hai Van and discussed the situation with them in detail. It was my belief that an attack on Ban Me Thuot would have strategic significance in the present phase of the war and that it must be considered. They agreed that we should abandon Duc Lap and launch an attack directly against Ban Me Thuot. We recommended that Pham Hung discuss the matter with the comrades in the Political Bureau.

On 18 December 1974 a joint meeting of the Political Bureau and the Military Commission of the party Central Committee, attended by representatives of the theaters in South Vietnam, began in an atmosphere of victory which had spread from the B2 theater. By that time the entire B2 theater had begun the first phase of the dry season and had won many victories. In the Mekong Delta the enemy's pacification plan had been shattered. We had liberated many villages and hamlets and expanded the rural liberated areas at Tieu Can, Tra Cu, Cau Ke, and Duyen Hai in Tra Vinh, Mo Cay and Giong Thom in Ben Tre. We had liberated the Hung Long subsector in the Hau Giang area and the Tuyen Nhon district seat in the Tien Giang area. That was the first time we had taken and held a subsector and district seat. We had wiped out a battalion, and inflicted heavy losses on three other battalions, of the puppet 21st Division reaction force sent to Hung Long. We had mastered segments of the Ong Doc, Cai Tau and Bay Hap Rivers in Ca Mau, the Xa No Canal in Can Tho, the Co Co River in the My Tu District of Soc Trang Province, the Vam Co Tay River in Kien Tuong, etc. In eastern Nam Bo we had liberated Route 14 north of Dong

Xoai, taken the Lo O-Mt. Giam high point, liberated a number of villages in order to isolate the Hoai Duc and Tanh Linh district seats in Binh Tuy Province, surrounded the Mt. Ba Den position, and wiped out a number of enemy outposts in Tay Ninh Province. In the outskirts of Saigon, the forces of the Saigon provincial unit, along with the sappers, had stepped up their activities against the enemy, overran outposts, created enclaves in the Cu Chi, Hoc Mon, Go Vap, Binh Chanh, southern Thu Duc, Long Thanh, and Nhon Trach area, and shelled and interdicted the Bien Hoa air base. Only 2 weeks into the dry season in the B2 theater good results had been attained in annihilating the enemy and liberating areas, and in popular uprisings to achieve mastery, which indicated the resounding victories that were to come and the clear decline of the puppets. Those actual developments on the battlefield said more than any reports or interesting theories.

The conference concentrated on discussing the 1975-1976 2-year strategic plan to complete the national democratic revolution which the Political Bureau had posed during the rainy season. COSVN and the Regional Military Party Committee (i.e. the B2 theater) had also discussed that plan since our regular session held to review the situation during the first 6 months of 1974. The foresight of the supreme leadership and the thoughts of the lower echelon of a typical battlefield coincided. Theory and practice were in synchronization. But the specific developmental process, the steps that were to be taken, and the measures that were to be applied required much more discussion if unanimity was to be achieved. That was inevitable. If everyone agreed readily to a proposal or if there were no differing opinions, that would be proof of a pitiful poverty of intelligence and thought.

At the beginning of the conference the representatives of the B2 theater and Military Region 5 reported on our situation and that of the enemy, on the actual situation on the battlefield, on the direction and prospects of their future activities, and on their recommendations and requirements. For B2's part, we presented a succinct briefing on developments since Resolution 21 of the party Central Committee, during the dry season--and then the rainy season-- of 1974 and the specific results in the Mekong Delta, in military Region 6 and 7, and in Saigon itself. I reported in detail on our objective of preventing the Saigon puppets from strengthening their defense lines and from being able to withdraw into an enclave in the future, by activities in the Route 7-Ben Cat area and by liberating Rach Bap. We brought the conference up to date on the development of our political and military forces, especially the organization and deployment in the outskirts of and inside Saigon, which formed a tight encirclement of the puppet capital. We reported on COSVN's assessment and evaluation of the recent situation and the new factors that had appeared, and concluded that we were strong and on the rise and the enemy was weak and on the decline. We reported especially on the 1975 dry season: we had to attack strongly and win big victories all over South Vietnam in order to victoriously conclude the war in 1976. Finally, we did not forget to recommend that B2 be provided additional materiel, weapons and personnel--requests to which COSVN had agreed--first of all a main-force division at the beginning of the 1975 dry season in order to strengthen the 4th Corps. We recommended that a plan be drafted to coordinate the activities of all theaters in South Vietnam, and that the High Command order the organization of a strong strategic reserve force in order to promptly win a decisive victory when the opportunity arose in the main theater. We recommended that since the eastern Nam Bo battlefield, which included Saigon, was one on which large numbers of the enemy would be annihilated and on which the war would be concluded, and the reserve force would surely be used there, it should be deployed immediately in the Central Highlands so that it could act promptly when necessary. We emphasized that our 1975 operational plan was based on the results that were attained in 1974, and on a situation which had developed in a manner extremely advantageous to us, and that its guiding principle was that we must rapidly and continually develop our attack and place the enemy in peril. We must not hold back, lest we miss the opportunity.

After the various theaters reported, comrade Le Ngoc Hien, on behalf of the General Staff, presented a briefing on the 1975 operational plan. The plan was based on the assessment that the enemy had to remain on the passive defensive and try to defend what places it could defend. They had weakened organizationally and with regard to morale. We were winning victories but still had deficiencies and weaknesses. The plan set forth a whole series of norms for the battlefields with regard to liberating land and people; annihilating and routing the enemy; decreasing their troop strength, and preventing them from making up their losses; wiping out the enemy's material-technical reserves, etc. The plan included provisions regarding the building up of our forces during the year, the creation of unimpeded corridors, and materiel reserves and rear-area services in the various areas. In 1975 we had to do a truly good job of completing all preparatory tasks in order to insure that we could fight on a large scale and that the General Offensive and General Uprising would be victorious in 1976.

He reported in detail on the current status of our military forces on the battlefield and at the central level, and on the quantity of technical equipment and ammunition available in the various areas and in reserve and their planned allocation and use on the battlefields during the 2-year period. With regard to heavy artillery shells, he reported that of the total on hand (100 percent), more than 10 percent would be used in 1975, 45 percent would be used in 1976, and the remainder, nearly 45 percent, would be kept in reserve.

Thus as it began its deliberations the conference had been fully briefed on the battlefield situation and had been briefed on the 2-year plan and the 1975 plan by the General Staff and the battlefields. The conference debated in an atmosphere of vigor and enthusiasm. I don't know what the others were thinking, but I was moved beyond words. That conference would determine the conclusion of the nation's 30-year war. Had there been any other people who had to take up arms and endure terrible death and destruction over a period of 30 long years of bitter, endless struggle, as had the Vietnamese people? In our war against the United States to liberate and unify the homeland there were many instances of three generations—grandfathers, fathers and sons—rushing to the front, sometimes in the same unit. There were many instances of whole families or groups of families being killed by the bombs and shells of the enemy during sweeping operations. And in our country there is practically no family, from Hoang Lien Son and Cao Lang to the Ca Mau Peninsula, Phu Quoc, and Co Dao, which has not lost at least one member. We had endured countless sacrifices and hardships for that day, the day that would determine a glorious feature. What a heavy responsibility we had! Every thought and every opinion expressed during the conference seemed to bear the weight of 4,000 years of history, of tens of thousands of sorrowful burdens, and to be watched by millions of pairs of eyes of the Vietnamese people, the oppressed people of the world, and our friends in all five continents. Many of the comrades spoke enthusiastically, and some spoke many times.

Everything evolved around our assessment and evaluation of the situation at home and abroad. If we attacked strongly, how would the puppets react? What would the United States do? Would it dare intervene, or did it have other schemes and plots? What were the best revolutioary methods we could apply? What steps should be taken during the 2-year period? How about 1975? And 1976? Two years of fierce fighting would not be brief, but they would be the last 2 years of more than 30 difficult years, so the end seemed so near. When concluding the conference, brother Ba said, "Prepare yourselves: 2 years are short but sometimes they can be long." And when expressing his opinions, brother [Pham Van] Dong said, "When will the puppets collapse? We may not have to wait until 1976. It may come quickly, and not gradually." [Vo Nguyen] Giap and many others stressed, "The decision to complete the national democratic revolution in the 1975-1976 2-year period is correct. But our planning must provide for the contingency that it could end in 1975, or perhaps not until 1977. Only then can we be prepared to take the initiative."

Pham Van Dong paced back and forth, thinking and then stopping to express an opinion, his face always rosy, his voice firm. He said, "In evaluating the enemy, we must answer a few questions, but without thinking in an outmoded way. We are in a new phase. The United States has withdrawn its troops in accordance with the Paris Agreement, which it regards as a victory after suffering many defeats with no way out. Now, there is no way that they could intervene again by sending in troops. They may provide air and naval support, but that cannot decide victory or defeat." Then he laughingly said, "I'm kidding, but also telling the truth, when I say that the Americans would not come back even if you offered them candy." Everyone laughed in delight. He continued, "For our part, the most important factor is that a revolutionary movement has arisen in the south. It is very new, and is both military and political. Military violence at the highest level is accompanied by political violence. Both Military Region 8 and Military Region 9 have reported thusly, which is very good. The situation will develop very rapidly. Truong Chinh arose, put on his glasses, glanced at a notebook he was holding in his hand, and began to speak in a solemn voice. He was always like that. He was always careful, as if not wanting to make even a small mistake. He paid attention to each word and comma in his articles. His speeches always had a beginning, a main part, and a conclusion. I did not take notes, but will here mention only a few of his ideas. He said, "The enemy is under pressure from three sources: our military attacks, the military struggle of the masses, and economic-technical difficulties. Therefore the enemy has weakened very rapidly. The enemy army has not been able to resolve the contradiction between holding on to land and people and fighting a war of mobility. But it is still viable, had not yet suffered heavy losses, and can still obtain recruits. It still receives large amounts of U.S. aid and holds the important strategic roads. For our part, we have grown stronger in all regards. We have the initiative on the battlefield. In 1974 we fulfilled our plan. If we can also take Phuoc Long, that will be eloquent proof that we have become much stronger. The enemy has the tendency to form defensive enclaves. It will be difficult for us to prevent them from withdrawing into enclaves around the large cities. It will be difficult for us to attack the enemy once they have withdrawn into large, fortified enclaves, and attacks on cities are very complicated. Will the United States step in? In fact, it still has 25,000 military advisers in civilian clothing. If the United States senses danger it will intervene, but it will be difficult for them to intervene with infantry and their use of air and naval forces must be circumspect and limited. We must create conditions for striking a strategic annihilating blow, but we must not limit ourselves to just one annihilating blow."

Every day news was received of victories in the B2 theater. Most encouraging was the news from Tra Vinh, a delta province and a principal focus of the first phase of the dry season, that we had annihilated many of the enemy, overrun many outposts, and liberated many villages and many people. Everyone attending the conference, especially, of course, the B2 delegates, were very pleased. The actual events on the battlefield had verified our evaluation of the situation as if the soldiers and people of that distant battlefield were particularly directed in the discussions at that conference. When making his speech, Le Duc Tho presented the following evidence: "In December our forces in the Mekong Delta eliminated more than 500 enemy positions and in a period of only a month attained 70 percent of the norm for the 6-months-long dry season.... In eastern Nam Bo, we have taken all of Tanh Linh District and a number of villages in Hoa Duc District in Binh Tuy Province. In Tay Ninh we have surrounded the Mt. Ba Den base and wiped out a battalion of the 49th Regiment of the puppets' 25th Division. In Phuoc Long Province we have taken the Phuoc Binh airfield and subsector and Mt. Ba Ra, and are now attacking the city." Everyone attending the conference was anxious to learn the results of the Phuoc Long battle. Suddenly, one day, while we were in session, a comrade from the Operations Section of the General Staff, brought and read a message from the battlefield which reported that "Because the enemy has sent in the 81st Airborne Ranger Brigade to reinforce the city and have put up a stiff resistance, we have temporarily withdrawn our troops to reorganize and study the situation before resuming the attack." I was astonished and unbelieving. I was sitting almost opposite brother Ba who, after he had listened to the reading of the message, looked directly at me as if to ask why. I had requested permission to attack Phuoc Long and to use some heavy artillery and tanks. I had assured him that we were certain to win a victory and that the enemy could not reinforce the city. If we failed to take the Phuoc Long provincial capital, it would be difficult to conclude that my other evaluations were correct. The operational ability of our main-force troops in eastern Nam Bo would clearly have been proven to still be very low. Actual results on the battlefield are the most accurate yardstick for measuring the level and leadership-command ability of the cadres and the fighting effectiveness of the armed forces. But I still thought that the situation was not that way at all, and still had confidence in the B2 troops and cadres and was certain that Phuoc Long would be liberated.

There was a basis for my confidence. I had lived with the B2 main-force troops from the time of the formation of the first battalions and regiments more than a decade ago. I had contributed my small part by looking after each cadre and weapon, and being concerned with training and combat, during one period after another and onto the present time. I had participated with them in nearly all of the important campaigns in the B2 theater. I understood them as I understood myself and had as much confidence in them as I did in myself. I regretted that I could not be present to share the hardships with them in that strategic battle for Phuoc Long. But I always believed that with me or without me they would be what they were: resolute and determined-to-win main-force units.

How about the command cadres? A unit is no better than its cadres, people who had become steeled and had come of age in the course of hundreds of large and small battles, and most of whom served in two resistance war periods. I had assigned them very difficult missions, given them extremely strict orders, and shared with them difficult, dangerous moments as well as glorious victories. I based my thoughts and actions on them. Each of my lower-echelon cadres who fell represented the loss of part of my body and soul. Until the day I die I will never be able to erase the image of comrade Tran Dinh Xu, a commander who was calm and steadfast under all circumstances and who sacrificed his life heroically while serving as the commander of the Saigon Special Zone in 1969, or of comrade Nguyen The Truyen, a very brave division commander who entered the puppet capital during Tet Mau Than in 1968 and later died during the fierce fighting in the outskirts. Nor could I forget comrade Nguyen Van Nho (Hai Nho), from Tan An, who was a resolute old guerrilla who participated in the Nam Ky uprising in 1940. He disregarded all hardships and dangers. In 1968 he set up his headquarters on Route 1 near Ba Queo to command the troops attacking Tan Son Nhat airfield from the west. He sacrificed his life heroically in 1969 while serving as the deputy commander of Military Region 8. There were many other such cadres. The person directly commanding the Phuoc Long battle was comrade Hoang Cam, who had been the commander of the first division formed in the B2 theater and who was now the corps commander. Over a long period of combat he and his unit had fulfilled even the most difficult missions assigned them. The person who had replaced me as regional commander, comrade Le Duc Anh, had many times served as my chief of staff. In 1973, while serving as commander of Military Region 9, he resolutely retaliated against the enemy and won glorious victories. The other cadres who were then on the battlefield were also resolute cadres who had passed many challenges. I was able to evaluate their capabilities and deficiencies, so my confidence was well founded.

I knew that our first attack to liberate an entire province, with complicated terrain and strong defensive works, would not be easy and that there would be difficult moments and that the battle would ebb and flow. But the ultimate result would be that our men would win. Convinced of that, I calmly expressed my opinion to the conference that once we had taken Phuoc Binh and Mt. Ba Ra the enemy could not make a stand in the city for long and it was certain that they could not send large numbers of troops there. I was still confident that our troops would take Phuoc Long within the next few days. I immediately sent a message to the theater inquiring about how the battle was really going and stating that it was necessary to send in sufficient reinforcements to overwhelm the city. The next day we received a message from the B2 Command stating that our troops had not been withdrawn, but that there had been an erroneous report from a cadre at the front, and that the independent 16th Regiment and the 2d Regiment of the 9th Division were being added to our forces in order to annihilate the enemy troops in the city. I felt relieved. Before brother Ba concluded the conference we received the following message from the B2 theater: "During the afternoon of 6 January 1975 our troops eliminated all of the pockets of resistance that the enemy had retaken on 5 January by using 250 airborne rangers who had just been sent in.... Our policy is to continue to mop-up the enemy remnants defending the city and in the rest of the province. If the enemy launch a counterattack, we will annihilate each enemy regiment and division, both those sent in by air and those arriving by road. We will create conditions for our attacks in areas that threaten the enemy, hold down our losses to a minimum, and protect the lives and property of the people." We also received a message from the B2 Staff: "During the early morning of 3 January we launched an all-out attack on the Phuoc Long subsector and city, and by 1530 hours on 6 January we had killed or captured all of the enemy troops and completely liberated Phuoc Long Province."* I sighed a sigh of relief and was liberated from all of my worries of the past few days.

The news that we had completely taken Phuoc Long City arrived while we were in session. Everyone jubilantly stood up and shook hands with one another to celebrate the victory. The B2 delegates were not the only ones whose hands were shaken. That showed that the victory had a common significance, not just for the B2 theater. It signified something about the fighting capabilities of our army and the weakness of the enemy army. A new page of history had been turned and a new phase had begun. No one directly expressed what he was thinking, but facial expressions and mannerisms said more than words, and everyone seemed to be in agreement. After several minutes, everyone returned to their seats. Brother Ba said, "For the first time a province in South Vietnam has been completely liberated. That province, furthermore, is near Saigon and we have expanded our important base area in eastern Nam Bo. That event reflects more clearly than anything else our capability and the reaction of the puppets, and especially of the United States." Everyone expressed agreement with and approval of that statement. Did the cadres and men who participated in the battle of Phuoc Long--the 7th Division, the 3d Division, the 9th Division, the sappers, and the local forces, guerrillas, and people in Phuoc Long--especially the comrades who fell there, understand the value of their feat of arms? Did they know that they and the soldiers and people of the Mekong Delta, by their actions during Phase 1 of the dry season, and not our B2 delegation, had reported most specifically and eloquently about the actual situations of ourselves and the enemy in the present strategic phase of the war to the Political Bureau of our party Central Committee, which is the supreme revolutionary leadership organ and determines all victories of the revolution. I sent back a message lauding the victory, but could not fully describe the scene at the conference and my own emotions.

---

*Archives of the B2 War Recapitulation Section of the Ministry of National Defense.

What was the enemy's assessment of the Phuoc Long affair? According to the U.S. study "The Collapse of South Vietnam," "The report thereafter tried to outline the collapse of that 'hard defense line' structure, beginning with the loss of the Phuoc Long provincial capital on 6 January 1975. According to many respondents, the loss of that city meant that South Vietnam had begun to disintegrate...."

Buu Vien regarded the loss of that province as having an important significance.

"To test the resolve of the armed forces of the Republic of Vietnam, and especially to probe the reaction of the U.S. Government, the truth is that the communists selected an easy objective. The loss of Phuoc Long had a great significance. It was the first time in the history of the Vietnam war that a province had fallen to the communists."

Immediately after Phuoc Long was lost, what did the Americans and puppets in Saigon think and do, and what did the puppet generals think? Duong Hao, in his book "A Tragic Chapter [Mot Chuong Bi Tham], published by our People's Army Publishing House in 1980, wrote that:

"Later, when relating the consequences of the Phuoc Long defeat, Col Pham Ba Hoa, chief of staff of the puppets' Logistics General Department, said that "The frantic days of the fighting at Phuoc Long were tense days for all officers at the GHQ of the puppet army, especially after Phuoc Long fell. It may be said that all of us were stunned. An atmosphere of worry enveloped everything, and grief pressed heavily on everyone. Grief not only because of the defeat at the very gateway to Saigon, but also because the loss of Phuoc Long resulted in large losses: 6,000 to 7,000 troops killed or routed.

"The main factor was that the Phuoc Long defeat reflected the position and strength of the ARVN forces. They were attacked at only one place but didn't have enough forces left to cope with the attack, so what would happen if they were attacked in many places? Phuoc Long was an event that demonstrated quite clearly the effectiveness of the 'Vietnamization' strategy that had been carried out during the past 6 years. In the past, the ARVN was able to escape from many perilous situations because it was saved by U.S. aid. The United States supplied all kinds of equipment to make up for losses and provided powerful fire support, even infantry support, so that the ARVN could have the strength to resist. Now, after the painful defeat and the loss of a province, the United States did nothing, although Mr Thieu often met with Martin to request intervention by the United States. The Ministry of Foreign Affairs of the Republic of Vietnam also sent an official diplomatic note, then General Khuyen held a conversation with Smith (head of the DAO). All of those efforts amounted to nothing.

"That situation made us extremely confused and pessimistic. It may be said that Phuoc Long was a test of strength between the two sides and that the result was evident."

The conference continued. Le Thanh Nghi, as was his custom, spoke softly and slowly; regardless of the attitude expressed by those around him, he continued to speak until he had said all that he wanted to say. After analyzing the situation he commented on the plan, and emphasized that additional forces should be sent to the B2 theater, the sooner the better. There had to be general strategic reserves and reserves for each of the important theaters. But how could the corps making up the general reserves be sent to the main theater in time if it is kept in the north? Le Duc Tho stressed that it is necessary to pay adequate attention to coordinating the three fists. Only if we attacked strongly and won big victories in 1975 could we be in a better position in 1976. Van Tien Dung said that forces could not be sent immediately, that it was necessary to build up our forces and give them combat training, then there were the problems of materiel and rear services, roads, etc. Furthermore, additional forces could not be sent to the B2 theater until the Central Highlands campaign was over, and no other divisions were available. The 316th Division could not be sent to eastern Nam Bo until May 1975. Upon hearing that brother Ba looked at us and said, "We fight in our own way, which is to combine the political, military and strategic fists. Otherwise we cannot be victorious. Because of the common difficulties, a few months' delay won't hurt anything. We must not disrupt the Central Highlands plan." I remained silent but I said to myself: we'll continue to fight in the way popularly known as "having the right ratio of rice and fish," i.e. no matter how many forces we had we would use them in the most appropriate way. But we were determined to win a big victory.

On 8 January 1975 brother Ba concluded the conference. To paraphrase him, he said, "The conference included the participation of Military Region 5 and Nam Bo, and it is very encouraging that there was a high degree of unanimity and determination to complete the democratic national revolution in the 1975-1976 2-year period, as proposed by the Political Bureau. We have thought a good deal and discussed a good deal, and we have reached a higher degree of unanimity among the battlefield commanders.

--In 1959-60 the mass movement was very strong but our military forces didn't amount to much.

--While fighting the United States we were strong militarily but the enemy used all barbarous methods to suppress the masses.

--Now we are stronger both militarily and politically, so we are capable of creating combined strength.

"Therefore, it is necessary to grasp even more firmly the laws of revolutionary war and the mass revolutionary movement. They are one in the same....

"At present we have the initiative on the battlefield in winning control of the people and the right of mastery. We have created an integrated strategic position extending from Tri Thien to Nam Bo, and on to the Mekong Delta. We have created very strong and mobile main-force fists. We have created such fists in the Mekong Delta as Military Regions 9 and 8, which are continuing to develop. We have created an overwhelming staging area around Saigon, which is a very great strategic advantage. A mass movement has begun to arise in the cities. Those things prove that we are strong. On the basis of those strengths, we are preparing to carry out our 2-year plan.

"The puppets are on the decline in all ways, militarily, politically and economically, because of our attacks and because of their inherent weaknesses.

"How about the United States? It has suffered many defeats, including the defeat of its global strategy. After it became involved in Vietnam, the United States became weaker and found itself endangered. If it returns now, it will lose everything. Even so, we must be on guard. The United States might use its air and naval forces to a certain degree. If we do not attack strongly and rapidly, but prolong our attacks, the United States will intervene to a certain extent to save the puppets from total defeat.

"But something that must be stressed is that even if the United States intervenes we are still determined to fight and are still determined to liberate the south and unify the homeland, for the simple reason that we do not want to be enslaved and lose our country. We want freedom, independence and unification.

"Our revolutionary guidelines and methods are as follows:

"Attacking and uprising, uprising and attacking, the three offensive spearheads, the three strategic areas, annihilate and achieve mastery, achieve mastery and annihilate, and advancing to a general offensive and general uprising.

"What must we do in 1975?:

"--The eastern Nam Bo main-force units must win a clear-cut victory in the Nam Bo lowlands in order to create an integrated liberated area from eastern Nam Bo to the Mekong Delta. We must liberate more rural areas and liberate more people. We must tighten our encirclement around Saigon and wipe out the puppet main-force units defending Saigon, so that even greater pressure can be exerted on Saigon. We must enable each locality to become stronger and fulfill their missions and be sufficiently strong to take advantage of the opportunity. We must strike a strong blow in the Central Highlands, and attack Ban Me Thuot. Military Region 5 must pay attention to the Binh Dinh, Da Nang-Tri Thien and Hue areas.

"We must take subsectors and district seats and then take district seats and cities.

"Only if we can accomplish those things in 1975 can we achieve our objectives in 1976, so 1976 will be a result of 1975.

"We still have difficulties, but we are determined to overcome them in order to advance to fulfilling our missions. For the sake of national independence, socialism, and peace in Southeast Asia and the world, we must win a complete victory. We have a responsibility to our people and to the people of the entire world."

When concluding the conference, brother Ba did not mention what decision had been made about the attack on Ban Me Thuot. I thought that perhaps he was leaving that decision up to the Military Commission of the party Central Committee prior to that. I had the opportunity to explain to him that in order to liberate all of Phuoc Long Province, which had complicated terrain and which the enemy paid attention to defending, B2 used a total of two divisions, in combination with the local forces. Those two divisions were under strength and had been formed by combining independent regiments. They were not strong units and they were supported by very few heavy artillery pieces and tanks, but we were able to fight over a prolonged period and launch one attack after another, even after we had lost the element of surprise. If we attacked Ban Me Thuot, we would have three divisions and strong tank and heavy artillery forces, so we were certain to win a victory.

After the conference I was extremely enthusiastic and confident. It was now only a matter of waiting and hoping that the Military Commission would decide whether or not to attack Ban Me Thuot so that we would have a basis on which to draft B2's plan for the second phase of the dry season, for the decision about whether or not to attack Ban Me Thuot would affect all theaters in the south. I believed that if we attacked Ban Me Thuot the pace of the war would be greatly accelerated. Thus the B2 plan had to be well coordinated or we could not promptly take advantage of the situation. I decided to find out about that before returning to the B2 theater.

On 15 January our delegation met with brother Ba to receive our final instructions. This time he went into very specific detail about the fighting methods, the annihilation of enemy units, and the depletion of their reserves. With regard to the deployment of our forces in the Saigon area, our commandos and sappers had to be strong. He continued to stress the necessity of combined forces and a combined strategy. He spoke about the nature of the main-force fist, the lowlands fist and especially the cities. He said that it was necessary to pay all-out attention to the mass movement, which had to become a high tide, the spearheads of which were the women, youths, middle school students, college students and trade union members. In political leadership and guidance in Saigon we had to be very alert for the political situation changed very rapidly, every day and every hour, so we had to be resolute and acute as was Lenin.

It was difficult to win political power, but it was a hundred times more difficult to maintain political power so we had to begin to think about that problem immediately. We had to be determined and be confident of winning big victories in 1975.

On 20 January we met with Le Duc Tho so that he could give us additional advice about a number of matters. He said, "Our leadership and guidance experience has always been to evaluate fully the enemy and ourselves. Then he told us that a decision had been made about Ban Me Thuot. He said, "I attended the regular meeting of the Military Commission and informed it of the Political Bureau's decision to attack Ban Me Thuot. The Commission only received the order, and did not further discuss it."

In his book "The Great Spring Victory," Senior General Van Tien Dung wrote that "Just after the meeting began comrade Le Duc Tho suddenly opened the door, entered and sat down. We were aware that the Political Bureau was not satisfied when it saw that the decision to attack Ban Me Thuot was not yet an explicit content of the operational plan. Thus comrade Le Duc Tho came to emphasize to us that it was necessary to attack Ban Me Thuot. He said very emotionally, "We absolutely must liberate Ban Me Thuot. We have nearly five divisions in the Central Highlands, so surely we can take Ban Me Thuot."

We were very pleased by that decision and thereafter we continually thought about the possible developments in South Vietnam as a whole and how to draft the B2 operational plan so that we could coordinate activities in the delta, in eastern Nam Bo and in Saigon. It was certain that we would have to run and could not take our time. I remembered brother Ba's unforgettable expression during an urgent period of the war, "We must run while forming ranks and not wait until we form ranks before running."

On 24 January 1975 our delegation set out to return to the B2 theater, full of animation and excitement. I could not stop thinking about the objectives we had to attack and on how to use forces. A very difficult mission awaited us. We had to get back to the B2 theater quickly.

The results of the activities of the first phase of the 1974-1975 dry season all over the B2 theater were truly brilliant. We had won big victories and surpassed all norms that had been assigned. I had been worried that if only the B2 theater was active during that phase we would encounter many difficulties because the enemy could concentrate on countering our moves, but that did not occur because the enemy was clearly confused and passive and had seriously weakened. Although the enemy had concentrated the air power of the 2d and 4th Military Regions on countering our attacks in Military Region 3--at Phuoc Long and Binh Tuy they flew more than 100 fighter-bomber sorties a day and used as many as 160 helicopters--they could achieve nothing on the battlefield. They transferred the 4th Ranger Group from Kontum to Long Binh, which was then replaced by the 8th Ranger Group which came down from Duc Duc, and sent the 4th Airborne Brigade and then the 2d Airborne Brigade from Da Nang to the Hoang Hoa Tham base and the 4th Marine Brigade from Tri Thien to the Song Than base, not to carry out a counterattack but to strengthen their defenses north and northeast of Saigon. The results we attained during the phase from December 1974 to February 1975 were greater than in any previous phase. We completely liberated a province, 4 districts, 72 villages and 489 hamlets, and essentially liberated 52 other villages. We liberated 584,800 people. We wiped out 22 battalions, inflicted heavy losses on 25 puppet battalions and overran 1,548 military posts, including a sector, 8 subsectors, 3 strategic zones and 88 subsector branches. We destroyed 108 airplanes, 110 boats and 494 vehicles, killed 56,315 of the enemy and captured 12,122 weapons, 786 radios, 118 vehicles, and 2 airplanes.

Although those figures were very significant, they still did not fully reflect the value of the victories won during the first phase of the 1974-1975 dry season in the B2 theater. Those victories were results not only of the first phase but also the entirely logical development of the victories of the 1974 dry season and rainy season. COSVN and the Regional Military Party Commission foresaw those victories when they realized the transformation that had taken place on the battlefield with regard to the balance between ourselves and the enemy by the end of the 1974 dry season, after which we continued that trend by means of our activities during the rainy season and the first part of the 1974-1975 dry season. The soldiers and people of the B2 theater understood the enemy's situation and their own, so they attacked and arose tirelessly from the 1973-1974 dry season to the 1974-1975 dry season; the more they fought the stronger they became, and the greater their strength the more their position improved. During that time the puppets, who began to decline during the 1974 dry season, were attacked continually all over the place; the more they declined the less capable they were of reviving. The actual situation proved that COSVN's assessment and evaluation of the situation was correct, and that therefore its policy was correct.

For the first time in decades of war a province (Phuoc Long) had been completely liberated. That province, furthermore, was a border province of the enemy's Military Region III, the strongest military region, which had the mission of defending the U.S.-puppet capital and war headquarters. That event occurred at a time when the puppets still had forces totaling more than 1 million troops in theory and nearly 1 million actual troops, who were strongly armed with U.S. weapons and facilities, and were built up, trained and commanded by the United States in order to carry out its strategy of Vietnamizing the war. Even so, the Americans and their puppets could not send a main-force unit to respond to our attack and defend the gateway to Saigon. As for the United States, it had to stand to one side and look at the puppet regime, a child it had painfully given birth to decades ago and which now was on the threshold of a dangerous period of rapid decline. The liberation of Phuoc Long was no different from a sword pointed at the throat of Saigon. The Saigon puppet regime, like an obstinate, excessively parsimonious person who would rather die than lose an inch of ground, spread out its troops to defend every faraway place. As a result, it was defeated everywhere it was attacked and could send no reinforcements. Instead, it ordered 3 days of national mourning for Phuoc Long! In fact, that was the funeral of the traitorous Thieu regime, the terminal period of which began with Phuoc Long.

Also during the first phase of that dry season another outstanding event terrified the Americans and puppets: the offensive and uprising of our soldiers and people in the Mekong Delta, which demonstrated that the ability of villages to liberate villages, districts to liberate districts, and provinces to liberate provinces was real and that that was a correct policy. In a little more than 2 months we wiped out 15 enemy battalions, knocked out of action more than 34,000 of the enemy, and overran 168 military posts, including 2 subsector-district seats, 2 strategic zones, 11 bases and 65 subsector branches. By the attacks of the armed forces and the 3 types of troops, in coordination with uprisings by the popular masses, 51 villages and 414 hamlets were completely liberated and 49 other villages were essentially liberated. Some 48,900 people were liberated. Especially, the area in which the greatest victories were won and in which the revolutionary movement was strongest was the Tra Vinh-Vinh Long area, the No 1 focus of Military Region 9 and a vital area of the Mekong Delta. If General Gavin was closely following the course of the fighting, he was aware that his strategem of withdrawing into a strategic enclave in the Mekong Delta had been bankrupted and could no longer be carried out.

Even in Saigon and its outskirts, in which the enemy paid much attention to strengthening defenses and suppressing uprisings, an area to which the enemy sent more and more forces as they were increasingly defeated in order to save their necks, the revolutionary movement was also seething during that phase and we won notable victories. During that period, in the outskirts we completely liberated 3 villages, 37 hamlets, and 17,000 people, and essentially liberated 4 other villages. The enemy had to withdraw into their outposts and in many places did not dare sleep in the posts at night and did not have confidence in their fortifications and weapons. The control of the puppet regime was weakened and the people could move about more freely, to the degree that the people living in the city came to the outskirts to contact the revolution and receive missions from the revolution. That situation was almost identical to that of Tet Mau Than. Those activities did not involve main-force troops, tanks or heavy artillery. He had only sapper units, commandos, local troops and guerrillas, but those small, elite units exerted an effect because they knew how to cooperate with the people who thirsted for freedom and peace and who arose to achieve mastery.

During that dry season we also liberated the Tanh Linh and Hoai Duc areas in Binh Tuy Province to serve as a future staging area to cut Route 1 and as the starting point for the attack on Bien Hoa and on Saigon from the east. We also took a relatively broad strip along the Van Co Tay River to create conditions for our forces to cut Route 4 when necessary and to surround Saigon and cut it off from the delta.

We also began to effectively interdict Bien Hoa AFB and the enemy could do nothing about it. Especially, to the north of Saigon, which had enormous strategic importance, we rendered the enemy deaf and blind by taking both of the important observation and communications relay stations--in fact two enemy fortresses--Mt. Ba Ra and Mt. Ba Den, two high points.

The victory of the 1974-1975 dry season helped us to have better understanding of the enemy and ourselves, and of their strength and ability to act, while at the same time helping us to understand ourselves and our actual capabilities, the Revolutionary measures that had to be taken, and where we stood in the final stretch of the long path we had traveled over 10,000 days of warfare.

CHAPTER SIX

A Once-in-a-Thousand Years Event:
The Spring General Offensive and Uprising

A people who know how to arise and take up arms and wage a life-or-death war to liberate themselves from the yoke of slavery must also know how to conclude the war in the most advantageous way. Under the wise leadership of the party, we had sacrificed and fought staunchly and had signed the Paris Agreement in hopes of ending the war in an atmosphere of national reconciliation and concord and end U.S. intervention with honor. But our enemies thought differently. They turned to an insidious plot intended to cause the war to "fade away" so that they could win complete victory. But in life, people who play with fire get burned. The United States was able to evaluate our fighting strength and courage, but it did not yet understand the cleverness and intelligence of the Vietnamese people, and thought that it could deceive us. If the legality of the agreement could not end the war, the only method would be the use of revolutionary violence. Our people were much in need of peace, but true peace that was tied in with freedom and national independence and was in accord with the conscience of mankind. With a strong sense of responsibility toward our people and the people of the world, the Political Bureau of the party Central Committee issued a resolution calling for the completion of the national democratic revolution throughout our nation and the eventual unification of the homeland during the 1975-1976 period. Implementing that resolution, the Political Bureau made a specific decision: to attack Ban Me Thuot and the Central Highlands, in order to create a favorable opportunity for the concluding phase of a fierce war that had lasted 30 years.

Two years had past since the Paris Agreement. But the sound of gunfire had not ended on any of the battlefields. Vietnamese blood continued to flow. The Americans and their vassals could return safely to their countries because we observed the agreement, while the Americans continued to carry out their strategy of "Vietnamizing the war" and not "bringing peace to Vietnam." That "2 years" figure had a double meaning. The Geneva Agreements decreed that after 2 years there would be general elections to unify our country, but the Americans and Diem tore the treaty to shreds before the ink had dried on it. During those 2 years the guns of Diem's army never fell silent, as it shot and killed patriots in the "denounce communists" and "kill communists" campaigns. But there was a fundamental difference between those two 2-year periods. After the Geneva Agreements our entire army had to regroup in the north, so in the south there was only the Diem army, which was free to fire on unarmed people. But after the Paris Agreement our army remained in place and its positions were interspersed with that of Thieu's army in the jungles-and-mountains, lowlands and urban areas. The enemy could not freely violate the agreement without being punished. None of their nefarious plots could escape the vigilant eyes of our people and our liberation armed forces. Throughout the 1973-1974 dry season, then the 1974 rainy season, then the 1974-1975 dry season, there was one violation after another and one punishing blow after another, and now the positions and strengths of the two sides had changed: we were stronger than the enemy. The liberation of Phuoc Long Province was a blood-red milestone, so both we and the enemy could see it clearly. But although it could be seen, it was necessary to do something. Up to that time there was enough time to strictly implement the agreement and end the war, or so I thought. Both of our diplomatic delegations continued to "hold their ground," one in elegant Paris and the other at Tan Son Nhat, "a socialist concession in the middle of Saigon," as it was called by Western journalists. But time was passing, one day after another, and long after the gunfire stopped at Phuoc Long it had to resume at Ban Me Thuot. So it was all over: the truck was racing full speed down a steep incline and could not be stopped.

I thought of the Ban Me Thuot battle in that way: the truck had started its engine. Its effect could be compared to a fuse which would detonate the "firecracker" of the puppet army and regime, which had weakened seriously but were strangely still subjective and obstinate.

From the time I learned that the Political Bureau had ordered the attack on Ban Me Thuot I was certain that we would win a brilliant victory in that battle, for the forces we would use were many times superior to those of the enemy, both quantitatively and qualitatively. We would strike an unexpected lightning blow in their undefended rear. Most of the puppet troops there were stationed in the division and regiment rear-area bases. The enemy had concentrated their military forces in, and paid much attention to, the forward areas: Pleiku and Kontum. That defensive deployment of the enemy was based on their assumption that our main attack would be in Kontum, a view they continued to hold until the day Ban Me Thuot fell. And as stated above, like a tree that had been cut down at the base, after Ban Me Thuot fell there would be no way to hold on to the Central Highlands. If Thieu did not immediately order the evacuation of Pleiku and Kontum to obtain the troops to defend the coastal provinces, before long those two provinces would also be lost. Later, when the Central Highlands were lost, which led to the disintegration of the coastal provinces and to complete defeat, the United States hastily covered up the main reason for its painful defeat in the Vietnam war and in Indochina, which weakened and troubled the United States, by blaming Thieu for abandoning the Central Highlands on his own accord, without asking the opinion of the United States. A number of Western journalists echoed that U.S. propaganda argument, and even some of our cadres thought that that was the truth, for they did not clearly understand the campaign and strategic significance of the attack on Ban Me Thuot. The disastrous U.S.-puppet defeat was due to the unjust, antiprogressive, anticonscience of mankind aims of the barbarous war of aggression, manifested by a passive defensive strategy of keeping control of the population, setting up outposts and holding ground everywhere. Once the enemy had awakened and wanted to withdraw their forces to form an enclave in an important strategic area with rich population and material resources--the old Nam Bo area--it was too late. We had calculated our moves in advance so that the U.S.-puppets were no longer free to withdraw into an enclave, but were cut up into fragments and were subjected to attacks and uprisings all over at the same time, which disintegrated the puppets' entire 1-million-man army.

Comrade Le Duan had asked a strategic question, which I quoted above, "Attack to annihilate all or to disintegrate all?" To "attack to annihilate all" does not mean to annihilate the enemy to the last soldier and the last unit, but to strike one or a series of blows to annihilate the enemy's principal forces, for only then can we cause the enemy to lose all capability to resist and enable ourselves to win total victory. To "attack to disintegrate all" does not mean not striking a shattering blow to cause the rapid decline of the enemy, until they no longer have the will and capability to resist or counterattack, which leads to complete disintegration and complete defeat, even though they still have many troops and large quantities of weapons and equipment. The shattering blow does not necessarily have to annihilate the principal enemy troop concentrations, but annihilate a certain part of the enemy forces and take a number of strategically important localities, thus creating a decisive situation by causing the enemy to lose all of their morale and will to fight, become chaotic, and when subjected to repeated attacks and uprisings will disintegrate into large segments and then completely collapse. The policy and methods to be selected depend on each specific war and on the specific strategic phase. It may be said that that is an art in the conduct of war. That art is manifested specifically in the organization and division of the battlefield and organizing the deployment and use of combined forces, and the fighting method of coordinating the various kinds of forces and the localities in each period of time. That is the art of creating and developing to a high degree the combined strength of the nation and the strength of the era. It is the art of leading and guiding general offensives and uprisings in a revolutionary war and armed uprising waged by our party. When one understands those secrets one will understand that the U.S.-puppet defeat was in no way surprising or strange. Their destiny was determined by a solidly deployed strategic position which gradually put them onto a path which led to a grave that had already been dug. It definitely was not caused by any one erroneous decision by Thieu in the Central Highlands campaign or in any other previous or succeeding campaign. Both the United States and Thieu started the war, were subjective and obstinate, committed political and strategic mistakes, and were buried together in the pit of defeat, so they cannot blame each other. As for us, the wisdom of the party and its correct revolutionary objectives, strategic line, revolutionary struggle methods, and manner of concluding the war led our country along the glroious path of total victory.

When thinking about the Ban Me Thuot battle, the Central Highlands campaign and the development in South Vietnam as a whole after the Central Highlands campaign, especially the possible developments in the B2 theater, I was both enthusiastic and very anxious. I understood that the situation would develop very rapidly and that our theater would be profoundly influenced. The opportunity would be priceless, and would require us to take bold and prompt action. But we had so little time--it had been only a month since we returned to the base area from Hanoi--to disseminate the Political Bureau resolution and make all necessary preparations so that we could open fire on "D Day" with coordinated actions in all parts of the region, as ordered by the High Command.

Two days after returning home, on 3 February, I worked with the Regional Staff, rear-services, and political organs and with the 4th Corps to grasp our situation and that of the enemy in the military regions, and reviewed B2's plan for the second phase of the dry season, in order to prepare for the meetings of COSVN and the Regional Military Party Commission. Fortunately, B2's dry season plan was essentially on the right track. During the COSVN conference from 13-16 February, many specific problems were posed and discussed so that they could be resolved. In the process of approving B2's plan for the second phase of the dry season plan, the comrades in COSVN worried about the units that would put pressure on and attack Saigon from the south. They stressed the necessity of quickly stepping up our activities in the Cho Gao, Go Cong and southern Long An areas because our movement was not yet strong there and it was not yet assured that our armed forces could move up close to Saigon's 4th, 7th and 8th precincts. Another source of worry was the armed forces, especially the main-force units, in the theater, a key theater which was at that time still too weak. The additional forces we had requested from the central echelon had not yet arrived, and the strategic reserves were deployed too far away. In addition to the military plan, the conference stressed the necessity of immediately drafting plans for mass uprisings, to insure the use of the combined forces of the people and the armed forces, and to organize a unified command made up of comrades in the party committees, military units, governmental administrations, youth, women's and peasants associations, and military proselyting organs in each village, district and province, especially in Military Regions 8 and 9 in the Mekong Delta. That truly was a plan for a general offensive and uprising: it was necessary to insure that the villages could liberate villages, the districts could liberate districts, and the provinces could liberate provinces. The conference also discussed in detail the organization and work of the military management committees after the liberation of towns and cities. On the basis of the experience we had gained in solving problems in Phuoc Long City just after its liberation, such as organizing and insuring safety, caring for the lives of the people, insuring ordinary activities and production, punishing spies and saboteurs, etc., we would provide prompt guidance for the localities. Finally, the conference discussed measures for disseminating and explaining the Political Bureau resolution without exposing secrets. It was necessary to maintain military secrets and national secrets in all phases in order to insure success. Failing to carefully discuss measures to maintain secrecy, being found out before one could act, and everyone knowing about a decision just after it was made were reasons for failure and could not be forgiven. That was a difficult problem. The echelons and sectors had to thoroughly understand their missions, be inspired so that they could endeavor to win the greatest possible victory, and carry out plans as well as possible without letting the enemy know and make countermoves. Brother Bay Cuong emphasized emphatically that it was necessary to act without saying anything, or very little. We had to oppose exaggeration, revealing one's intentions before acting, and promising much but delivering little. It was necessary to resolutely:

--Say nothing about the completion of the democratic national revolution.

--Say nothing about the 1975-1976 2-year plan.

--Say nothing of the general offensive and general uprising.

--Say nothing about the new resolution; act as if there was only Resolution 21, the resolution of which the enemy was aware. Disseminate the work step-by-step, under tight control but promptly.

In accordance with the spirit and contents of that COSVN conference, we held a Regional Military Party Commission conference at the end of February to initiate all military tasks.

Before we began the second phase of the dry season in March, in accordance with the order of the High Command, the situation of the enemy forces in the B2 theater had undergone a number of changes. Most painful for the Americans and puppets was the fact that the pacification on which they had spent so much effort and money had been heavily defeated. The most evident defeat was in the Mekong Delta, which was highly populated and rich and which they hoped to make their final redoubt. After going all-out in January to carry out operations to retake land and relieve sieges along the border in Kien Tuong, in the Cho Gao area in My Tho, in the Thay Pho area in Tra Vinh, in the Thoi Binh area in Ca Mau, and in the Rach Gia-Ha Tien area but achieving no results, and indeed suffering losses in the lowlands, the enemy had to shift over to opposing our new offensive phase, which they expected before or after the lunar new year (about 10 February). In eastern Nam Bo they intended to concentrate troops and attempt to retake Phuoc Long City by means of their "Operation 271," but they were unsuccessful because since they were being attacked everywhere they could not put together sufficiently strong forces. They shifted the focus of their efforts on taking Mt. Ba Den, a position that was vital to them not only with regard to the defense of eastern Nam Bo and Saigon but also for the defense of Kampuchea and Phnom Penh (Lon Nol). Between 20-26 January the puppet III Corps, in the presence of a representative of CHQ, used forces of the Tay Ninh Sector and the 25th Division, with strong artillery support (an average of 6,000 rounds a day) and air support (84 sorties per day), launched an extremely vicious attack on the mountain. They used 29 helicopters to land many waves of troops to retake the position atop the mountain, but met fierce resistance and lost much manpower and many airplanes and helicopters. Ultimately the enemy had to accept defeat and withdraw to defend Tay Ninh.

The very significant victory of the battle to take the Mt. Ba Den position and the fighting to hold that position in the face of a fierce enemy counterattack was an extremely brilliant feat of arms of one of our small but elite units: the 47th Reconnaissance Battalion of the Regional Staff, reinforced by 2 sapper companies of the 429th Regiment, an antiaircraft machinegun unit, and a mortar unit, a total of 300 cadres and men. Clearly understanding the value of the battle, the Regional Command designated comrade Ba Tran, the regional deputy chief of staff, and comrades Son Bich and Chin Loc, commander and political officer of the intelligence branch, to approve the operational plan, and assigned comrade Huynh Long, deputy intelligence commander, and comrade Hai, commander of reconnaissance forces, to directly command the fighting. During the night of 3 December our units attacked the Mt. Ba Den position from three directions. To the southwest the main unit, led by comrade To and his deputy comrade Thang and with five enlisted men, penetrated to the center of the strongpoint and killed many of the enemy. But the enemy, aided by airplanes and helicopters, counterattacked and retook the position. Toan died heroically. Under the guidance of the upper echelon, the unit changed over to laying siege to the position, cutting off all sources of supply and not allowing a single helicopter to land troops. The imperiled enemy troops had to withdraw at the end of December, but nearly all of them were killed or captured. Because it was an important strongpoint with modern equipment used to monitor a large area and with a communications station that relayed messages to battlefields in both Vietnam and Kampuchea, both the puppet GHQ and III Corps were determined to retake it by means of extremely fierce attacks. But our small reconnaissance-sapper unit defeated a combined enemy force dozens of times larger. That was a victory of both position and force, of cleverness, intelligence, courage and combat skill, will and determination, willingness to bear difficulties and hardships, and selfless sacrifice for the great undertaking of the people and the nation. In that sense, was the battle not a microcosm of our liberation war against the U.S. imperialists? Few defeated many, small defeated large, the benevolent defeated the uncouth and the brutal, and justice defeated perversion. The battle was even more valuable because it took place in the last phase of the war and rendered the enemy deaf and blind so that we could attack their final lair.

During that period, our intelligence reported that the enemy learned of our intentions for the 1975 dry season high point, from Tet to June 1965: we would concentrate on disrupting their pacification program, the focus of which was in the Mekong Delta; weaken the puppet army; force Thieu to resign; and achieve a political solution by forming a coalition government. Or perhaps we would launch a general offensive to take such cities as Quang Tri, Kontum, Tay Ninh, Long Khanh, Kien Tuong, and Chuong Thien. On 18 December, at the Presidential Palace, the puppet Ministry of National Defense reported on the military situation and predicted that:

--In Military Region 1 we would attack to force the withdrawal of the district seats near the mountain region, threaten the lowlands, shell the Da Nang airbase, and take Hue.

--In Military Region 2 we would seek to permanently cut routes 1, 19, 14 and 21, to isolate and attack Kontum and Pleiku Provinces.

--In Military Region 3 we would attack to take Tay Ninh City, force the abandonment of Chon Thanh, Phu Giao, and Tri Tam, and isolate Saigon by blocking routes 1, 4, 20 and 15.

Then it concluded that we would begin our spring-summer campaign in March 1975 to implement our key plan for 1975: strongly attacking the pacification program, winning control of additional land and people, and depleting their military potential. The other military regions would coordinate their activities. The "communists" had nearly completed their activities.

On all battlefields they strengthened their defenses and sent out reconnaissance troops to spy on and monitor our forces. They urgently restored the units that had recently suffered heavy losses or been wiped out. The enemy continually alerted the various echelons that we would attack during the lunar new year period, then announced that our attack would begin on 14 February, then that it would begin on 20 February, etc. They paid special attention to Chuong Thien in western Nam Bo, Kien Tuong in central Nam Bo, and Tay Ninh, Hau Nghia, and Long Khanh in eastern Nam Bo. Most of the forces of the 25th Division were concentrated in the vicinity of Tay Ninh City. The entire 18th Division was sent to the area east of Saigon, around Xuan Loc. The airborne and ranger troops were sent to search the northern outskirts of Saigon.

In general, in late February and early March the enemy was certain that we would launch a dry season offensive and had a plan to counter it. But they still were not certain about the scale of the offensive and by what means we would carry it out, did not know when it would begin, and guessed wrong about the focus of our offensive. Meanwhile, the morale of their officers and men continued to weaken; they were very tense and did not believe that they were capable of coping with us. There was also disorder in the ranks of the puppet army and administration. Thieu and Khiem were at odds and Ky was eagerly awaiting an opportunity to carry out a coup d'etat and take power. The United States had to seek all ways to help Thieu and avoid a dangerous political upheaval. Martin, the U.S. ambassador, and Polgar, head of the U.S. CIA in Saigon, acting feverishly, stayed the hand of Ky, advised Khiem to suppress the opposition parties, protected Thieu, covered up for the Thieu regime in the United States, and came to grips with U.S. public opinion and the U.S. Congress.

In Saigon, the mass struggle movement became increasingly strong: there were demands for relief from hunger, the workers opposed layoffs, and "refugees" demanded rice. The women's movement demanding the right to live also struggled seethingly. Newspapermen protested the closing of five opposition newspapers and the arrest of dozens of journalists. There were demonstrations and fasts demanding the release of political prisoners, that Thieu resign, and that a government be formed to carry out the Paris Agreement.

After the loss of Phuoc Long and the Mt. Ba Den strongpoint, Tan Ninh Province was threatened and there were many rumors that we would liberate Tay Ninh so that it could become the capital of the PRG and the RSVN. The situation in that city was very chaotic. Some of the people, fearing that they would be killed in the fighting, fled to the countryside, to areas controlled by the revolution, or even to Saigon. The people living near the puppet military strongpoint left the area so that they would not be caught up in the fighting. The Cao Dai leaders, realizing that the puppet army could no longer protect them and the Holy See was in danger of being destroyed, declared their "neutrality" and encouraged the puppet regime to withdraw its military forces, including the civil guards, from the "holy ground," although they had long relied on those forces to oppose the liberation troops.

In An Giang, the Hoa Hoa sect organized its own armed forces to defend itself and to carry out its own political scheme once the Thieu regime collapsed. On 30 January 1975 Thieu issued a decree dissolving the Hoa Hoa militia, for he could not allow "an army within an army." Therefore there were clashes between the Hoa Hoa armed forces and the Thieu police in Sadec, Kien Phong and Long Xuyen. Thieu's bloody suppression resulted in many deaths and hundreds of Hoa Hoa militiamen were captured, including its leaders.

Thus by the beginning of the second phase of the 1974-1975 dry season, all over South Vietnam, and especially in the B2 theater, the puppet Thieu regime was faced with an extremely confused situation militarily, economically, politically and socially.

On the basis of the plan for the second phase of the dry season that had been approved by COSVN, the Regional Command assigned missions to and approved the plans of 4th Corps, the divisions and the military regions. Comrade Tam Phuong, i.e. Maj Gen Le Quoc San, commander of Military Region 8, personally accepted his mission. He was very enthusiastic and confident of being able to correctly implement the plan of both liberating the provinces in his military region by means of attacks and uprisings and fulfilling the important mission assigned him by the Regional Command: insuring the success of the theater as a whole, using his forces to participate in the all-out assault on Saigon from the south and on the main objective--the puppet national police headquarters--and taking and cutting strategic Route 4 in order to cut off the puppet capital from the south. He said to the Regional Command, "The soldiers and people of Military Region 8 have the great honor of being able to participate in the historic campaign to take Saigon, the final U.S.-puppet lair. Only after many years of war could we arrive at this glorious hour. On behalf of the armed forces of Military Region 8, I promise to carry out the plan that has been approved and win the greatest possible victory, in order to be worthy of the confidence of the upper echelon.

As for Military Region 9, although he had to travel a long way and overcome many difficulties, comrade Ba Hai, i.e., Maj Gen Pham Ngoc Hung, commander of the military region, also went to the Regional Command to personally accept his mission. He had taken the risk of traveling openly, but his trip was very meticulously organized. He promised to select the 1st Regiment, the strongest regiment in the military region, which along with the provincial 3d Regiment and the local militia forces, were liberating the strategically important Vinh Binh-Tra Vinh area, and cutting Route 4 and the Mang Thit River, if so ordered, to join the forces of Military Region 8 in attacking Saigon from the south. Although difficulties were involved in interdicting the Le Te airfield, he promised to go all-out to fulfill that mission in order to contribute to the common victory. Meanwhile, comrade Sau Hat, i.e. Senior Colonel Nguyen Trong Xuyen, commander of Military Region 6, was very worried about his difficult mission of liberating an area from Binh Tuy Province to Di Linh, Dalat and the coastal provinces in his military region, for in that military region we had many difficulties in all regards. The organized mass forces were not yet sufficiently strong and with regard to armed forces there were still very few local troops, there were not many guerrillas, and there was only one main-force unit: the 812th Regiment. His careful weighing of his strength in comparison to such a great mission was entirely appropriate to the sense of responsibility of a cadre with actual combat experience. On behalf of the Regional Command I analyzed the situation in the B2 theater as a whole and the advantageous factors in the present strategic phase that would create very great strength with which the military region could fulfill its mission. In coordination with the other forces, troops and people in the military region, the main-force 812th Regiment would make a worthy contribution and would win a big victory, as in other parts of the theater. He felt more at ease and promised to make a maximum effort, but I sensed that he was still quite worried. Even so, I knew that he would fulfill his mission because he had confidence in the upper echelon and in the overall efforts of the theater as a whole in that important phase.

Senior Colonel Le Van Ngoc, commander of Military Region 7 and, comrade Dang Ngoc Si, deputy commander of the military region and commander of the 6th Division, were present at the Regional Command to accept their missions. They briefed us on the weakness of their understrength divisions and requested the Regional Command to urgently provide additional troops and equipment, but made a firm promise to overcome all difficulties in order to correctly implement the plan. The military region's most important mission was coordinating with the 812th Regiment of Military Region 6 in rapidly mopping up the enemy in the Tanh Linh and Vo Dac areas of Binh Tuy Province to create a convenient staging area from which the 4th Corps could attack Xuan Loc, Bien Hoa and Saigon, and cut Route 1 between Xuan Loc and Rung La in order to isolate Saigon from the coast of central Nam Bo, cut Route 15 between Saigon and Vung Tau, and join 4th Corps in attacking the enemy.

With regard to 4th Corps, it still consisted only of the 7th and 9th Divisions and its combat arms were still very weak. Initially, as requested by B2, the General Staff intended to send the 968th Division from the Central Highlands to reinforce 4th Corps, then decided to replace it with the 316th Division, but it could send neither. Finally, it decided to send the 341st Division, which was undergoing training in our Military Region 4. On 11 February I sent a message to the High Command recommending that the division be sent south urgently: "Recommend that brother Tran (i.e. the commander of the 341st Division) be sent south early. Only if half of it arrives by the first part of March can it arrive in time." We must assign in advance a number of cadres who are familiar with the battlefield and are combat experienced so that as soon as the unit arrives, they can reinforce it and provide urgent tactical training (the division had not had much actual combat experience). We also readied a technical reconnaissance unit consisting of experts and the light equipment and machinery needed for their work, to be turned over to the disposal of the division staff. In general, the 4th Corps was still understrength with regard to both infantry and combat arms. Even so, the operational plan assigned it by the Regional Command divided it into two areas of operation: Binh Long, Binh Duong and Tay Ninh, and Route 20, Long Khanh and Bien Hoa. Each of those two areas required a division from the corps, combined with the forces of Military Region 7 and the local provincial forces. The comrades in the Corps Command expressed their aspiration of being able to concentrate the entire corps in one area of operations so that it could have stronger combat strength with which to strike an annihilating blow in order to create a common transformation in the theater. We at the Regional Command had thought about and reflected upon many aspects of that problem. The principal reason we formed the corps was to use it in a concentrated manner so that it could have the strength to strike annihilating blows, in order to both win big victories and steel the units, so we were completely sympathetic with the worries and thoughts of the corps. But, regrettably, we were in a period in which there would be very rapid changes on the battlefield. The Ban Me Thuot battle was certain to create a strong transformation all over South Vietnam and force the enemy troops on the eastern Nam Bo battlefield, which included Saigon, to urgently take up strong defensive positions. It was an area in which the enemy would react quickly and strong, with maximum effort, to save themselves. In order to defeat we had to know not only how to concentrate large strong forces, but also, and especially, to take steps and carry out schemes to disperse the enemy, deceive the enemy and prevent it from discerning our intentions, so that we could launch surprise attacks and win certain victories. We were already behind schedule in forming our corps. We had not yet received the additional forces we had requested to deploy in the various areas in accordance with a strategic-campaign position that provided for all contingencies, including sudden military and political developments. Therefore, we had to know how to deploy and use the forces we had on hand in the most effective way in order to win the greatest, most timely victories. The B2 theater had the enormous responsibility of insuring that the final, decisive attack on Saigon was launched at the right time and won a certain victory. If it was to fulfill that responsibility it was necessary to create at an early date favorable conditions for deploying forces; to move up close to and tightly encircle Saigon; to create staging areas from which to launch attacks from the various directions; to be prepared for all contingencies; and to be able to act immediately once the opportunity arose and the order was given. If we had to start thinking about a plan for an offensive against and an uprising in Saigon during the rainy season of 1974 in order to draft a plan for the 1974-1975 dry season, now it was even more important that we be prepared to carry out that offensive and uprising. Although the corps was still understrength, it was made up of elite divisions which were very familiar with the battlefield and of experienced cadres, and it was the main force available to the Regional Command. Therefore, we had to make very careful calculations when using it, so that it could be used very properly from both a campaign and strategic point of view, and in accordance with the extremely important current phase. On the eastern Nam Bo theater, if at that time we had concentrated in one area the enemy would have concentrated their forces in the same area and fiercely opposed us. We had to flexibly maintain the initiative so that we would not be caught up in a tug of war between ourselves and the enemy. If we were to strike effective manpower-annihilating blows we had to attack the key points and draw in the enemy in order to annihilate them, but the enemy would defend those key places to the end. Therefore, the Regional Command decided to use the corps in two different areas to expand the staging areas north, northwest and east of Saigon, and launching surprise attacks on and annihilating the enemy in places very advantageous to us without having to clash with the enemy in places vitally important to them, while at the same time deploying our forces so that they could launch an offensive when necessary. Our forces were small but would become strong and would win one victory after another.

Another important focal point of the B2 theater's activities was to annihilate the enemy and expand the liberated area in western Tay Ninh and in the Ben Cau-Queo Be area in order to create a staging area for the attack on Saigon from the west and for blockading Saigon from the southwest and cutting it off from the Mekong Delta. Therefore, the Regional Command decided to use the 5th and 3d Divisions in those areas. Later, in order to insure the success of the attack from the west--a very difficult but very important direction--the Regional Command decided to form Group 232--corresponding to a corps--to unify the command of both divisions, the local forces, and the subordinate combat arms. Comrade Nam Nga, a diligent and brave cadre who had high regard for justice and who had gained much experience in commanding main-force units during the anti-French resistance war in southernmost Central Vietnam, had personally commanded the fighting in Binh Tuy during the first phase of the dry season and had been on the staff of the Regional Command for years, was appointed Group Commander. His political officer was comrade Tam Tran, i.e. Maj Gen Tran Van Phac, and his deputy commander was Maj Gen Nguyen Van Nghiem.

With regard to the sappers and commandos in the Saigon area, in order to achieve unified, close command in the various directions the Regional Command decided to set up commands for each of them. Those north of Saigon were commanded by comrade Muoi Co, i.e., Nguyen Thanh Tung and comrade Nguyen Van Tang, an Army Hero; those to the southwest were commanded by comrades Nguyen Van May and Guyen Van Hat; and those to the east were commanded by comrades Tong Viet Duong and Le Ba Uoc.

D Day of the second phase of the 1974-1975 dry season campaign--in fact the beginning of the general offensive and general uprising all over South Vietnam--had been set by the High Command: "The night of 9 March and the early morning of 10 March 1975." That day had arrived. In coordination with the B2 theater, from the mountains and jungles of Military Region 6 to the Mekong Delta and the area around the capital, and the main-force troops, local troops, militiamen, and guerrillas, enthusiastically rushed forward together to annihilate the enemy. The entire B2 theater simultaneously arose and attacked! Except in a few areas in which we encountered initial difficulties, our attack slowed down, and our victories were limited, such as in the Hau Giang area of Military Region 9, and in Ben Tre Province (Military Region 8), our attacks went well and everything went according to plan. We were winning a resounding victory.

In the Saigon area the forces of the municipal unit and the sappers, by launching absolutely secret surprise attacks, and insuring their victories without harming the theater as a whole, were authorized to open fire during the night of 8 March and the early morning of 9 March. A large number of enemy outposts, in the directions that had to be cleared for the movement of our forces and for activities the sappers and commandos were about to carry out, were wiped out. The civilian self-defense forces, which became demoralized after they were attacked and were educated by the people, largely disintegrated during that period. The enemy's control in many areas in the outskirts of the city was weakened. Outstanding victories were won in the taking of a number of enemy outposts around Hoc Mon on Route 8 and in the Rach Tra area, which were important to the enemy defenses north of Tan Son Nhat airbase and Saigon. In Binh Chanh, the headquarters of the 86th Ranger Battalion at Tan Tuc suffered heavy losses. At Thu Duc, about 40 percent of the enemy's Sicona chemicals depot was destroyed. On 20 March the Quyet Thang Battalion, in cooperation with the local troops and guerrillas, wiped out an escorted 51-truck convoy taking ammunition to Cu Chi along Route 1, and wiped out or inflicted heavy losses on four enemy companies sent to relieve the convoy.

In the Mekong Delta the 4th Division of Military Region 9, along with the local forces and guerrillas, liberated Kinh Xang, O Mon, and Thi Doi, moved up close to Thoi Lai and Kinh Xang Xano, wiped out or forced the withdrawal of many outposts, and liberated a number of villages. In Vinh Tra the 1st and 2d Regiments cooperating closely with the on-the-spot forces, surrounded the Thay Pho strategic zone, wiped out the outposts on the Vinh Xuan road, wiped out two enemy battalions sent as reinforcements, forced the enemy in that strategic zone fo flee, inflicted heavy losses on the Cai Nhum and Cai Von subsectors, cut Route 4, and essentially mastered the Mang Thit River. In Long An, beginning on 9 March the 1st Provincial Battalion annihilated an RF Battalion in Ben Luc District. The 8th Division of Military Region 8, which began its second-phase activities on 11 March, wiped out the Nga Sau base, an important position in the Cai Be area, bordering the Dong Thap Muoi region, in My Tho Province. The enemy used the 10th Regiment of their 7th Division to carry out a fierce counterattack to retake that position on 14 March, but we wiped out two battalions and the remainder of a third battalion was wiped out when we retook the base.. Many other posts in Cai Be and Cai Lay Districts were wiped out or forced to withdraw. Meanwhile, between 11-14 March, the 3d and 5th Divisions, annihilated enemy troops and completely liberated the Ben Cau, Moc Bai, An Thanh, and Tra Cao areas. By 20 March they had overrun the enemy position at Queo Be in Duc Hue District, extended our corridor in western Tay Ninh Province down to the Dong Thap Muoi area, and mastered a broad strip along the western bank of the Van Co Dong River in Tay Ninh and Long An Provinces, just as planned. That was the famous "Parrot's Beak" area which the Americans had greatly feared, for they regarded it as a vital staging area from the "Viet Cong" could threaten Saigon from the west. They launched many operations in that area, and dropped many bombs and laid many minefields in trying to transform that area into a killing zone. Especially, in 1970, U.S. and puppet troops passed through that area and penetrated deeply into Kampuchea, thus beginning the period in which the Vietnam war was expanded into the Indochina war. Now that "Parrot's Beak" area had been cleared of enemy troops, had been expanded eastward to the Van Co Dong River and southward to near the Van Co Tay River, it had become a staging area for us that was much more solid than in the past. When Queo Ba was threatened during the 1974 dry season the puppet III Corps urgently sent six task forces to sweep and defend that area at the same time. Now that their position and strength had weakened, the puppets viewed the enemy's staging area, which had been extended closer to Saigon from the west, as being many times more dangerous than in the past.

Thus less than a month into the second phase our soldiers and people in the Mekong Delta had attained notable accomplishments and were continuing enthusiastically and effectively to disrupt pacification, win control of the population, and win the right of mastery. In eastern Nam Bo, on the western bank of the Saigon River, on 11 March the 16th Regiment wiped out the Suoi Dong Hung position and on 12 March the 9th Division took the Tri Tam Subsector and on 13 March liberated all of Dau Tient District east of the Saigon River and the Ben Cui area west of the river. On 17 March the Cau Khoi position was taken and we gained control of a segment of Route 26 in Tay Ninh Province. Thus we had liberated a vast area along both banks of the Saigon River to form a staging area for the attack on Saigon from the northwest. The enemy used the 3d Cavalry Brigade and a 25th Division force to counterattack along Route 2 at Suoi Ong Hung. That presented us with a good opportunity to annihilate an important part of the armored forces of III Corps, but due to deficiencies in our preparations and combat operations we could only inflict heavy damage on the enemy and force them to withdraw them to defend the area south of Bau Don. The armed forces of Tay Ninh Province during that time coordinated very well by attacking directly Route 22, cutting that road from place to place and from time to time, thus forcing the puppet 25th Division to defend that road in order to insure that Tay Ninh would not be isolated. To the east, between 15-18 March the 6th Division of Military Region 7 extended the liberated area along Route 2 from Xuan Loc to Ba Ria and completely liberated Route 3 from Hoai Duc to Gia Ray. On 20 March it took the Ong Don intersection and Suoi Cat, and by 28 March it had mastered a 50 kilometers-long segment of Route 1 from Suoi Cat to Rung La, thus cutting the lifeline connecting the central Vietnam coast with Bien Hoa-Saigon. The 812th Regiment of Military Region 6 completed the annihilation of Vo Duc and liberated a large area in Binh Tuy Province and the districts of Hoai Duc and Tanh Linh, thus creating a good staging area from which the 4th Corps could later attack Xuan Loc and Bien Hoa. Then the regiment, according to plan, moved quickly to coordinate with the 7th Division on Route 20 in the direction of Dalat. On 15 March the 7th Division launched its attack and by 18 March had completed the taking of the Dinh Quan district seat, a fortified strongpoint which backed up to a store outcropping and controlled important Route 20. After taking Dinh Quan the division took the Da Oai strategic zone and, along with the local forces mopped up the enemy, expanded the liberated area and mastered Route 20. On 28 March it launched a lightning-fast mechanized attack which liberated the city of Lam Dong in only 2 hours. Thus we had completed the expansion and connecting of an important, integrated and solid base area extending from Dong Thap Muoi west of Saigon, running from the western and northern parts of Tay Ninh Province to Phuoc Long, War Zone A in northern Bien Hoa, and to Binh Tuy and Ba Ria on the South China Sea. Saigon had in effect been surrounded from the west, north and northeast. The 812th Regiment, reinforced by an element of the 7th Division, took advantage of the opportunity and occupied the town of Di Linh. Thus all of Lam Dong Province had been liberated. That represented a great victory on the eastern Nam Bo theater during that period. It greatly strengthened our position north and east of Saigon and defeated the enemy's scheme to form a defensive enclave.

In Part II ("The End") of his book "Decent Interval, Frank Snepp wrote that "The next day the communist forces opened a new front in the southern part of that area (the puppet Military Region II) and advanced to Lam Dong City, 3 hours from Saigon by road, without meeting any resistance (more accurately, resistance had been quickly crushed). At that very moment Thieu and his generals were once again debating and weighing the possibility of setting up a defense line immediately north of the city (Saigon), extending from Tay Ninh to Nha Trang. Before nightful, Polgar (the U.S. CIA chief in Vietnam) personally went to the Presidential Palace to inform Thieu and his generals that their plan had been smashed, for Lam Dong Province, the backbone of that defense line, had fallen into the hands of the North Vietnamese troops."

With the loss of Lam Dong and Route 20, the city of Dalat and all of Tuyen Duc Province (as it was called by the puppet regime) were isolated. Route 11, which connected Dalat with Phan Rang on the coast, was a very dangerous, twisting up-and-down road that could not be used to save the city. The liberation of Dalat was the responsibility of the B2 theater, but B2's forces were small and it had to move in close to Saigon and thus could not move up to liberate Tuyen Duc Province. After the Central Highlands were liberated our strong forces there could come down to take Dalat, then continue on to eastern Nam Bo, very conveniently and promptly. Therefore I sent a message to Van Tien Dung, then the commander of our forces on the Central Highlands battlefield, recommending that he send forces down to liberate Dalat because our forces had to advance toward Saigon and could not go to Dalat. Brother Dung replied in the affirmative. But the enemy troops, very confused and terrified, and threatened by our local armed forces there, fled from Dalat. An element of the 812th Regiment, along with local forces, took over Dalat on 4 April, pursued the enemy, and liberated Route 11 as far as the Thanh Son airfield. All of Tuyen Duc Province, including the important city of Dalat, had been liberated.

North of Saigon, after Cau Tieng was liberated the city of An Loc in Binh Long Province (to use the puppet regime's term) was tightly surrounded. There we had used forces drawn from the organs of the Regional Command, in coordination with the local forces and guerrillas, to threaten and attack the enemy from the beginning of the second phase of the dry season. On 23 March the enemy troops withdrew to Chon Thanh, a district seat far to the south on Route 13. By that time part of the 341st Division sent by the central echelon had arrived. We used a regiment of that division, along with an element of the 9th Division, to pursue the enemy and attack Chon Thanh. During the night of 31 March, after suffering heavy losses, the enemy troop remnants abandoned Chon Thanh. All of Binh Long had been liberated. Our main base area had been expanded and filled out until it reached close to Saigon, near the bases of the puppet 5th Division at Lai Khe and Phu Loi and of the puppet 25th Division at Dong Du, which became the outposts for defending Saigon from the north and the northwest. Even so, the enemy was still blindly trying to defend Tay Ninh, a city that had become distant and isolated, merely because it was afraid that it would become the capital of a revolutionary government.

In March the B2 theater had won great victories, thanks to active coordination with the principal battlefield--the Central Highlands--and by taking full advantage of the turmoil caused by the Ban Me Thuot battle and the succeeding battles. The harmonious coordination of all theaters in the south during the strong simultaneous attacks and uprisings were the result of the rapid decline and disintegration of the puppet army and regime. In Hanoi, the Political Bureau and the Military Commission of the party Central Committee had very closely monitored the overall situation and the situation on each battlefield, promptly reported on all developments in each area, and promptly guided and corrected the activities in each direction. It may be said that the Political Bureau and the Military Commission guided, and in fact exercised coordinated command of all the battlefields and guided the activities of all the offensive columns.

By 11 March we had essentially taken the city of Ban Me Thuot. When he was informed of that victory by the High Command, comrade Le Duan said, "We previously had estimated 2 years but now, after Phuoc Long and Ban Me Thuot, we may step up the pace. Is this the beginning of the general offensive and general uprising?" Flexibility in such a situation is always the key to timely actions. The reporting of that victory was a great source of inspiration, but the Military Commission continued to urge the battlefields to launch strong attacks and win big victories. On 12 March comrade Vo Nguyen Giap sent a message to comrade Van Tien Dung in the Central Highlands which included the following passage:

"The Political Bureau and the Military Commission have determined that if a large part of the enemy's manpower is annihilated, the city of Ban Me Thuot and many district seats are lost, and Route 19 is cut, the remaining enemy forces in the Central Highlands will form an enclave at Pleiku and may be forced to carry out a strategic evacuation of the Central Highlands. Therefore, the Political Bureau and the Military Commission have directed that it is necessary to immediately surround Pleiku, cut off both the enemy's air route and land routes, and make good preparations to annihilate the enemy in both contingencies."* Clearly, we accurately predicted, at an early date, the enemy's actions. Not until 15 March did Thieu, because of the desperate situation, meet with his generals at Cam Ranh and decide to abandon the Central Highlands. On 15 March they secretly, and in an arduous and chaotic manner, began to implement their plan, and on 16 March Hanoi reported that the forward headquarters of the puppet II Corps and the U.S. Consulate had been shifted from Pleiku to Nha Trang. Between 18-24 March, the withdrawing enemy troops were completely annihilated or routed. The Central Highlands has been liberated!

The entire B2 theater was happy and enthusiastic and its activities were stimulated by news of the victories on the other battlefields, which was promptly reported. In coordination with the other theaters, the soldiers and people of Tri Thien also arose to carry out strong attacks and uprisings, and on 19 March liberated Quang Tri. The puppets' Military Region I was shaken and began to prepare to abandon Hue on 18 March. The High Command ordered the Tri-Thien Military Region to cut Route 1 south of Hue to prevent the 1st Division from withdrawing to Da Nang. The puppet troops were in a state of panic. Their only way out was to flee via the Thuan An river mouth, but they were wiped out by the 2d Corps and the forces of the Tri-Thien Military Region there on 25 March. The ancient capital of Hue was liberated for the second time (the first time was during Tet Mau Than in 1968) and for good. Similarly, with regard to Da Nang on 18 March the High Command ordered Military Region 5 to attack urgently and bold in and cut Route 1 south of Da Nang in order to surround and annihilate the enemy and prevent them from withdrawing into an enclave at Da Nang and moving to the south. In view of that favorable situation, and carrying out the orders of the upper echelon, the military region's 2d Division, along with the local forces, resolutely attacked and annihilated the enemy and liberated Tam Ky, Tuan Duong and Chu Lai. The soldiers and people of Quang Ngai, combining attacks and uprisings, completely liberated their own province. Thus a vast area and Route 1 south of Da Nang were

---
* "The Great Spring Victory" by comrade Van Tien Dung, pp 104-5.

liberated. The enemy troops in Da Nang had been surrounded and could escape only by sea, but were annihilated and disintegrated by 2d Corps and the forces of Military Region 5 on 29 March in an extremely tragic spectacle, no less so than in the Central Highlands and in Hue. We soon learned of all of that news, except that about an event rare in the history of warfare: the best puppet general dived into the South China Sea and swam out to a ship in order to save his life. (Related by Frank Snepp in op. cit.)

"On the morning of 23 March General Ngo Quang Truong, reputed to be the most skilled commander of the South Vietnamese army, had to tread water in the waves, totally incoherent, in order to escape from Da Nang. He was not a good swimmer, so an aide had to help him swim to a South Vietnamese patrol boat. The next 2 days he spent on a ship watching the remnants of his once-proud army burning and pillaging South Vietnam's second largest city. Perhaps later some of his comrades in arms would accuse him of the ultimate crime of not fulfilling his responsibility as commander by remaining behind to fight to the death. Of the 2 million refugees who were still in Da Nang, there were at least 100,000 deserters from the 1st, 2d and 3d Divisions and from the famous Marine Division, who were now no different than mice caught in a trap. Now they were ready to do anything, including betraying, stealing from and killing one another, to find a way of escape for themselves and their family."

The acute assessment of the situation and accurate, timely forecasting, flexible guidance, and resolute, skilled command of the Political Bureau and the Military Commission of the party Central Committee upset all U.S.-puppet strategic-campaign plans. We used the method of cutting down the tree at the roots, so "the mice were trapped" in the Central Highlands, at Hue, at Da Nang, and in the south. Our method of organizing forces was to move forces prepositioned in each area, in coordination with extensive local and militia for forces on all battlefields of an extremely potent revolutionary people's war. Everywhere the enemy was attacked and surrounded in a very timely, rapid manner and could not flee or form into enclaves. Our use of combined forces-- both armed forces and the political forces of the people--in a widespread general offensive and uprising created a peerless strength which struck down the enemy at a time when they still controlled a million well-equipped troops and whose master stood behind them and served as a pillar of support.

While that was happening in the north, in the B2 theater we were kept well informed by the Political Bureau and the Military Commission about the situation and were provided specific guidance encouraging bold attacks against the enemy to make certain that they could not form enclaves anywhere. We strictly implemented that guidance and won a great victory in the specific situation of the theater and in the balance of forces between ourselves and the enemy. A U.S. CIA specialist observed, "Far to the south, in III Corps, the government troops also continued to go downhill, perhaps not as precipitously, but the results were the same: there was a loss of land and a loss of tactical flexibility. Around 20 March an ARVN division became bogged down in defending Tay Ninh and the area northwest of that city. Some government commanders wanted to withdraw or bring in another division from the Delta to serve as a mobile reserve. But Thieu rejected both proposals. He believed that the loss of Tay Ninh would weaken the morale of the troops and civilians in the other areas, and that to bring in forces from the Delta would mean abandoning a vast area to the enemy, for the three ARVN divisions there had already been stretched to the limit.

"If that had been a chess move, Thieu would have already lost. He was about to be checkmated on all fronts." (Frank Snepp, op. cit.)

The overall situation in the south developed very rapidly, much more rapidly than we had anticipated, which created very favorable conditions for the theaters to win the greatest possible victories. We in the Regional Military Party Committee and COSVN worked very urgently and night and day closely monitored the military regions and units. News of victories flowed in and we sent out a stream of combat guidance messages. But we felt that we were still making slow progress and that our armed forces were not strong enough to fully exploit the situation. Brother Bay Cuong sent several messages requesting the Political Bureau to urgently send additional forces. On 23 March I received message No 81/TK from Van Tien Dung informing me of the overall situation and outlining the development of the attack after the liberation of the Central Highlands: advancing along routes 9, 7 and 21 with the objectives of annihilating the 22d Division, liberating Binh Dinh and Phu Yen, then liberating Khanh Hoa and Dien Khanh. The message stated, "We do not yet have forces to send you. By the time we are able to send them to you the opportunity to launch the final, war-deciding battle will be at hand. If we are to take advantage of that opportunity, the battlefield must be prepared in advance." At the end of the message he told me to begin thinking about the final battle so that I could come to meet with him and brother Sau (Le Duc Tho).

After reading the message, I felt disappointed. First, we could not yet be provided additional forces. Second, I had learned that the divisions in the Central Highlands would develop their attack eastward toward the sea. I thought that that was contrary to what had been decided during the Political Bureau meeting in January 1975. I remember that at that time brother Ba concluded that after the Central Highlands had been liberated our forces would rapidly develop their attack southward. As he spoke he spread out his hand and swept it down the map from the Central Highlands to Saigon. I could not forget how that image moved me, for that was what I was also thinking. I thought that if our entire 3d Corps came down into eastern Nam Bo immediately we could attack Saigon earlier and better take advantage of the opportunity. The enemy troops in central Vietnam would not have time to withdraw south. Furthermore, along the coast we already had the 2d Corps and the forces of Military Region 5, which were sufficiently strong to annihilate the enemy. But the next day I received a copy of a message from brother Sau Many (Le Duc Tho) to brother Bay Cuong (message No 71, 23 March):

"Have sent brother Tran (i.e. the 341st Division). That cadre (i.e. division) is skilled and capable. That does not include a number of other cadres to support those cadres (i.e. combat arms attached to the division that would be sent down). Those cadres will be sent immediately from the place where I am now. Prepare to make use of them as soon as they arrive."*

---

*Document of the War Recapitulation Office of Military Region 7.

I was delighted, but was worried that because those units had to travel a long distance they would arrive late.

On 25 March 1975 the Political Bureau met and decided to liberate Saigon before the rainy season (which began in early May).

On 29 March brother Ba sent a message (No 928/KT) to brother Bay Cuong which included the following passage:

"In view of our great, overwhelming victories and the extremely serious and unforeseen defeats of the enemy, the U.S.-puppet gang is faced with the peril of rapid collapse militarily, politically and with regard to morale.

"I strongly agree with you that at this time it is necessary to act very promptly, resolutely and boldly. In fact, the battle of Saigon has already begun.

"While urgently and promptly carrying out the strategic decision that has been made, I want to stress an urgent requirement: boldly increasing forces in order to immediately fulfill the mission of carrying out a strategic interdiction and encirclement, and cutting off Saigon to the west in the area of My Tho and Tan An."*

On 30 March brother Van (comrade Vo Nguyen Giap) also sent me a message:

"We have sent a message to brother Tuan (comrade Van Tien Dung) informing him that he should send forces south as soon as possible and make the best use of time. New technical equipment units are also now enroute south to reinforce the B2 theater. We have prepared a corps, which will soon head south to the B2 theater to serve as a reserve force."**

After the guidance message from the Political Bureau and the Military Commission of the party Central Committee, COSVN and the Regional Military Party Committee met to discuss an implementation plan. COSVN Resolution 15, which resulted from that meeting, assessed and evaluated the situation as follows: "The revolutionary war in South Vietnam has not only entered a period of rapid development, but the strategic opportunity for carrying out the general offensive and general uprising to take the enemy's lair is ripe. From this moment the final, war-deciding strategic battle of our people, to complete the people's democratic national revolution in the south and achieve national unification, has begun."

With regard to missions, the resolution stated: "The direct, urgent missions of our entire party are to mobilize the entire party, the entire army and the entire population to concentrate their morale strength and forces, develop to a high degree the combined strength of the three offensive columns, the three types of troops and the three strategic areas, advance to a general

---
*Document of the B2 War Recapitulation Section of the Ministry of National Defense.
** Ibid.

offensive and general uprising, bring about the rapid and complete overthrow of the puppet army and puppet regime, win political power for the people, with a spirit of resolute, marvelously rapid and bold offensive, and be determined to liberate the villages, districts and provinces all over South Vietnam." The resolution encouraged the various echelons, "Make the best use of time, for at present, time is strength...." "We must truly concentrate each hour, each day and each month, beginning with April 1975...."

During that COSVN conference we discussed at length how the situations might develop in the B2 theater. If we won additional victories on the battlefields, Saigon itself might be thrown into chaos. In that event, we cannot wait until a plan is drafted to grasp the opportunity before acting. Brother Ba's message to COSVN affirmed that the situation would develop rapidly, and that it was necessary to step up our attacks on the enemy and move up closer to Saigon. If our victory advanced a step further, a change might be brought about in Saigon. Time was strength. After carefully studying the guidance opinions of the Political Bureau and the Military Commission of the party Central Committee and carefully weighing the situation, our Regional Military Party Committee and Regional Command drafted a plan to attack Saigon with the existing forces. The plan was approved by COSVN and reported to the central echelon. The five-pronged attack on the city had been drafted, and the enemy units that had to be annihilated and the objectives that had to be taken had been determined. The problem was how to deploy and use our forces. The objectives in the city had been assigned and the sapper and commando forces that would attack from within had been deployed. Now it was a matter of forces attacking from the outside.

According to our plan, the eastern column, commanded by 4th Corps, made up the 7th, 341st and 6th Divisions; the northwest would be the responsibility of the 9th Division, and the 16th and 271 B Regiments; and the west would be the responsibility of Group 232, made up of the 5th and 3d Divisions. The attack from the south would be undertaken by the 88th and 24th Regiments of Military Region 8. To the north, we would deploy the Gia Dinh Regiment. If there were additional outside forces, they would be added to that direction. The forces for those directions had been assigned and we were closely monitoring developments in order to determine the best time to carry out that attack. In the immediate future it was necessary to annihilate additional enemy manpower defending Saigon, cut Route 4 and the Long Tau River, and interdict the airfields, to tighten the noose on Saigon so that the enemy could not form an enclave at the last minute and especially to drive a wedge between the puppet III Corps and IV Corps and tie down the enemy everywhere. COSVN agreed with the Regional Military Party Committee that it was necessary to launch an immediate attack on Xuan Loc and annihilate the puppet 18th Division and Cavalry Brigade, strong III Corps forces, and move up close to Bien Hoa. Group 232 was ordered to prepare to attack Moc Hoa and win control of the only road--Route 12--that could be used to send the 5th Division and technical military equipment down to cut Route 4 and, along with the 8th Division of Military Region 8, annihilate the puppet 7th and 9th Divisions. If that step were carried out well, we would win a big victory all over the theater and the puppet army and regime would vacillate and become chaotic and not be able to defend Saigon effectively, or else there would be an important political upheaval within the ranks of the puppets or between the puppets and the Americans, in which case we would immediately grasp the opportunity and launch an offensive and uprising, combining military attacks and mass uprisings, and combining inside-out and outside-in attacks on the five most important objectives: Tan San Nhat air base, the puppet GHQ, the Capital Special Zone headquarters, National Police headquarters, and Independence Palace, in order to liberate all of the B2 theater.

On 31 March, I and Lt Col Nguyen Van Minh, an operational cadre with the Regional Command, and a number of other cadres came to Military Region 7 headquarters to assign missions to the military region and to 4th Corps. Before setting out I had sent a message convening the cadres and stating that I would arrive on 1 April. In March it had been sunny and dry. The road passing through War Zone A was only a dirt road but there were no obstacles. Our cleverly camouflaged command car moved rapidly through the jungle. It was the beginning of spring and the plants were in bloom. The flowers of spring blossomed everywhere; along the road purple pansies were mixed with golden apricot blossoms, green leaves and white leaves. It was also in the midst of the combat season, and the sounds of bombs and artillery shells were bursting in all directions around Saigon. It was a scene that was both attractive and martial, and moved one's soul. I emotionally remembered the victorious springs of our forefathers and of ourselves. Vietnam was still Vietnam. I recorded in my diary:

> Golden apricots embellished the route,
> The rustling jungle breeze crackled along with the guns
> of spring surrounding the city.
> Then as now the mountains and rivers are ours.
> The brilliantly gifted Nguyen Hue, in love with
> Princess Ngoc Han.

We traveled all day and into the night. The headquarters of the military region was situated on the bank of the Dong Nai River in the Vinh An area. The jungle there had been devastated but because the trees were large it still provided some cover. When I arrived there it was late at night. The enemy did not suspect that location, so it was regarded as being relatively safe. But night and day artillery shells fired from Hoc Ba Thuc and Cay Gao still exploded incessantly around the area, at times in large numbers and sometimes sporadically. All of the comrades who had been called in were present. Comrade Nam Cuc, i.e. Nguyen Nhy Y, secretary of the Military Region Party Committee, who was short and slim but had a resolute will, was arrested with me by the French in the Catinet secret police station and we were imprisoned together in the Saigon prison in Saigon in 1944-1945. When he saw me he was overjoyed and confided, "The situation is very encouraging. I'm anxious to return to Saigon and visit the poor neighborhood in Tan Dinh, where we set up a secret organ and were captured together by the French secret police, to see how it changed during the U.S.-puppet period...." Comrades Sau Trung, a member of the standing committee of the Military Region Party Committee; Duong Cu Tam, the military region's political officer; Le Van Ngoc, commander of the military region; and Dang Ngoc Si, deputy commander of the military region and commander of the 6th Division, appeared to be happy and enthusiastic. The 4th Corps comrades--Hoang Cam, commander; Bui Cat Vu, deputy commander; and comrade Tran, commander of the 341st Division, which had become the 1st Division, had arrived during the afternoon. Although it was late at night we sat talking with one another, forgetting sleep and even fatigue. Early the next morning we held a meeting. I reported on the overall situation and on the situation of each battlefield in South Vietnam, the assessment and evaluation of the Political Bureau and COSVN, and the specific guidance of the Political Bureau and the Military Committee of the party Central Committee. I reported on the essential points of the attack on Saigon that had been drafted by the Regional Military Party Committee and approved by COSVN, so that they could understand the overall missions. Finally, we announced the decision of the Regional Command to attack Xuan Loc and annihilate the 18th Division and the 3d Cavalry Brigade and assigned missions.

We carefully discussed the specific plan for the battle, the capabilities for the situation to develop favorably or unfavorably, and the necessary measures. The comrades pointed out that the enemy had paid attention to defending Xuan Loc and that the fighting was certain to be fierce. If, after taking Dinh Quan, we attacked Xuan Loc right away and did not attack Lam Dong, that would have been very strange. I defended the decision to liberate Lam Dong for the following reasons:

--We had only mastered a segment of Route 20 between Dinh Quan and Phuong Lam, the corridor connecting 4th Corps and the War Zone A rear area, in the immediate future and in the long range, could not be insured. We were experiencing difficulties with regard to ammunition, so if we fought on a large scale it would be even more necessary to insure that corridor. If we mastered Route 20, we would not only have a road along which to advance toward Bien Hoa and Saigon, but also create considerable difficulties for Dalat from the south. If we do not expand our hold on the road immediately, the enemy might risk their lives and counterattack to retake it so that they could withdraw into a solid strategic enclave in the Saigon area and in Military Regions III and IV.

--Xuan Loc was an important strongpoint in the Saigon defensive system, and although the enemy had strengthened its defenses in comparison to the past, the enemy defenses there were not weak because they had deployed all of the 18th Division and 3d Cavalry Brigade there since February.

Everyone agreed that an attack on Xuan Loc had to be regarded as an attack on a blocking position that was extremely important to the enemy, so it had to be assumed that they would try to defend it and would send in strong defenses, and that the battle would be very fierce. Everyone discussed tactics and techniques very carefully and requested additional artillery shells and technical support facilities for the tanks. While we were meeting news was received that we had completed the liberation of Qui Nhon and Tuy Hoa, which made everyone determined to achieve merit. The situation was developing very rapidly. We had set 10 April as the opening date of the battle so that there would be time to make meticulous preparations, but then we agreed to make 9 April "D-Day."

I also discussed with the comrades in the Military Region Party Committee and the Military Region Command the advance preparation, and organization and working methods, of the military management committees of the cities of Long Khanh, Ba Ria, Vung Tau and Bien Hoa.

Before returning I ordered Group 75--i.e., the Regional Artillery Command--to immediately set up a long-range 130mm artillery fire support base at Hieu Liem, at the intersection of the Be and Dong Nai Rivers, in order to effectively interdict the Bien Hoa airbase and support the 4th Corps attack. For a long time, the 113th Sapper Regiment had been responsible for attacking the Bien Hoa airbase with rockets and mortars. Now conditions were good so we added a 130mm artillery base, so the fate of that airbase had been decided. The region's 75th Artillery Group had been the nemesis of the Bien Hoa airbase. It fought its first artillery battle there in December 1965, when it was armed with only 57mm recoilless rifles and mortars of various kinds, and along with the sappers destroyed a large number of enemy aircraft, including more than 20 B57 bombers that had just been sent over from the United States. That battle had been commanded by comrade Luong Van Nho, in charge of artillery, and comrade Hai Ca, i.e., Senior Colonel Tran Cong An, commanding the sappers. That was the first time the U.S. Air Force had been struck a painful blow. Maxwell Taylor, then the U.S. ambassador in Saigon, hastened to the airbase and looked disappointedly at the American eagles, with broken necks and smashed wings, strewn about in piles of scrap steel. Twelve years had passed, an extremely valuable period of maturization in an extremely fierce war. During that period the artillery cadres were steeled, the unit developed, and the upper echelon provided additional artillery and equipment. Especially, it captured enemy artillery--from 106mm and 107mm DKZ to 105mm and 155mm howitzers. Now it had 130mm guns with strong firepower, long range and great accuracy. It had contributed to all campaigns in the B2 theater and now it had the mission of paralyzing one of the large airbases during the decisive phase. The comrades who had commanded Group 75, from its first commander Luong Van Nho to comrades Dao Son Tay and Bui Cat Vu, and then comrades Son Tieu, Nguyen Tam, So, Lai, etc., may take pride in their contributions to developing the units and our creative use of artillery, including artillery captured from the enemy and both small and large artillery, in fighting in combination and independently, in attacking both fortified and field positions, and in shelling enemy aircraft at airbases and enemy boats operating on rivers, by all methods and under all circumstances.

When the work was done I hastened back to the Regional Command headquarters. When passing by the Rang Rang airfield in the midst of our War Zone A, I viewed the criminal scars caused by the puppet air force's continuous bombing practice there since the Paris Agreement. But the runways were still intact and when necessary our small aircraft could still use them which demonstrated the lack of skill of the puppet pilots. Just beyond the airfield, when our car was crossing the Ma Da River at a ford, two enemy fighter-bombers circled overhead: they had discovered our small convoy crossing the river. Our car sped ahead and turned into the jungle. I hid in a trench on the riverbank, watching the enemy aircraft diving and dropping bombs around us. Our antiaircraft machinegun spewed out bullets at the enemy airplanes, one of which was hit and, trailing smoke, flew away. The convoy which had not been hit continued on.

After returning home at 0100 on 4 April I learned that Van Tien Dung's party had arrived the previous afternoon and had been provided living and working areas. I was very pleased, for the chief of staff and the entire foreward headquarters of the High Command--codenamed Group A75--had arrived. They had arrived in time for the strategic, war-determining attack on the final U.S.-puppet lair. As usual, when I returned from a trip, no matter what the hour, my secretary brought me the urgent news and messages from the battlefield, the units and the central echelon. A long message from brother Ba which had been received on 1 April immediately caught my attention:

"The Political Bureau met on 31 March and listened to a Military Commission report on the developing situation of our general offensive during the past 3 weeks, especially during the recent period.

1. It agreed unanimously that:

"After our great victories in Military Region 9 and eastern Nam Bo, the liberation of Phuoc Long Province, and the great victory on the Central Highlands battlefield, our strategic general offensive began and within a brief period of time won extremely great victories.

"...2. Our country's revolution is now developing more seethingly than ever, at the rate of 1 day equalling 20 years. Therefore, the Political Bureau has decided to further exploit the strategic opportunity, with the guidance thoughts of marvelous speed, boldness, surprise and certain victory, with strong determination to carry out a general offensive and general uprising as soon as possible, during April at the latest. The factors of certain victory and surprise at present lie principally in making the best use of time and attacking the enemy while they are in a state of disarray and collapse, and in concentrating our forces to a greater degree on the main objectives at each time and in each direction.

"...3. In order to carry out the strategic motto along those lines, and to meet the requirement regarding time, beginning immediately it is necessary to draft a bold plan of action with the existing forces on the eastern Nam Bo battlefield.

"...The Military Commission of the party Central Committee has decided to rapidly shift the forces of 3d Corps and their weapons and equipment, southward from the B3 theater, and has ordered the reserves corps to move south.

"...In order to make the maximum use of time, we should not wait for all of the reinforcements to arrive and avoid irrational troop movements which affect the action time."*

There was also a long message from the Military Commission of the party Central Committee, signed by brother Van, which included the following passages:

---

*Document of the B2 War Recapitulation Section of the Ministry of National Defense.

"...At present, surprise is mainly a matter of time. We must move forces with marvelous rapidity and use the existing forces to act promptly, without waiting until all forces are concentrated before acting. In that sense, the Political Bureau has affirmed that the strategic, war-deciding battle for Saigon has begun.

"...C. The eastern prong, made up of the divisions now on the spot (we should avoid upsetting, time-losing troop movements), augmented by the necessary forces, especially technical military equipment, must first of all annihilate the 18th Division, take Xuan Loc, and move up close to Bien Hoa airbase as soon as possible....

"It would be best if the local troops were assigned the mission of surrounding Moc Hoa, while all of the regional main-force units there should, along with the main-force units of Military Region 8, immediately concentrate and move down to cut Route 4 between Ben Luc and Tan An and between Tan An and My Tho...."*

I went to bed with my mind full of thoughts. Over a period of 30 years there had been many long sleepless nights, but no night had been like any other. I thought about the enemy forces deployed on the inner and outer perimeters and our forces in each area of the campaign. I closed my eyes and imagined the approach routes into Saigon, the rivers and canals, the fields and the high-and-dry or muddy terrain. I agreed about the attack on Xuan Loc. But if we abandoned Moc Hoa and advanced to Route 4, how could we take the technical equipment along? I also imagined the enemy's reaction when we attacked. Saigon, a large city that was complicated in many regards, and the final lair of the enemy, had been surrounded and had no way out, which forced the enemy to hold out until there was no longer any hope before surrendering or disintegrating. It was also our beloved city. Its large population had to be protected and had to prevent the enemy from sabotaging the streets, buildings and social property. The terrain around the city was, by and large, high and dry, with many wide roads, unlike those in Central Highlands, which passed between high mountains, or those along the central coast which were long but narrow and easily cut which caused the enemy to panic and disintegrate. Since the enemy was collapsing, the existing B2 armed forces could, in coordination with the uprising masses, launch a direct attack on and liberate Saigon, but they were not strong enough to attack sufficiently rapidly and strongly to keep the city intact.

When I encountered problems I could not solve I often thought of Uncle Ho and silently recited a stanza from his Chinese poem "Studying Chess":

> "One must have a broad view and think carefully,
> And be resolved to keep up the attack.
> If they are not used well two rooks are worthless,
> But when there is an opportunity, one
> well-used rook will insure success."

―――――――――――――
*Document of the B2 War Capitulation Section of the Ministry of National Defense.

I told myself that although our forces were small the opportunity had arrived: when there is an opportunity, one well-used rook will do, and we should not slow down the attack when the enemy is confused. I smiled to myself contentedly and dropped off to sleep. When I awoke it was dawn. I went to meet brother Dung, who had also awakened. We happily embraced each other. I asked, "How does it feel to be in Nam Bo for the first time?" He replied, "Moved and happy beyond description."

Then the conversation turned to the victories on the battlefields and we discussed what should be done.

Then we went to visit and shake hands with the comrades in the "forward headquarters." Comrades Le Ngoc Hien and Le Quang Vu had served as regional deputy chiefs of staff, so I already knew them. Comrade Doang Tue, artillery commander of the High Command, had come south for the second time. Many of the combat arm commanders, staff cadres, and operations cadres, who had come to the B2 theater, with its strange scenery but familiar people, were happy and enthusiastic. Thus the opportunity was at hand and our ranks had been strengthened. Once sufficient main-force units had been concentrated certain victory would be ours. It was truly a once-in-a-thousand-years opportunity.

That day we divided the work among two elements: the organs of the Regional Command and those of Group A75. I assigned to the B2 staff, political and rear services organs the mission of briefing the comrades in the forward headquarters fully and in detail on the battlefield situation, especially in the Saigon area, from the composition and value of the important enemy objectives to their defensive deployment, from the terrain of the various areas to our forces, large and small, inside and outside the city, the psychology, way of life, and capabilities of the people of Nam Bo and Saigon, the plans that had been drafted and the battlefield that had developed. The briefing had to be completed in the briefest possible time. From that movement on we were in a race with time!

In the afternoon of 7 April comrade Le Duc Tho, representing the Political Bureau, after a nonstop trip from Hanoi arrived at the Regional Command, then located west of the city of Loc Ninh, which later became the headquarters of the campaign to liberate Saigon. In the morning of 9 April, at a meeting attended by the comrades in COSVN, the Regional Military Party Commission, and the B2 Command, and key cadres of the regional and A75 organs, comrade Tho gave a briefing on the newest resolution of the Political Bureau. The resolution systematically assessed and evaluated the situation on the battlefield since Resolution 21, the outstanding developments on each battlefield, the relevant situation in the United States and in the world, and the decision to liberate the south before the beginning of the rainy season. He said, "The situation has developed very rapidly and the opportunity is extremely favorable, so our 1975-1976 2-year plan can and must be achieved within a few months. The Political Bureau has directed that 'At present, time is strength,' We must act quickly, boldly and unexpectedly, and win certain victory."

Then the conference reached a decision on the working method and on an explicit division of labor among the elements:

COSVN, the Regional Military Party Commission and the Regional Command kept their responsibility of guiding and commanding the general offensive and uprising throughout the B2 theater, especially close guidance of the uprising of the masses in Saigon.

The offensive campaign against the city of Saigon, which the Political Bureau later named the "Ho Chi Minh campaign," was commanded by comrade Van Thien Dung, a decision everyone supported. Meanwhile, the Regional Command continued to carry out its B2 responsibilities. Some of its comrades participated in the campaign command: comrade Pham Hung served as political officer, and comrade Le Duc Anh and I served as deputy commanders.

The regional staff, political and rear services organs had to fulfill two functions: one was to continue to help the Regional Command in the B2 theater; the second was becoming an organ of the Ho Chi Minh Campaign Command which was augmented by cadres and facilities of Group A75. The Regional Staff had to select cadres who thoroughly understood the situation, the terrain and the localities, and with many years of experience in commanding main-force units in the B2 theater, to help the corps of the High Command which would participate in the campaign but were confronted by extremely urgent circumstances: sometimes they had to join the fighting immediately, even before all of their units had arrived. Comrade Dinh Duc Thien, director of the Rear Services General Department who had accompanied comrade Dung, went directly to the Regional Rear Services Department, blended in with our comrades there, and worked with them in providing all necessary material-technical resources for the campaign.

Comrade Nguyen Van Linh, deputy secretary of COSVN, was especially responsible for mass uprisings, especially in Saigon. Comrade Vo Van Kiet, a member of the Standing Committee of COSVN, was responsible for guiding the takeover of the organs in Saigon and for guiding the planning and organization of the Municipal Military Management Committee. As a representative of the Political Bureau, comrade Le Duc Tho contributed opinions to all tasks of COSVN as well as the campaign command.

The Loc Ninh jungle, which was already famous, now had even greater historical importance and was bustling with activity night and day. Under the remaining canopies of leaves and clever camouflage nets, cadres, enlisted men and motorbicycles went from one tent to another without stop. At night rays from the carefully masked electric lightbulbs fell on bright faces, maps containing countless secrets and many kinds of equipment and machinery, both old and new, thus giving a mysterious but modern, urgent but deliberate appearance to the supernatural jungle that contained both the Regional Command and the Campaign Command. Electric wires spread out in all directions, from one tree branch to another. And flashing over the horizon were the invisible signals of messages being sent to all areas. Comrade Xuan Dao,* in charge of communications in the B2 theater continued to complain about the chronic lack of machinery and facilities, and the lack of cables and overhead wires, but he was always proud of

---

*Senior Colonel Nguyen Xuan Dao (now head of the Communications Section of Military Region 7).

his brave cadres and men, who had done everything possible to insure unimpeded communications between the Regional Command and all of the military regions and units in all main-force campaigns in the B2 theater. Now Xuan Dao was delighted to be augmented by the communications facilities of the High Command at a time when requirements had doubled or tripled.

On the basis of the resolution and directives of the Political Bureau, the conference also concluded that the situation on the battlefield had continued to change rapidly. It was necessary to assume that at a certain time there could be a sudden change in Saigon, the final lair of the enemy. Therefore, in order to take the initiative under all circumstances we had to have a plan to act immediately when the opportunity presented itself with the forces on hand, without awaiting the arrival of the High Command corps. In the event that there was no sudden change, we would wait until all of our main-force units had arrived in order to have the superiority with which to overwhelm the enemy troops and strike an unexpected lightning blow in order to eliminate all resistance, prevent destruction and sabotage, and insure the safety of our largest, most heavily populated city. The conference unanimously approved the plan to attack Saigon by using the existing forces in the B2 theater that had been approved by COSVN and had begun to be implemented, and which we had carefully explained.

While B2 began to implement the strategic interdiction and surrounding of Saigon in accordance with the above-mentioned plan, the Political Bureau and the Military Commission of the party Central Committee resolutely concentrated all available forces on the Saigon front, in the final, strategic, war-deciding battle. Carrying out urgent orders of the upper echelon and with the fire of enthusiasm burning in their hearts, unit after unit rushed south in order to be in time to participate in the "national liberation celebration." Corps and divisions from the Red River Delta and Military Region 4 carried out a mechanized movement day and night along the Truong Son route. Main-force units of Military Region 5 and the High Command, technical military equipment which the soldiers and people of Military Region 5 had taken from enemy supply depots, advanced southward down the central Vietnam coast under the command of comrades Le Trong Tan, Le Quang Hoa, Hoang Minh Thao and Nam Long, who had been appointed by the Military Commission of the party Central Committee, annihilated the enemy as they urgently moved down to reinforce the prong that would attack Saigon from the east. Following them were supplementary troops from Hanoi, Tay Bac, Viet Bac, and the provinces of the socialist north, who were ready to sacrifice their lives so that our people could advance to dazzling new heights. Meanwhile, in the B2 provinces, especially in the Mekong Delta, many youths enlisted, joined the guerrillas and formed new units in order to create the strength with which, along with the people, to attack and arise to liberate their home areas. In Saigon, one regiment became two regiments--Gia Dinh 1 and 2--and in Military Regions 8 and 9 provinces, such as Ben Tre, Tra Vinh, Can Tho, etc., practically all districts had a battalion. Some provinces had five or six battalions. Tens of thousands of youths returned to the military regions to supplement the main-force units. The spirit of the masses was seething. It was truly heroic: the whole nation was on the move, the whole nation was fighting, and the whole nation was arising. Oh! How sacred our homeland, how heroic our people!

During that time, for the enemy's part, they were very confused because they had suffered heavy defeats. The forces of I Corps and II Corps had essentially been annihilated and disintegrated. But they had still obstinately and hastily reassembled their forces and reorganized their defenses in Military Region III and Military Region IV. Thieu came up with a new strategy he called "light at the top and heavy at the bottom," i.e. he withdrew from the remaining areas in Military Region I and Military Region II in order to defend Military Region III and Military Region IV in accordance with the plan proposed by Gavin. If in the past Thieu had mercilessly cursed that plan, now he regarded it as a plan to save his regime, which was in its death throes. But unfortunately, it was too late! Even the Americans were still very subjective, especially Martin, the U.S. ambassador in Saigon. "Martin replied to the (U.S.) Senate that the South Vietnamese forces had carried out an orderly withdrawal from the Central Highlands, although there were reports to the contrary. And when the deputy head of the Vietnam section (of the U.S. Department of State) protested that optimism, Martin promised that within a year he would invite that deputy section head and his wife to visit Ban Me Thuot. Martin also appeared to be annoyed by his aide Al Francis. After reading a gloomy message from Da Nang, Martin cruelly commented that 'It appears that Francis' thyroid glands are acting up again.' Martin did not think that way because he did not understand the truth. He was always telling the pessimists--one after another--in Washington, that he regarded the loss of the northern part of South Vietnam as insignificant and that it had been a drain on the government's resources. The rest of the country was much richer and formed a unit that could be more effectively defended."* Even the CIA and Pentagon analysts took the view that: "Although admitting that large parts of Military Region I and Military Region II had been permanently lost, they argued that the government forces in the other parts of the country were sufficiently strong to at least hold the defense line north of Saigon until the rainy season began in May, after which the North Vietnamese offensive was certain to encounter difficulties because of the weather and the government would have time to reorganize and reassemble its forces and could participate in negotiations from a position of relative strength."**

In the morning of 25 March, a meeting of U.S. bigwigs held in the White House was attended by President Ford, Kissinger, Martin and Weyand, chief of ground forces and former U.S. commander in Indochina, to assess the situation and discuss a plan to counter the military developments in Vietnam. The meeting got nowhere because of conflicting reports, so it was decided to send Weyand to Saigon to personally evaluate the situation and discuss effective countermeasures with Thieu.

On 28 March, Weyand, Martin and an important delegation arrived at Saigon and began work immediately. "As soon as he arrived in Saigon Weyand focused his attention on a few basic objectives. In addition to the specific task of studying the situation, he concentrated on drafting a new strategy to save

---

*From the book "Decent Interval," Random House Publishers, 1977, New York.
**Op. cit.

South Vietnam. The key to that plan was to change Thieu's structure of 'light at the top, heavy at the bottom.' At first, Thieu, in accordance with that concept, hoped to set up an outer line to defend Saigon extending from Tay Ninh in the west to Nha Trang on the coast. But now that the communists had penetrated deep to the southern part of Military Region II, it was clear that some adjustments would have to be made. Weyand suggested as an alternative a new defense line anchored by Phan Rang City to the east, with Xuan Loc serving as the central base, and anchored by Tay Ninh in the west. Since Thieu had little choice he immediately accepted that recommendation."* Weyand emphasized to Thieu, "Xuan Loc must be held at all costs. To lose Xuan Loc is to lose Saigon."

"As the first step in implementing that new defensive plan, Thieu sent General Toan to defend Phan Rang (General Toan was III Corps commander) and in turn Toan directed his old friend Gen Nguyen Van Nghi (a former IV Corps commander who had been dismissed the previous fall for corruption) to set up forward headquarters there, along with part of the mobile division. He also sent an armored brigade and a few ranger units to eastern III Corps to strengthen the South Vietnamese division at the key city of Xuan Loc."**

Although he made those moves and gave the appearance of wanting to fight to the end, in their hearts neither Thieu nor the United States believed that the plan would work. That was demonstrated on 2 and 3 April, when Thieu secretly sent treasures he had pillaged from our people to Taiwan and Canada so that he could live the life of a king when he had to flee abroad. As for the United States, it also prepared a plan to take vengeance after it had to withdraw from Vietnam. "When the Weyand delegation visited Saigon, Johnson (CIA station chief in Saigon) requested permission to select some people to 'remain behind' and set up an organization of Vietnamese refugees in Bangkok, to serve as a bridge to the spy networks to operate permanently in Vietnam. In concept, that was a relatively simple problem. The CIA had already done so with groups of exiles in Eastern Europe many years ago."***

People of good conscience all over the world should, from that perfidy, understand the truth about the Vietnamese refugee problem, which the U.S. propaganda loudspeaker has ballyhooed for a long time. It is in fact part of a revanchist plan of the United States and the Chinese expansionists, who have formed an alliance after the bitter, disgraceful defeat in Indochina. It should also be amply clear that Bangkok is in fact a U.S. staging area for attacks on Indochina, where it hired Thai soldiers to participate in the fighting during the recent war, is also a base for training spies and sending them into Indochina to carry out the revanchist plan of the imperialists and expansionists, and the point of origin of all schemes to sabotage peace in Southeast Asia in the postwar period.

According to the new defensive plan, in addition to the puppet 25th Division at Cu Chi northwest of Saigon, the 5th Division at Lai Khe to the north, and

---
*Op. cit.
**Op. cit.
***Op. cit.

the 18th Division, 3d Cavalry Brigade, 2d Marine Brigade and 1st Airborne Division to the east, they urgently rebuilt the 22d Division and deployed it at Long An in the west to link up with the 7th, 9th and 21st Divisions in the Delta. In the outskirts of Saigon they also had an airborne brigade, three ranger groups and a number of RF groups. Inside the city they organized their forces into three defense zones manned by Police Field Forces and civilian self-defense forces in the precincts and subwards.

In order to give a meaningful send-off to the Weyand delegation, on 1 April we liberated Quy Nhon and Tuy Hoa, on 3 April 23 took Cam Ranh and Nha Trang and moved closer to Saigon to the north by taking Chon Thanh on Route 13, and on 4 April we liberated the city of Da Lat. Another noteworthy event was that on the morning of 4 April the Weyand delegation flew back to the United States to report on its completed mission at the White House and Thieu's Independence Palace was bombed by an airplane on 8 April. That airplane was F-5E piloted by Air Force Lieutenant Nguyen Thanh Trung, who took off from Bien Hoa air base and very accurately dropped two bombs on the place of the president of the puppet regime, foreshadowing the coming collapse of the lackey regime. Trung was a patriotic youth, the son of one of our comrades in Ben Tre, who had long been planted in the puppet air force. The time had come when we needed Trung to train our pilots to use the various kinds of airplanes and ordnance we had captured from the enemy so that they could be used if needed. The Phuoc Binh airfield in Phuoc Long Province was activated and guided the F-5E, the enemy's most modern airplane, to a safe landing. Nguyen Thanh Trung who achieved merit and was appropriately rewarded, fulfilled a glorious mission in the bosom of the enemy and returned in victory. That was one of the many-faceted countenances of the liberation soldiers, who operated wherever there were Vietnamese during the glorious anti-U.S. war for national salvation.

CHAPTER SEVEN

The War-Deciding Strategic Battle:
The Historic Ho Chi Minh Campaign

After the first part of April, the political stage in Saigon was seething with urgent activity. The people demanded the overthrow of Thieu in order to have peace, in accordance with the request of the PRG of the RSVN. Weyand and Martin wanted to keep Thieu in order to avoid political upheaval, but to expand the government to include many elements, including the opposition, in order to negotiate with the NLF in hopes of avoiding the complete defeat of the "Republic of Vietnam," the so-called "Senate" of South Vietnam also issued a resolution which although it had no value, demanded a change of leadership in order to "save the nation!" Khiem toadied the United States and completely approved of its opinions, but Nguyen Cao Ky invited Cao Van Vien, Le Minh Dao, commander of the 18th Division at Xuan Loc, and a number of others, to stage a coup d'etat. As everyone knows, everything that occurred in Saigon, from military plans, the "Phoenix" plan to kill Vietnamese, and internal and external policies, to the infighting among the lackeys, was decided by the U.S. master. Thus Ky had to seek permission from the United States, but Polgar, the CIA station chief in Saigon, strictly forbade the coup. The straw hero, air force general Cao Ky, had to remain at his home in Tan Son Nhat airbase, awaiting the day he would flee. Of course, with U.S. support Thieu remained in power. He thought that Khiem belonged to Ky's faction so he dismissed Khiem as premier and minister of defense and brought in a lackey, Nguyen Ba Can to head a so-called reorganized government called the "Government of Combat and National Solidarity" and named Tran Van Don vice premier and minister of defense. It was truly a case of not knowing when to quit. Their end was near but those power-hungry men tried to hang onto their positions, while the opportunists continued to be obsequious toward their masters or get ahead by stepping on others. But they continued to mouth the words "nation" and "people."

By then, Martin realized that only by negotiation was there a chance of saving the situation and gain time to save tens of thousands of Americans and their trusty lackeys of long standing, so that they would not be trapped in Saigon.

During the time Ambassador Martin and CIA station chief Polgar contacted the other diplomats and politicians in an effort to search out all ways to arrange those anxiously awaited negotiations, our delegation to the Two-Party Joint Military Commission at Camp David suddenly became extremely important. Occasionally, prominent Saigon figures also arrived to request a meeting and inquire about the military situation, the attitude of the PRG, and the possibility and conditions for talks to avoid a direct attack on Saigon. That was easily understood. The members of our delegation were the only people in the frightened "capital" who were calm and self-confident, like people who were now the real bosses, who understood the true combat situation better than anyone else, and who clearly understood the positions of the revolutionary government. During that period we remained in constant contact with our delegation, and under the direction of the Political Bureau quickly replied to the messages and guided every thought and act so that they could be appropriate to diplomatic atmosphere and to the developments on the battlefield.

Meanwhile, the White House was extremely anxious: "During the past several days, since Weyand had gone to Saigon, the White House had not dared comment directly on the crisis in Indochina. But on 3 April, when fierce fighting broke out around Saigon, President Ford could no longer remain silent. During his vacation at Palm Springs, Ford spoke with reporters and criticized Thieu from having withdrawn his troops from the Central Highlands too hastily and said that the evacuation of 6,000 Americans from Vietnam was under consideration. In dealing with one of the most delicate matters, he said that as he understood the War Powers Limitation Act he was authorized to use force to assist in the evacuation of Americans from any war zone in the world.*

"His remarks about that matter were not surprising. For in addition to the tense situation around Saigon his administration had to cope with a disaster that was occurring in Kampuchea. The military situation in Phnom Penh had reached the danger point in the past few days. The White House had finally decided to withdraw all U.S. troops there."**

Thus Dean, the U.S. ambassador in Phnom Penh, on 12 April boarded a helicopter, an American flag under his arm, and fled before Martin did. Lon Nol, the leader of the Kampuchean puppet regime, under the guise of going on an official trip abroad, had gone to the United States at the beginning of the month. On 17 April all of Kampuchea was liberated by the revolutionary forces of the heroic Khmer people. It was beautiful coordination between two battlefields that had long been linked together, in a strategic position of the three Indochinese countries relying on one another in order to exist and grow stronger, a solid strategic position that was as unshakeable as the Truong Son range and the great Mekong River.

While the Americans were carrying out the "Operation Eaglepull" evacuation by helicopter from Phnom Penh, in Saigon the pace of the evacuation also steadily increased. "After 7 April the number of U.S. transport aircraft arriving at and departing from Tan Son Nhat airbase greatly increased. Nearly a dozen C141 transport aircraft left every day, along with a smaller number of C-130 aircraft which landed at night to transport cargo."***

"From the very beginning, flights departed like a shuttle to Clark Air Force Base, mainly carrying DAO personnel and their families. Nonessential personnel would have to leave the country by commercial aircraft so that the

---

*Frank Snepp, op. cit.
**During the past few days the White House lawyers had prepared a report to Ford on the legal debate about the War Powers Act. In addition to other matters they pointed out that when the act was discussed in committee and on the floor even its sponsors agreed that armed force could be used to rescue American citizens abroad in an emergency. Since they had no other authorization, Ford decided to use that point to justify his use of Marines stationed aboard ships in the South China Sea.
***Frank Snepp, "Decent Interval."

evacuation could proceed rapidly. A State Department official contacted PANAM on 7 April and requested that company to increase its flights to Saigon. The officials of that company did not want to do so, for that would mean that they would have to pay out more to insure the Indochina flights. But they agreed to provide more seats by providing 747 aircraft for the evacuation from Saigon.*

In Washington, high-ranking officials were arguing about providing Thieu with emergency aid of $722 million, which was regarded as a dose of medicine that would bring him back to life. Secretary of State Kissinger wanted to provide maximum aid, but Secretary of Defense Schle   protested, for he regarded South Vietnam as already lost.

Against such a background, we began to carry out the strategic encirclement of Saigon according to plan. On "D-Day," 9 April, battles to cut Route 4 west of Saigon and the attack on Xuan Loc, the key strongpoint on the life-or-death defense line of Saigon and Military Region III, began.

To the west, the plan had envisioned using forces of Group 232 to take the town of Moc Hoa, then advance along Route 12, and a combined arms unit advancing to cut Route 4 between Cai Lay and Tan Hiep and, in coordination with the 8th Division of Military Region 8, annihilate the puppet 7th and 9th divisions. But the situation had developed too slowly and the Regional Command was because our forces were not large they could be held up for a long time at Moc Hoa if the enemy concentrated forces and put up a stiff defense, so it recommended to the upper echelon that the plan be changed. While it was keeping the enemy tied down at the Kampuchean border the 5th Division unsuccessfully attacked the town of Thu Thua and the city of Tan An because the puppet 7th and 22d divisions had prepared fortified defenses and put up a resistance, while our division had only infantry and weak fire support. The Group 232 Command ordered the division to attack to annihilate the enemy reaction force and eliminate the enemy's system of outposts north of Route 4 in order to create a staging area from which to control that road and cut it whenever necessary. During the next few days of the fighting the division inflicted heavy casualties on the 1st Infantry Regiment of the puppet 7th Division and an armored regiment and liberated a broad strip along the Van Co Tay River and the Bo Bo Canal immediately north of Route 4, thus directly threatening that road. The forces of Military Region 8 from time to time cut Route 4 between Tan Hiep and Cai Be in My Tho Province, while the forces of Military Region 9 attacked the Cai Von-Ba Cang segment in Vinh Long.

To the east, during the night of 9 April and the early morning of 10 April, 4th Corps, made up of the 7th and 1st (formerly 341st) Divisions and the understrength 6th Division of Military Region 7, attacked the city of Xuan Loc in Long Khanh Province. The powerful attack broke through the city's defenses in many places and rapidly developed to the center of the city. At 0740 on 10 April we planted our flag on provincial headquarters and took a number of other bases and positions, such as the Police Service, the U.S. advisers' compound, the CIA intelligence compound, the ranger base, the railroad station, etc. The enemy still held the subsector and immediately concentrated two

---
*Op. cit.

regiments of the 18th Division, along with the remnants of the RF, ranger and armored battalions to put up a defense and launch one counterattack after another. On 10 April the enemy used helicopters to land an airborne brigade in the outskirts of the city to reinforce and shore up the morale of the 18th Division. By 15 April they had sent there two additional Marine brigades, a ranger group, a regiment of the 5th Division, an artillery battalion, and two armored regiments. Thus they concentrated 50 percent of the regular troops, about 60 percent of the artillery, and nearly all of the armor, of III Corps, and the equivalent of a division from the airborne and Marine strategic reserves during the first days of the fighting. They also provided intensive air support for their infantry and armor counterattacks, while also bombing the areas we had taken and our troop formations, as well as our supply lines and rear areas.

They used two types of very lethal bombs, the "Daisy Cutter" and the "CBU,"[*] used to clear landing zones for helicopters and for mass murder, which the U.S. troops used for many years in Vietnam and surreptitiously turned over the puppet troops after leaving Vietnam in accordance with the Paris Agreement. (After the liberation we captured a CBU bomb depot and are exhibiting that weapon in the Museum of U.S.-Puppet Crimes on Vo Van Tan Street in Ho Chi Minh City.) That was the first time since 1973 that puppet airplanes had dropped those bombs on targets. It may be said that the puppet troops used everything they had and all strength they could assemble to defend Xuan Loc. Was it that they feared the shocking statement made by their mentor Weyand when he drafted the final defense plan: "To lose Xuan Loc is to lose Saigon." The puppets not only went all-out to defend Xuan Loc, the key, central point of their final strategic defense line, but also hoped to win a major psychological and political battle during that perilous time. During that period the puppet and foreign press propagandized and ballyhooed the fighting ability of the revitalized puppet troops, and that the puppet troops were not in such dire straits and were still strong enough to defend the regime, etc. The U.S. UPI news agency on 12 April, thinking Xuan Loc could hold, said that the puppets had selected Xuan Loc as "a testing ground for the fighting ability of the South Vietnamese troops." That was partly true: the outcome of the battle for Xuan Loc would decide the fate of the puppet army and regime. Thieu very much needed such a victory so that he could appeal for maximum U.S. support and aid, in order to rebuild the puppet army, shore up the morale of their officers and enlisted men and, especially, so that Thieu could remain in power. The United

---

*The high-ranking CIA officer Frank Snepp in his book "Decent Interval" described those two types of bombs as follows: "The Daisy Cutter was a type of bomb used to blow down trees in helicopter landing zones. It exploded in the air above the objective and cleared an area of up to 100 meters square. The CBU was an even more terrible weapon. It exploded at a predetermined height, creating a billowing cloud with a radius of up to 100 meters and more than 2 meters thick. When it encounters flame the cloud gives off intense heat and creates pressure of tons per square centimeter that disintegrates everything. Anyone surviving that ring of fire will still be suffocated after the bomb explodes, thus creating a vacuum. In the U.S. arsenal, the CBU bomb is the most murderous weapon outside nuclear weapons."

States hoped that the puppets could hold out for a time so that they could have something with which to bargain should negotiations be held.

At the Regional Command headquarters we closely monitored each development of the battle. The reports of 9 and 10 April were very encouraging. The columns were developing their attacks well and we had occupied many objectives. But beginning with the evening of 10 April the situation became tense. The enemy counterattacked insanely even though they had suffered heavy losses. The enemy airplanes attacked fiercely, as if they wanted to destroy the positions they had lost. The Corps complained about shortages of ammunition of all kinds, and especially that the 1st, 6th and 7th Divisions were understrength because they had fought continuously since the fighting along Route 20 began. Then there was a report that the positions we had taken had to be given up one by one. Some positions changed hands several times. The losses of the 1st Division were heavier than those of the other units because it did not have much experience in intensive combat. The situation was very difficult.

Comrades Pham Hung, Van Tien Dung, and even Le Duc Tho were very worried when they saw that the enemy was concentrating increasingly larger forces and we appeared to be slowing down and had failed to take our objectives rapidly and effectively, or had been pushed back. The fighting was very fierce and we were afraid that we would suffer heavy losses at an inopportune time. Thus they suggested that our men be withdrawn from the city and annihilate the enemy troops all around the city, concentrating on annihilating them bit by bit. I recommended that I go there in person to grasp the situation first-hand and work with our men there to find a way to win victory. They agreed.

Thus on the afternoon of 11 April I headed straight for the 4th Corps headquarters. Our vehicle crossed the Dong Nai River by ferry at the Ta Lai ferry crossing and met Route 20 at Phuong Lam. The Corps headquarters was situated on the bank of the La Nga River, a name which entered history with the great La Nga victory during the 9-year anti-French resistance. That battle was commanded by comrades Huynh Van Nghe and Bui Cat Vu. Now comrade Vu was deputy commander of 4th Corps. When I met him on the bank of the La Nga River I happily admonished him to win a second La Nga victory. In fact, I was confident that we would.

After being briefed on developments in the battle and personally inspecting a number of areas, monitoring the enemy's air and artillery activities, reviewing the situation of the enemy troops, and assessing our actual strength, on 13 April we discussed alternatives. By that time the Corps had been reinforced by the 95B Regiment, which had just arrived, a tank company, and a number of field artillery and antiaircraft pieces, and had urgently brought in reinforcements and ammunition, so we still had good fighting strength. The enemy troops were counterattacking to retake the lost positions in hopes of regaining all of Xuan Loc City. The intensity of antiaircraft and air activities was great.

Comrade Hoang Nghia Khanh, the Corp's chief of staff, concisely analyzed the situation and then recommended that Long Khanh be abandoned and that all of our forces circle around to take Trang Bom and then Bien Hoa. Comrade Hoang

Cam, the Corps commander, suggested that we wipe out the puppet 52d Regiment at the Dau Giay intersection and at Nui Thi. Then we would take Xuan Loc. Bien Hoa would be attacked in coordination with attacks in other areas. Many others, such as Hoang Cam, agreed differing only on what forces should be used.

After listening to all opinions I analyzed a number of points and reached a clearcut conclusion: Xuan Loc was an extremely important point on the enemy's defense line, so they had concentrated many forces to defend it. At that time the enemy forces were superior to ours. We no longer had the element of surprise. Thus, it was not to our advantage to continue to attack Xuan Loc. We controlled Route 20 as far as Tuc Trung. Between Tuc Trung and the Dau Giay intersection (the intersection of Route 20 and Route 1) the enemy was not strong. We had to fully utilize our advantage on Route 20 and the enemy's weakness in the area around Dau Giay.

If we took and held the Dau Giay intersection--which we were capable of doing because the enemy there was weak and would be taken by surprise--Xuan Loc would no longer be a key strongpoint because it would lay outside the defense line. Bien Hoa would immediately be threatened. After we had taken Dau Giay the enemy in Xuan Loc would be confused and in a state of chaos because they would be cut off from their rear area, and become surrounded and isolated. The III Corps would be terrified, for large forces would be trapped outside the defense line. Thus we would make two moves. One, we would concentrate our attack on Dau Giay from two directions: Xuan Loc and Trang Bom. Second, we would withdraw from Xuan Loc and advance toward Ba Ria and Bien Hoa. Therefore, we could not take the pressure off the enemy in Xuan Loc but carefully keep them contained and annihilate them if they counterattacked or fled in panic.

On the basis of that analysis, it was decided to:

--First of all, use the 1st Division to annihilate the 52d Regiment at Dau Giay and Mt. Thi, a dominating high point there, liberate a large area, and defend at all the Dau Giay intersection, a position which would become a key position as well as for the enemy. We would stop and annihilate the enemy troops counterattacking from Trang Bom.

--The strong forces of the Corps would keep up the pressure on and annihilate the enemy in Xuan Loc, especially in the area between Xuan Loc and the Day Giay intersection, to support the Dau Giay blocking position.

--Send a force to lay an ambush on Route 2 to block that road, the only road to Ba Ria, and annihilating enemy troops fleeing along it.

--Rationally deploy antiaircraft firepower in order to effectively counter enemy airplanes. Meanwhile, the Hieu Liem artillery base and Group 113 would effectively interdict Bien Hoa air base, from which enemy airplanes equipped with powerful bombs had been taking off to attack us.

Everyone agreed with that operational plan and urgently prepared to carry it out, under the specific guidance of the corps.

I then discussed with the Corps and Military Region 7 the direction of attack after Xuan Loc was liberated, how the eastern column would attack Saigon once the order was received to do so. When we were discussing that matter we did not yet include in our calculations the forces commanded by comrade Tan, which were advancing south along the central coast. We were still working with the plan of attacking Saigon by using the existing B2 forces.

I made a careful analysis: The city of Bien Hoa, along with the air base and the headquarters of the puppet III Corps, had many complicated structures and fortifications. The enemy would take advantage of them to stop our advance on Saigon. After the loss of Xuan Loc was lost, Bien Hoa would be the most important point in that direction. By attacking Bien Hoa we would attack the "hardest point on the enemy's defensive shield, which would be to our disadvantage and slow us down. The enemy would be weaker--and unexpecting--along Route 15 flanking the Long Binh supply depot to the Saigon-Bien Hoa highway. We would then follow that broad highway and rapidly take the principal objective: Presidential Palace. Our advance in that direction would be mechanized, with tanks leading the way--and would develop very rapidly and have good support once we had established a 130mm artillery base at Nhon Trach. Meanwhile, part of our forces would keep the enemy tied down at Bien Hoa, which would be taken care of later.

Everyone agreed with that analysis. I also discussed with those comrades a plan: the 6th Division of Military Region 7, which was familiar with the area, would be reinforced by artillery and tanks and would move secretly and unexpectedly to liberate a segment of Route 15, penetrate through to Provincial Route 19 running through the Nhon Trach depression, quickly liberate Nhaon Trach, and set up a 130mm artillery base there. From that artillery base, before the order was received to attack Saigon, we would shell and interdict Tan Son Nhat air base. When the various columns had advanced into the city it would no longer fire on objectives in the city but would give effective support to the eastern column.

In coordination with that column, we would use the 10th Sapper Regiment to block the Long Tau River to prevent any traffic to or from the city, and send a force across the Dong Nai River to liberate Precinct 9 in Saigon in coordination with the local forces.

The 1st Division was responsible for pinning down and wiping out the enemy at Bien Hoa, and for protecting the Corps' flank.

The principal force of the Corps--the 7th Division, with the 95B Regiment in reserve--would circle around Bien Hoa, advance along Route 15, then attack directly toward Saigon and take Independence Palace, the Corps' main objective.

The comrades in the Corps all approved of that plan and were enthusiastically confident of victory. Comrades Le Van Ngoc, commander of Military Region 7, and Dang Ngoc Si, deputy commander and commander of the 6th Division, enthusiastically accepted both the immediate mission of wiping out the 52d Regiment and forming a blocking position at the Dau Giay intersection and later taking Nhon Trach in order to set up an important 130mm artillery base to interdict Tan Son Nhat airbase and support the Corps' attack on Saigon.

We parted company with confidence in victory. My party urgently returned, at a time when everyone was urgently preparing for that enormously important battle. Meanwhile, the puppet troops who had been drawn into Xuan Loc and were trying to win a "world famous" Xuan Loc victory did not suspect that they were about to become "mice caught in a trap."

During the mid-April period all of us were anxiously following every move of the 3d and 1st Corps and the combat arms units, which were coming south to participate in the campaign to liberate Saigon. Groups of cadres were sent to guide the columns. Each unit followed a different route and had a different departure date. The 1st Corps would depart from the Red River. With regard to 3d Corps, some divisions would come from the Central Highlands and some would turn from the coastal road onto Route 11 to Dalat, then follow Route 20 south. The 2d Corps and the 3d Division of Military Region 5 would fight their way down the coast. Some units arrived before the ammunition did, and when some tanks arrived they were out of POL and had only one or two rounds. Some units needed to be supplemented and reorganized. The staff and rear services cadres were buried in work. Everyone worked much longer than normal, night and day. Enthusiasm and energy were multiplied and tasks were completed cleverly and quickly.

Except for the coastal column, each corps sent in advance a group of cadres to the campaign headquarters to receive missions. The groups had to study in advance the assembly areas, and assault positions their units had to occupy, the enemy units they had to wipe out and the main objectives for which the units were responsible. Then they organized coordination among the various areas and columns, among the combat arms, between the main-force units and the local units, etc. The staff cadres of the Regional Command, led by comrade Dong Van Cong, working together with Group A75 cadres commanded by comrade Le Ngoc Hieu, briefed them on all details of the operational plan and thoroughly answered their questions. Comrade Tran Van Dinh organized cooperation between the corps and areas and the sappers and commandos, and assigned to each corps, each deep-penetration division, and the sapper and commando cadres and units guiding the attacking units, objectives that had to be attacked. Everyone went all-out and contributed all he knew to the victory.

Because of the demands of the situation, and because the corps were arriving at the battlefield piecemeal, COSVN and the Campaign Command, with the participation of Sau Tho, decided to wait until all units of the corps had arrived so that we would have absolute superiority over the enemy, launch a rapid, strong, certain-victory attack on the final U.S.-puppet lair, and keep the city intact. The Political Bureau agreed with that decision.

We concerned ourselves with adjusting the campaign plan. On the basis of the plan drafted by B2 to attack Saigon with its own forces, which had been approved by COSVN and agreed to by Van Tien Dung and Le Duc Tho; on the basis of the forces that had been predeployed in the various areas and to avoid unnecessary, time-losing upsetting deployments; and with the spirit that the B2 forces, which were familiar with the battlefield, had to be responsible for areas in which the terrain was complicated and there were many difficulties, it was necessary to reserve the most forward positions for the forces arriving from afar which arrived in time to be deployed. The plan was adjusted, and the forces assigned missions, as follows:

The northern prong, which would originate its attack from Cu Chi and Ben Cat, attack the puppet 25th Division, and advance mainly along Route 1 to take the main objective--Tan Son Nhat airbase--would be the responsibility of 3d Corps. We had originally intended to assign that direction to the 9th Division and the 16th and 271B Regiments, but now those units were transferred to Group 232.

Group 232, as originally planned, would attack from the west, mainly along Route 12, with the objective of taking the Capital Special Zone headquarters. The 271B Regiment was transferred to the southern prong.

The organization of the attack from the south, which was still the responsibility of the 88th and 24th Regiments--now with the addition of the 271 Regiment--was the responsibility of Military Region 8, which designated comrade Ba Theng, i.e. Maj Gen Vo Van Thanh, commander of that column; comrade Tu Than, i.e. Maj Gen Huynh Van Men, deputy commander; and comrade Chin Pham, a member of the standing committee of the Military Region 8 Party Committee, political officer Comrade Tu Chieu, commander of the Long An Province unit, was named a deputy commander of the prong. The main line of advance from that direction was along Route 5, north from Can Giuoc. Its main objective was National Police Headquarters.

Comrade Le Duc Anh, deputy commander of the Regional Command, was designated a deputy commander of the Campaign Command, and comrade Le Van Tuong, deputy political officer of the Regional Command, was designated to exercise direct, unified command of both the western and southern prongs.

The northern column which would attack the 5th Division and advance along Route 13 to take the puppet GHQ, was the responsibility of 1st Corps. The Gia Dinh Regiment was responsible for the Saigon outskirts in that direction.

The eastern prong was previously the responsibility of the 4th Corps, which was now reinforced with part of 2d Corps and the 3d Division of Military Region 5. Comrade Le Trong Tan, deputy commander of the Campaign Command, was designated to command both corps and make the specific decisions in that direction.

Thus all five directions were reinforced with very strong forces, including both infantry and the combat arms. However, there was a shortage of military engineer units and facilities, especially river-crossing facilities. The eastern, western, and southern prongs were strengthened by the addition of strong commands because they were made up of many units and had many complications.

The forward headquarters of the Campaign Command was located in the Van Tam area southwest of Chon Thanh and north of Ben Cat, immediately to the rear of the 3d Corps. The Regional Staff had prepared that site in advance.

On 18 April comrade Sau Tho, representing the Political Bureau, along with the Campaign Command reviewed the campaign for the final time. Everyone expressed a high degree of determination to correctly implement the motto of the

Political Bureau and the Military Commission of the party Central Committee: "Marvelous speed-boldness-surprise-certain victory." With regard to main-force units, we had a three-fold advantage over the enemy numerically and were many times superior with regard to quality. We had to deploy forces to annihilate the enemy troops defending the outer perimeters and also strong forces to penetrate directly and rapidly to the main objectives in the city. We had to attack rapidly and strongly from the outside, in close coordination with attacks and uprisings inside the city, so that the enemy would not have time to react or carry out sabotage. The troops would coordinate with the uprising revolutionary mass forces to quickly take all installations and neighborhoods in the city in the briefest possible time. That was the content and significance of marvelous speed. It was decided that the five columns would have to coordinate closely in combat and that the five main objectives assigned to the five columns would have to be taken almost simultaneously, but that the Independence Palace would be the central, final objective. When a column had taken its main objective it would have to advance immediately on the Independence Palace. If none of our forces had already taken it, that column would have to take it and raise our flag of victory. If our forces had already taken it, the column would immediately return to its original position.

"D Day" for the attack on Saigon would depend primarily on the arrival of most of 3d Corps and 1st Corps. Previously, in message No 07, brother Ba had given the following instruction: "I have discussed the situation with brother Van and feel that several more days of preparation are necessary. When most of the forces of 3d Corps and 1st Corps arrive (both infantry and technical military equipment) the large-scale attack can begin. It should not be launched now."* On the basis of that directive we monitored, ever hour and every day, the movement of each unit of the various corps, especially 1st Corps, which was traveling the longest distance. Furthermore, we sent groups of staff and rear services cadres to be on hand at the assembly areas to help the corps inventory their forces, rectify their organization and supplement their ammunition and rear services. The Regional military engineers had to prepare the Ben Bau ford across the Be River northwest of Tan Uyen for 1st Corps, insure that the 3d Corps could cross the damaged Nha Bich bridge and the Saigon River, etc. It was truly a race against time. The situation in general was urging us on and the upper echelon was urging us on. On 22 April brother Ba sent a message which included the following passage:

"The military-political opportunity for launching an attack on Saigon has arrived. We must take advantage of each day in order to promptly launch attacks on the enemy from all directions and not dally. Delay would be disadvantageous both politically and militarily. Acting promptly at the present time is insuring to the greatest possible extent that we will win total victory.

"Immediately instruct the columns to act promptly and stress combining military attacks with mass uprisings and coordination among the various columns as well as between attacks and uprisings during the action process.

---

* Document of the B2 War Recapitulation Section of the Ministry of National Defense.

"If we grasp the great opportunity, we are certain to win complete victory."*

That message arrived at a time when all enemy troops at Xuan Loc had been annihilated, routed at Xuan Loc and Thieu had been forced to resign as president of the puppet regime.

During the night of 13 April and the early morning of 14 April, in accordance with a new decision made by 4th Corps the 6th Division had wiped out a battalion of the 52d Regiment of the 18th Division and an armored squadron, and had liberated the Dau Giay intersection. The next day we took Mt. Thi, Tuc Trung, and Kiem Tan, the last positions on Route 20 and wiped out the remainder of the 52d Regiment. The 6th Division shifted over to the strong defense of those areas and to wiping out the enemy troops who launched continuous counterattacks from Trang Bom. The 7th and 1st Divisions of 4th Corps wiped out bit by bit the enemy forces at Xuan Loc belonging to the 48th Regiment, the airborne regiment and the armored units.

After the enemy failed to retake the Dau Giay intersection and they lost all of Route 20, Bien Hoa became a front-line position but the enemy did not have sufficient forces to defend it. On 18 April the puppet III Corps had to use helicopters to extricate a number of forces from Xuan Loc and take them to Bien Hoa-Trang Bom to bolster a new defense line, and on 20 April the troops remaining in Xuan Loc fled the city along Route 2 past Ba Ria and back to Bien Hoa. We were able to wipe out only part of the fleeing troops because our unit which the Ba Ria Military Command had assigned responsibility for blocking Route 2 was careless and failed to prevent the enemy from fleeing.

Frank Snepp, in the book noted above, related that "On the morning of the 21st the remaining defenses of the Government at Xuan Loc collapsed. The four surviving battalions of the 18th ARVN Division, with its commander, General Dao, were removed from the devastated city by helicopter."

At noon on the 21st Thieu called ex-Premier Khiem and Vice President Huong to his office and sadly told them that he was resigning. Thieu said, "Because of the military situation, which he described as 'hopeless' (Khien and Huong agreed) there would be no point in his remaining in office, and his doing so would only impede a settlement."**

That afternoon Thieu announced his resignation and turned over his office to Vice President Huong. "During his solemn inauguration ceremony, Tran Van Huong, who was 71 years old, had arthritis and was nearly blind, promised to hold out until 'the troops are killed or the country is lost.'"

The experts at the U.S. Embassy laughed at those hard-line declarations. They regarded them as "a pacifier for Ky and his clique, so that they would not jump in."***

---

*Document of the B2 War Recapitulation Section of the Ministry of National Defense.
**"Decent Interval," by Frank Snepp
***Ibid.

"A few months later he (Thieu) told a friend on Taiwan that "Yes, my timing was right. I waited until the disease progressed to the point that he was bedfast. No one can surpass me in what I did for my country."

That was truly the style and thought of a president of the puppet regime.

While waiting for the forces of 3d Corps and 1st Corps to arrive we were concerned with the synchronized guidance of the Military Region 8 column attacking Saigon from the south. As stated above, that direction was the most difficult one because the terrain was very difficult, our staging area was very far away and our approach route passed through areas long held by the enemy. Some segments had to be traversed secretly at night, and in other places it was necessary to wipe out enemy outposts and wipe out counter-attacking enemy troops in order to reach the outskirts of Saigon. We had to travel a long way, through a highly populated area in which the supporters of the revolution did not always outnumber the families of puppet troops. The masses had not been awakened. It was an operation in which we would have to fight our way through. We had to be good at mass proselyting and at proselyting among enemy troops. Carelessness could cause the defeat of our operation before it had a chance to participate in the attack on Saigon. If our timing was not precise and if our deployment was not solid, we could upset the plan and not meet the D Day attack date. And if we were too early we would reveal the overall scheme and harm the campaign as a whole.

After careful deliberation, during the first week of April we ordered the Military Region to deploy the column. The Military Region had received its mission in February and had organized in advance and prepared its command, forces and plan, but maintained secrecy until an order was received from the upper echelon.

I have received permission to excerpt a few pages from the diary of comrade Tran Ham Ninh, the operational aide and secretary of comrade Ba Thang, i.e. Maj Gen Vo Van Thanh, commander of that column.

The brief, succinct lines of those diary pages, although not giving the whole picture, help us imagine the organization and implementation methods of a small offensive column of the Ho Chi Minh Campaign. I say "small" because to the south we were forced to use forces smaller than in the other directions: only three regiments and two light infantry battalions made up the prong's formation. There were no clamoring tanks or armored vehicles and there was no heavy artillery or antiaircraft artillery. In addition to those units there were other units and organizations, including those of the people, which did not participate directly in the column but contributed considerably to its success. In order to fight their way through, the forces in that direction had to wipe out 45 enemy outposts, liberate 12 villages, fight the enemy on the outer perimeter, penetrate directly to the center of the city, and take by the stipulated time one of the five key objectives in order to overwhelm the enemy with marvelous speed. The key objective they had to take was National Police Headquarters, the innermost defense force and the force which guarded against and quelled the uprisings of the people. It was a key objective of our strategic general offensive and uprising.

Comrade Tran Ham Ninh recorded:

On 6 April 1975

--2330 hours. Everyone is asleep. Why do I keep tossing around, unable to sleep?

--From the fields I could see the light of a flashlight coming toward me. I got up and turned on the lantern. A courier from the cryptography section arrived. It was 12 midnight.

--"What message could be so urgent."

--"A message from ZN."

--"I'm going back now, brother Sau (i.e. Ninh)."

I opened the envelop, took out the message, and glanced at the sheet of paper. There were many instructions. The message was signed by Bay Hong* and Tu Nguyen.**

I put the lantern in a corner so that less light would be visible from outside. I read the instructions. There had been a major change. A flashlight lighting my way, I went to see brother Hai Phat (head of the operations section), who was asleep. I gently shook him and he awakened. "I've received a message changing our mission." Those words were sufficient to set up and get out from the mosquito net. After reading and rereading the message, he picked up a flashlight and went immediately to the command headquarters. It was 0100 in the morning.

9 April 1975:

I again left the beloved 20-7 area (an area in Cai Be and Cai Lay in My Tho Province, between Route 4 and the Mekong River), as I had many times before. Why did I feel so hostalgic this time? I had left the area only a week before but had returned after a few days. After I left this time, when would I return? I didn't know. I left my bag of (vegetable) seeds with brother Ba Lac.

My boat passed by the My Long base, which an enemy battalion had abandoned 2 days previously. The half-red, half-blue flag flapping in the breeze was a beautiful sight. The current flowed lazily, as if not caring that in a corner of that base there was still a body of a mercenary.

When we reached Nhi Qui, the sun had not yet gone down. Guerrillas had surrounded the Bo Keo post, so enemy mortar shells were falling haphazardly. The enemy infantry had not yet withdrawn from Route 4, so we could not yet cross the road. At 2100 hours I established contact with the provincial

---
* Pham Hung
**Tran Van Tra

unit. We organized a road crossing. Thus by 2400 hours, far from the 20-7 area, we rested for the night.

10 April 1975:

Tan Hoi, a staunch area, the inviolable base of the My Tho provincial unit. Of the command staff only Tam Cong was present. The commanders of two battalions who had an appointment to meet with the Command were present, and after having waited a long time were only able to meet with the E2 chief of staff.

At 1500 hours I set out for Tam Hiep, where I met E3 (E88). They were ready.

At 1900 hours I again crossed Route 4. To the right was the Trung Luong intersection, to the left was the Ben Chua bridge. With the help of the people, our column crossed the road safely.

While passing through the Bao Dinh area I met someone I knew. But we didn't have time to talk because the column continued to move forward. My friend's mission was to remain behind and defend that area. We followed a footpath passing in front of many houses. Inside the houses there was complete silence. But it was certain that the women and children in them could not sleep, for the sound of footsteps, although very light, echoed in their hearts. It was a moving, memorable scene.

Due to a lack of close coordination, the column went down to Luong Hoa but went to the wrong place and met no one. It was too late at night, so we slept among the roots of popinac bushes.

11 April 1975:

We arose early in the morning and went up to Song Binh, where we met everywhere. It was reported to J10 (the Military Region 8 Command) and Group 232 that the command of the southern prong had arrived safely. During the late afternoon the command crossed the Ong Vau road and went down to Quon Long (Cho Gao). When we arrived there, it was very difficult to find a level place to spread a plastic sheet on which to sleep. But it wasn't really much of a problem.

12 April 1975:

Quon Long. After a day we still hadn't learned about the whereabouts of E2, E4 (i.e. the 24th Regiment). We also could not learn about the location and activities of E3. We waited anxiously.

The determination of the southern column, to make its way to the assembly position by the stipulated time, was reported to R, Group 232 and J10.

13 April 1972:

The cadre team of E2, E4 arrived. But we still did not know the location of E3 and brother Tu Than.

Two My Tho battalions were operating strongly at the Cho Gao Canal. The enemy resisted fiercely. The enemy was drawn to that area so that we would not be bothered.

That night the division (5th Division). After the other units had launched their attacks, we would have an easier time of it.

E3 was encouraged to go all-out to attack Tan Tru during the night of 14 April.

14 April 1975:

Because of a lack of close cooperation, when the E4 cadre team arrived at Rach Tram no one was there to meet it, so it was unable to cross Route 21 and had to return to Quon Long.

E2 was ordered to return. There had been a change regarding the use of forces. What unit would replace E2 in the formation of the southern column?

The 279th Battalion wiped out the Ong Bai post, thus expanding our corridor.

All of E4 arrived.

Brother Hai Phat's team arrived. Thus only now could the column's command organ assemble. With regard to forces, by that time we had 2E and ed (i.e. the 3d Battalion). As for d10, d14, and another E, we didn't know when they would arrive.

15 April 1975:

Today we left Quon Long and at 1700 hours we arrived at the fields. We organized the formation and set the departure times.

We left Quon Long. It was unimaginably muddy. I didn't suspect that we would be in mud and water up to our waists. Following water coconut trees, we made our way to Rach Tram. When we crossed Route 21 it was nearly 2400 hours. There were no junks to cross the Van Co Tay River. We lay in the field and waited. Nearby was the Thuan My outpost. A little farther was Thanh Vinh Dong. On the other side of the river was Cho Dinh. How bold we were! It had been 15 years since I was there. I had very fond memories. My mother had passed on and was buried near there. My elder brother had fulfilled his mission during the anti-French resistance war. He had sacrificed a few years ago. Only my father and I survived. No! There was still a whole nation.

16 April 1975:

Nhut Ninh. We weren't able to cross the river until 0400 hours. When we took our first break the sun was up. Our clothes were covered with mud. The troops passing by looked strangely peaceful.

22 April 1975:

The command headquarters was still at Tan Phuoc. Thieu had resigned. The command sent message No 72ZN to E3 and E4 instructing them to both step up their attacks and do a good job of proselyting enemy troops. E3's attack was going well at Can Gioc (it had wiped out four outposts). E4 had also wiped out four outposts in Can Duoc.

Difficulties had been encountered in all aspects of rear services support for the past week. Too few supplies were being sent to the forward areas. During the day the column's command sent five ZN messages regarding rear services.

The command established contact with brother Tu Chieu (commander of the Long An provincial unit and deputy commander of the southern column) through E3.

23 April 1975:

Vam Rach Ca (Tan Phuoc). The command assigned E4 the following mission: "The line of development of E is Phuoc Hau and Long Thuong (Can Giuoc, bordering Binh Chanh) in order to fulfill the principal mission."

Rear services were very difficult. We knew that J10 was also experiencing difficulties but in order to insure victory we recommended that J10 (brother Ba Dao) send Nam Tri of Ba Thi to replace Ba Canh (who had not fulfilled his mission) and that J10 report the situation to J50 (the command of the southern column).

During the day E4 liberated Long Cang (Can Duoc) and was surrounding and attacking d2/E42.

Brother Thu Than went to Group 232.

The situation of the southern column was reported to R, Group 232 and J10.

24 April 1975:

The units temporarily halted their rapid advance and reformed their ranks to the spot. The positions of the E and d were reported to R, Group 232 and J10.

The reinforcements for J50 had not yet arrived. Recommended that brother Ba Dao (J10) look into that problem.

Recommended that brother Tu Chieu and E3 send a cadre from Can Giuoc to the command headquarters.

The command asked Tu Chieu whether he had been able to establish contact with the party committees and district units of Nha Be and Binh Chanh.

R ordered Ba Thang to go to Group 232 to receive a mission. A message was sent to Long An instructing him to go to a location on Route 4 in Binh Duc. We waded across the muddy and mosquito-infested Nhat Tao River at 1800 hours.

When we neared Route 4 the rice had been harvested and the fields were dry. We felt very comfortable. We lay waiting until 2200 hours but the situation was changing and we could not establish contact with Long An. We had to return to command headquarters.

25 April 1975:

Long Son. The fields were dry and the rice had been harvested. Received message 111ZN from Group 232 about the campaign's D Day. Repeat, D Day. The awaited day had arrived.

Directed E3 to do a good job of coordinating combat and the proselyting of enemy troops. The command agreed to leave d4/E4 behind, and have E3 take Long Thuong. A message was sent to Tu Chien and Bon Do (E3) instructing them to come to the command headquarters. The Long An D1 unit blew up the Rach Dao bridge.

26 April 1975:

Long Son: Starting today, messages would be numbered from 01. Message 01ZN was sent to Group 232 repeating the D Day date a second time (in reply to Group 232's message 442N).

Reported to R, Group 232, and J10 that we had encountered difficulty en route to the meeting. Recommended that Group 232 assign mission via message. Said that brother Tu Than could not go either.

Received message No 452N from brother Sau Nam (Group 232) assigning mission to the column, which expressed determination to fulfill its mission.

Still unable to make contact with Nha Be and Can Giuoc.

The command reminded brother Phong, commander of the 271B Regiment, to organize a march because the time was pressing.

Reminded brother Nam Nghi to go to Long An to defend the area 1 kilometer from the Cho Dao post to insure the command's movement.

1800 hours. The command headquarters departed Long Son in the direction of Can Giuoc. Passed through a populated area. Most of the people stayed put.

2200 hours, arrived at Phuoc Lam (Can Giuoc).

2300 hours, the southern column command met to evaluate E3's fulfillment of its mission and to review the good points and deficiencies. Brother Tu Do (regimental commander) and Nam Tu (political officer) of E3 participated in the meeting.

Note: Fulfilled missions, opened up approach route, and prepare to launch a rapid attack.

Stress teaching mass viewpoint to the units: fight for the people, protect the people, liberate the people, motivate the masses to participate in the revolution, and dig shelters for the people.

--Pay more attention to proselyting among enemy troops.

27 April 1975:

Phuoc Lam.

Recommended that Group 232 and R allow us to contact E117 (sappers).

0730, the southern column command met to discuss the attack plan and organization.

Received message No 53ZN from Group 232 stating that Group 232 had instructed brother Nam Man (of the Saigon municipal unit) have Binh Chanh and Ha Be contact the southern column.

--1d/E529 (Chin May) now in the Cau Nhi, Thien Duong area.

0920, the column command assigned mission to E4, accepted by Ba Thuyen, the regimental commander, and Hai Van, the regimental political officer:

--The Ho Chi Minh campaign will liberate Saigon.

--The principal objective: the National Police Headquarters.

--Time: night of 27 April, the advance element arrives in Binh Dang. Night of 28 April, the entire regiment arrives at Binh Dang. Night of 29 April, the attack begins.

--The command headquarters of the southern column: Nam Cau Mat. Field hospital will set up near the headquarters.

--Beginning on 27 April, no firing while en route, until the attack begins. The 1st Long An battalion will serve as the regimental reserve.

--The objectives of E3 are to attack Qui Duc, Hung Long, Phong Duoc and Binh Dang.

--Slogan:
  Question: Ho Chi Minh
  Answer: Long live!

--Code signs:

--Carry liberation flags.

--Wear red armband on left arm.

28 April 1975:

The command headquarters did not know the location of the 271B Regiment. The regiment had only recently come down to the delta, where the going is very rough. The command sent a message to the 271B Regiment and also a message to J10 recommending that it inform us about 271B.

Message was sent to J10 and Group 232, informing them that our supplies were very low and requesting additional supplies.

We sent someone to establish contact with brother Chin May.

Night. The command headquarters and the units left Phuoc Lam-Thuan Thanh with the units, crossed the Quan Com River and advanced to Hung Long. After traveling all night we arrived there and by the time we completed our fortification it was morning.

29 April 1975:

Hung Long: When they awoke in the morning and saw the liberation troops everywhere, the people were extremely enthusiastic. One old woman went out into the field and dug up a red flag with a gold star. I don't know when it had been buried, but it looked very new.

Message No 15ZN, to Tu Nguyen, Sau Nam and Tam Phuong, reported that the command headquarters of the southern column, E4, E3, and d10 had arrived at Hung Long during the night of 28 April. E4 would take Precinct 8 (Y Bridge) and E3 would take Route 5. The column command would also use the 2d Long An battalion.

The command sent a message to the 271B Regiment: "The time for fulfilling your mission has arrived. Move out rapidly."

Message No 16ZN to Tu Nguyen, Sau Nam and Tam Phuong reported that the 1st Battalion of the 3d Regiment would be used to attack the Hung Long subsector.

The command met to discuss the attack plan. Brother Tu Chien reported on the terrain east of Route 5 and on our situation and that of the enemy in the Binh Chanh and Nha Be areas.

In the Rach Cay area the terrain was very wild and belonged to neither us nor the enemy. It was very marshy and impassable.

The deployment of E4 was changed a little. Instead of the whole regiment crossing over to the area east of Route 5 and advancing from Rach Cay to Y Bridge, we would use only the 1st Battalion of that regiment to carry out that plan, while the 2d Battalion of the 24th Regiment would attack along Route 5 to the Nhi Thien Duong bridge, turn and go to the Pham The Hien ferry landing, and from there go to Y Bridge.

E3 would remain unchanged:

Message No 18ZN to brothers Tu Nguyen, and Tam Phuong reported on the liberation of Hung Long, the receipt of the 731 message and attack plan.

1900 hours. The command headquarters moving toward Da Phuoc. The regiments were moving according to plan.

2100 hours. Arrived at Da Phuoc. All elements dug fortifications. The masses at first would not let us dig, perhaps because they were afraid of "disturbing" the soil. We explained that the positions were being dug both so that the troops could fight and so that the people could take shelter from the bombs and shells. If there were no fortifications, the troops and the people would be endangered. Ultimately, they not only let us dig but gave us wood to make covers and glutinous rice for the troops to eat.

After 2400 we had completed the digging of fortifications. All of the fortifications were full of water. Some collapsed after being dug.

30 April 1975:

Da Phuoc. Early in the morning the sound of vehicles could be heard on Route 5. The command headquarters was situated 500 meters from the road.

Liberation Radio broadcast the communique of the PRG and the communique of the Saigon Front Command. I felt very excited when I heard it.

The command sent messages guiding E3 and E4 and relaying the two communiques, and a message reporting the results of the fulfillment of missions.

At 0800, message No 23ZN to brothers Tu Nguyen, Sau Nam and Tam Phuong reported that E3 and E4 had taken up positions at the designated time and had begun their attacks.

At 1000 E4 reported that it had crossed Y Bridge. There was another report: it was advancing to take the column's main objective: National Police Headquarters. The time was exactly 1030.

After 1000, the triangular Da Phuoc post surrendered. The command headquarters moved out to Route 5.

From Da Phuoc the masses used buses and commercial trucks to transport the entire command organ to the Y Bridge. The time was 1130 hours.

1200. The command headquarters of the southern headquarters arrived at the National Police Headquarters, an hour and a half after E4.

The final message, No 24ZN, to brothers Tu Nguyen, Sau Nam and Tam Phuong, reported the taking over of the Municipal Police Headquarters and the National Police Command.

One of the most difficult problems during the period of final preparations for the Ho Chi Minh campaign was that of military engineers taking the advancing columns across rivers so that they could advance into the city. For example, we had to find a way to take Group 232 across the Vam Co Dong River so that the entire formation could arrive at the assault position. Group 232 had been reinforced with additional infantry forces, field artillery--including heavy 130mm artillery--and antiaircraft artillery--and a tank-armored regiment one-third of the tanks of which were T54's. In all, there were nearly 800 vehicles and artillery pieces, but the region only had half of a heavy ferry (the Soviet TPP model). An additional half had been requested from the central echelon but it had not yet arrived. In all other directions there was also a shortage of military engineer forces. The staff carried out a review and concluded that the High Command had reinforced the Saigon Front with the following military engineer forces:

--The 279th Construction Regiment had arrived.

--The 574th Road-Building Regiment of the 599 Command had arrived and would be put at the disposal of the Rear Services Department.

--The 249th Ferry Regiment had four companies and one-fourth of a TPP heavy ferry set. It was estimated that the unit would arrive on about 20 April but it had not yet arrived.

We had decided that the first ferry unit to arrive would be sent immediately to Group 232, for its forces had to cross a river before the others, and may be the only direction to require such facilities if the enemy could not blow up the bridges. The 1st Corps had to cross the Be River, but during that season that river's water level was low and the regional military engineers had already prepared a ford at the Bau ferry landing. For the immediate future, Group 232 would have to rely on the existing forces and mobilize on-the-spot facilities in order to cross the Van Co Dong River.

For that reason, a question that was posed at that time was what we would do if the enemy withdrew rapidly into the city and blew up the bridges on the roads leading to Saigon. Anything could happen, so we had to have contingency plans. We knew that Saigon was situated in an area with many rivers, streams and drainage ditches. The rivers and streams were deep and marshy. The rivers were marshy and the banks were marshy; after one went ashore it was sometimes necessary to cross marshy fields. The enemy had sufficient explosives and know-how to carry out sabotage. In their death throes they had all sorts of insidious plots.

That was a very great obstacle for bringing into play the offensive strength of the combined combat arms' heavy technical equipment. In all directions we had to cross at least four or five bridges. If the bridges were blown up, would our vehicles and artillery be stopped in the outskirts? We could overcome those problems, but the enemy would have time to build fortifications and obstacles and organize a defense, and our commandos attacking objectives inside the city would be isolated and the people could not arise. We would have to attack each defense line, street and house, so we would no longer have the element of surprise or rapid speed, and the city would no longer be intact.

At that time our troops did not have the capabilities of the other modern armies, and could not send in airborne units or land troops by helicopter to take the bridges by surprise before the main body of troops arrived. But that was not a simple matter, for it was necessary to attack and take dozens of bridges at the same time in many different directions.

We had a total of six sapper regiments, added to dozens of commando units which were on a state of readiness in the outskirts and in the city. Those were elite units which had been steeled and challenged over the course of many years of fighting the Americans and had achieved many brilliant feats of arms. Many units had been awarded the "hero" designation. The 3d Corps also had its own sapper regiment. Thus we were fully capable of preventing the enemy from blowing up the bridges and of insuring that the corps could advance directly to their objectives unimpeded.

But it was necessary to change the missions of the sapper-commando units. The Regional Command had previously assigned them the mission of taking the objectives for which they were responsible, from the five key objectives to the other important objectives, while the corps were entering the city, in order to coordinate attacks from within with attacks from the outside. Now their principal objective became taking and holding the important bridges in the various directions until the corps passed. Although there were many commando units and a number of sapper units which were still responsible for objectives inside the city, the strong units had to shift over to the new missions. The change of principal missions had to be carried out very urgently, within 4 or 5 days. The units had to study and draft combat plans while on the move. Another difficulty was that after taking the bridges it was necessary to defend them and repulse enemy counterattacks. That was a tactic the sappers had seldom used, and there was no time for retraining. Even so, confident in the capabilities and traditions of the sappers and commandos, and confident in their strong will and courage, on 25 April we decided to change the missions. The bridges had to be taken and held immediately before H-Hour on D Day, when simultaneous attacks would be launched on the city. If we were tardy the vanguard units and the success of the entire campaign would be jeopardized. But if we were too early our units would in many instances be in great danger, for the sapper units, which made use of the tactic of surprise attacks and not defensive tactics, and who were not equipped to launch direct attacks, would have a hard time holding bridges for a long period of time or retaking them a second or third time. Furthermore, the enemy could launch strong counterattacks before our corps had arrived and then blow up the bridge. The time when a bridge should be taken was determined by the rate of advance of the corps. The campaign command assigned to the commands in the various directions responsibility for assigning times to the sappers.

The direction with the most large bridges was the east. In addition to the bridges across the Dong Nai River, such as the Dong Nai highway bridge and Ghenh Bridge, and bridges across the Saigon River, such as the Newpost highway bridge and the Binh Loi bridge there were other smaller, but no less important bridges, such as the Rach Chiec bridge. In the other direction the bridges were not very large but there were many of them and if they were destroyed we would encounter considerable difficulties.

Group 232 had to cross the Van Co Dong River before launching its attack, but it encountered many difficulties. And because it had to maintain secrecy before attacking it had to cross the river at night and take up its assault positions at night in an area still controlled by the enemy: the My Hanh area near the intersection of Route 9 and Route 10 (Duc Hoa in Long An). The point where the Vam Co Dong River that had to be crossed was in the village of An Ninh, more than 10 kilometers northwest of Bao Trai (i.e. Khiem Hanh, capital of the puppets' Hau Nghia Province). If necessary, the Group was prepared to cross the river by force, advance directly to the town of Hiep Hoa, and then follow Route 10. Along that stretch of the Vam Co Dong River both banks were marshy and it was very difficult to find firm terrain. The area west of the river, which we had liberated during the first phase, was in the "Parrot's Beak" area, part of Dong Thap Muoi. It was a largely marshy area with some high-lying area and was sparsely populated. Trees were very scarce. During the wars, both the anti-French war and the anti-U.S. war, when our troops went there the people could provide us with much rice and food, especially fish, but we couldn't touch the firewood, which was precious. All of the troops brought along a small bundle of firewood for his own use. Along the bank of the river, an area controlled by the enemy, we occasionally had guerrilla bases. An Ninh village was a village with a revolutionary tradition. During Tet Mau Than our 9th Division bivouaced there before attacking Saigon during the second phase of the offensive and uprising. The terrain there was relatively good. There was a strip of high-lying land extending to Route 10, down to Bao Cong hamlet, and then on to My Hanh village, the first village base of the "Hoc Mon-Ba Diem-Duc Hoa Interdistrict Liberation Unit" in 1945--during the anti-French war--and a village of a heroic liberation soldier during the anti-U.S. war: Nguyen Thi My Hanh. Thus at the river crossing point we could cross from our area, which was marshy, and land on the enemy-controlled opposite bank, which was relatively high, and launch the attack immediately. The route from the rear area to the river-crossing point was very muddy and if steps were not taken to correct that problem it would be difficult to use vehicles. The cadres of Group 232, working with the cadres of the neighboring localities, mobilized the people to cut and bundle thousands of bushes and conceal them in many places. As stated above, wood was scarce there so only if the people were mobilized early and over a large area could we have sufficient wood by the deadline. The results were satisfactory and the enemy knew nothing.

Comrade By Triet (Vo Minh Triet), director of military engineers in the Regional Command, who was appointed as commander of military engineers in Group 232, related the following:

"The day before the river crossing the first rainstorm of the season poured water down over a large area. The road became increasingly flooded and muddy. At night the troops moved up to the river and sat on the bank. Everyone, from Brother Nam Nga to the staff, military engineer, artillery and tank cadres, were worried and anxious. There was the noisy sound of vehicles over a stretch of road several tens of kilometers long. When the first vehicle reached the crossing point the last vehicle was still at the starting point on the Vietnam-Kampuchea border. In the darkness, the people came up to the road from all the hamlets and placed on the muddy segments the bundles of bushes they carried on their shoulders with every vehicle and every artillery piece, especially T-54 tanks and 130mm guns, that passed by the road was further churned up and the mud became increasingly deeper. More bundles of bushes were placed on the road and the vehicles and artillery continued to pass.

> "If the task is easy, the people will do it,
> If it is a hundred times harder, they will also get
> the job done."

That saying is correct both tactically and strategically and is correct in wartime as well as in peacetime construction.

If conditions were bad on the road, on the river they were even worse. If there were sufficient modern ferries there would have been no problem. Comrade Sau Nhan (Bui Huu Tru), deputy commander of the regional military engineer office, who was responsible for the river-crossing ferries that day, told me that "All of the vehicles and artillery were taken across the river on makeshift ferries: in the middle there was a modern ferry platform, but on both sides there were floats we had made. During my several decades as a military engineer I had never worried about so many things as on the day the forces of Group 232 crossed the Vam Co River. That day brother Nam Nga came to make an inspection. The tank slowly crawled aboard the ferry. The more the ferry sank only the faster my heart beat. Fortunately, just as we had calculated, the ferry sank only to the expected level and remained afloat. If the tank had sunk along with the ferry, perhaps my heart would have stopped beating altogether.

"At the designated time the ferries were taken by truck to a point five kilometers from the river and lowered into a stream. Each ferry platform was poled and pulled to the river and then quickly assembled into makeshift ferries. We had to maintain secrecy and work urgently, and technical expertise was required on the part of each man. The commands of each cadre had to be very expert. Then there was the matter of propulsion. The river was broad and the wind was strong, so the "Seagull" motors of the military engineers were insufficient and the ferries tended to drift downstream. Only because the 230th Rear Services Group supplied us with some 50-hp motorboats were we able to cross safely."

That was a river crossing under noncombat conditions. If we had to cross many rivers or under combat condition, it would have been very difficult indeed. The corps and tank and artillery brigades that advanced rapidly across the bridges to make a brilliant entrance into the city could not but recall the contributions of the sapper units. And each feat of arms of a unit or combat arm would have been impossible without the contributions, of one kind or another, of the people.

In the plan for the attack on Saigon, our Regional Military Party Committee had one more problem about which it had to worry: its responsibility toward the cadres and men in our military delegation at Camp David, which was surrounded by enemy troops. The puppet troops had many times made crude threats against the lives of our men. Even after we had just arrived, during Tet of 1973, when I was still a member of the delegation, they used tanks to surround and initimidate us, and threateningly flew armed helicopters over our roofs merely because the DRV flew its flags in order to celebrate a national Tet. Around Camp David the enemy set up 12 tall guard towers and continually pointed gun barrels at our men. There were many other ugly acts. Thus when we attacked would the puppets leave our men alone? It seemed unlikely. In order to seek revenge, and because there were few of our men and most of them were cadres, the enemy might well carry out a cowardly attack and murder all of them. We felt that we had a responsibility to protect our men there.

At the end of March I invited comrades Ba Tran and Bui Thanh Khiet to discuss that problem and concluded that before we launched our attack on Saigon we had to send a sapper unit that was skilled and familiar with the area around Tan Son Nhat airfield to take all of our men to the liberated zone. The plan was discussed in detail, a unit was selected and I assigned those two cadres responsibility for carrying out the plan.

The plan was urgently put into action and the members of our delegation were informed so that they could coordinate their actions. But while the plan was being carried out we continued to think about the problem and were worried. Most of the members of our delegation were cadres and there were very few enlisted men. They had insufficient combat weapons. And although our sapper unit was an elite one, it was small and was accustomed to attacking, not defending. There were many enemy troops around Tan Son Nhat and they were strongly equipped and had air and armor support. The fighting to break through the encirclement would be very one-sided, on a battlefield that was not to our advantage, and could easily result in regrettable losses. Thus we ultimately canceled the plan. Especially after the decision was made to wait until most of the units of the corps had arrived, after which we would attack rapidly and strongly from the outside, combined with uprisings inside the city, we were certain that the fighting would not be prolonged. If they made careful preparations, our men in Camp David would be capable of defending themselves successfully until Saigon had been completely liberated.

We immediately contacted the responsible cadres in Camp David and informed them of the opinion of the Regional Military Party Commission that the delegation had to have a plan to fight to defend themselves throughout the period of our attack on Saigon. The on-the-spot combat plan had to be based on a system of bunkers and trenches dug with utmost secrecy. They had to be solid bunkers and trenches that could withstand the explosive force of the enemy artillery and also of our 130mm artillery. That task had to be carried out very urgently, and the entire delegation had to be organized into a tightly commanded combat unit.

Comrade Muoi Suong (Col Ngo Van Suong), the political officer of the delegation, related the following:

"When we learned that a sapper unit would come to take us to the liberated area we were all very moved, for we realized that the party was always concerned about us, although there were few of us compared to the many large units. But although not saying anything, everyone had the same thought: when our columns were rapidly advancing into the city we would be a unit already inside. Why shouldn't we participate in the fighting instead of leaving the city? Why could we not be regarded as an on-the-spot sapper-commando unit? We intended to send a message requesting permission to voluntarily remain behind and fight to the end. So when we were ordered to remain and fight everyone, both cadres and enlisted men, were very enthusiastic. Everyone stayed up all night digging bunkers. To avoid giving away our secret, we dug at night and rested during the day. We dug carefully and avoided making loud noises. The dirt that was dug up was hidden under the floors. Some was put into steel lockers, which became the roofs of the bunkers, thus further fortifying them. Within only a week the men dug a trench network hundreds of meters long, with bunkers and interconnected fighting trenches extending from the house of brother Tuan (the delegation head) to the units and even to the rear services element, and connecting with the remaining (graves registration) part of the DRV delegation. There was even a place for holding meetings and a place for the wounded. During the last days of the war some emissaries from the Saigon puppet regime who had come to take a respite and negotiate with us took refuge with us in those bunkers until Saigon was liberated. They were well protected."

During the Ho Chi Minh campaign our delegation at Camp David shed blood for the historic victory: an engineer captain and a master sergeant were killed, and five or six other comrades, including a lieutenant colonel, were wounded!

On 26 April 1975 a number of jeeps carried Van Tien Dung and I, along with the command organ, southward. The forward headquarters began to work.

Two days later Sau Tho and Pham Hung also arrived there so that we could quickly reach collective decisions regarding the major questions.

By that time the situation was clear. Saigon had been completely besieged.

To the west, on 26 April the 5th Division of Group 232 began its attack on the 22d Division, wiped out its regiments one by one, and completely mastered Route 4 between Tan An and Cau Voi. The 16th Regiment took the Binh Dien and An Lac bridges. The 115th and 117th sapper regiments took Phu Lam. Farther to the west, Route 4 was also cut in the Diem Hy-Nhi Qui-Nhi Binh area of Cai Lay District. That was accomplished by the My Tho provincial forces, including the Ap Bac Battalion--which was awarded the Liberation Army Hero designation and was led by comrade Le Quang Cong, which cut the road during the night of 26 April and the early morning of 27 April. Also on 26 April the 8th Division of Military Region 8 cut Route 4 between the Trung Luong intersection and Tan An. The forces of Military Region 9 also completely dominated the Cai Von-Ba Cang segment. The only strategic road running through the Mekong Delta had been chopped into pieces.

To the east, on 26 April 2d Corps attacked the Nuoc Trong armored training base and the Long Thanh subsector. On 27 April it took the city of Ba Ria. Route 15 was completely blocked. Also during the night of 26 April the 116th Sapper Regiment launched its attack on the Dong Nai highway bridge. On 26 April the 10th Sapper Regiment attacked enemy ships on the Long Tau River Phuoc Khanh and the mouth of the Dong Tranh River and blocked the river when it sank a ship the next day.

The Bien Hoa air base had been shelled by 130mm artillery at the Hieu Liem artillery base since 15 April. Many airplanes were destroyed and the air base was in a state of chaos. On 18 April the enemy had to send their F5 aircraft to Tan Son Nhat and their A-37 aircraft to the Lo Te airfield in airfield was closed, along with the U.S. Consulate in Bien Hoa City. The enemy had only two airfields left: Lo Te and Tan Son Nhat. Tan Son Nhat was sporadically hit by 122mm rockets fired by the 117th Sapper Regiment to the west and by the sappers of the northern column at Quoi Xuan. After the 2d Corps' Nhon Trach 130mm artillery base was completed and opened fire in the evening of 28 April, and the unique attack by the Vietnamese Air Force on the same day, in which five A-37 jets captured from the enemy and led by comrade Nguyen Thanh Trung, Tan Son Nhat was no longer of use to the puppets. The Lo Te airfield was shelled by artillery of Military Region 9 beginning on 28 April, but because that area was controlled by the enemy, we experienced difficulties and the enemy could use the airfield until 30 April, although their use was limited.

Both the Americans and the puppets realized that the situation was hopeless.

"Within the walls encompassing his life, Thieu himself had also begun to realize the inevitable. He could hardly avoid it. Before dawn on the 18th a communist sapper squad attacked the Phu Lam radar station in the western outskirts of Saigon. Thus the fighting was brought to the threshold of the city. About an hour later, General Toan, the III Corps commander, flew in from his headquarters at Bien Hoa to report to Thieu that, in fact, the war was lost, that the army was in disarray and was hopelessly outnumbered. There was no hope of holding out for more than 2 or 3 days."*

Martin, the most unrealistic and subjective of all, now also had to realize that defeat was inevitable and tried to persuade Thieu to step down so that a political plot could be implemented which would, with any luck, stop the advance of our troops. Martin, who jumped from one unrealistic proposal to another, was truly a person who lived in a world of illusion.

"Martin drove to the Presidential Palace to meet with Thieu on the morning of the 20th, after having met with Merillon (the French Ambassador) on the same subject and to the same end. He said to Thieu, 'I said that my conclusion was that nearly all of the generals, although they could continue to fight, believe that resistance would be hopeless, unless there is a negotiated ceasefire, and that negotiations could not begin unless the president resigned or steps were taken immediately to initiate negotiations.'"**

On 21 April Thieu resigned. It is not known whether or not that was a result of Martin's efforts.

Also on 28 April Tran Van Huong, who had been the puppet president for a week, was weak and feebleminded but thought that he was "destined" to move heaven and

---

*Frank Snepp, op. cit.
**Frank Snepp, op. cit.

earth, voluntarily or under pressure, turned over the "golden throne" to Duong Van Minh. As for Minh, perhaps because of his naive nature, he believed in the sorcery of the sorcerer Martin and his assistant Merillon, and although he had long since been pushed out of the picture, at the last minute tried to accept the burden of unconditional surrender.

On the same day, the puppets' III Corps headquarters at Bien Hoa completely fell apart and withdrew to Go Vap so that the next day its commander, General Toan, could flee to the United States with Chief of Staff Cao Van Vien. The military command of the Saigon regime had lost its head.

For our part, we urgently relayed to all cadres and men on the Saigon Front, the following message of encouragement, dated 2200 hours, 28 April 1975:

"The Political Bureau and the Military Commission of the party Central Committee send their determined-to-win greetings to all cadres and men, party members and Youth Union members. Let us heroically advance to winning total victory in the historic campaign bearing the name of the great Uncle Ho.

CHAPTER EIGHT

Final Hours of a Regime:
The Ho Chi Minh Campaign Wins Total Victory

H-Hour of D Day had arrived. The time was 0000 hours, 29 April 1975, the designated hour for all of our columns in five directions to simultaneously launch their attacks on Saigon, annihilate the rest of the enemy's defensive troops, and penetrate directly to the five key objectives. It was the designated hour for all of the commando teams and sapper units to emerge from their hiding places in and around the city, attack the enemy from the inside, take the objectives assigned them, and establish contact with the column advancing into the city from the outside. It was also the designated hour for the party cadres and political cadres to lead the patriotic masses in uprisings to kill the tyrants, disintegrate the puppet administration, encourage the puppet troops to throw down their weapons and surrender, win political power for the people, bring about an earthshaking upheaval, and eliminate oppression, injustice and slavery.

H-Hour of D Day was a common starting point the Ho Chi Minh Campaign Command set for the entire Saigon Front. It was the reference point for calculating every task and act, no matter whether the unit was far or near, whether the unit's conditions were difficult or easy, whether the unit was encountering obstacles or going smoothly, and whether it had begun its activities before or after, early or late. At that hour, everyone would have to make the maximum effort to take their objectives and converge at the central point: the Presidential Palace of the puppet regime.

H-Hour, D Day was also the time the B2 Regional Command had set for all military regions, provinces, units and areas in which the enemy was still present, so that they could simultaneously arise to gain political power and determine their destiny. Villages had to liberate villages, districts had to liberate districts and provinces had to liberate provinces.

There had seldom been an H-Hour more eagerly waited by millions of animated, excited hearts waiting worriedly and happily. It was the H-Hour we had awaited during decades of fierce warfare. It was a D Day made possible by millions of people who fell, every day and every hour, over a period of 10,000 days of fierce fighting.

Those of us waiting at the campaign headquarters waited anxiously. I naturally felt oddly tranquil. By that time there was nothing to worry about. All of the columns reported that things were going well and they were ready. The military regions and the distant units repeated the H-Hour, D Day date so that there would be no confusion. All orders were sent out and correct replies were received. How about the coming tasks? Wait until the guns exploded like new year's firecracker. Those tranquil moments were too brief, but were precious.

They helped us purge ourselves from the residual poisonous air of the past and to breathe in pure air for the coming urgent tasks.

It was just like new year's eve. The sound of firecrackers could be heard from all directions.

To the northwest, our 3d Corps attacked and overran Dong Du, the base of the puppet 25th Division, and captured Ly Tong Ba, the division commander. The Corps' sapper regiment took in advance and held the Bong bridge on Route 1 and the Xang bridge on Route 15. The corps advanced toward the city along two roads: the main road was Route 1 and the secondary road was Route 15. But when our troops were crossing Xang bridge it collapsed and two tanks fell into the river, so the Route 15 column had to switch over to Route 1 and advance on Hoc Mon. The forces of Tay Ninh Province coordinated by preventing the 25th Division from withdrawing from the province, and helped the people to liberate their province. Cu Chi coordinated with the main-force troops in attacking Dong Du and taking the subsector. The people in the Cu Chi area, led by mother Bay Nguyen Thi Lanh, a 76-year-old party member whose three sons had sacrificed their lives for the revolution, took the police headquarters and then occupied all of the Cu Chi district seat, kept everything intact, and turned it over to the local troops. Mother Bay herself climbed up to plant a flag on the police headquarters while the enemy was still there. The police were terrified by the vengeful glare of an old, gray-haired mother and the unarmed uprising people, and threw down their weapons and fled.

In the 3d Corps' path of advance, on 29 April the 14th Sapper Battalion took the Cho Moi bridge, the Quan Tre broadcasting station, the police branch, and the Quang Trung Training Center in Hoc Mon. The 1st Gia Dinh Regiment liberated the villages of Tan Thoi Nhat and Xuan Thoi Thong, and took the Tham Luong bridge, the 4th Battalion of the Gia Dinh Regiment, along with the 115th Sapper Regiment, liberated Tan Thoi Hiep village and made two breaches north of Tan Son Nhat airfield so that the forces of the Corps could come in to attack it. During the early morning of 30 April the 3d Corps advanced from Hoc Mon to take its main objective, defeating the enemy's counterattacks and taking the entire airfield by 1400 hours that day.

To the north 1st Corps took the town of Tan Uyen, surrounded the Phu Loi base, and penetrated straight through to Lai Thieu in order to advance into the city. The entire puppet 5th Division was surrounded and isolated between our two columns--3d Corps and 1st Corps--and had no way out. Attacked by the local troops in coordination with the corps, it hoisted the white flag and surrendered. All three regiments--the 7th, 8th and 9th--threw down their weapons and surrendered on the spot. The Binh Duong subsector also raised the white flag in the morning of 30 April. The 1st Corps crossed the Binh Phuoc bridge and advanced to its main objective: The GHQ. The Binh Phuoc Bridge, which had been taken by the 115th Sapper Regiment on the morning of 29 April, was retaken by an enemy counterattack. When our headquarters learned that the enemy had placed explosives and intended to blow up the Binh Phuoc bridge, we immediately sent an urgent message to the 115th Regiment: "Take and hold the Binh Phuoc bridge at all costs.... Immediately cut the wires to the explosive charges the enemy had placed at the bridge...." In the early morning of 30 April the Regiment retook the Binh Phuoc bridge and held it until the 1st Corps passed over it. Ahead of 1st Corps, the 80th Sapper Battalion, along with commando units, during the night of 28 April attacked the Co Loa artillery base at Go Vap, which they were unable to take until the morning of 30 April. That same morning, at 0920 hours, the battalion took the "Phu Dong" armor base. At the puppet GHQ, in the morning of 30 April there were no longer any commanders. The puppet troops had lost all their morale, and some had fled. But the 81st Airborne Ranger Brigade continued to defend the gates obstinately. At 0830 on 30 April the Z28 commando regiment commanded by comrade Bay Vinh unsuccessfully attacked Gate 1, so it changed over to Gate 3. Near there were some abandoned enemy tanks. A team took a fully equipped enemy gun, mounted it on a Jeep, and broke through to the Electronic Computer Center. Colonel Ho, who was in charge there, turned the entire installation over to them. The IBM computer system and all puppet personnel management and equipment inventory tapes were intact. The time was 1000 hours. The team drove the Jeep to the main building of the GHQ. All of the enemy troops had fled. There remained only a corporal, who greeted the team and turned over to it a bunch of keys. All documents and property were intact. That puppet corporal was comrade Ba Minh, a regional intelligence agent who had been planted in the GHA long before (he is now a captain with the staff of Military Region 7). Our flag was flown from the main flagpole and the roof of the main building at 1030 hours. At exactly 1200 hours on 30 April comrade Vinh (now Lt Col Le Van Vinh, a Hero of the Armed Forces and now deputy chief of staff of Tay Ninh Province, greeted the forces of the Corps and turned over the objective to them. Along that column's route the people arose and coordinated with the commandos, especially in An Phu Dong village, wiping out the puppet organs and village police and immediately setting up a new administration. At 0930 hours on 30 April, under the leadership of the local party cell, the people took Subward 2 in the town of Go Vap. Prior to that, in the afternoon of 29 April, comrade Thuan, a district cadre, led the masses in taking and flying a flag from the headquarters of Subward 12 in Phu Nhuan District.

To the west, in the morning of 29 April, Group 232 took the city of Hau Nghia, thus insuring its left flank. One element wiped out the puppet 22d Division and took the city of Tan An and the towns of Ben Luc. And Cau Binh Dien, then advanced toward Saigon along Route 4, insuring its right flank. The main deep penetration element--the 9th Division, advanced from My Hanh and Vinh Loc to the Bay Hien intersection and took its main objective, the puppet Capital Special Zone headquarters. The time was 1030 hours, 30 April. In the area of the Bay Hien intersection the enemy put up a stiff resistance and used A-37's to bomb our troop formations, inflicting a number of losses.

The 429th Sapper Regiment and the 117th Regiment, coordinating with the western column, on 29 and 30 April took a number of key objectives, such as the Phu Lam radar station, the Tan Tao strategic zone, the Vinh Loc intersection, the Phu Tho Communications Center, Ba Hom bridge, and Nhi Thien Duong bridge.

The people in the villages of Hoc Mon and Ba Diem, and especially in the village of Phu Tho Hoa, arose, encouraged the enemy to put down their weapons and surrender, smashed the puppet administration, and flew liberation flags. Many villages set up revolutionary administrations. In Precinct 11, sister Ut Van and brother Sau Hoang, local party cadres, led the masses in arising to take over the administration in Subward 8 at 0900 on 30 April, and took over the administration headquarters of the precinct at 0915, before our troops arrived.

The southern column, as stated above, despite many difficulties, arrived at its objectives by the stipulated time and quickly took its main objective, the National Police Headquarters. The files, records and documents, some still on desks, were all intact.

To the east, the 4th Corps, following Route 1, advanced directly to Bien Hoa air base and the headquarters of the puppet III Corps. The remaining forces of the 18th Division, the 3d Armored Brigade, and Marines tried to stop us and launched continuous counterattacks. The deep penetration forces included the 7th Division and its reserve unit the 52d Brigade. Early in the morning of 30 April the lead element reached Ghenh bridge but saw that it was weak and feared that tanks could not cross it, so it returned to the Bien Hoa highway and followed the 2d Corps into Saigon and took the puppet Ministry of Defense, the naval base, and the radio station.

The people in Binh Thanh District, led and mobilized by sister Ba Lieu, took the headquarters of Subward 13 at 0930 hours on 30 April. One column of the 2d Corps took Ba Ria and Vung Tau (the 3d Division of Military Region 5). Another column attacked Long Thanh, took the Nhon Trach war zone, set up a 130mm artillery base there, and prepared for an element to cross the Dong Nai River to coordinate with the sappers and commandos in attacking Military Region 9. The main column advancing on Saigon was led by the 203d Tank Brigade. When it arrived at the Buong bridge it discovered that it had been blow up. All day on 29 April the 203d Tank Brigade was unable to cross the river. Only around midnight was it able to cross the Buong River and advance straight toward Saigon along the Bien Hoa-Saigon highway. There the 203d Tank Brigade established contact with our forces holding a bridge. An element of the 116th Regiment responsible for holding the Dong Nai bridge expanded the area under its control and occupied a corner of the Long Binh supply depot (liberated the villages of An Hoa and Long Hung villages). The 116th Regiment immediately built defensive works in that area. After midnight the 203d Tank Brigade, firing furiously, advanced toward Saigon. Thinking that they were enemy tanks, the sappers defending the bridge fired back with B40 and B41 RPG's. Fortunately, they were inaccurate. But thanks to the light produced by the exploding shells, our men recognized the NLF flags on the tanks (0050 hours, 30 April) and asked for the password, "Ho Chi Minh?" The tank driver, recalling the password used when he was in Military Region 5, responded, "19 May." He was asked a second time, "Ho Chi Minh?" This time the driver responded, "Long live." Our men were ecstatic and waved NLF flags.

On that highway there were three key bridges: The Dong Nai bridge, the Rach Chiec bridge, and Newport bridge.

During the night of 26 April the 116th Sapper Regiment took the Dong Nai bridge but the next day the enemy counterattacked and retook it. During the night of 28 April our unit retook the eastern end of the bridge, then attacked the western end and organized defensive positions. During the afternoon of 29 April our men could hear the sound of many vehicles coming from toward Saigon from the direction of Long Thanh. Our reconnaissance reported that in all there were 15 enemy vehicles, led by five tanks and armored vehicles with trucks full of troops, women and children, and that they were infantry on both sides of the road. Over a U.S. PRC-25 field radio the regimental radio heard a brief conversation:

"When the last vehicle has crossed the bridge, use 5 tons of explosives to blow up the bridge."

"How about the units behind us?"

"This road is no longer usable. That's an order from our commander. The Viet Cong are pursuing you. Blow up the bridge right away!"

Our troops had not given away their ambush positions. The unsuspecting convoy reached a point about a kilometer from the bridge. We immediately opened fire with B40 and B41 RPG's. The first five vehicles were wiped out. Some of the enemy troops climbed over the fence of the Long Binh supply depot and fled on foot. The vehicles in the rear of the convoy turned around and headed for Bien Hoa.

Exploiting its victory, our unit took a corner (in the west southwest) of the Long Binh depot. The bridge was kept intact to the end.

At the Rach Chiec bridge the fighting was also very fierce. The Z23 commando unit, along with the 81st Sapper Battalion, the commander of which was Nguyen Hoang An, the deputy commander of which was Tran Kim Thinh, and the political officer was Nguyen Van Tu, were responsible for taking and defending that bridge. At 0300 hours on 27 April they opened fire and after an hour of fighting they took the entire bridge and carefully cut all electric wires under the bridge. All day on the 27th the enemy troops, in coordination with boats on the river, counterattacked fiercely. By 1500 on 28 April, steadfast Z23 had lost 20 comrades. Our forces had to temporarily withdraw to a channel, in which many nipa palms and holly plants were growing, about 500 meters away.

Determined to fulfill its responsibility, during the night of 28 April Z23 carried out another attack. But it was unsuccessful. Only by the night of 29 April was the unit able to take the bridge for a second time. It held the bridge until our tanks crossed it at 0930 30 April.

During the night of 28 April the 4th Thu Duc Battalion was unsuccessful in its attack to take the Newport bridge because the enemy was strong there and the bridge was near Saigon.

When the 203d Tank Brigade of 2d Corps reached the Dong Nai highway bridge the infantry had not yet caught up. At the bridge comrade Tai, the brigade commander, met comrade Tong Viet Duong, an Army Hero, commander of the sapper-commando forces of the eastern column (now a colonel and deputy commander of the Dong Nai Province military command); Vo Tan Si, commander of the 116th Sapper-Commando Regiment (now a lieutenant colonel and commander and political officer of the 304th Police Regiment of the Ho Chi Minh City Public Security Service). Comrade Tai said that the Corps had ordered that Independence Palace be taken that day. But the infantry had not yet arrived, it was not clear where the enemy was. The unit was not familiar with the streets, which it knew only from the map.

Comrade Duong said immediately, "It will be too late if we wait for the infantry. We have a strong sapper regiment. I was for many years an intelligence cadre in Saigon and know the streets very well. I know all of the enemy areas. I even know all about Independence Palace. Go ahead and attack."

Comrade Si added, "Our regiment had been assigned the mission of attacking in the outskirts and was only recently reassigned here. Many of and was only recently reassigned here. Many of our cadres and men are familiar with the area. Our regiment is also capable of fighting as infantry and is experienced in attacking the enemy's bases and rear area. Go ahead and launch a coordinated attack!

Comrade Tai considered their opinions and agreed.

Some time was lost in reorganizing the tank formation and in concentrating the sapper regiment.

Except for two companies which remained behind to defend the bridge, the troops of the 116th Regiment climbed aboard the tanks of the 203d Brigade. Cooperating in combat, the two units bravely advanced toward the presidential palace of the puppet regiment.

Comrade Duong sat with comrade Tai and comrade Minh (political director) in the command car of the brigade commander, the sixth vehicle in the formation. Comrade Si, commander of the 116th Regiment, traveled in the third vehicle. Comrade Pham Duy Do, acting commander of Company 1, 19th Battalion, traveled in the second vehicle. The convoy left the Dong Nai bridge at 0600, 30 April.

When the convoy passed by Suoi Cai in Thu Duc puppet troops in enemy's Joint Officer Training School poured artillery fire into our formation. One tank was hit and its crew was killed. The 37mm antiaircraft guns were damaged. Following the directions of comrade Duong, comrade Tai ordered two tank columns--one crossing a field and the other circling around in the direction of Nho Market, to immediately wipe out the artillery positions in the school (in Tang Nhon Phu village).

When the convoy crossed over the Rach Chiec bridge, comrade Tu Thinh reported on the bridges and enemy troops in the area. As it neared the Newport bridge, suddenly many rounds were fired at our troops from the buildings on both sides of the road. One vehicle was damaged and one comrade was killed. The sappers immediately jumped down from the tanks and searched out and captured many heavily armed enemy troops still wearing their camouflaged uniforms. Then two A-37 airplanes dived down to drop bombs, then flew away. We were safe and continued to advance.

When the convoy passed over the Newport bridge the people poured out of the houses along the road. The nearer it came to Saigon the more people there were, waving flags and hands to greet the liberation troops. Foreign journalists taking moving and still pictures led us into the city. Near Thi Nghe bridge three enemy M113 armored personnel carriers appeared. We fired, setting one afire. The crews of the other two abandoned their vehicles on Thi Nghe bridge and fled.

The T54 tank in the lead rammed into the iron gate of Independence Palace and entered at 1110 hours. The tanks advanced directly to the flagpole in the center of the grounds. Another tank went left, then right, then came to a halt. The 116th Regiment troops jumped down from the tanks and surrounded the building, rounding up and arresting the guards and personnel and led them out and ordered them to sit on the grass. A tank crew led by comrade Bui Quang Than and a sapper team consisting of comrades Pham Duy Do and Pham Huy Nghe, took a flag to the balcony in front of the puppet Presidential Palace, waved it for a long time, then ran it up the main flagpole on the balcony. The time was 1130 hours.

The sapper team ran downstairs to and searched the rooms. On the first floor, they pulled aside a curtain at the entrance to a room on the right. Inside the room the entire cabinet of the puppet regime was sitting around an oval-shaped table in the government conference room. Comrade Do pointed his AK rifle and shouted, "You've been surrounded. If anyone has a weapon, throw it down and surrender."

No one moved. No one said a word.

Do ordered comrade Nghe, who carried an AK rifle, to stand guard at the door: "Stand guard here, comrade. No one may leave this room!" Then Do ran out to find the commander. At that moment, comrade Tung, the political officer, and comrade Tai, the commander, of the 203d Brigade, along with Minh Chu, political director, and Duong, commander of the eastern column's sapper-commando forces, had just arrived at the gate. Do led the cadres inside.

Everyone in the room stood up. Duong Van Minh, president of the puppet regime, who sat at the head of the table, said,

"We have been waiting for you so that we could turn over the government!"

"You have nothing left to turn over. You can only surrender unconditionally. I invite you to come to the radio station to announce an unconditional surrender," said comrade Tung in a stern voice.

At command headquarters we attentively followed, hour by hour, the progress being made in each direction. On a large table there was spread out a large map of Saigon and its environs. Everyone watched the red lines drawn on the map by a staff cadre on the basis of reports from the columns. The cadre marks the points to which our troops had advanced and the objectives we had taken. Suddenly a cadre gleefully brought in a tape recorder and placed it on the table: it was the voice of Duong Van Minh announcing his unconditional surrender over the radio and ordering the puppet troops to throw down their weapons and surrender. Everyone gathered around, listening silently.

Everyone jumped with joy. Le Duc Tho, Pham Hung and Van Tien Dung, who were very moved, hugged and kissed one another and firmly shook hands. There are few moments in life when one is so happy that they want to cry. I suddenly felt as if my soul was translucent and light, as if everything had sunk to the bottom. The war was nearly over. It had been a long, fierce war, and many of our comrades and compatriots were not around to share that happy moment. They had fallen so that we could enjoy that moment.

On 30 April Saigon was bright and sunny. Of all the streets half-red, half-blue liberation flags, mixed in with gold-starred red flags, flapped in the breeze. Everyone poured out onto the streets, pulled down the puppet flags, ran up our flags, appealed for the puppet troops to throw down their weapons and surrender, dissolve the puppet regime, and set up revolutionary administrations. The entire city arose, maintained order, and protected the factories and installations for the revolution and for themselves. Only after many years could there be that day. I remember that 25 August 1945 was a similar day, echoing with revolutionary footsteps. I happily looked at the liberation troops, the troops of Uncle Ho, and at the gigantic tanks and the enormous artillery pieces. Were your children or elder brothers among those troops? Were your uncle or aunt sitting on the tanks or artillery movers heroically spreading out in all directions? On all streets there were crowds surrounding the liberation troops, asking questions and talking. "Oh! They aren't at all like the puppet troops." "You are so nice and so handsome!" "You are so young and lovable."

In Saigon it was a day of action; indeed, it had been several days of action. It was not merely a matter of shouting, celebrating and greeting, like some historic days in the past. On 31 January 1789, during Tet Ky Dau, the people of Hanoi poured out onto the streets, happy, proud and confident, to greet the victorious troops of the national hero Nguyen Hue, who had come to liberate the capital. The poet Ngo Ngoc Du described the animated atmosphere on that victorious day:

> "The clouds dispersed, the fog lifted, the sky brightened.
> "All over the city, old people and young, faces like flowers."

On that day, in the city of Saigon, the largest city in the nation, a city that had fought for many years under the leadership of the party, there was a similar animated atmosphere. But there was also a seething atmosphere of enthusiastic uprising. Everyone had contributed to the brilliant feat of keeping the city intact for the benefit of the people.

Did ordinary activities in Saigon differ before and after 1130 hours, 30 April? It differed in that before the fighting began every family was worried and everyone was agitated. Afterwards, when flags were flying on all streets, the atmosphere suddenly became festival-like. There were large crowds everywhere, but they were orderly and happy. Every house had ample electricity and water, and there was not a minute's interruption. Has a war ever concluded in such a manner in a city of 3.5 million people? On was that an accomplishment rare in history? That accomplishment was due to our party's leadership skill in combining attacks and uprisings, uprisings and attacks, and in combining attacks from without and attacks from within. If that had not been so, we could not have won victory. The actual results were evident.

At the city's waterworks in Thu Duc the Uprising Committee led by comrade Nguyen Van Muong mobilized the masses, frightened and chased away the enemy, and took over the plant many hours before our troops arrived there. In and around the plant the enemy had stationed a Marine battalion, an antiaircraft battalion and an RF battalion, and on 28 April they sent there about 40 tanks and armored vehicles. The enemy supplied 30 weapons to the self-defense forces, but most of them were in the hands of our organized masses. Comrade Muong was very worried. The trade union of Thu Duc District, represented by comrade Thanh Do, had assigned him the mission of organizing the workers and keeping the plant intact.

On 30 April, when he heard thst our tanks from Bien Hoa were approaching comrade Muong led the worker masses in spreading rumors to frighten the puppet troops. He went up to the roof of the plant and raised a large flag he had readied in advance. The puppet troops were terrified and thought that the liberation troops had entered the factory. They disintegrated and ran. Some abandoned their vehicles and fled on foot. Comrade Muong organized an armed protection unit and a Plant Self-Management Committee, and continued to operate as usually, supplying water to the city without an hour's interruption.

The Thu Duc power plant was taken by commando unit Z23. After fulfilling its mission at the Rach Chiec bridge, Z33 was ordered to take the Ha Tien Cement Plant, the warehouse area, the Zetco mill (now Combine No 4), and the power plant, and to insure their safety and guide the workers in continuing to operate the plants. Electricity in Saigon was interrupted only 2 hours on 30 April. Thereafter there were always lights in all houses, government offers and streets.

In practically all factories--textile mills, food products plants, machinery plants, etc.--the workers helped protect the factory and insure the safety of machinery and facilities until an official management committee arrived to take over management. In all public offices at the central and municipal levels the personnel and officials kept intact the files, documents, and facilities so that they could be turned over to the revolutionary administration.

It was a truly magnificent transition from one regime to another. There were no serious foul-ups. There was not a single act of petty revenge. That was made possible by true revolution and by true people's war, in which all the people followed our party's guidance. Our people's armed forces and the heroic people of Ho Chi Minh City are worthy of being commended for their brilliant accomplishments.

We were happy to relay to the cadres, men party members, Youth Union members, and people of Saigon the congratulatory message of the Political Bureau of our party Central Committee on 30 April:

"The Political Bureau warmly congratulates the soldiers and people of Saigon-Gia Dinh and all cadres and men, party members, and Youth Union members of the main-force and local units, the elite troops, and the militia and self-defense forces, who fought very heroically, achieved brilliant feats of arms, annihilated or wiped out large numbers of the enemy, forced them to surrender unconditionally, liberated Ho Chi Minh City, and advanced the historic campaign bearing the name of the great Uncle Ho to total victory.

"All of you must manifest a determined-to-win spirit and, together with the people, continue to attack and arise to fully liberate the beloved south of our homeland."

Political Bureau*

While such attacks and uprisings were taking place in Saigon and eastern Nam Bo, in the provinces of the Mekong Delta and even on such distant islands as Phu Quoc and Con Son the revolutionary wave of the people was billowing up. The soldiers and people cooperated very closely in carrying out attacks and uprisings, mopping up the enemy troops, and liberating one province after another. The movement was prepared and launched at a very early date, beginning in October 1974 with COSVN's instruction that villages should liberate villages, districts liberate districts and provinces liberate provinces. The provinces, cadres and people ardently responded to that correct stand. Tens of thousands of youths joined the armed combat forces. Hundreds of thousands of the masses participated in civilian labor, transporting ammunition and the wounded. All masses organizations, under the tight leadership of the local party committees, mobilized their forces to prepare to participate in the simultaneous uprising. The revolutionary tradition of the Mekong Delta has been demonstrated in the course of many movements, from the August Revolution in 1945, through the anti-French period, to the "simultaneous uprising" in 1960, and throughout the anti-U.S. period. Now, millions of people who were grateful to the party because they had land to till and prosperous lives, were awaiting the day of their home area's liberation.

The first province to be liberated was Tra Vinh, in Military Region 9, now a part of Cuu Long Province. The province was awarded the designation "The leading province in the two-months campaign during the 1974-1975 dry season" by the Western Nam Bo Zone, and was awarded a First-Class Bulwark Medal by the PRG.

At 1500 hours on 28 April the order of the Combined Provincial Campaign Command was promulgated. The cities and districts enthusiastically went into battle. During the night of 29 April the province opened fire.

By 0700 on 30 April, the RF posts, artillery bases, and airfield in the city were liberated. The people in and around the city, totalling more than 30,000 people of Vietnamese and Khmer descent, took to the streets to disarm the puppets and dissolve the hamlet, village and subward administrations. In all the districts, 180,000 people participated in arising to win political power. There remained only the headquarters of the puppet regime. The provincial forces, including the local troops, the sappers and the armed public security forces, led by Muoi (Nguyen Tan Tai) and Hai Tri, fought very fiercely. As many as 50 of our comrades died on the fence around provincial headquarters. Brother Hai Tri, a resolute commander, also fell there. At 0800 hours on 30 April the fighting there was still fierce and the headquarters was surrounded. At that time the superior bonze Son Xut of the Xon Rom Pagoda volunteered to win over the obstinate province chief and give him a way out and a way to redeem

---

*Document of the B2 War Recapitulation Section of the Ministry of National Defense.

himself with the people. At 1030 all puppet forces laid down their weapons and surrendered. At 1100 hours the revolutionary flag fluttered above provincial headquarters. The Tra Vinh provincial capital was liberated a little earlier than Saigon.

Another exemplary event in the uprising in the province took place at the My Khe post in Can Long District. Unarmed people surrounded and attempted to enter the post. A puppet police lieutenant set off a Claymore mine, killing four people and wounding four people and wounding four others. Immediately, hundreds of people surged into the post and captured the enemy troops. The police lieutenant was executed in the presence of the people.

The last place to be liberated in the province was Duyen Hai District. The time was 2000 hours, 30 April.

A province with an important position in the Mekong Delta, one that was not far from Saigon and was a staging area from which the enemy could aid the capital if they were capable of doing so was Tien Giang Province, made up of the former My Tho and Go Cong Provinces. There the enemy had concentrated nearly all of their 7th and 9th Divisions, with strong armor and artillery forces. They went all-out to defend Route 4, their lifeline, but beginning on 26 April, as stated above, Route 4 was cut in many places and the enemy was broken up into many fragments. Another strategic route passing through the province was the Cho Gao canal, which connected the Ca Mau area with Saigon and had always been an extremely important rice route. The people of Tien Giang had participated in many movements against foreign aggression, beginning with the arrival of the first French troops, and then against the Siamese troops brought in by Nguyen Anh (which was like bringing a fox into a chicken coop). There was a famous part of the Dong Thap Muoi which had a movement for the past 30 or 40 years. In April alone 40,000 people participated in civilian labor and in transporting weapons. Beginning on 15 April, 4,000 participated in cutting roads and in erecting obstacles on the Cho Gao canal. Tens of thousands of people took to the streets to participate in attacks and uprisings to liberate their province.

The first place to take over political power in the province was Cho Gao District. The local troops, along with the armed security forces and commandos annihilated the enemy and completely liberated the town at 1330 hours on 30 April. Then our troops mobilized the people to arise, shatter the puppet regime and army, and spread out to liberate the entire district.

In Go Cong events developed differently. The provincial capital was situated deep in enemy territory, there were few provincial troops, and they were far to the west. When they learned that the puppet army and regime in Saigon had surrendered, the popular masses flocked to Go Cong City and used hand-held megaphones and electronic loudspeakers to appeal to the enemy to lay down their weapons and return to their home areas to earn a living. Soldiers' families rushed into the posts, brought out their relatives and forced them to throw down their weapons and come home. The local party cadres and political parties cleverly led the people in dissolving the puppet administrations, dismantling guard posts, and confiscating weapons and ammunition. An entire enemy provincial capital completely fell apart. The people mastered all of the capital by 1300 hours on 30 April. Then three-wheeled Lambrettas and trucks carried our troops from the city to Vinh Huu so that they could take control. The entire province of Go Cong was liberated at 1430 hours on 30 April.

Go Cong had a tradition of using the strength of simultaneous uprising by the people to oppose the enemy. In 1954, immediately after the signing of the Geneva Agreements, a single local company, along with the militia and the people, wiped out or forced the surrender of 30 to 40 outposts, and by the time a ceasefire was imposed the enemy controlled little more than the city. Such incidents occurred many times--in the simultaneous uprising year of 1960, the elimination of village administrations and the dismantling of strategic hamlets in the Diem period, the expansion of the people's mastership right of mastery to many areas in 1974, and then their liberation of their province.

In the city of My Tho, a commando company of the municipal Labor Youth Union, relying on the revolutionary infrastructure, mobilized the masses to arise in the subwards, forces the civil guards and police to turn their weapons over to the revolution, and appealed for the puppet troops to lay down their weapons and surrender. At 1600 hours on 30 April a large liberation flag was raised from a high flagpole at the Nguyen Dinh Chieu High School. Subwards 1, 2, 4, 5 and 6 were the first to be liberated. But there were still troops holding out in the military compound near the soccer field. Members of the commando company, riding six Jeeps and holding high revolutionary flags, circled around to the riverbank and used loudspeakers to appeal for the enemy to surrender. When the convoy passed by Chuong Duong the enemy poured heavy fire into the vehicles. One Jeep was hit and Tran Van Tram was killed. The commandos, fighting back by firing pistols and throwing grenades, continued on and took the northern bridge in order to establish contact with Ben Tre. At 2400 hours on 30 April the 1st Regiment of the 8th Division of Military Region 8 arrived and fought to wipe out the puppet 6th Armored Squadron, which was still holding out at the old market. At 0500 hours on 1 May the city of My Tho was completely liberated.

On the morning of 30 April very large numbers of people poured out onto Route 4. While the province's armed forces were wiping out the enemy troops and capturing the Bung Mon bridge, from the direction of Binh Phu the people frightened the puppet troops and captured intact six M113 armored personnel carriers and an artillery base at Thuoc Nhien, along with two 155mm howitzers and four 105mm howitzers. The 12th Regiment of the puppet 7th Division completely disintegrated there.

In My Tho Province there was still a large enemy military base at Binh Duc, formerly the base of the U.S. 9th Infantry Division. After the Americans withdrew they turned the base over to the puppet troops. The Americans had spent much effort and money, brought in much machinery, confiscated the fertile rice land, and leveled the houses and gardens of the people living along the Mekong River, to build the base. They confiscated property and killed innocent people in the locality in order to transform the fields into a military base. The crude U.S. General Westmoreland not only realized that he was a war criminal but bragged about that project:

"The (U.S.) navy and army engineers created an island of sand which in the dry season became one of the greatest sand-rich places in the world.

"I personally selected the name for that base to typify the cooperation between America and South America: 'Dong Tam' [Common Effort]."*

Furthermore, that general admitted that he had used chemical warfare against our people. He said:

"Chemical defoliants were used to kill the enemy's rice in remote areas controlled by the enemy. Although the border between the government-controlled area and the area under Viet Cong influence was not clear, that type of defoliant was frequently used. No one is certain whether the defoliant causes biological damage, how much harm it does or what its long-range effects are."

In the morning of 30 April, in that Dong Tam base there was held an urgent meeting between the command of the puppet 7th Division and the neighboring subsectors to discuss "defending to the death." They thought that the fortified defensive works and complicated barbed wire fences left behind by the Americans could save their lives. At noon they ordered the regiments still north of Cai Lay and Chau Thanh to pull back to that base. The armor was spread out along Route 4 to direct the troops. However, while withdrawing back to the base many of the troops deserted. Others deserted when they returned to the base and saw the chaotic conditions. All along Route 4, up to the road leading to Gate 2, everyone who met the armed soldiers asked, "Why do you want to die when you can enjoy the peace? Why are you still armed?" or, "Saigon has fallen, didn't you know that? My goodness! The Dong Tam base can never hold out against the liberation troops. You should go home and take care of your affairs!" Furthermore, when the troops pulled back the people followed them into the base. By 1900 or 2000 hours guerrillas had infiltrated the base. Around midnight provincial troops and troops of the military region were also inside the base. All of the puppet officers and men deserted or were captured. By 0000 hours on 1 May the "Dong Tam" base was completely liberated.

In all of the Mekong Delta provinces there were similar attacks and uprisings. The tempo was greatest on 29 and 30 April and 1 May. Although Saigon had to surrender unconditionally at noon on 30 April and the puppet IV Corps command surrendered late that day, the leaders of the puppet regime and army in the provinces continued to put up an obstinate resistance, to "hold out" in hope of obtaining U.S. aid.

But because of the storm-like attacks and uprisings of the armed forces and revolutionary masses, some of the enemy were killed, others surrendered or deserted, and nearly all of the provinces were completely liberated on 30 April and 1 May.

At the command headquarters of the Ho Chi MInh Campaign we had readied a powerful force of infantry, tanks, field artillery and antiaircraft artillery to

---
*From Westmoreland's memoirs "A Soldier's Report."

move down into the delta to help the soldiers and people of Military Regions 8 and 9 to rapidly wipe out the enemy troops who were still obstinately holding out. We understood very clearly that after the head of the puppet army and regime in Saigon had been smashed, and the Americans had to climb up to the rooftops to flee, the decisive blows had been struck to completely liberate all of South Vietnam. But the liberation of Saigon did not mean that the other places would automatically be liberated, that we had to do nothing but sit and wait for the ripe fruit to fall into the basket.

During his last days Thieu said to his subordinates, "If we lose the east and Saigon we must by all means concentrate the remaining South Vietnam, withdraw into the Mekong Delta and make a stand there. We must defend the islands to the south more tightly.

"Can Tho will be the capital of the Republic of Vietnam."

In fact, Saigon had surrendered but the puppet troops were still holding out at Dong Tam and Can Tho, and even after Can Tho surrendered the puppets in some localities still hoped to hold out. If we had not taken steps in advance to smash the plot to form an enclave in the delta, and if we had not had a revolutionary strategy which combined a series of attacks and uprisings by combined political-military forces, it is certain that the situation would have become even more complicated. The soldiers and people of the Mekong Delta, who realized at an early date their historic responsibility of arising to liberate their home areas, shed much blood in the final battles. Following the wise guidance of the party and coordinating their fighting with the Saigon front, the delta provinces simultaneously attacked and arose. Some provinces were liberated before Saigon, and some were liberated at the same time. When the central puppet administration had to surrender unconditionally, millions of soldiers and people, taking advantage of that valuable opportunity, stepped up their attacks and in a period of only 2 days, 30 April and 1 May, liberated nearly all of the delta provinces.

The combined arms force we had made ready in eastern Nam Bo did not have to engage in combat. Both the 8th and 9th military regions sent messages to regional headquarters: "We can handle things by ourselves." Indeed, the delta, using its own forces, efficiently mopped up the enemy troops and liberated itself.

Military Region 9 by itself took the headquarters of the enemy's Military Region IV, liberated the "Western Capital" [Can Tho], and coordinated in a timely manner with the Ho Chi Minh Campaign by cutting the Mang Thit canal and strategic Route 4, and interdicting the large airfield in Can Tho.

On 25 April the Military Region received Message No 693/ZN(24-4) from the Regional Command:

Beginning on 28 April the Military Region must resolutely attack and cut Route 4 at many important points, which have already been designated. Also beginning on 28 April, we used sapper units to carry out continuous small and large attacks on the Tra Noc airfield, accompanied by the use of mortars and artillery to interdict the runways and control tower so that the enemy cannot take off from or land at that airfield. Then, if conditions permit, attack and take the city of Can Tho."*

On 28 April the Military Region, obeying the order of the Regional Command, continually shelled and attacked the airfield, and on the morning of 30 April, when Duong Van Minh was announcing the surrender, the military region's mainforce 20th Regiment launched a direct attack on the airfield and took the Tra Noc airfield at 1400 hours on that day. All of the enemy troops there surrendered, including the command of the 21st Infantry Division and the 4th Air Division. We captured 113 airplanes of various kinds.

Meanwhile, in the city of Can Tho the political cadres led the masses in an uprising to take the subwards in the center of the city: An Cu, An Nghiep and An Hoa in Precinct 1; An Hoa and An Thanh in Precinct 2; and Binh Di hamlet and Xa Long Tuyen in Precinct 3, etc. Our troop proselyting infrastructure, along with the people, took the radio station at 1415 hours and broadcast the revolution's appeal for the puppet troops to surrender.

At 1500 hours on 30 April the armed forces of Military Region 9 tightened their encirclement of and directly attacked the headquarters of the puppet IV Corps. Faced by a hopeless situation from which there was no escape, the puppet general Nguyen Khoa Nam, commander of Military Region IV, had to surrender. A few hours later he took his own life, ending a dirty life of a lackey. We took all of the city of Can Tho during the night of 30 April.

Then the command of Military Region 9 used 24 M113 armored personnel carriers that had just been captured from the enemy and some trucks to take the mainforce 101st Regiment toward Long Xuyen and Chau Doc, the last places in the Mekong Delta to be liberated. But it was not strong military forces alone that resolved the complicated situation in that area. There was also clearly manifested cooperation between attacks and uprisings and between military forces and mass political forces. That clearly reflected unity between the intentions of the party and the hearts of the people, and the strength of the revolutionary case.

It was not true that that entire area was liberated late. On 25 April Thanh Binh District, on the eastern bank of the Tien River, was liberated. Then all of the enemy in the area east of the river was mopped up. The rest of the enemy withdrew to form an enclave at Hong Ngu but, because of our pressure, they had to surrender at 0800 on 1 May.

At Chau Doc City, during the night of 30 April the enemy in the subsector was ordered to withdraw to the "Hoa Hao Holy Land" to fight to the death. Before they withdrew they set fire to the treasury and to the documents and files, but the local people put out the fire in time, saving 11 crates of money and papers and files needed by the revolution.

---

*Document of the Military Science Office of Military Region 9.

The "Hoa Hao Holy Land" was the prayer-and-sacrifice place of the Hoa Hao religion in the village of Hoa Hao, the birthplace of the person who founded that religion: Huynh Phu So. The village was situated on the Vam Nao River, a small river which connected the Tien and Hau Rivers. The puppets had relied on a number of bad people among the leaders of that religion, who took advantage of the Buddhists and Hoa Hao adherents by concentrating a million followers in that area to carry out a long-range patriotism and opposition to oppression of the adherents, most of whom were working peasants. They also could not understand the roots of the religion and the true aspiration of the "Master" (i.e. Huynh Phu So). In 1964-1947 Huynh Phu So, a scholarly man with a long neck and bright eyes who had regarded me as a friend and had believed in and accepted by explanations regarding the revolution, and who had often confided in me many times during our meetings. I was then commander of Military Region 8 in Dong Thap Muoi during the anti-French resistance war. Huynh for a time lived in the base area with me. Huynh confided in me, "I am a patriot. I can't stand France's expropriation of our country and its oppression of our people. But how can we resist? I worry myself sick night and day. If only I had met you earlier so that I could know what path to follow." He paused, looked at me, and said smilingly, "But it's not too late." Then he continued, "I thought out one way: many of our people are still superstitious, so I founded a religion to rally the people and trick the French and their secret police. Once we have large forces we will be strong, and then we will act and regain our country." He again paused, appeared to be deep in thought, and said, "Now that I have listened to you, I think you are right and I believe you. Only if the whole country, tens of millions of Vietnamese, act in concert can we succeed. If one stresses duty to our homeland our people, who have always been patriotic, are certain to work together in fighting the French.... It's true that we shouldn't let our people be superstitious forever...." Regrettably, later, after being away from us for a while, he was exploited and dominated by bad people, who tried to pull him far from the path he had found. Then when he died the bad people used his name to exploit his followers. But the just cause always triumphs. That is a truth.

So the enemy troop remnants went from those places to the "Holy Land" and formed an enclave there with more than 10,000 troops deployed in battlefield positions.

After we liberated Tan Chau near the Kampuchean border 1st Battalion and 2d Battalion of the local provincial troops, along with the district troops, advanced into the "Holy Land" along two routes: the eastern bank of the Tien River and the eastern bank of the Hau River. When the 2d Battalion neared Kinh Xang An Long and was about to cross over to Cu Lao Tay the enemy fired furiously to stop it. The unit also lacked means to cross the river. The people mobilized boats for our troops. They also sent a number of old men and women and the families of the troops in advance, directly toward the enemy positions, to appeal for them to surrender. The enemy fled. Our troops crossed safely. The 2d Battalion went to An Phu, killed a number of the enemy, and established contact with the other column so that they could attack the main enclave. The time was 1400, 2 May. When our troops were reorganizing their formation in preparation for the attack Miss Ut Nhang, a member of the provincial party committee in charge of proselyting among the religious adherents and had always lived in that area, arrived and said that "The enemy is confused. You must attack this afternoon." She went in advance, encouraging the people to cooperate with our troops in putting pressure on the enemy and encouraging the puppet troops to surrender. Miss Ut Nhang met and won over Luong Trong Tuong, one of the Buddhist-Hoa Hao leaders. Tuong surrendered to the liberation troops. Our troops entered the area. More than 10,000 puppet troops laid down their weapons and surrendered. We mastered the entire area by 1700 hours on 2 May.

But that was not the end. A number of obstinate troops fled to join forces with a larger, more heavily armed group of enemy troop remnants which had formed an enclave at the old Tay An pagoda in Cho Moi District, also calling themselves the Buddhist-Hoa Hao Army.

Before dealing with that enclave we liberated the city of Long Xuyen, an attractive city with many modern buildings on the bank of the Hau River. There, teacher and student circles paid an important role in the uprising movement to take power.

At noon on 23 April the teachers and students took over the schools and punished the tyrants who had oppressed and arrested them over the course of many years. Then, making use of the existing infrastructure, they took the communications station, the treasury and an enemy artillery base. Revolutionary flags which had been hidden were brought out and flew everywhere. The people were encouraged to sew others. They immediately organized armed forces, which were equipped with some weapons captured from the enemy. The situation became complicated after Radio Saigon broadcast Duong Van Minh's unconditional surrender statement, when a number of bad elements, reactionaries and opportunists, taking advantage of the fact that our troops had not yet arrived, carried out a coup in the name of the Hoa Hao. Thus in the city of Long Xuyen there were two uprising forces: the uprising people and the so-called "uprising Hoa Hao." The latter group, which was fully armed, began to pillage and seek revenge. The people's armed forces were weak and they had not yet made contact with our troops on the outside. The teacher-student forces, which controlled the communications center, contacted Can Tho and requested aid. They also sent some people with great prestige in the city to meet with the coup leaders and tell them, "Don't be so stupid! You are only a small group of people and cannot stand up to the liberation troops. You will only cause the people of Long Xuyen to have to coninue to shed blood at a time when all other places, including Saigon, are at peace and happy. The whole nation will soon be at peace, so why should you create more enmity? Tanks from Can Tho will be here soon. The people have filled the streets waiting to greet the liberation troops. If you take a look around, you will know what you must do."

"How far away are they now?"

"About 6 or 7 kilometers."

Then they ordered their forces to disband. Weapons were strewn all over the place and their ranks disintegrated. Most of the enemy mingled in with the people. Some went to join forces with those at the Tay An pagoda.

Long Xuyen was completely liberated at 0900 hours on 2 May.

As for the Tay An pagoda, the enemy had planned in advance that if we attacked and liberated the other places they would concentrate in the "Holy Land" and the Tay An pagoda. When the "Holy Land" was lost they regarded the pagoda as their final redoubt. There were an estimated 14,000 fully armed puppet troops there. In addition, many boats carrying weapons, equipment, food, etc., were anchored on the river. The pagoda area became crowded and there was not enough space or water for any more troops.

But the pagoda's board of governors, which was made up of old men and truly religious people, was unwilling to accept such a misdeed. They said, "There is an opportunity to restore peace. That is the aspiration for peace that was cherished by the founder of our religion and passed on to his followers everywhere. Therefore, continuing to shed blood is contrary to his wishes." The Hoa Hao people agreed with them. Furthermore, when the ragtag troop remnants assembled there were many instances in which the people were subjected to robbery, rape and murder and were even worse off than when they were under the control and suppression of the puppet regime. The popular masses, under the leadership of the revolutionary cadres in the surrounding area, arose to shatter the local administration, disband the civil guards, confiscate weapons, fly revolutionary flags, hang up banners proclaiming "Political power to the people," and encourage the enemy troops to lay down their arms and return home to earn a living and avoid being killed. Rumors spread that the liberation forces were coming from Sadec, Long Xuyen, and Can Tho on foot, on tanks, on naval boats, etc. The enemy leaders were terrified and highly confused. In fact, they could no longer command their troops, who had become a disgusted and completely demoralized lot. They fled, every man for himself, with the people helping them to flee and pointing out escape routes. Within an instant that mob had dissipated as quickly as foam.

On 6 May 1975 the bright red liberation flag above the Tay An pagoda flapped in the breeze. The last place in the B2 theater of South Vietnam had been liberated.

While we attacked and arose on the mainland, there were also uprisings and attacks on the islands. The two largest, most important islands in the south were Con Son and Phu Quoc. Because of their strong naval and air forces the enemy regarded those islands as being their safest places. They had transformed those islands into enormous prisons. Tens of thousands of patriots were imprisoned and mistreated, and many died there. Those beautiful places, with rich natural resources and cool sea breezes, had for many years been places full of resentment and hatred, and the people there only waited for the day they could tear asunder the jails and smash their bonds.

On Con Son, as well as Phu Quoc, in March and April 1975 there was no lack of encouraging news coming from the mainland. In the political prisons the inmates had concealed small radios and continually monitored each of our victories and each place that had been liberated. The comments of the puppet officers and enlisted men were also sources of inspiration: "The liberation troops have taken Phuoc Long"; "The Central Highlands have been lost"; "Lam

Dong Province has been lost"; "They are so strong and their artillery is very long-range and very accurate, and one shell can blow apart a house.... Their tanks crush everything beneath them, and no American tank can stand up to them"; "I hear that all their weapons are Russian.... Maybe they have already sent submarines here."

On 30 April, in political prison camp No 7 on Con Son a number of our people were gathered around a radio listening to a Radio Hanoi broadcast: "Saigon has been liberated.... Duong Van Minh, the puppet president, has surrendered unconditionally." The news quickly spread through the camp. Meetings were held to analyze the situation and discuss what to do. Suddenly the door opened and a few puppet officers, no longer arrogant, stuck their heads in and said, "Did you know that Saigon has been liberated? There's no longer any reason to keep you in here." Doors were opened all over the camp and the inmates poured outside. The liberation flag and the gold-starred red flag, which had been secreted away, were raised on the flagpole in front of the camp. Our people went to camp No 1, then to all the other camps. A sea of people swirled about and a forest of flags fluttered in the breeze. All over the island there arose an atmosphere of celebrating the victory, giving rise to bright rays of peace.

Con Son was completely liberated at about 1600 hours on 30 April.

A liberation committee was set up to temporarily manage the island and wait to establish contact with the mainland.

Meanwhile, a naval convoy we had to send to liberate the island was spreading across the South China Sea.

Phu Quoc Island was nearer the mainland, was larger, and had a larger civilian population. Over the course of many years the local party organization had built up a resistance war base, had continually led the masses in struggling against the enemy, had organized an armed force amounting to almost a company, and actively coordinated in attacking the enemy during the spring of 1975. At Duong Dong we shelled and attacked many enemy outposts, forced the abandonment of one outpost, and overran a police station. On that island most of the prisoners were our cadres and men who had been captured on all fronts. They had often retaliated against the cruel puppet troops and many groups had escaped from prison to come to the base area, listened to their reports on the situation in the prison, set forth action guidelines, and provided facilities for them to return to the island to work and serve as an echelon connecting the island with the upper echelon. The enemy continued to take the struggle movement there lightly, perhaps because they thought it was small, weak, isolated and easily suppressed. Thus they still regarded the island as their last safe haven. On 20 April, when Saigon was under strong pressure, the CIA immediately sent all personnel, families, and equipment of the secret CIA-operated radio stations codenamed "House No 7" to Phu Quoc Island. Those five stations, which broadcast in both Khmer and Vietnamese and included "Sacred Sword Radio" and "Sweet Mother Vietnam," were located at No 7 Hong Thap Tu Street (now Nghe-Tinh Soviet Street). Thus the code designation "House No 7." Those stations, which were very reactionary and anticommunist and the contents and forms of which were determined by the CIA, were intended to weaken the morale of patriotic Vietnamese and were yet another weapon used in Kissinger's insidious plots to win total victory and keep South Vietnam forever as a new-style U.S. colony. Kissinger himself had ordered the formation of those stations after the Paris Agreement was signed. That reflected the insincerity of Kissinger and Nixon when they signed the peace treaty and also the U.S.-puppet sabotage of the Paris Agreement.

But those stations and the thousands of people who had recently gone there had to be put aboard U.S. ships and flee to Guam at the end of April.

At noon on 30 April the forces inside the prison and our armed people outside the prison coordinated with the local people in arising, wiping out guard towers, dismantling the prison, routing the puppet troops and taking power on the island. The revolutionary administration took over management of the island at about 1700 hours on 30 April.

Later, a number of puppet naval ships and some Hoa Hao reactionaries also came to the island with the intention of forming an enclave there. But we had already liberated the island, so they again fled and some of the puppet ships returned to their base and surrendered.

Thus the entire island, which was separated from the mainland, also attacked and arose to liberate itself very early, in the afternoon of 30 April 1975.

The entire B2 theater had fulfilled its historic mission. The soldiers and people of B2 had confidence in, and closely followed, the leadership of the party in maintaining the tradition of revolutionary struggle with two legs, three spear-heads, and attacks and uprisings, from the jungles-and-mountains area to the delta and islands and from the rural areas to the cities, including Saigon, the puppet capital. The soldiers and people of B2, who always remained loyal, were the first to go and the last to return, and are justifiably proud of being a Bulwark of the Homeland.

LAST CHAPTER

The Municipal Military Management Committee

I met with another surprise.

On 1 May, at the forward campaign headquarters, I was urgently carrying out several tasks: monitoring the attacks and uprisings which were taking place in the Mekong Delta; completing the organization of the column that would aid our forces in the Delta; reorganizing and redeploying the military forces in Saigon and eastern Nam Bo; and continuing to guide the mopping up of the remaining troop remnants scattered about in company--in places battalion--sized units in the jungles and maquis around Saigon.

Brothers Sau Tho and Bay Cuong arrived and announced that "Brother Ba has sent a message which said that the Political Bureau has decided that you will serve as chairman of the Military Management Committee of Saigon-Gia Dinh. You'd better leave now so you arrive in time."

Since the beginning of April, under the guidance of the Political Bureau and COSVN, and with the participation of Sau Tho, we had made provisions for everything. A detailed work plan had been drafted for the Military Management Committee and the committees to take over management of the installations in the city. The apparata had been organized and appointments had been organized to personnel. The chairman of the Military Management Committee and the head of the Transition Committee had been appointed (I was not appointed to either position). The Political Bureau gave its approval and sent many cadres from the central echelon in Hanoi to the south so that we could have the capability to handle the enormous volume of work. As the columns were advancing on Saigon from all directions, the military management and transition apparata followed close behind. Perhaps they had already begun work. Thus from the beginning of April, when the deployment of the combat units and uprising forces had been completed, the city's military management and transition forces were also organized. When the offensive and uprising plan was drafted the transition and military management plan was also drafted. Before one task had been completed another would have to be carried out. We were determined to win total victory and were fully confident of winning victory, so everything was provided for in advance.

I could not remember how many times I had been surprised in my work, but I was certain that I had not been surprised for the last time. There would be many more surprises, both good ones and bad ones. That was a truth of life, nothing out of the ordinary when there is work to be done and we are still breathing and able to work. Even when we are no longer capable of working, when we have "fading eyes, graying hair, a bent back and slow speech,"* that is also nothing out of the ordinary. There will be surprises until we return to dust, for only then will it all be over.

---
*"Nom" poem by Nguyen Trai, "Tales of Travel" (Poem No 14), from "Quoc Am Thi Tap."

Our convoy left the command headquarters, passed through the Dau Tieng rubber plantation, crossed the Saigon River, went to Ben Cui, and then to Trang Bang along Route 1 and to Saigon past Cu Chi, Tan Phu Trung, Hoc Mon and Ba Queo. Oh! The fruit orchards, the rows of luxuriant green bamboo, the fields on the edge of the village and the flowers. I felt so familiar with those surroundings, as if I had lived there only recently. The people we encountered along the way, in groups or standing in front of their houses or in their gardens, all friendly faces and bright eyes, as if we had met at least once before. I felt very moved. I wanted to visit each house and hug and kiss everyone I met. I wanted to photograph with my eyes and imprint on the bottom of my heart everything I saw that day, from the spacious fertile fields to the pure blue sky. It wasn't important what village, hamlet, subward, or neighborhood it was, or whether the person's surname was Nguyen or Le. They were all our relatives and villages, and they were all us! Thirty years ago we had been apart, near yet so far, close but seemingly strange. Now the sky and earth belonged to us. We were free and independent. Did everyone understand that?

When I remembered how I felt then I praise the poet Xuan Dieu, who wrote the poem, "I Want To Visit All of South Vietnam," the last lines of which are as follows:

> "Oh! On the splendid wings of the phoenix bird of victory,
>
> If only I could, I would imitate Khuat Nguyen and ride the phoenix through the pass, taking along a rainbow as his cockscomb.
>
> To express my joy toward the nation,
> I want to visit every village and house, every flower-
> fenced village in the south.
> I want to turn my head and greet every mother,
> And shout 'Forever!' to all appeals of our country."*

Coincidentally, my route into Saigon that day was almost the same one I took from Saigon to the resistance area in September 1945. Then I went to Go Vap and Ba Queo, then stayed for a while in Hoc Mon and Ba Diem. I then went to An Nhon Tay, Cu Chi, Duc Hoa, My Hanh, etc., and had to leave my beloved city to the occupation of the French and English. We were armed only with sharp stakes and a few muskets, and some Japanese rifles taken from the enemy. Before I left I participated in the fighting at Cau Bong, Ba Chieu, and Phu Nhuan, with a staff in my hand and a pistol under my belt. Many brave youths, shoulder-to-shoulder, marched to the cadence of a song everyone knew by heart: "Brothers! Let us set out together to attack the enemy." I cannot forget the image of the old man Pham Thieu, a famous teacher in Saigon at that time who, wearing a bamboo hat and holding a sharp stake, attacked the enemy along with us youths. Many of our comrades and compatriots fell and found their permanent resting place in Saigon. As for us, we set out empty-handed,

---
*From "Vietnamese Poetry, 1945-1975" [Tho Viet Nam, 1945-1975], New Works Publishing House, Hanoi, p 85.

rich only in spirit. We had confidence in the party and in a brighter future. We fondly bid adieu to the city, pledging to ourselves that we were going so that we could later return one splendid day to liberate our city and people. We were certain that that day was not far away. That turned out not to be the case: that day would be more than 10,000 days away. Time can be measured in terms of nights and days, rainy seasons and dry seasons, but I challenge anyone to recall how many kilometers our path had taken us. From village to village and hamlet to hamlet I, like countless others of our comrades, had lived with the loving care of the people in the outskirts of Saigon, then in all of the provinces of eastern Nam Bo, the marshy maquis and the jungle-and-mountains area, then in central and western Nam Bo and amidst the rivers and streams of Dong Thap Muoi. How can I recall the names of all the hamlets and villages or of the mothers, brothers and sisters. The young couriers of that time, who were only about 10 years old, today, if they are still alive, have gotten married and have children. Those hamlets and villages were named "Vietnam" and the family members were named "Mother Nam," "Mother Tam," "Uncle Hai," "Uncle Bay," "Master Ba," and "Master Tu," all of whom I regard as my relatives. The undertaking of one person is an undertaking of all. If I accomplished anything it was with the help of the people. After I returned to the city I would never forget the maquis, the sea, the jungle and the mountains. I had been able to fulfill my mission thanks to the people and now my mission was above all to serve the people. I was successful thanks to my friends, and now I would not forget them. Vietnamese virtue is love and justice, and is loyalty between people. Our eyes and hearts must be clear and pure: that is the law of a person's life.

But after having traveled every path in our country and having endured every hardship and danger, now we were returning. I automatically ran a hand over my body: luckily, I was still in one piece. I had encountered bombs and shells many times, but they had been very considerate toward me. Perhaps if I didn't think about them they would avoid me. But it was really just a matter of luck. Nguyen Trai once wrote the line, "When the warfare is over there is great happiness." In his poem, "Writing Poems on Mt. Con After the Battle," Nguyen Trai wrote:

> "Ten years away from home,
> The pine tree will be ragged when I return.
> I've promised the forest and the streams
>   that I won't break my oath.
> How pitiful are those who endure hardships.
> I dreamed that I had returned home,
> Happy to still be alive, although the fighting hasn't ended.
> When will we erect our huts down from the mountains?
> A rock is my pillow and I brew my tea with stream water."
>
>   (translated by Khuong Huu Dung)*

---

*From "Poems and Prose of Nguyen Trai" [Tho Van Nguyen Trai], Education Publishing House, Hanoi, p 83.

But not everyone comes through a war unscathed. Many of my comrades and friends gave their lives in one part of the country or another. They gave their lives so that we could return and, on behalf of those who left in the fall of that year, tell the people that we had kept our word. Families that have suffered losses and have members who have not returned should regard us as their children, brothers and sisters, and work with us in building the new life we have long desired.

I still remember, as if they were extremly pretty pictures, the villages of Vietnam every time there is foreign aggression. That year groups of young men and women of all strata--workers, intellectuals, etc.--with strong hatred and determination greater than a mountain, left the city. Some went to central Vietnam--to which the French had not yet gone--to request the Central Committee to equip them and organize units so that they could return to kill the enemy and defend the nation. Others remained behind, banded together, equipped themselves with weapons captured from the enemy, and attacked the enemy, even in the outskirts of the city. I and my younger brother Viet Chau joined the latter group. There were nights when I and sister Nam Bi (i.e. Colonel Ho Thi Bi, now retired) went to the Ba Diem area, entered the former base of the Japanese troops, and dug up dry wells to search for Japanese weapons in that manner. I met with the Provincial Party Committee of Gia Dinh Province and issued a resolution regarding the organization of guerrillas from Hoc Mon, Duc Hoa, and Ba Diem districts to form the "Hoc Mon-Ba Diem-Duc Hoa Interdistrict Liberation Unit" based at My Hanh village. The people in that beloved area called us "our troops" to distinguish us from the troops who refused to fight the enemy but often harassed the people. From that time on our men fought continually, with the support of the people, developed into detachments 12, 14 and 15, then into Military Region 7, Military Region 8, etc., and became increasingly powerful. Now we were returning, returning with artillery paratroops. On the sidewalks there were even more: backpacks, caps, and cartridge belts had been thrown everywhere. Hundreds of thousands of puppet troops had fled to Saigon in terror, and there could be seen in all parts of the city the disastrous disintegration of a mercenary, hired-murderer army of a traitorous regime. Anything that is not virtuous or beneficial to the people, or is unjust, although prospering for a time, is only temporary and superficial. Such was their fate.

Our car sped along on the asphalt road. Then we turned onto broad Thong Nhat Boulevard (now 30 April Street) and went directly to Independence Palace. There our cadres had already set up the headquarters of the Municipal Military Management Committee. Everyone was there. But before beginning work I went all over Saigon for old time's sake. Nothing could have been happier than driving around in the tanks of sharp stakes and muskets. We had returned to overwhelm enemy forces which were also much stronger than those in the past, and to defeat an imperialist chieftain that was much stronger than the French colonialists in the past.

That was revolution and the just cause.

Obeying Uncle Ho, under the leadership of the true party, with pure hearts and iron will, we had the strength to move mountains, fill in the ocean, and do anything we wanted.

As I traveled that day I was deep in thought. It was a moving experience to look at the city and the people. Now I returned. I elatedly looked at the streets red with flags of victory. Everyone's face looked as fresh as a flower. From Hoc Mon into the city our car ran over clothing, shoes and socks that had been strewn along the road by puppet infantry and middle of our free, recently liberated city, looking at one street after another and at our people, who were gleeful and happy, and who saw in me a liberator who had just returned, as a liberator with "half a head of gray hair." Perhaps I was looking for relatives who had become lost in the course of events. A number of people reluctantly asked me if that was the case. It was far different in 1973, when I was head of the military delegation of the DRG of the RSVN at Camp David at Tan Son Nhat airfield. Then, every time I went into my city I had to be "escorted" by puppet MP's, who prevented me from freely moving about or from meeting the people. An MP jeep would lead the way, its siren screaming, past the vehicles and people along the way, and running red lights at intersections, out of fear that the people would gather around the liberator.

First of all, I went directly to the bank of the Ben Nghe canal, crossed Quay bridge, and went on to Ben Nha Rong. I was there, where Uncle Ho set forth in the past; his feet walked but his eyes nostalgically looked at his beloved city, and at a part of the homeland that our ancestors had built up over the course of several thousand years. Uncle Ho was distressed over having to leave our people, who were still in wretched straits and in chains. Swallowing his hatred and steeling his will, Uncle Ho departed to find a way to save his country and people. Uncle Ho delineated that path. We followed that path and resolutely and bravely pursued the truth illuminated by his truth. Now we had reached our goal and had retraced Uncle Ho's footsteps. We were there!

"Uncle Ho is like the light of morning, illuminating the path I am taking."*
"Give me big mountains and long rivers, give me the sword that has been honed a thousand years."**

I remembered the first time I met Uncle Ho, in 1948, at Viet Bac. Since the outbreak of the Nam Bo resistance on 23 September 1945, that had been the first time a Nam Bo delegation, including military, political and Front cadres, and headed by myself, had gone from Dong Thap Muoi to Viet Bac to report to Uncle Ho and the party Central Committee. Our route passed largely through areas temporarily occupied by the enemy. We had to organize ourselves into a well-armed combat unit so that we could be prepared to defend ourselves and fight our way through when necessary, although when passing through the localities gave us their all-out assistance. We walked all the way along the eastern side of the Truong Son range, climbing mountains and crossing rivers and streams. Along some sections we had to travel at sea, such as at Cam Ranh Bay and Nha Trang, and traveled 6 months without rest. The French were monitoring us very clearly, and tried to block and ambush us, such as in the mountain region of Phan Rang, at Doc Mo, and in Khanh Hoa. Finally, they parachuted

---
* and ** From the poem "Send My Heart to Father," by Thu Bon. "Vietnamese Poetry 1945-1975" [Tho Viet Nam 1945-1975], New Works Publishing House, Hanoi, pp 30-31.

troops at Van Dinh west of Hanoi, hoping to capture our entire delegation by surprise, but each time they failed. Uncle Ho and the Central Committee sent people to meet us. When we reached Viet Bac we were anxious to meet Uncle Ho to satisfy a long-held desire. When we met Uncle Ho, we were all moved: there was our teacher, our father, the incarnation of the homeland, the image of our people. He had a high forehead, a thin beard, a pair of bright eyes, a kind face and a fragile, relaxed demeanor. I did not yet know about his great ideas and his noble virtue. Just looking at him, I suddenly felt that I had limitless confidence in him, respected him, and felt very close to him. His skill conquered all. He was the quintessence of talent. It was so fortunate that our people gave birth to such a person, whom millions of people followed and loved. On the day our delegation returned south, Uncle Ho, the Central Committee and the government held a going-away dinner. In the presence of everyone, Uncle Ho called me over, presented me with a very attractive sword, and said in a warm voice that reached the bottom of my heart:

"I'm giving you this valuable sword so that you can take it back to the people of Nam Bo and use it to kill the enemy. Tell the people the party and I will always be beside them. If we are united in serving the country we are certain to win!"

His words have never faded from my mind or from the hearts of the people of Nam Bo.

On another occasion, in 1963, I returned south to fight the Americans. I had been named commander of the liberation armed forces in South Vietnam. Uncle Ho invited me to his house for dinner before I set out. He handed me a box of cigars made in Cuba and said to me, "I only have this gift--sent to me by comrade Fidel--to give you. Take it with you and pass them out to the cadres in the south. When you smoke them, remember my ardent interest--and that of our Cuban brothers--in the South. Do your best to enable me to visit our people in the South."

I could never forget his admonition. Now our country had been completely liberated and Uncle Ho was resting in peace. I am neither a writer nor a poet, so I cannot describe my feelings. Thu Bo expressed my feelings in his poem "Send My Heart to Father":

> "Give me an arrow
> That I can fire from the rampart.
> Oh Vietnam! Descendant of the celestial dragon.
> Four thousand years of making flowers of rosy blood.
> Send my heart to father,
> The nation's victory is a great bouquet"*

When I left Ben Nha Rong I went all over Saigon and then to old Cho Lon. When we reached Thuan Kieu Street we got out of the car to commemorate comrades Le Thi Rieng, member of the Saigon Municipal Party Committee, head of the Women Proselyting Section of the Municipal Party Committee, and a member of the

---
*From "Vietnamese Poetry 1945-1975" [Tho Vietnam 1945-1975], New Works Publishing House, Hanoi, p 32.

Central Committee of the NLFSVN. I had known her since the arduous but heroic anti-French resistance war years in eastern Nam Bo. I met her again in the jungle base area of eastern Nam Bo during the years of the anti-U.S. war. She volunteered to go into the city and proselytize among the women and organize them to struggle against the enemy and to protect women's rights. Brother Kieu was also a member of the Municipal Party Committee and was deputy head of the Municipal Worker Proselyting Section. Unfortunately, the enemy captured them and imprisoned both in Chi Hoa Prison. During Phase 1 of the Tet Mau Than general offensive and uprising the puppets brought Sister Rieng and brother Kieu from the prison to that street and murdered them. Such a cowardly act against unarmed people is totally incomprehensible. They committed many other barbarous acts, such as the puppet Gen Nguyen Ngoc Loan shooting a bound prisoner on the streets of Saigon. The puppet troops chopped their bodies into many pieces, as if they were butchering animals. It does no good to speak of the inhuman Vietnamese traitors, but ask the Americans, their teachers and father, who often speak out on human rights, what they would call such acts? Today we are the victors. How did we treat the million puppet officers and enlisted men, many of whom could be regarded as war criminals? There was no revenge and no bloodbath as they had ballyhooed. Who is civilized? And who knows respect for mankind?

I went to Minh Phung Street and the surrounding area, which was the scene of fierce fighting during the second phase of Tet Mau Than, during which our regiments came in and occupied that area. The enemy used helicopter gunships in combination with armor and artillery in insane counterattacks. Comrade Hai Hoang sacrificed his life there. As commander of the "Gironde" Battalion he victoriously commanded the famous Ap Bac battle at the beginning of 1963, in which we successfully countered the enemy's tactic of moving troops by helicopters and armored personnel carriers for the first time. In 1968, when commanding the Long An Province troops, he lost his life in that area. Also in that area, on Minh Phung Street, comrade Nguyen Thi (Nguyen Ngoc Tan), a talented writer and a brave soldier, fulfilled her duty to the nation during the second phase of the general offensive and uprising in 1968. Comrade Nguyen Thi had been present during the anti-French resistance war period in eastern Nam Bo and at that time took up arms to kill the enemy and began to write short stories which all of our soldiers liked. During the anti-U.S. resistance war period she continually volunteered to go to the front and live and create with the liberation troops and under combat conditions. Was she not exemplary of the qualities and souls of Vietnamese writers during the nation's glorious war years?

All over Saigon-Gia Dinh, practically every place was the scene of a glorious feat of arms of our sappers, commandos and armed young men and women. There were not only such famous attacks as those at the presidential palace, the U.S. Embassy, the radio station, the puppet GHQ, Y Bridge, etc., during Tet Mau Than, but also during both the anti-French and anti-U.S. resistance wars. In all periods there had been resounding victories in Saigon. Not only armed soldiers, but also political cadres and cultural cadres, had struggled in all ways in the city of Saigon-Gia Dinh against the country-stealing, country-selling troops. It is not possible to speak of all the many and varied feats of arms, or know all of the unknown soldiers who sacrificed their lives in that beloved city for our total victory of today.

They were the people who brought about the victory. They sacrificed so that the S-shaped country on the western shore of the Pacific Ocean could become increasingly advanced and strong. They wrote pages in the dazzling, heroic history of Vietnam. We must be eternally grateful to them in future generations, when we can stand equal to others, holding our heads high and watching the sun shed its rays on the splendid scenery of our country. We must also be grateful to the fathers and mothers of those who gave their lives for the great spring victory. Never forget the past, so that we can build a brilliant, secure future. If there has been no past there can be no future.

I returned to Independence Palace. In accordance with the instructions of the Political Bureau, I declared the release of all key members of the puppet regime, who had been detailed by our troops in a room in the palace since the day Saigon was liberated. I met with only the leaders: Duong Van Minh, the president; Nguyen Van Huyen, the vice president; and Vu Van Mau, the premier, of the puppet regime. I explained to them that the policies of the revolution were just, upright, moderate and lenient. "It uses justice to defeat brutality and replaces cruelty with humanity." I emphasized that everything that had happened would be relegated to the past. We would be concerned only with their future attitude and actions. I hoped that they could understand the great national victory that had just been won and be proud that they were also Vietnamese.

They appeared to be moved. Duong Van Minh said, "I am happy to be a citizen of an independent Vietnam." Nguyen Van Huyen said, "As a citizen of Vietnam, I can be proud of the glorious success and victory of the nation. However, when I look back I can see that I was in error." Vu Van Mau also appeared to have become enlightened: "April 30, 1975, the day the revolution was successful, was also the day I escaped from my delusion. I am happy and proud to be a citizen of an independent, unified Vietnam."

We took them for their word. How sincere they were depends on the virtue of each of them. The policy of the revolution was carried out.

That was also in accordance with the humanitarian line of the party and the tradition of our forefathers, about whom Nguyen Trai wrote, "Since heaven opposes killing, we give the enemy a way out." And Uncle Ho, with his limitless mercy, said the following of people who had gone astray, "Among them, no matter what, patriotism cannot have been completely extinguished, but is still glowing like an ember. We must help them kindle it into a flame." The Military Management Committee announced the registration and reporting of all generals, officers and enlisted men, as well as the personnel at the various echelons of the puppet regime, and arranged study for them regarding the revolutionary line, their attitude toward the homeland and the people and the concepts of independence and freedom. All of those things were intended to contribute toward achieving national solidarity and developing the nation.

We had shed much blood to arrive at that glorious day, and we wanted to waste no more Vietnamese blood. We are a heroic people and are also a civilized people. We know how to value the dignity of mankind. We want to do everything possible to enable everyone to be friends and to have a society made up entirely of good people. That was far different from the people who, thinking that everyone else was like them, thought that there would be a terrible "bloodbath" of vengeance. That was far from the Americans and puppets who, when one of their adversaries fell into their hands, barbarously mistreated him or tortured him so cruelly as to be beyond imagination. They regarded people as animals, murdered people at will and deliberately crippled--both physically and mentally--the people they captured. Once again we have the right to pose the question: who is civilized? who knows how to respect mankind?

On 7 May 1975 the Military Management Committee held a ceremony to present itself to the people of Saigon-Gia Dinh. Throughout the night of 6 May and the early morning of 7 May the entire city was excited and all of Saigon spent a sleepless night. Every person and every house prepared and every mass organization and precinct prepared. Everyone anxiously awaited a tomorrow bathed in rosy rays of sunlight. It would be an epoch-making moment. It had taken our country 117 years to arrive at that day, which was the greatest event in that city on the Ben Nghe River during the past 400 years. Although it was an initial military management administration, it was a revolutionary administration which had been built on the sacrifice of the people of our nation and of Saigon. It was our army and our administration, one of the people and for the people. Beginning early in the morning, groups of people coming from all precincts and districts inside and outside the city, with banners, flags and slogans celebrating the victory of the revolution and the Military Management Committee, filled the grounds of "Independence Palace." Saigon was truly a big festival, a festival celebrating total victory after more than a century. The happiness and pride of a people, the joy and delight of people who had truly become the masters of their beautiful country, spread all over the city. On the grounds of Independence Palace, where in the past large numbers of puppet MP's and police chased the people away from the restricted area, there were orderly groups of people. Old people with wrinkled skin and white hair, who had lived through the dark periods of suppression by the colonialists, brought their grandchildren to witness a scene which manifested what was most precious and sacred: the freedom and independence of the nation and of the people. Young children enjoyed themselves because nothing threatened their happiness and their lives. But the largest group, that with the fullest realization of their splendid future, was made up of young men and women. They wore their most attractive clothing and held fresh flowers and entered the palace grounds shoulder-to-shoulder, as if ready to follow in the footsteps of their fathers and elder brothers in order to write additional pages of history, no less majestic, in building and defending the country.

On behalf of the Military Management Committee I read the coming-out speech and appealed for everyone in all strata to participate in all ways in maintaining order and building a well-off, happy life. I stressed:

"Vietnam, from Lang Son to the Cau Mau Peninsula, is for the first time in more than a century, completely free of the malevolent shadow of foreign aggressor troops.

"The entire nation has won complete independence and freedom....

"Our people will from now on certainly endure and develop....

"No reactionary power can impede the progress of our people who are advancing and creating for themselves a well-off, happy life....

"Only the U.S. imperialists have been defeated.... All Vietnamese are victors....

"Anyone who has Vietnamese blood has the right to defend the nation's common victory.

"All Vietnamese who think about their compatriots and their country cannot but be very happy over the expanded horizon of their homeland.

"The grandchildren and children of all strata of the new society will from now on be able to grow up with a spirit of national pride, hold their heads high, be happy, be provided for, and be able to work in the most brilliant period of development of their country....

"We are not ashamed of the thousands of years of our past history....

"We have not betrayed the love and respect of our brothers and friends all over the world....

"Our historic victory is a victory for our people's heroic tradition, which had been built up in the course of our 4,000-year history of struggle to found and defend our nation. The revolution has gone all-out to maintain that tradition and has continually developed it....

"Our epochal victory is a victory of the only correct revolutionary line and completely accurate revolutionary guidance, which led our country's revolution from one victory to another, to total victory and to a splendid future....

"At this sacred moment the hearts of all of us focus on the divinity of the great President Ho Chi Minh, and remember his enormous merit....

"The glory of today belongs above all to the people of our entire nation, who for 30 long years sacrificed and struggled for our people's great cause, and did not fear bombs, shells or jail....

"Glory belongs to the heroic people's armed forces, which have been completely loyal, fulfilling all missions, overcoming all difficulties and defeating all enemies....

"The people of Saigon-Gia Dinh have become the complete masters of their city....

"The revolution has brought about and developed the people's mastership right and has liberated the limitless creative capability of the masses....

"Everyone understands that after 30 years of continuous warfare, in the initial period after the restoration of peace, it is not possible to avoid difficulties in life and work. The war crimes of the U.S. imperialists will adversely affect the lives of our people for many years to come. The chief traitor lackeys of the U.S. imperialists, who for their own vile, selfish benefit, brought a fox into the chicken coop and brought an elephant into the graveyard, must accept full responsibility for the long-range serious consequences of the neocolonial policy of the U.S. imperialists in our country....

"All patriotic Vietnamese must work together to rebuild their home area and quickly bind the wounds of war, and resolve all serious consequences of the many war crimes committed by the U.S. imperialists and their lackeys, which caused suffering for every person and every family....

"No matter how great our present difficulties are, they are no greater than fighting and defeating the U.S. imperialists....

"Our people, who have defeated the U.S. imperialists, certainly have sufficient spirit, intelligence and capability to resolve all problems in order to rapidly recover and solidly develop the life of the nation....

"To have independence and peace, and for the people to have conscience of mastery, is to have everything...."

Clearly, we knew that there were many difficulties, even during the days of the resounding victory. We were also aware of the unavoidable missteps in the initial period, which is always the case. The 30-year war which was concluded by the great spring victory in 1975 had its origins in the difficult days of 1945, 1957, 1959, etc. The many missteps and errors in each period of progress provided us with additional experience. If we had had no sharpened stakes we could have had no artillery or tanks.

> "Without the desolate scenes of winter
> There could be no brilliant scenes of spring."
>
> (from Uncle Ho's poem "Self-Advice")*

We were determined to bring about the great spring victory of the socialist revolution and create a well-off, happy life, so there is no reason why we cannot overcome the difficulties and missteps of the first years after the victory. That is the will of Vietnam.

Spring of 1982

---

*"Compilation of Vietnamese Literature" [Tong Tap Van Hoc Viet Nam], Social Science Publishing House, Hanoi, p 662.

Pages 225 through 243 Omitted

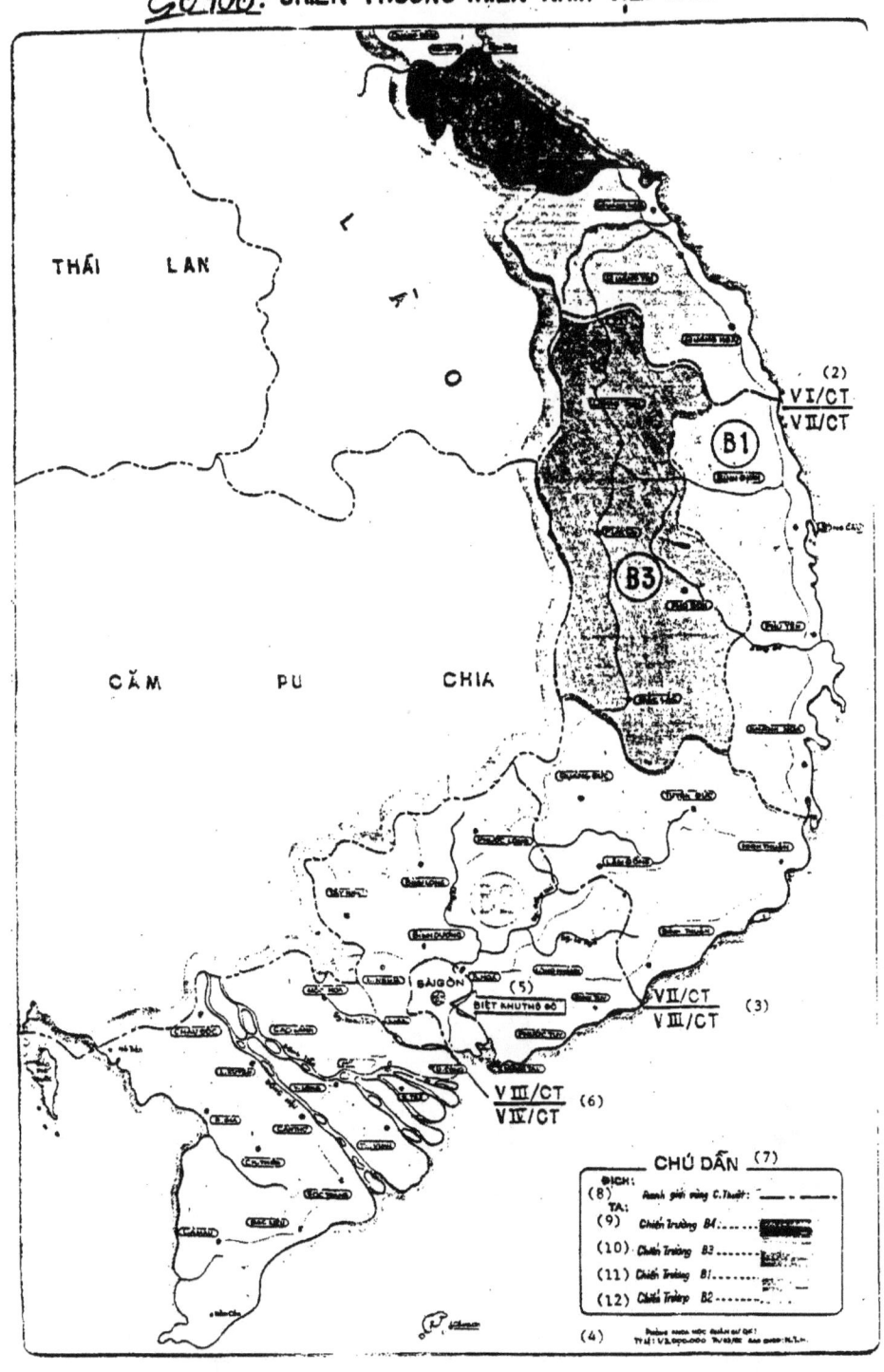

Map 1

Key to Map 1

1. The South Vietnam Theaters
2. I Corps Tactical Zone/II Corps Tactical Zone
3. II Corps Tactical Zone/III Corps Tactical Zone
4. Military Science Office of Military Region 7
   Scale: 1/3,000,000   March 1982
   Cartographer: N.T.H.
5. Capital Special Zone
6. III Corps Tactical Zone/IV Corps Tactical Zone
7. Legend
8. Enemy: Border of tactical zones
9. B4 Theater
10. B3 Theater
11. B1 Theater
12. B2 Theater

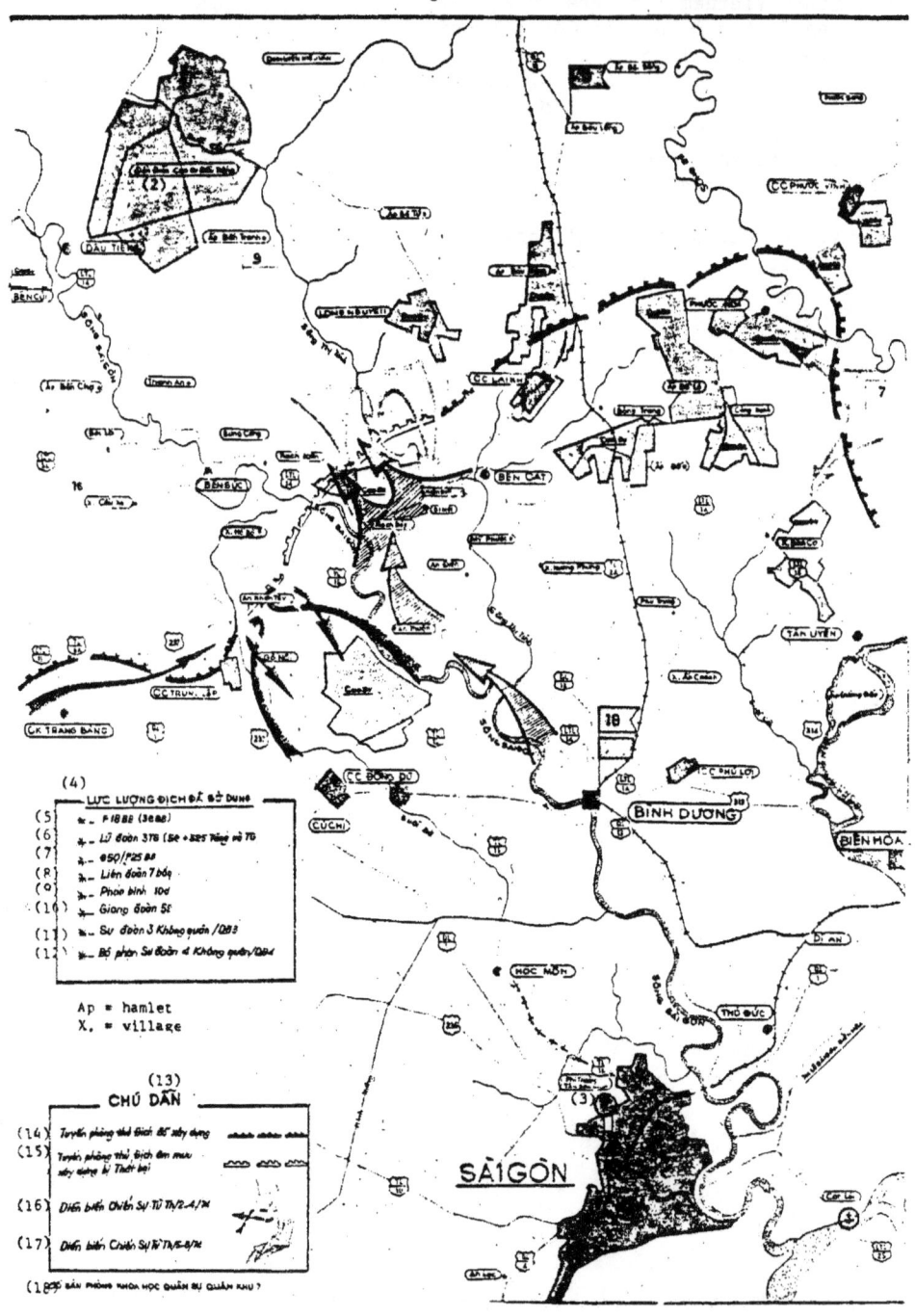

Map 2

Key to Map 2

1. The Lateral Route 7 Fighting (Ben Cat-Bung Cong), May-June 1974
2. Dau Tieng Rubber Plantation
3. Tan Son Nhat Airfield
4. Forces used by the enemy
5. 18th Infantry Division (3d Infantry Regiment)
6. 3d Armored Brigade (5th Regiment plus 325 tanks and armored vehicles)
7. 50th Regiment/25th Infantry Division
8. 7th Ranger Group
9. 10th Artillery Battalion.
10. 52d River Flotilla
11. 3d Air Division/III Corps
12. Element of 4th Air Division/IV Corps
13. Legend:
14. Defense line set up by enemy
15. Defense line enemy failed to set up
16. Combat developments, February-April 1974
17. Combat developments, May-August 1974
18. Map by Military Science Office of Military Region 7

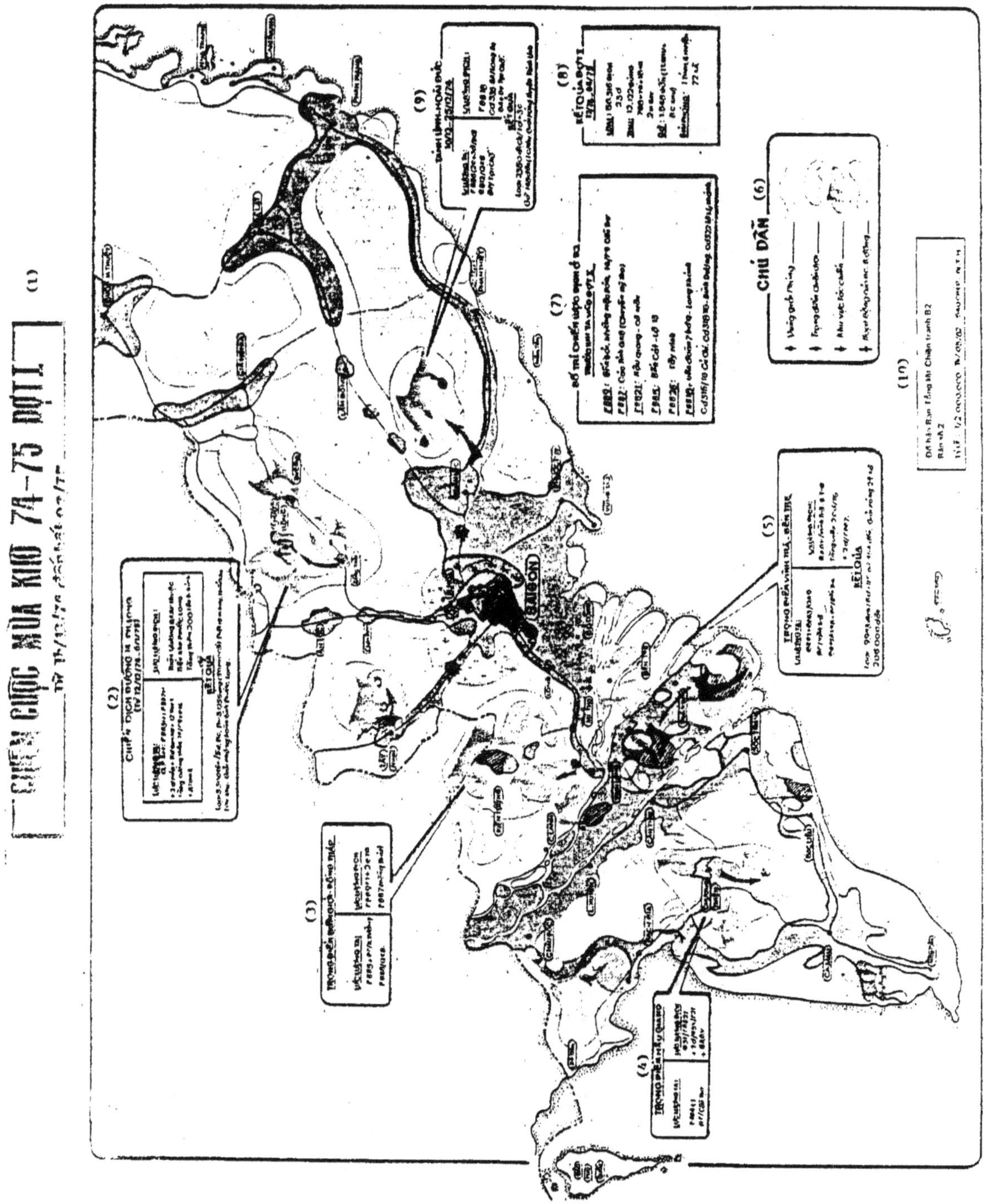

Map 3

Key to Map 3

1. 1974-1975 Dry Season Fighting, Phase 1
2. Route 15-Phuoc Long Campaign (12 Dec 74-6 Jan 75)
   Our forces:
   4th Corps: 3d Infantry Division (minus); 7th Infantry Division (minus). 2 artillery battalion plus 5 antiaircraft battalions plus 12 tanks. Reinforced by 1st Division/9th Division and 16th Regiment plus 8 tanks.
   Enemy forces:
   All Phuoc Long Sector RF and civil defense units, reinforced by 200 airborne rangers.
   Results:
   Knocked out of action 3,300 of the enemy, 5 battalions, 8 companies; captured 3,125 weapons (50 artillery pieces and mortars); shot down 15 airplanes; took 1 sector and 10 subsectors. Completely liberated Phuoc Long Province.
3. Border-Dong Thap Focal Point
   Our forces: 5th Infantry Division plus Kien Tuong local troops
   Enemy forces: 9th Infantry Division (minus) plus 2d Armored Regiment; 7th Infantry Division (Dong Thap).
4. Hau Giang Focal Point
   Our forces: 4th Infantry Division (minus); Can Tho local troops
   Enemy forces: 31st Regiment/21st Infantry Division; 1st Battalion/33d Regiment/21st Division plus RF and civil defense forces.

   Vinh Tra-Ben Tre Focal Point
   Our forces: 887th and 883d Regiments/Military Region 9; Vinh Tra local troops; 881st Regiment/Military Region 8 plus Ben Tre local troops.
   Enemy forces: Vinh Tra-Ben Tre RF and civil-defense forces, reinforced by 2 armored brigades and 2 battalions of 7th Infantry Division.
   Results: Knocked out of action 9,943 of enemy, 6 battalions, 11 companies; overran 454 posts; liberated 24 villages and 206,000 people.
6. Legend
   Liberated areas
   Focal points of campaign
   Operational zones
   Sapper-Commando activities
7. Enemy's Strategic Deployments in B2 Theater (Before we began phase 1):
   9th Infantry Division: Ben Soi, Kien Tuong-Moc Hoa; 1st Regiment/9th Division, Can Tho
   7th Infantry Division: Provinces of Military Region 8 (focusing on My Tho)
   21st Infantry Division: Hau Giang, Ca Mau
   5th Division: Ben Cat-Route 13
   25th Division: Tay Ninh
   18th Division plus 7th Ranger Group: Long Khanh
   315th Armored Brigade: Cu Chi; 318th Armored Brigade, Binh Duong; 322d Armored Brigade, Route 1-Long Khanh
8. Results of Phase 1 (December 1974-April 1975):
   Knocked out of action: 56,315 enemy troops, 23 battalions
   Captured: 12,122 weapons, 768 radios, 18 vehicles, 2 airplanes
   Overran: 1,568 military posts (1 sector and 8 subsectors)
   Liberated: 1 province, 4 districts, 72 villages
   Tanh Linh-Hoai Duc (10 December-25 December 1974):
   Our forces: 6th Infantry Division (2d Regiment plus 3d Sapper Battalion)
   Enemy forces: 18th Infantry Division, 335th Long An RF Brigade, local forces
   Results: Knocked out of action 2,350 enemy troops, 1 battalion, 3 companies. Overran 148 posts (1 subsector); liberated Tanh Linh District
9. Map No 2, B2 War Recapitulation Section
   Scale: 1/2,000,000   March 1982
   Cartographer: N.T.H.

- 249 -

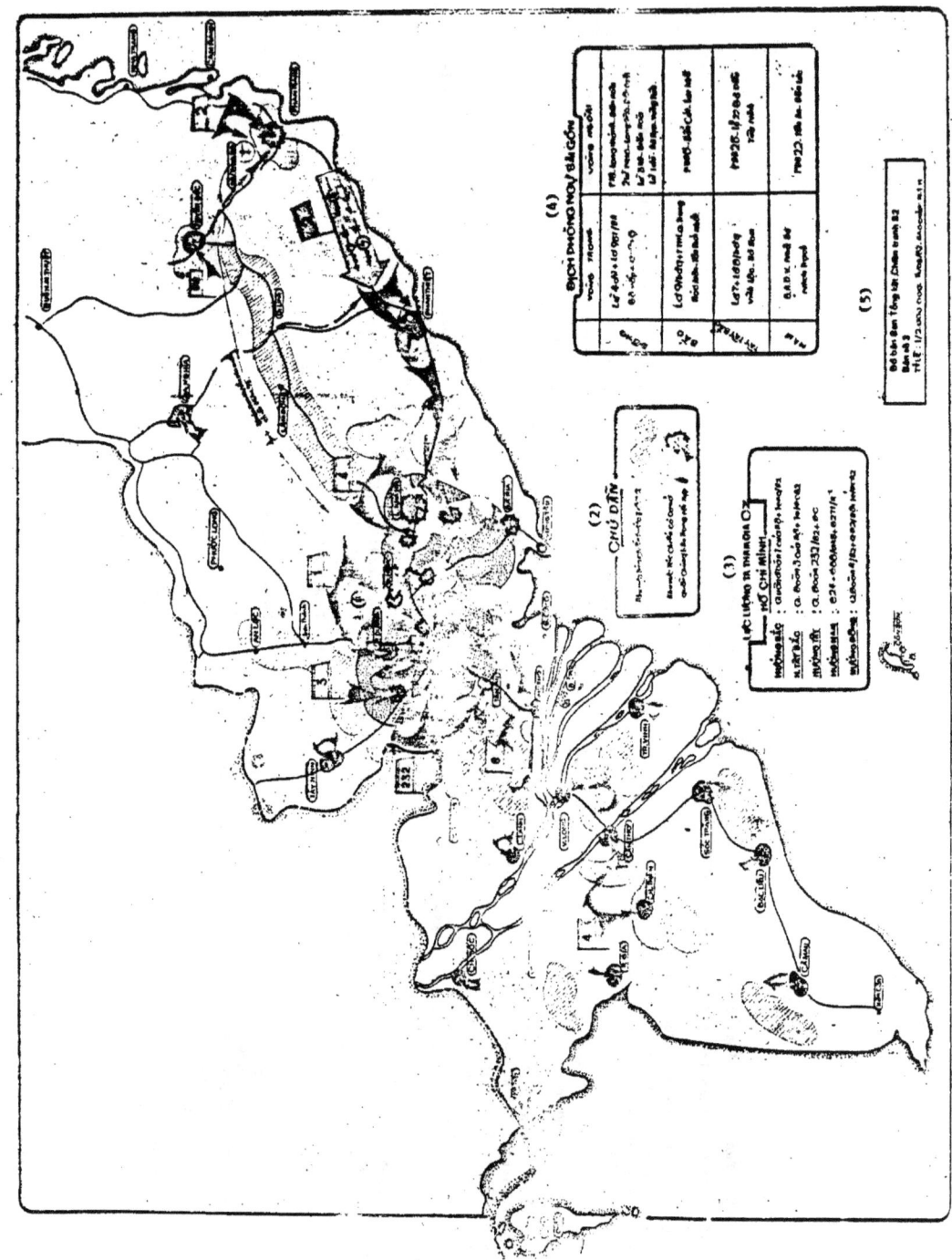

Key to Map 4

1. 1974-1975 Dry Season Fighting (Step 2, Phase 2)
   Beginning in April 1975, Ho Chi Minh Campaign

2. Legend
   Operational zones, Step 1, Phase 2
   Operational zones with coordination of internal mass infrastructures.

3. Our forces participating in Ho Chi Minh Campaign:
   North: 1st Corps of High Command plus one B2 sapper regiment.
   Northwest: 3d Corps of High Command plus one B2 sapper regiment.
   West: 232d Corps/B2 plus sappers.
   South: 24th Regiment plus 88th Regiment of Military Region 8 plus 271st Regiment of Regional Command
   East: 4th Corps/B2 plus 2d Corps of High Command plus one B2 sapper regiment.

4. Enemy troops defending Saigon

   Inner Perimeter
   East: 4th Airborne Brigade plus 951st RF Group of Go Vap plus Precinct 9
   North: 9th Ranger Group plus Quang Trung Training Center, Hoc Mon-Tan Thoi Nhat
   Northwest: 7th, 8th ranger groups, Vinh Loc-Ba Hom
   South: RF and civil defense forces of Nha Be and Nhon Thanh

   Outer Perimeter
   18th Division: Long Khanh-Bien Hoa
   2d Marine Brigade: Long Binh-Bien Hoa
   3d Cavalry Regiment: Bien Hoa
   1st Airborne Brigade: Ba Ria, Vung Tau
   5th Division: Ben Cat, Lei Khe
   25th Division: Route 22, Go Dau, Tay Ninh
   22d Infantry Division: Tan An, Ben Luc

5. Map No 3, B2 War Recapitulation Section.
   Scale: 1/2,000,000   March 1982
   Cartographer: N.T.H.

5616
CSO: 8058/0292   - END -

www.ingramcontent.com/pod-product-compliance
Lightning Source LLC
Chambersburg PA
CBHW050459110426
42742CB00018B/3304